TIBETAN SKY-GAZING MEDITATION AND THE
PRE-HISTORY OF GREAT PERFECTION BUDDHISM

Also Available from Bloomsbury:

Buddhism and Waste, edited by Trine Brox and Elizabeth Williams-Oerberg

Buddhism, Education and Politics in Burma and Thailand, Khammai Dhammasami

Rethinking 'Classical Yoga' and Buddhism, Karen O'Brien Kop

TIBETAN SKY-GAZING MEDITATION AND THE PRE-HISTORY OF GREAT PERFECTION BUDDHISM

The Skullward Leap Technique and the Quest for Vitality

Flavio A. Geisshuesler

BLOOMSBURY ACADEMIC
LONDON • NEW YORK • OXFORD • NEW DELHI • SYDNEY

BLOOMSBURY ACADEMIC
Bloomsbury Publishing Plc, 50 Bedford Square, London, WC1B 3DP, UK
Bloomsbury Publishing Inc, 1359 Broadway, New York, NY 10018, USA
Bloomsbury Publishing Ireland, 29 Earlsfort Terrace, Dublin 2, D02 AY28, Ireland

BLOOMSBURY, BLOOMSBURY ACADEMIC and the Diana logo are trademarks of
Bloomsbury Publishing Plc

First published in Great Britain 2024
Paperback edition published 2025

Copyright © Flavio A. Geisshuesler, 2024

Flavio A. Geisshuesler has asserted his right under the Copyright, Designs and Patents Act,
1988, to be identified as Author of this work.

For legal purposes the Acknowledgments on pp. vii–viii constitute an extension
of this copyright page.

Cover image: An abstract painting of pink, yellow and blue. © Jr Korpa/Unsplash

This work is published open access subject to a Creative Commons
Attribution-NonCommercial-NoDerivatives 4.0 International licence (CC BY-NC-ND 4.0,
https://creativecommons.org/licenses/by-nc-nd/4.0/). You may re-use, distribute, and
reproduce this work in any medium for non-commercial purposes, provided you give
attribution to the copyright holder and the publisher and provide a link to the Creative
Commons licence.

Bloomsbury Publishing Plc does not have any control over, or responsibility for, any
third-party websites referred to or in this book. All internet addresses given in this
book were correct at the time of going to press. The author and publisher regret any
inconvenience caused if addresses have changed or sites have ceased to exist,
but can accept no responsibility for any such changes.

A catalogue record for this book is available from the British Library.

Library of Congress Cataloging-in-Publication Data
Names: Geisshuesler, Flavio A., author.
Title: Tibetan sky-gazing meditation and the pre-history of great perfection Buddhism :
the Skullward leap technique and the quest for vitality / Flavio A. Geisshuesler.
Description: 1st. | New York : Bloomsbury Academic, 2024. |
Includes bibliographical references and index.
Identifiers: LCCN 2023026056 | ISBN 9781350428812 (hardback) |
ISBN 9781350428850 (paperback) | ISBN 9781350428836 (epub) |
ISBN 9781350428829 (adobe pdf)
Subjects: LCSH: Rdzogs-chen. | Meditation–Rdzogs-chen. |
Rnying-ma-pa (Sect)–Doctrines–History. | Buddhism–History.
Classification: LCC BQ7662.4 .G45 2023 | DDC 294.3/4435–dc23/eng/20230626
LC record available at https://lccn.loc.gov/2023026056

ISBN: HB: 978-1-3504-2881-2
PB: 978-1-3504-2885-0
ePDF: 978-1-3504-2882-9
eBook: 978-1-3504-2883-6

Typeset by Newgen KnowledgeWorks Pvt. Ltd., Chennai, India

For product safety related questions contact productsafety@bloomsbury.com.

To find out more about our authors and books visit www.bloomsbury.com
and sign up for our newsletters.

CONTENTS

Acknowledgments	vii
INTRODUCTION: SKULLWARD LEAP MEDITATION AND THE QUEST FOR VITALITY	1

Part I
THE MYTHICAL-HISTORICAL CONCEPTION OF VITALITY

Chapter 1
THE SKY AS SOURCE OF VITALITY IN ANCIENT TIBET 13
   Dzogchen Conceptions of Origins 13
   The Descent of the Celestial Kings 19
   The Cult of the Sky-Deer 21

Chapter 2
THE TIBETAN EMPIRE AND THE (INCOMPLETE) BUDDHICIZATION OF VITALITY 27
   The Spherical Vitality of Buddhism 27
   As Above, So Below 32

Chapter 3
THE RISE OF THE NEW SCHOOLS AND THE CIRCULARITY OF VITALITY 41
   Tantric Vitality 41
   Dzogchen Riddles 45
   Crisis and Crisis Management 48
   Ambiguity and Circularity 53

Part II
THE EMBODIED-TECHNICAL CIRCULATION OF VITALITY

Chapter 4
THE FOUR VISIONS AND THE MEANING OF VITALITY 59
   An Experimental Study of Perception 59
   Seeing the Mythical Self 67

Chapter 5
THE PRELIMINARY PRACTICES AND THE DOMESTICATION OF VITALITY — 71
- The Activation of Vitality — 71
- The Yogi as Hunter and Herder — 76

Chapter 6
THE DZOGCHEN BODY AND THE INTERNALIZATION OF VITALITY — 83
- The Six Key Points — 84
- Embodying Myths — 85
- Lassoing Vitality — 89

Part III
THE INSTITUTIONAL-MATERIAL CRYSTALLIZATION OF VITALITY

Chapter 7
VITALITY AND THE BUDDHIST PATH — 95
- Longchenpa and the Systematization of Dzogchen Buddhism — 95
- Strategies for the Buddhicization of Dzogchen — 99
- Traces of the Quest for Vitality — 106

Chapter 8
THE INTRODUCTIONS BETWEEN LANGUAGE AND VITALITY — 113
- Experience and Language in Dzogchen Buddhism — 113
- The Introductions and the Quest for Vitality — 118

Chapter 9
DZOGCHEN YOGIS AND THE FORGOTTEN SHAMANS — 127
- Playing with the Mirror of the Shaman — 128
- The Interiorization of the Shaman's Headdress — 131
- The Indigenous Tibetan Practice of Transference — 134

CONCLUSION: MEDITATION AND THE ADVENTURE OF LIFE — 141

Notes — 145
References — 191
Index — 221

ACKNOWLEDGMENTS

As is customary for a research project of such proportions, I would first like to extend thanks to the many people, relationships, and institutions that have supported me over the past years. As a student, I had the privilege to be instructed by some of excellent scholars in Tibetan Studies: learning the fundamentals of Tibetan language and culture from Tom Tillemans and Pascale Hugon at the University of Lausanne, developing a sense of the vibrancy of the field of Indo-Tibetan Studies under the guidance of David Germano, Kurtis Schaeffer, Michael Sheehy, Karen Lang, Sonam Kachru, and John Nemec at the University of Virginia, and finally finding my place within this rich academic *maṇḍala* through my interactions with Yael Bentor, Eviatar Shulman, Ian MacCormack, and Dan Martin at the Hebrew University of Jerusalem.

This study, more specifically, would not have been possible without the help of David Germano, my PhD advisor, who first introduced me to the Great Perfection more than a decade ago during one of his graduate seminars. Although some of my interpretations of the tradition's history and teachings have started to deviate from his own understanding over the years, he has gained my lifelong allegiance for his sharp intellect and genuine generosity. This monograph is also the result of sustained conversations with Dan Martin, oftentimes taking place in his living room in Jerusalem, a sort of Middle Eastern museum of Tibetological texts and artifacts. During my time as postdoctoral researcher in Israel, he has not only inspired me with his vast knowledge and his intellectual flexibility, but also with a selfless and sustained mentorship that I will cherish forever. Finally, I am also humbled by the support and encouragement of Emeritus Professor Geoffrey Samuel, whose belief in this project was particularly important in moments when I myself started to lose faith in its viability.

Of course, I was also lucky to cross paths with many colleagues and friends in less formal ways. All of them have made academia a warmer—and more interesting—place over the past decade. Many thanks go to Jens Schlieter, Donatella, Rossi, Karénina Kollmar-Paulenz, Anne Klein, Matthew Kapstein, Janet Gyatso, Ingo Strauch, Jim Rheingans, Mark Allon, Georges Dreyfus, James Gentry, Jacob Dalton, Dylan Esler, Carmen Meinert, Roy Tzohar, Jean-Luc Achard, Henk Blezer, John Dunne, Volker Caumanns, Nick Trautz, David Divalerio, William McGrath, Natasha Mikles, Christina Kilby, Eva Natanya, Naomi Worth, Kali Cape, Dominic Sur, Ben Nourse, Adam Newman, Daniel Hirshberg, Katarina Turpeinen, Jue Liang, and Frédéric Richard.

Additionally, I am thankful to the US Department of Education for providing me with a Fulbright-Hays Dissertation Research Abroad Scholarship to undertake sustained fieldwork in Nepal. Living among various communities in the Kathmandu valley and the Himalayan mountains has allowed me to gain early glimpses of what would later become a core idea of this book: Indo-Tibetan Buddhism is an extraordinarily diverse and eclectic cultural phenomenon that grew out of the encounter of a wide variety of peoples and religions—many of which had originally very little to do with Buddhism. After finishing my dissertation, my postdoctoral research at the Hebrew University of Jerusalem has been funded by the Khyentse Foundation, the Lady Davis Fellowship, the Mandel Scholion Center, and the Azrieli Foundation. While all of them have provided me with the generous financial support to finish this book, I am particularly indebted to the team of the Azrieli Foundation. They not only enabled me to live in Tel Aviv—without a doubt one of the world's most dynamic cities—but they also stood fully behind my interdisciplinary research endeavor. I also express my gratitude to the editorial team at Bloomsbury, particularly Lalle Pursglove, who has been both professional and kind over the course of our collaboration.

Last but not least, a shout-out to my younger self! Vividly remembering childhood moments during which I was lying on an Italian beach while instinctively following the continuous flickers of *mouches volantes* dancing across my field of vision, I can only marvel at how much even the most rigorous science is fundamentally fueled by the power of intuition.

The ebook editions of this book are available open access under a CC BY-NC-ND 4.0 licence on bloomsburycollections.com. Open access was funded by the Swiss National Science Foundation.

INTRODUCTION: SKULLWARD LEAP MEDITATION AND THE QUEST FOR VITALITY

On the side of a mountain in the great Himalayas, there sits a yogi in a meditation pose. Surrounded by a stunning panorama of snow-capped peaks, he meditates by gazing into the deep blue of the cloudless Tibetan skies. Present yet relaxed, he holds his posture and gaze without moving, until he suddenly starts to perceive specks of light against the dark blue background of the open sky. At first, the lights just flicker and oscillate hectically. Then, they naturally start to form strings resembling sheep strung together by a rope. The meditator then gathers these luminous sheep together as if corralling them in a fence. Subsequently, the animals gradually shape-shift into more elaborate patterns, grow spectacularly in size, and configure other motifs, such as rainbows, lotus flowers, and even large *stūpas*, hemispherical structures containing relics of great Buddhist masters. Finally, without the slightest effort of active visualization, he finds himself in the midst of a magnificent *maṇḍala*, a world of gods. Instantly recognizing his own true nature as an enlightened being, he understands that the luminosity is nothing else than his own primordial wisdom, the nucleus of Buddha-nature located within his body. Implanted in his heart, this awareness is spontaneously mobilized to course through a series of light-channels consisting of white silk threads, crystal tubes, or far-reaching lassos that pervade his body. Like a lasso, the luminous energy is flung out of his eyes onto the canvass-like blue sky, and instantly recognized through his sight in the form of a magical display of lights. Ultimately, the visions swirl back into the expanse of the pure sky, evaporating just as miraculously as they appeared, and the physical body of the meditator dissolves into rainbow-colored lights.

The yogi performs "Skullward Leap" (*thod rgal*, Tögal),[1] the famous Tibetan sky-gazing meditation. It is the most secretive meditation practice of one of the most esoteric traditions of Buddhism,[2] namely the Heart-Essence (*snying thig*, Nyingthig) "Great Perfection" (*rdzogs pa chen po* or *rdzogs chen*, Dzogchen).[3] Because of its great importance, Dzogchen is recognized as the highest teaching of both the "Ancient" or Nyingma (*rnying ma*) School of Tibetan Buddhism as well as the tradition known as Tibetan Bön, both of which claim to be among the most ancient religious schools on the Tibetan plateau.[4] It is no coincidence that the meditation is centered on the open cloudless sky of Tibet as this openness perfectly represents the tradition's emphasis on freedom as a fundamental teaching. Indeed, the Great Perfection is notorious for relying on the idea of spaciousness—such as the "sky" (Tib. *nam mkha'*, Skt. *ākāśa/ gagaṇa*), the "expanse" (Tib. *dbyings*, Skt. *dhātu*), or "space" (Tib. *klong*, Skt. *dhātu*)—to represent the fundamental freedom underlying all of human existence (Rossi 1999, 35; Hillis 2002). While "freedom" (Skt. *mokṣa, mukti*, from *muc*, signifying "release," Tib. *thar pa*) is a core persuasion of Indo-Tibetan religions, it is particularly developed within the Great Perfection. The tradition articulated a robust vocabulary and grammar of "freedom," and even went as far as popularizing an ontology of natural freedom. David Higgins identifies this fundamental attitude by noting that Dzogchen Buddhism is profoundly pervaded by the idea of "primordial freedom" (*ye grol*),[5] and argues that it performed a radical transformation of the ancient Indian understanding of freedom, as it is "construed as a primary mode of being rather than as a teleocratic goal" (Higgins 2013, 219). "Humans," so Higgins summarizes the fundamental mindset of Dzogchen, "are fundamentally always and already free" (213–14).

Of course, this philosophical resonance of human nature is echoed in the tradition's meditative rhythm. Because freedom describes "how we are," rather than "capacities and properties of agents" (Higgins 2013, 219), it is not accidental that Dzogchen meditations are dominated by such themes as spontaneity, naturalness, and effortlessness. This becomes even more apparent if we look at the other primary meditation technique performed by Great Perfection yogis, namely Breakthrough (*trekchö, khregs chod*). If Skullward Leap—undoubtedly the highest Dzogchen technique—is a practice that involves the application of simple yet disciplined postures, gazes, and breathing patterns leading to the gradual evolution of visions, Breakthrough is a sort of non-practice, frequently simply described as resting within the mind's natural state (*gnas lugs*).[6] Longchenpa (1308–1364), the tradition's most eminent scholar-practitioner who is also known under his full name Longchen Rabjam Drime Özer (klong chen rab 'byams pa dri med 'od zer),[7] correlates "freedom" to "simply letting be" (*bzhag pa tsam*) and "simply being aware" (*shes pa tsam*) (*The Treasury of the Supreme Vehicle*, vol. II: 1613.2).

> Because "freedom" (*grol*) is not the same as "liberation" (*bkrol*), there is no need to make efforts in view and meditation. Since freedom abides as one's natural mode of being, this means that [freedom] is "unmodified" and "unfabricated." As a consequence, letting body, speech, and mind simply relax in their natural condition and abiding in the natural state of mind itself is called "freedom." (*The Treasury of the Supreme Vehicle*, vol. II: 1615.2-4)[8]

The increasing popularity of Dzogchen Buddhism among contemporary practitioners is also related to a larger phenomenon known as the rise of Buddhist Modernism.[9] As David McMahan argued, Buddhist modernism led not only to the unprecedented identification of "meditation as the essential Buddhist practice,"[10] but it also exhibits our culture's fascination with freedom. The term *mokṣa* invokes "tremendous cultural resonances" in the modern West as "it inevitably rings the notes of individual freedom, creative freedom, freedom of choice, freedom from oppression, freedom of thought, freedom of speech, freedom from neuroses, free to be me—let freedom ring, indeed" (McMahan 2008, 18).

More specifically, we could summarize the main characteristics of this modernist construction of meditation under the aegis of freedom by means of three processes, namely, demythologization, psychologization, and detraditionalization (McMahan 2008, 42).[11] First, demythologization results in cultural freedom as it constructs meditation as largely decontextualized practice detachable from the wider mythical, cosmological, and social context of Buddhism. Instead of being rooted in a particular place, time, and community, meditation is seen as a universal practice that is ubiquitous, present-centered, and focused on our individual selves. Second, psychologization brings with it a psychological freedom as meditation is seen as a process concerned with our "internal" realities and the experiential transformation of our consciousness, rather than the external reality of our bodies and the material universe surrounding us. Instead of being seen as a practice that involves all our somatic energies to explore the relationship between our internal awareness and the material world around us, meditation is a technique of relaxation that serves the recognition of our true inner self. Third, detraditionalization leads to institutional freedom as meditation is oftentimes practices outside of the institutional structures of traditional religion. Instead of being understood as a practice that is grounded in larger ritual, ethical, and philosophical structures established by tradition, meditation is regarded as a spontaneous and creative inner experience largely independent of institutional and social realities.

If Buddhist modernism embraces the ethos of freedom and encapsulates it in a description of meditation as something that is demythologized, psychologized, and detraditionalized, this book offers a systematic analysis of Skullward Leap meditation as a corrective. Specifically, it understands meditation as part of a larger "contemplative system," which consists of multiple components that surround the actual practice like frames that border a painting. In so doing, the book not only eschews the three reductive moves of Buddhist modernism, but it repairs them by restoring the frames of myth, embodiment, and institution. If the modern conception of meditation is largely free-floating,[12] the core structure of this study—consisting of three major parts—provides a tight framework to approach meditation in a methodologically sound way. Indeed, neutralizing the modernist construction of meditation under the aegis of freedom, each part of the tripartite structure restores one of the frames that have too frequently been overlooked, namely mythical-historical narratives, technical-embodied instructions, and institutional-material tradition.

Such a comprehensive investigation into the contemplative system of Dzogchen requires a fundamentally interdisciplinary and comparative methodological attitude. Inspired by a long-standing tradition of historians of religions, particularly prominent in the Italian School of the History of Religions,[13] the study traces large and seemingly universal ideas such as the centrality of the sky and explores them in a variety of contexts. This exhilarating journey leads us to sample distant worlds that span across time and space, from the very creation of the cosmos out of eggs to archeological traces in burial mounds of Tibetan kings, from early indigenous myths of flying deer to the elaborate anatomy of yogic bodies gradually accrued over centuries of embodied practice, from Stone Age rock paintings of antlered figures to MRI scans of human brains produced in cutting-edge laboratories, from the hunting behaviors of traditional peoples living in the Siberian steppes to the lives of renowned philosophers in bustling monasteries in Central Tibet, from the seekers of enlightenment in the years after the introduction of Buddhism to Tibet in the seventh century to the contemporary clinical studies of perceptual hallucinations among migraine sufferers, from the practices of witchcraft among contemporary religious communities of the Himalayas to the serene scenes of hermetic meditators sitting in isolated places. Such a journey could potentially lead to a flattening of the topographies of these varied contexts. To avoid this, the approach in this study is best described as a "contrasting comparison," which pays equal attention to resemblances and divergencies. In fact, despite the discovery of fascinating similarities in these colorful environments, our investigative itinerary is also marked by forensic attention to details that serve to highlight the idiographic dimension of each unique cultural manifestation. To continue with my illustration, while the conception of the sky maintains certain stable characteristics, each context substantiates unique peculiarities that depend on factors like available evidence (e.g., archeological ruins vs. MRI scans), disciplinary perspective (e.g., ethnography vs. philology), historical change (e.g., ancient myths written in the ninth century vs. philosophical treatises written in the fourteenth century), and so forth.

Moving beyond the archetypical symbol of the sky and the modernist ethos of freedom to study Tögal as part of a complex contemplative system has far-reaching consequences for our understanding of the Dzogchen tradition. It is no exaggeration to say that *Skullward Leap* represents a watershed moment in the reception history of the Great Perfection with potentially powerful repercussions for our understanding of both Tibetan religion and meditation practice more generally. Just like a depiction of animals in an ancient rock painting reveals an entirely different meaning if it is no longer approached like an artistic creation in the contemporary sense, but rather a symbol transmitting a semantic logic that is itself profoundly shaped by its cultural-religious context, Skullward Leap starts to change in appearance once it is placed within its unique universe. Today, the Heart-Essence tradition holds a prominent position in the world of Tibetan Buddhism, and scholarship generally argues that its scriptures grew out of the tantric traditions of India imported to Tibet during the time of the empire between the seventh and the ninth centuries.[14] While the post hoc self-narration of the tradition emphasizes its thoroughly Indic and Buddhist nature, a deeper look into the mythical, technical, and institutional dimensions of Dzogchen leaves us perplexed as we encounter an overabundance of idiosyncratic motifs that seem completely foreign to Buddhism and unique to the practice of Tögal.[15]

The characteristics are too many to list them comprehensively here. Nonetheless, some of the most perplexing peculiarities can briefly mentioned: the overwhelming prioritization of the sky as a source of enlightened energy that manifests simultaneously in the sky, in our bodies, as well as the space in between;

the description of this circulating energy as sheep that are chained together; the yogi's contemplative interaction with such animalistic beings, which involves the imitation of their behavior and the visionary attempt to capture them in fence-like structures; the luminous pathways inside the meditator's body—described as deer-hearts, silk-channels, buffalo-horns, or far-reaching lassos—which reproduce the terminology of the hunting of animalistic vitality as if internalizing the quest for precious substances; accompanying techniques such as the preliminary practices and introductions to the nature of the mind, which involve the use of contemplative paraphernalia associated with such animals and their most characteristic traits like silk; and the culmination of the practice, during which the body of the practitioner is said to turn into a rainbow body, dissolving into the sky by transforming into light. Although these idiosyncratic motifs have puzzled experts in the field in the past, scholarship has generally avoided the thorny question of their origin. By contrast, and this is the first argument of *Skullward Leap*, I believe that these traits point to the Great Perfection's true identity as a tradition that is not suffused by a Buddhist or Indian ethos of freedom, but rather by indigenous Tibetan priorities centered on the "quest for vitality."

One could, of course, object and suggest that the presence of pre-Buddhist motifs in Dzogchen does not necessarily mean that it emerged outside of the province of Buddhism. After all, "an entangled encounter between different religious traditions and cultural spheres," to put it in the eloquent words of Georgios Halkias, "generates a vibrant manifold of similarities and differences where both indigenous and imported elements and processes reveal their identities relationally, in their creative responses to the challenges of identity and continuity they faced" (Halkias 2016, 131). It is theoretically possible that a set of Indian practices entered Tibet and there found articulation in terms of locally inherited concepts and metaphors. This book, by contrast, vigorously ratifies the revolutionary theory of an indigenous origin. I agree with Dan Martin, who once wrote that an effective way to establish whether "particular items, practices and ideas are most likely to be indigenous to Tibet," is to simply "sift out those things that clearly came from India and see what remains" (Martin 2014, 79). In our case, the matter is astonishingly simple: Not only do we not find a sun-gazing technique in Indian Buddhist sources, but most of the items in the list of eccentricities that mark the Dzogchen contemplative system are equally absent.

Of course, other readers could object and suggest that just because a tradition appears in Tibet in the tenth century does not necessarily mean that it must be "indigenous." After all, Tibet—due to the introduction of Indian religious teachings in the seventh century—was already a "Buddhist" domain at that time. However, while it is, indeed, true that the main scriptures of the Heart-Essence Great Perfection appear suddenly in the form of so-called treasures (*gter ma*, *Terma*) in the tenth century, they seem too far removed from all of their potential Buddhist "ancestors." It is clear that they are neither directly flowing out of earlier forms of Dzogchen, such as the "mind series" (*sems sde*) or the "space series" (*klong sde*),[16] nor do they seem to belong to Chinese teachings like Chan Buddhism or specific tantric systems imported from India. At the same time, it is extremely unlikely that these texts were just the result of an impromptu invention by some renegade scholars, who came up with a series of random texts that they would call the Heart-Essence Great Perfection. The teachings offer us a picture of an established and complex contemplative system that is premised on extensive yogic experience acquired through many years of practice.[17] A more careful look at the evidence available to us does not only reveal that Dzogchen is an extremely ornate contemplative system—equipped with elaborate myths of cosmogony, detailed spiritual anatomies, phenomenological accounts of visionary journeys, and much more—but that it does not just suddenly appear in tenth-century Tibet. On the contrary, we are dealing here with a long-standing indigenous religious tradition that reaches back into a period that precedes the introduction of Buddhism in the seventh century before being transformed repeatedly through its contact with other teachings that flourished on the plateau.

The timing of this watershed moment in the study of the Great Perfection is felicitous as we have witnessed a sprouting surge in research into the indigenous traits of Tibetan culture, with more and more manuscripts of various provenance becoming available in recent years.[18] In this regard, I would like to highlight the importance of two scholars' interventions. First, the work undertaken by John Bellezza, who has relentlessly brought to light localized popular practices by drawing on textual sources about the pre-Buddhist society (written during the empire and the ensuing centuries), archeological evidence, and anthropological data from contemporary Tibetan communities. In so doing, he effectively succeeds in reconstructing an indigenous worldview and the mythical-ritual religion of pre-Buddhist Tibet (Bellezza 1999; 2000; 2002; 2005). The second endeavor worthy of note is Toni Huber's *Source of Life* (2020), in which he has recently exposed what is likely the driving theme of indigenous Tibetan culture, namely the quest for vitality. By combining ethnographic fieldwork among highland populations in Bhutan and Arunachal Pradesh with more extensive textual research that extends into the eastern Himalayas to include the Naxi and Qiang peoples, Huber offers unprecedented insights into how indigenous myths and rituals regulate fertility, virility, procreation by periodically revitalizing the human realm on earth with the life-sustaining energies emanating from the sky.[19]

The works of Bellezza and Huber also share another trait with my appreciation of early Tibetan culture, namely its close association with Bön. Although the religious tradition only self-consciously formulated its identity in the tenth century (Blezer 2011b, 212), it too existed much earlier and centered its focus on the quest for vitality.[20] As we will soon see, in the historical reconstruction of the earliest period of the Great Perfection, the distinction between Bön and Buddhism—particularly in the case of the Ancient School—is largely artificial (and anachronistic).[21] It is hardly a coincidence that both Nyingma and Bön share the practice of Skullward Leap,[22] the teachings of Dzogchen, and the literary medium of treasure revelation; all of which are directly or indirectly related to their pre-Buddhist origins. In fact, the two contemplative systems are profoundly intertwined, not only in these structural similarities, but also in their historical origins. Particularly the Bönpos are adamant that Dzogchen originated somewhere in Central Asia and certainly outside of India. To wit, the original scriptures were composed in the kingdom of Zhangzhung in a region in the Northwest of Tibet, frequently identified as Tazig, a term that points into the Iranian world.[23]

Hence, when I use the expression "indigenously Tibetan," I do not mean to say that these practices are exclusive to Tibet, but rather that they are indigenous in the sense that they were originally non-Buddhist.[24] To account for the fact that Tibet belonged to a wider cultural realm that included much of Central and Northern Asia, I frequently speak of the "wider Tibetosphere." The prehistoric inhabitants of the Tibetan plateau belonged to various different ethnic groups (Hazod 2012). These consisted not only of Turkic and Tibeto-Burmese peoples, but also had close contacts with Indo-Scythian communities (Hazod 2009, 175). Throughout the study, I will also make frequent references to parallel ideas and practices in Scytho-Siberian, Iranian, Turkic, and Mongolian cultures. It might be relevant to note that experts have collected more and more evidence—including prehistoric art, ancient texts, and contemporary ethnographical data—that point to the pervasive and long-standing presence of a cult of the sky associated with deer across much of the Eurasian steppes.[25] While it is beyond my capacity to reconstruct this Eurasian substratum,[26] and virtually impossible to demonstrate its possible historical influences on the development of early Tibetan culture, future research could explore such links in order to complement the focus on Buddhism in our understanding of Tibet. It could even be argued that studies of the abundant depictions of animals like deer and sheep in Tibetan rock art,[27] the discovery of a Himalayan cult of animal guides,[28] the study of ancient manuscripts regarding burial customs and postmortem journeys involving deer or sheep in early Tibet,[29] study of artifacts in silver, gold, and wood found during archaeological excavations of Tibetan tombs and from Zhangzhung and the Tibetan empire,[30] and the identification of the deer as a major structuring device for mythical-ritual practices among indigenous Tibetans[31] have allowed the field of Tibetan studies to adumbrate the first contours of a more local cult of the sky-deer.

This wider substratum brings us to another element that makes our venture into the origins of Dzogchen a bit tricky, namely the close association with "shamanism." While there are many definitions of this term and it has oftentimes been applied too widely in discussions of Tibetan religions (Achard 2022, 1–2), it is nonetheless a relevant and effective concept if defined appropriately.[32] In the present, shamanism finds its most vivid expression in the mythical-ritual world of Himalayan, Siberian, and North Asian religions. It involves the belief in the sky as the primary source of vitality, the conviction that vitality moves between the heavenly and the earthly realms by means of messenger beings like deer and sheep,[33] and the practical performance of ritual acts by figures known as shamans, who successfully appropriate the help of the animalistic emissaries of vitality to reinvigorate the community of humans in an effort to heal, protect, or solve other forms of crisis. Upon first blush, these pragmatic objectives of shamanism might seem far removed from the salvific ambitions of Dzogchen Buddhism. However, I will show that Skullward Leap is a meditation practice that operates along the same cultural continuum as shamanic traditions. While they are both deeply embedded within the quest for vitality and the sky-deer, they find divergent means to express their invigorating journeys to the heavenly realm.

Having shared my manuscript with experts in the fields of Tibetan and Buddhist studies, as well as beyond, I am under no illusion that my arguments will strike some readers as fanciful. I nonetheless invite you to suspend your judgment until the end of this book. It is no exaggeration to state that the sky-deer's role as the primordial source, transmitting messenger, and lasting object of vitality nourishes the Heart-Essence Great Perfection so deeply that this book's seemingly fantastical thesis cannot be dismissed easily. The animalistic emissaries of heavenly vitality do not just surface in some tangential reference in an enigmatic text, but rather permeate the entire contemplative system, from the mythical background, through the conception of the body, to the material universe.

Equally crucial, the resemblances are not only linguistic and thematic in nature but pervade the very structure and function of the practice of Skullward Leap itself. It is for this reason that I have decided to deviate from the existing translations of *thod rgal* as "Direct Transcendence" or "Leap Over" by proposing a more literal designation of the practice as "Skullward Leap."[34] It is likely that these translations are anachronistic reinterpretations based on the gradual transmission of the practice from its original indigenous context to Buddhism.[35] In light of the significant influence of the indigenous Tibetan substratum on the early development of the Great Perfection, it is much more likely that the expression *thod rgal* means something radically different. Literally, Tögal is an expression that consists of the Tibetan words *thod* ("above," "over," but also "head wrapper," "turban," "skull") and *rgal* ("to leap over"). In the larger Tibetan cultural area, in fact, it is the most elevated part of the human body—the skull or, its extension in the form of a turban-like headdress—that allows the religious practitioner to gain access to the source of vitality located in the heavens. Both the head and the headdress, as we will see, have deep resonances with animals—particularly deer and sheep—which are central for the sky-gazing practice because of their ability to ascend and descend vertically to move in between various realms of existence.

To be clear, contemporary experts on Dzogchen Buddhism did not simply mistranslate the expression *thod rgal*. On the contrary, they clearly rigorously followed the tradition's own self-representation as a unique religious movement that allows practitioners to simply "leap over." In contrast to the tedious processes of mental and physical transformation, advocated by other Buddhist traditions on the Tibetan plateau and beyond, Dzogchen meditation enables practitioners to directly "transcend" embodied human existence by becoming their truest selves as beings of light. This Buddhist reading of the term Tögal—which has also led to a search for Sanskrit equivalents like *avaskandha*, *viṣkanda*, *vyutkrānta*, or *vyatikrāntaka*—as an expression of simultaneist enlightenment is not to be neglected as it has come to dominate the Dzogchen system as we know it today.[36] This understanding, I must hasten to add, is the result of a long and opaque process involving the transformation of both the Dzogchen tradition and the meaning of vitality in Tibet. This brings us to another key objective of this study, namely the historical development of the cult of vitality and the sky-deer over time. As the discussion of the book gradually unfolds, it becomes ever clearer that the Dzogchen contemplative system, by and large, mirrors the cultural history of Tibet as a whole. The tripartite structure of this study transmits this historical development by reverberating the vicissitudes in the Tibetan conception of vitality.[37] Here, the sky-deer also reveals a heuristic function that is closely related to its identity more generally. The deer does not only possess a complex semantic status throughout this region. It is associated with the idea of "transition" between various worlds, a sort of mediator between the world of animals and humans, between heaven and earth, between life and death, and so forth. In this study, this dual nature of the deer reflects the status of Skullward Leap, which changes rather dramatically with time while simultaneously maintaining its core meaning across the centuries. At the same time, we have a movement in the opposite direction as the Buddhist orthodoxy struggles to integrate the pre-Buddhist tendencies present on the Tibetan plateau. Particularly, the moment of the introduction of Buddhism during the empire in the seventh century, the renaissance of Tibetan culture in the ninth century, and the rise of the scholastic tradition in the thirteenth and fourteenth centuries left decisive marks on the Dzogchen Great Perfection.

Part I opens with a major bang as it looks at the mythical-ritual foundations of the Great Perfection to suggest that it is a tradition that was originally neither Buddhist nor Indian, but rather formed in a cultural "substratum" of pre-Buddhist culture. In a journey filled with rich stories, we travel into territories that most readers have never even imagined. Specifically, it leads us into the world of early Tibet, which we access through a body of textualized ritual narratives, so-called antecedent tales (*rabs*). These texts were written over the course of many centuries, with the oldest ones dating to the ninth century and the newer ones, frequently by anonymous authors, still used in ritual traditions throughout the Himalayas today.[38] Despite this temporal and spatial distribution, however, the narratives have been studied by many scholars as a genre of texts because of their protagonists, themes, and structure. For heuristic reasons, these texts can be divided into two categories: first ancient texts found in the library cave at Dunhuang (敦煌) that was likely sealed in the early eleventh century,[39] on the one hand, and a broad collection of antecedent tales belonging to the wider Tibetosphere that vary greatly in their dates of redaction, ownership, and date of discovery, on the other.[40] Although the specific texts that I will discuss are not directly associated with the Great Perfection but circulated within the Ancient School of Buddhism and Tibetan Bön,[41] I allow myself to group them together for the simple reason that they represent a unified worldview centered on the quest for vitality and the cult of the sky-deer.

Part II moves beyond the mythical background stories of the heavenly origins of vitality to analyze the embodied technical aspects of Skullward Leap by offering a close reading of a group of texts known as *The Seventeen Tantras of the Esoteric Instruction Series* (henceforth: *The Seventeen Tantras*).[42] These texts, which the Buddhist tradition claims were brought to Tibet by an Indian monk known as Vimalamitra and later discovered as treasures in the late tenth century,[43] are the authoritative scriptures of the Heart-Essence Great Perfection.[44]

Although scholarship has a tendency to refer to them as a collection, a practice that I maintain in this study, it is likely that the scriptures were written by multiple hands and over the course of decades or even centuries (Cuevas 2003, 62).[45] I will not be able to reconstruct their precise redaction. However, I suggest that they were heavily influenced by earlier indigenous Tibetan beliefs and practices. More specifically, I demonstrate how the Great Perfection used Skullward Leap practice to mobilize the flow of life. The contemplative system, indeed, internalized the mythical universe, turning the body into the stage where the meditators would play out the quest for vitality and the cult of the sky-deer.

Finally, in Part III, we turn our attention to a third type of literature, namely the commentaries composed by the great fourteenth-century scholar-yogi Longchenpa. Most contemporary practitioners of Dzogchen are familiar with this buddhicized version of the Great Perfection as his extensive writings organized, unified, and systematized the tradition. Specifically, Longchenpa gave Dzogchen both internal definition—representing the core of its teachings in harmony with the Ancient School's exoteric (i.e., sūtric) and esoteric (i.e., tantric) teachings—and legitimacy toward other Buddhist schools of his time—situating it in relationship to the other major schools of Buddhism. While Longchenpa was an exceptionally prolific writer,[46] this part draws primarily on his most influential writings for the systematization of the Great Perfection, namely *The Treasury of the Supreme Vehicle* and *The Treasury of Words and Meaning*.[47] Analyzing these texts, we discover that Longchenpa was not only a great source of vitalization for the Dzogchen tradition, but also threatened to destroy some of its most characteristic traits. For one, Longchenpa simply brushes over some of the most idiosyncratic motifs related to vitality that abound in the earliest tantric scriptures, giving them little to no attention at all. Even more importantly, he sometimes radically alters the logic of the existing tradition by inserting the circularity of the quest for vitality into a linear Buddhist path that culminates in a state of final liberation.

We are now almost ready to embark on our quest for the astounding features in the Dzogchen system through the reconstruction of the pre-Buddhist Tibetan world and commencing our journey through the gradually intensifying buddhicization of the tradition that reached its climax in the systematization by the great Longchenpa in the fourteenth century. Before doing so, however, I encourage you to keep our opening reflections on the nature of meditation in the back of your mind while reading this book. If meditation is no longer simply about the fundamental freedom of the open sky above Tibet, but rather about facing the ever-recurring adventures of life—emblazoned in the indigenous Tibetan quests for various life-sustaining energies—then this book also offers us an opportunity to adjust our definition of this phenomenally popular contemporary practice. In other words, by rehabilitating the quest for vitality as primary impetus for Skullward Leap, the book also adumbrates an innovative model of meditation as an open-ended practice that animates practitioners to face the most challenging moments of their lives with courage and curiosity, imagination and creativity, and playfulness and excitement; qualities that are oftentimes overlooked in contemporary descriptions of contemplation.

Part I

THE MYTHICAL-HISTORICAL CONCEPTION OF VITALITY

As a minor tradition that developed on the margins of Buddhist culture, either simply overlooked or actively suppressed by the powerful orthodoxy, Dzogchen features significant—and generally underestimated—affinities with indigenous Tibetan folk religion. While this first part makes hardly any reference to Skullward Leap practice, the remainder of the book will offer many justifications as to why this thorough reconstruction of the indigenous Tibetan worldview is warranted. Myths are commonly held to be something akin to fiction. However, we must never forget that we enter a world in which such stories are real because they provide the framework for ritual and contemplative practices. Since our understanding of pre-Buddhist culture is still very limited, this part of the study turns to early Tibetan myths about the origin of life on earth in an attempt to reconstruct this early universe of beliefs and practices. Particularly in Bön sources, this conception of vitality boasts the preeminence of the heavens as a source of vitality, as well as the role of animals like sheep and deer as mobilizing agents that transport vitality between the realms of the sky and the earth. The quest for life was so central to early Tibet that it even gave rise to a unique vocabulary composed of words like *lha*, *bla*, *mu/dmu/smu/rmu*, *phya/phywa*, or *g.yang*, terms that can all be situated within the semantic field of "vitality." Myths, moreover, are real not only because they offer the blueprints for various religious practices like Skullward Leap meditation, but also because they are intimately linked to the historical circumstances in which they were composed. In our case, the stories point not only to an early Tibetan fascination with heavenly vitality, but also testify to the fact that this model of vertical vitality was challenged by worldviews that were likely imported from India. Indeed, the political context of early Tibet was rather tumultuous, including a series of cataclysmic events like the conversion to Buddhism during the height of the great empire in the seventh century, the collapse of the kingdom in the second half of the ninth century, and the Renaissance of Tibetan culture during the eleventh and twelfth centuries.

Chapter 1

THE SKY AS SOURCE OF VITALITY IN ANCIENT TIBET

The Great Perfection flamboyantly flaunts its thoroughly Tibetan temperament in the most obvious trait of *Tögal* meditation, namely its overwhelming fascination with the sky.[1] Indeed, it is hardly a coincidence that the most emblematic performance of Skullward Leap takes place in the open air. As yogis gaze into the sky above Tibet for extended periods of time, they gradually realize their true identity and reach a state of enlightenment that leads to the dissolution of their material bodies as if restoring them to their truest element as luminous beings of an ethereal realm. Arising on the Tibetan plateau, "the roof of the world," the place where the sky meets the earth, this chapter is dedicated to the Great Perfection's "prehistory" during which the heavenly world was the locus of a divine vitality that sustained life on earth. Exploring certain key motifs of this early mythical conception of the sky—such as the ethereal origins of kings and humans, the vertical movement of animals like sheep and deer, or the continued connection between those realms by means of a luminous sky-cord—I suggest that the quest for vitality represents the centerpiece of pre-Buddhist beliefs about the origins of life-giving energy. Furthermore, the chapter argues that the origin of the Tibetan infatuation with the sky as a realm of vitality might be sought in the Eurasian cult of the sky-deer. Although scholarship outside of the Slavic world has not yet paid much attention to this phenomenon—the overwhelming majority of serious discussions are written in Russian—the cult of the deer has a great significance in northern Eurasia, where it formed in the Paleolithic, developed through the Mesolithic, Neolithic, and the Bronze Age, and remains popular among shamanic societies of places like Siberia and Central Asia until today.

Dzogchen Conceptions of Origins

Tibetan religions are marked by a pronounced concern for origins. Such a "preoccupation, sometimes to the point of obsession," is particularly prevalent in the Ancient School, where we find extended "lines of continuity that link present institutions, or their scattered remains, to both divine and human origins" (Aris 1997, 9).[2] Identifying self-consciously as a Buddhist tradition, its adherents refer back to the "earlier spread of the teachings" (*bstan pa snga dar*) when the first Buddhist scriptures were introduced to the plateau during the height of the great Tibetan Empire (*bod chen po*, c. seventh century to 842). It was during this period that Tibet was converted to Buddhism under the aegis of the three Religious Kings (*mes dbon rnam gsum*) or Dharma Kings (*chos gyal*),[3] Songtsen Gampo (*srong btsan sgam po*, 569/605–649),[4] Trisong Detsen (*khri srong lde btsan*,[5] reigned 755–797/804) and Ralpacen (*ral pa can*, 802–838).[6] Among Tibetan Buddhists, this period is remembered as the most illustrious moment of their nation, and the extent of the kingdom was indeed very impressive, including parts of China, India, Nepal, and Mongolia.[7]

Critical scholarship generally agrees that Dzogchen is thoroughly Buddhist and that its scriptures grew out of the tantric traditions of India imported to Tibet during the time of the empire between the seventh and the ninth centuries. In fact, this was not only the period during which Tibetans developed their own writing system by adapting the Gupta script from northern India or Nepal (Scherrer-Schaub 2012; Schaik 2011; Schuh 2013), but also the time of a massive state-sponsored translation project that led to the creation of an impressive royal library that served as foundation for the establishment of Buddhism in Tibet (Scherrer-Schaub 2002). Although it is classed as Atiyoga, the highest of the three supreme forms of yoga, the Great Perfection's texts are said to have developed from the lower tantric vehicles, Anuyoga and, more specifically, Mahāyoga.[8] Samten Karmay, for instance, asserts his belief that it emerged out of the practice of the primary Mahāyoga tantra of the Ancient School, the *Secret Nucleus Tantra* (*Guhyagarbhatantra*). To wit, the Dzogchen teachings are supposed to have expanded upon a specific stage of meditation within this tantric school. Indeed, in the concluding moments of many tantric practices, after engaging in visual and physical practices, the yogis rest in the natural state of the pure and luminous mind that remains after the visualization is dissolved (Karmay 2007, 11–14). Sam van Schaik, building on this argument, even suggests that in the early tradition of the Ancient School, the presence of both Mahāyoga and Dzogchen does not point to the "existence of two separate traditions" (Van Schaik 2004a, 167), but rather interwoven approaches, with the former serving as somewhat of a philosophical backdrop for the latter.

In many ways, this idyllic picture of Great Perfection Buddhism fits well with what has been described as the "perfectibilism" of Buddhism.[9] "In the final analysis," so Matthew Kapstein writes, "yoga is always a sort of perfectibilism, which is clearly indicated by the characteristic term used to denote the successful adept, 'siddha' (Tib. *grub thob*), which means 'accomplished, perfected, completed'" (1992, 199). The idea of discovering a state of perfection—marked by dissolution and openness—is central to the Dzogchen tradition and correlated to its emphasis on inherent freedom. As its very name already indicates, the Great Perfection is premised on the belief that human beings are already inherently perfected and that they have access to a ground of "awareness" (Tib. *rig pa*, Skt. *vidyā*), without the need for transformation. In *The Mirror of the Heart of Vajrasattva*, one of the early Dzogchen scriptures, the etymology of Dzogchen is explained as follows:

> Because awareness is perfect primordial wisdom in the state free from action, it is perfection. Because meditation is perfect stainless wisdom without concepts, it is perfection. Because behavior is perfect all-pervasive wisdom in an uncontrived state, it is perfection. Because view is perfect non-conceptual wisdom in the realm beyond achievement, it is perfection. Because fruit is the perfect twenty-five wisdoms in the realm beyond frame of reference, it is perfection. (372.1–3)[10]

In the contemplative system of Dzogchen, this idea of inherent perfection, of an ever-present "ground of awareness," is also a central attribute of its mythological narratives. Arguably the most famous myth of the Great Perfection is its myth of cosmogony out of a vase of light, also known as the "manifestation of the ground" (*gzhi snang*). More specifically, the myth tells the story of the creation of our universe and the liberation of a primordial Buddha, whose name is Samantabhadra (lit. "All Good One," Tib. *kun tu bzang po*). Relying on a particularly striking image, the initial setting of the tale opens with the description of a perfectly self-contained and luminously shining "youthful body in a vase" (*gzhon nu bum pa'i sku*), which breaks open to shine forth rainbow-colored lights. If the body in a vase is a symbolic representation of the fundamental concept of the "ground" (*gzhi*), it is also linked to Samantabhadra, who is also known as the "First Buddha." Indeed, Samantabhadra, upon emanating from the source of light, is immediately liberated because he recognizes himself within the luminous display of light rays emanating from the vase of light. Since this innate wisdom, the capacity to recognize our true identity as already perfect beings is present in all sentient beings, Samantabhadra serves as an example for all the practitioners of Dzogchen until today.[11] This foundational cosmogonic myth of Dzogchen, recounting the story of a ground of awareness located in a luminous whole and the instantaneous self-liberation upon the emission of light rays, could serve as a sort of campaign slogan for the tradition as it perfectly encapsulates the Nyingmapa account of the Buddhist conversion of Tibet. Originating in the holy land of Buddhism, the Dzogchen teachings spread to the north where they get transmitted to the Tibetan people, who are immediately recognizing themselves in its doctrine of inherent perfection and effortless enlightenment, and manifest it sociopolitically in the glory of the prosperous realm of the Tibetan empire.

This mythical-historical self-representation of the Nyingma tradition, however, is so far removed from the historical reality of the formative years of the Dzogchen teachings that they must be recognized as a later construction of Buddhist exegetes.[12] Indeed, during the first centuries of its existence, the tradition developed on the margins of the Buddhist world, with many lineage holders struggling to find patronage and institutional support and the teachings being accused of being heretical and non-Buddhist.[13] There is little doubt that the tradition must have been a rather puzzling religious phenomenon that was marked by a fundamental tension—a sudden appearance of a seemingly long-standing tradition—adumbrated in the introduction. So how did the tradition move from such a paradoxical status of a "sudden appearance of something long-standing" arrive to a relatively standard self-depiction of its origination as an Indian Buddhist teaching? To say it in the words of the German Tibetologist Peter Schwieger, we could say that the great Buddhist empire and the tantric scriptures of India are the foundational stones in the "history of myth" of the Old School.[14] Schwieger uses this expression to argue that "history, understood as the remembered past, has the function in Tibetan culture of providing a solid basis for, and defining, sociocultural interrelationships in a monocentric culture" (Schwieger 2013, 66).[15] This process of "conversion" of Tibetan culture to a monocentric Buddhist worldview was anything but harmonious. On the contrary, I tend to believe that Bellezza's observations regarding the millennial historical revisionism involved in the Buddhist adaptation of spirit-mediums can be applied to the history of the Nyingma Great Perfection:

> Regarding the cultural orientation of Tibet, I present the standpoint that a reconfiguration of its historical discourse, resulting from an obscuring and dissolution of early religious and mythic forms, caused Tibetans to become ever more remote from their pre-Imperial cultural heritage. The cultural history of Tibet over the last millennium would seem to testify to a relentless suppression, assimilation and reconstruction of antecedent legacies in an effort to bring them in compliance with Buddhist sensibilities and tradition. (Bellezza 2005, 10)[16]

Unlike the inquiry of Bellezza, however, this study is not concerned with archeological evidence that can be dated and documented, but rather with texts that were in all likelihood redacted after the arrival of Buddhism in Tibet. The case of the quest for vitality and the cult of the sky-deer might be more akin to pre-Buddhist Tibetan ancestor cults. Here too, scholarship has pointed out that while its existence is almost certain, its nature remains enigmatic due to the scarcity of extant primary sources. Just like Bellezza, Erik Haarh attributed this lack of sources to the activity of Buddhist writers, who suppressed the indigenous trends of Tibetan religion, purging it of references to ancient ancestral deities (such as *mtshun*) from the textual record (Haarh 1969, 226, 316). In light of this literary expulsion, we need to ask ourselves whether we can excavate this ancient indigenous layer of Tibetan culture through a sort of textual archeology based on very limited and fragmented sources.[17] In response to this challenge, I would like to invoke the work of Hank Blezer, who has dedicated much effort to the reconstruction of early Tibetan history. In an article dedicated to the unearthing early history of the Dzogchen tradition, which he recognizes to be carrying an "aura of antiquity, which reaches back into an obscure 'pre-Buddhist' past, beyond the Neolithic even"—he summarizes his position as follows:

> Traditional Tibetan historical data and narratives, however unlikely they may appear, are not to be dismissed off-hand, they can only be assessed properly if it is clear why exactly Tibetan writers present and narrativise their data the way they do, or, in other words, if the wider two-sided narrativising historiographical context—of meaningful emplotment and identity—is properly understood, as it

is there, rather than with an approximately positivist factuality of the data, that the primal concern of traditional historical writing lies. (Blezer 2011b, 209)

Elsewhere, Blezer elaborates that the lack of "historical" sources does not necessarily mean that we cannot learn more about the tradition's history as the cosmogony of Dzogchen can be understood as a sort of historical self-description of the tradition. Specifically, he points to apparent correlations between the "cosmological parts" of the tradition's myths and "the architecture of the post hoc restructuring or even new invention of the earliest, transcendent origins" of its lineages (Blezer 2012, 127). In the first chapters, I will closely follow Blezer's approach by pointing to many parallels between the mythical narratives found in Dzogchen and the early history of Tibet, particularly surrounding the great empire. Indeed, although scholarship has frequently focused primarily on the cosmogony out of the manifestation of the ground, the Great Perfection scriptures consist of a variety of myths, many of which do not subscribe to the Buddhist soteriology of perfection, but rather an ethos of vitality. While the third chapter will deal with a series of such indigenous narratives in the Dzogchen scriptures, particularly those dedicated to the quest for precious substances, we do not need to go that far afield to find pre-Buddhist motifs. These ideas are so prevalent in the Nyingma Great Perfection that they even surface in the famous myth of cosmogony that we already looked at. Indeed, if the epiphany of the ground is oftentimes imagined as the breaking open of the youthful body in a vase, other Dzogchen scriptures associate the origin of the universe by relying on one of the most indigenous Tibetan motifs, namely the hatching of an egg. In one of *The Seventeen Tantras of the Ancients*, for instance, we read:

> Awareness abiding within the ground is the perfectly complete triad within wisdom's expanse, just like a peacock's egg endowed with the radiant clarity of the inner light of wisdom. Awareness shining forth on the path is like rainbow colors. Awareness reaching its extent resembles the peacock's chick bursting out of the egg. (*The Tantra of the Lion's Perfect Dynamism*, 372.4)[18]

There is no doubt that the vitalistic motif of a cosmogonic egg giving rise to our universe is a theme that is intimately associated with the ancient Tibetan universe (Bellezza 2005, 326). In fact, while the image of the primordial egg has a wide currency in China, North Asia, and elsewhere (Blezer 2000), it is nowhere as prominent as in the pre-Buddhist circles of the Bön tradition (Blezer 2012).[19] The fact that this profoundly non-Buddhist symbolism is discovered within the most fundamental myth as it expressed in the most sacred scriptures of Buddhist Dzogchen, obviously makes us wonder whether the historical circumstances of the tradition's formative years might have been less self-evidently Buddhist than is commonly believed.[20] Historical sources alone could make a convincing argument for such a revision. Almost contrary to the unified sphere of a perfectly self-contained vase of light, neither the prehistoric population nor the community during the Tibetan empire represented a unified group. The prehistoric communities belonged to a range of ethnic groups (Hazod 2009; 2012) that assembled in connected political units or vassal states (*rgyal phran*), which were kin-based. As Lewis Doney has put it, "the commonly understood extent of 'Tibet' has more to do with the incorporation of a number of ethnicities (most notably Turkic and Tibeto-Burmese) within a single cultural matrix over time than a shared genetic makeup, and the Tibetan Empire and its imposed lingua franca Tibetan spoken and written language (known as Old Tibetan) made a significant and long-lasting impact in this respect" (Doney 2023, 4). Yet even the Tibetan empire at its peak of extent and cosmopolitanism was far from a homogenous realm, and its creation was marked by sociopolitical upheaval as it consisted of various tribal and clan units fighting for power.[21]

Many of those groups, particularly those associated with the influential nobility, did not only not identify themselves with the imperial political and military entity but even actively resisted it. I believe that this is—despite the later identification with the imperial glory—likely true of many adherents of the Nyingma school. Since much of this prehistory has been lost or suppressed within the Buddhist tradition, we need to turn elsewhere to understand what Tibetan religion looked like during this early period. Consider, for instance, the histories of the Tang Chinese court, such as *The Old Book of the Tang Dynasty* (*Jiu Tangshu,* 舊唐書), where we find references to Tibetan practices, such as the "worship the *yuandi* god," which might be a reference to the psychopomp sheep, the "belief in witches and seers" (Schaeffer, Kapstein, and Tuttle 2013, 10). More specifically, in order to reconstruct the earliest layer of the history of the Dzogchen, we might turn to Bönpo texts. While evidence for their relevance will only gradually be revealed throughout this study, I am convinced that the Bönpo myths offer a more accurate description of the underlying worldview of the Dzogchen tradition, particularly its vitalistic thrust. According to the Bön tradition, and here its accounts differ drastically from the "myth of history" of the Nyingma school, the original scriptures were composed in the kingdom of Zhangzhung in Western and Northern Tibet and the origins of the teachings are frequently associated with a place known as Tazig, a term that points more West. Research by John Bellezza, who conducted extensive fieldwork *in loco*, documents hundreds of archeological sites that likely date back to the very beginnings of Tibetan history (Bellezza 1999; 2000; 2002; 2005). In many ways, his discoveries confirm alternative mythological accounts of an earlier mysterious polity known as Zhangzhung that was said to exist in the high deserts of far Western Tibet in the centuries before the establishment of the Tibetan empire in the seventh century. "Aside from the myth, legend and apparent mystery," so Aldenderfer and Yinong suggest, "Zhang zhung played a major role in central Asian prehistory and history."

> It appears to have acted as an important intermediary of trade and the diffusion of knowledge between the Indian subcontinent and the Tibetan plateau, and for a time, was a significant political rival of the emerging Tibetan empire. It also acted as a filter of knowledge and cultural influences from the distant west,

including Sogdiana, Persia, and the Hellenistic world. Perhaps of even greater importance was the sponsorship by Zhang zhung of Bon, a belief system thought by many to be the indigenous religion of much of the Tibetan plateau, and which had a profound influence of the development and evolution of Tibetan Buddhism. (Aldenderfer and Yinong 2004, 42)

While it is clear that we are dealing here with just another "myth as history" version, namely that of the Bönpo tradition, the remainder of this chapter takes this possibility nonetheless seriously and consequently explores a range of early Tibetan and particularly Bönpo texts about the origins of life. Reconstructing these stories, we will not only find evidence for a Tibetan deer-cult that shares many attributes with similar religious phenomena in the regions where Zhangzhung would have been located, but we also reconstruct a pre-Buddhist cultural "substratum" that lays the foundation for our understanding of the Dzogchen contemplative system; a system in which the pre-Buddhist influences remained present in the practical, somatic, philosophical, and material dimensions.

The Descent of the Celestial Kings

If we will see that the indigenous Tibetan conception of vitality is multifaceted, its most defining trait is the valorization of the sky as source of life. The trope of the vitality of the ethereal realm is so embedded within the DNA of pre-Buddhist Tibet that Stein once wrote that "the Bonpo love the sky" (Stein 1988, 40).[22] According to the psychoanalytic anthropology of Robert Paul, in Tibet, the sky is "associated with maleness, potency, eternity, and purity, and the 'reservoir' of Life in its pure, unlived state" (1979, 298). In this context of a more general vitality, another set of concepts takes center stage, namely *phya/phywa* and *g.yang*, words that scholarship has translated as "well-being," "prosperity," "fortune," or "quintessence." Entirely absent in Indic Buddhist texts, the concept features prominently in a series of Dunhuang texts, particularly those associated with divination.[23] From the early sources until today, it is quite clear that these terms belong to the wider semantic field of "vitality;" I will therefore translate them accordingly. The vertical descent, or katabasis, of vitality from the sky is a theme that remained particularly prominent among the followers of Bön, where it is still a core belief in folk religions. In a text belonging to a cycle of rituals associated with Nam Par Gyelwa (rnam par rgyal ba),[24] who was considered to be an emanation of the founder of the Bön religion, Shenrab Miwo (shen rab mi bo), we read:

> When *g.yang* descended for the first time, it descended from space, it descended from the womb of the Great Mother, the *dmu* rope and *g.yang* rope were woven into the sky, and the grasping rope of the sky was thus made, as if the sky would permeate through everything, the spacious, high, deep *g.yang*, flew from the sky like a seed, and rolled down onto the earth. [25] (*The Coiled up Sky Lasso Vitality*, 4b, 10)

Although mythical texts of this nature are particularly prevalent in Bönpo sources,[26] they also circulate in Buddhist circles where some of the rituals are performed until this day. In one Nyingma text, for instance, we read that the father and mother of *g.yang* were six-winged vultures, who flew to the sky and the earth, respectively, and that their union produced nine precious eggs from which the beings inhabiting our world were born (Berounský 2014, 68–9). Indeed, just like in the origin myth of Dzogchen that we encountered in *The Tantra of the Lion's Perfect Dynamism*, many of these mythical narratives surrounding "vitality" make explicit reference to cosmogonic eggs. In *The Ultimate Vitality: The Celestial Head-Ornament*, for instance, we encounter eight deities of *g.yang*, which are born from eggs made of precious substances: "The father is the highest tip of the rock of existence and the mother is the great trickster of the lake of existence. From the manifestation of the mind of these two appeared the eight eggs of existence" (18.1).[27] Their shared emphasis on cosmologies involving eggs is not the only way to connect the indigenous beliefs in a primordial descent of divine vitality to the myth of the "manifestation of the ground." In Tibetan language manuscripts from highland Nepal discovered by Charles Ramble,[28] we find many myths that lay out the cosmological foundation by emphasizing the importance of what can be called the "ground of vitality" (*g.yang gzhi, phya gzhi*). Consider, for instance, *The Great Main Text of the Vitality Ritual of the Lord of the Vitality* where we read:

> *Khuye!* Come undefeated and steady! Well, where do we search for the base of *phya* and base of *g.yang*? Where do we search for the substances of *phya* and the substances of *g.yang*? Kye! At the beginning of the earliest times, at the beginning of the earliest eon, at first, before anything had come into existence, there existed just the smallest dust-particle; from that there came into being a very fine dew drop; from that there came into being a vast ocean. In that ocean bubbles formed, and the bubbles rolled up into eggs, and nine precious eggs came into being. There came into being three conch shell eggs, three golden eggs and three iron eggs, nine in total. The conch shell egg dissolved into the sky, and from it there appeared the gods, the white [ones], and the support. From the golden egg that had appeared next there came into being humans, *smra*, and *gshen*; from the iron egg that had fallen down, there came into being the *'dre*, the *srin*, and the *'byur*.[29] (524)

The title's text reveals another element of central importance to the early Tibetan sky-cult, namely the association with royalty. Although I translated the title by invoking his most famous moniker, the "Lord of the Vitality" (*phywa rje*), the text speaks of a particular Bönpo ancestral god, namely the "Existence-Father-God-Six-Divisions."[30] This figure appears pervasively throughout Bön sources, both modern and ancient, and is generally identified as the ancestor of the kings, particularly Nyatri Tsenpo (gnya 'khri btsan po), the first Yarlung Valley Tibetan king.[31] Thus, while it is impossible to date such text with certainty, it is likely that they are imbibed with pre-Buddhist beliefs and practices.[32] The stories surrounding the Lord of Vitality, thus, point to a dominant trait of early Tibetan understandings of vitality, namely that its primary source is a multileveled sky world that is the realm of ancestral gods and kings.[33]

This understanding of the ancestral spirits and their descent from the celestial realm has important consequences for the Tibetan conception of kingship. Tucci, in what has been a watershed moment in the study of early Tibet, remarked that the king's role was "that of keeping off epidemics, causing the rain to fall, assuring fertility, in other words that of maintaining the cosmic and social order intact and in due working order" (Tucci 1955, 200).[34] More specifically, the early Tibetan kings are associated with the sky as they were extraordinary godlike individuals, who have descended from the heavens by means of a ladder or cord.[35] Thus, while the three religious kings mentioned previously fulfilled a civilizing function inasmuch as they introduced and propagated Buddhism in the realm of Tibet, the earlier "indigenous" kings had a fundamentally cosmological role as they brought life itself to earth. Many early manuscripts focus especially on the descent of Nyatri Tsenpo, explaining that he was born in the land of the *mu* (Tib. *dmu*).[36] The Zhangzhung term *mu* (also spelled as *dmu*, *smu*, or *rmu*), in fact, carries a variety of meanings in early Tibetan religion, but it is most prominently related to the Tibetan terms *mkha'*, *gnam*, or *dbyings*, and thus best translated as "heaven," "sky" or "space" (Martin 2010, 164).[37]

The Cult of the Sky-Deer

Existing scholarship has reconstructed the political myth of the kings and their association with the heavenly realm in great detail. Nonetheless, it has oftentimes underestimated another, likely older, layer of the Tibetan fascination with the sky, namely the persuasion that animalistic forces like sheep and deer (and sometimes other animals) allow for the movement in between the celestial and the terrestrial realms.[38] This relative neglect is somewhat surprising for several reasons: First, there is a lot of evidence that the pre-Buddhist Tibetan religion might have been heavily inspired by religious beliefs and practices that stemmed from other regions, particularly to the north of Tibet. Since the writings of Tucci, in fact, it is well known that the royal cult of ancient Tibet was not imported with Buddhism as it differs dramatically from that of ancient India. Instead, Tucci suggested that the Tibetan ideology of royalty is fundamentally inspired by the religious traditions of the pastoral Turco-Mongolian peoples to the north of Tibet (1949; 1955). Since then, scholarship has repeatedly pointed in the direction of this same geographic region, amassing astounding evidence that the centrality of the sky as a source of vitality is widespread among many cultures throughout the wider Himalayas and beyond.[39] Third, the association between the sky and these animalistic motifs is pervasive throughout cosmogonic stories surrounding vitality in Tibetan lore. The hunt for deer and sheep and their precious body parts reaches back to the earliest strata of Dunhuang texts,[40] and continues to persist in contemporary society where these animals are also known as the "ground of vitality" (*g.yang gzhi*) (Huber 2020, vol. I: 185-6). Fourth, and finally, both the ancient and the modern narratives concerning the sky-dwelling animal forces tie back to the cult of kings as an overwhelming proportion of the stories narrate how an offspring of royal family hunts the precious deer/sheep in the pursuit of vitality. In other words, it is quite possible that the royal cult represents a variant of a much larger religious phenomenon in pre-Buddhist Tibet, namely that of the sky-deer. While this endeavor will have to remain tentative for the time being, the following pages will offer a preliminary reconstruction of a cult that will be fleshed out more and more throughout the remainder of this book. In the process, we will also take into consideration Scytho-Siberian and northern Asian conceptions of the deer as it is quite likely that this cultural area marks the origination point of the cult as a whole (Fitzhugh 2009).

To begin, let us consider a typical Bönpo account of the origins of the world to explore this nexus of the heavenly vitality, the god-kings, and animals. *The Extensive Elimination and Offering Rites for the Gods of the Four Groups of Little Humans*, which Karmay described as being "of ancient origins" and Huber unambiguously identifies as part of the cult of the "gods of procreation" or the "gods of the phenomenal world" (*srid pa'i lha*) (Huber 2020, vol I: 38), contains not only detailed ritual instructions but also a cosmogonic prelude. Here, we read about two divine figures, who begat bird-like sons that hatched out a series of five eggs made from agate, conch, turquoise, copper, and iron. The creatures, ranging from an unidentifiable winged animal that is neither a bird nor a rat to a parrot, are encouraged to fly to the thirteenth level of the sky, where they should "act as messengers of human beings to the gods." They are then asked to "invite the gods to the [land of] humans,"[41] before the parrot answers as follows: "If we should go to invite the gods, then we request a mount for each of us. For this purpose, we request a token to reciprocate with."[42] In response, they are instructed to go to a mountain "at the base of which, there are white sheep with horns of conch" and to "ride upon those."[43] The five beings do as they are told:

> They rode upon five [sheep] with horns of conch. They kept close together like [a herd of] deer and went off. They soared like vultures and went off and arrived at the top of the thirteenth level of the sky world. They carried arrows decorated with five types of silk in their right hands. In their left hands, they carried mirrors (me long). They purified with the smoke of fragrant incense. (*Extensive Elimination and Offering Rites for the Gods of the Four Groups of Little Humans*, 1–2)[44]

In reading such passages, I have always been struck by the impression that we are dealing here not only with isolated ideas like a sky-dwelling vitality or a cosmogony out of eggs, but rather with a rich indigenous worldview that tells us a story about how animalistic forces play a crucial role in the transmission of heavenly vitality into the human world. The passage intimates the vitalizing thrust associated with sky-dwelling deer and sheep, who serve both as messengers of vitality and as its repositories because of their physical attributes like the silken coat or the conch-shell horns. In another manuscript from highland Nepal, we encounter a myth of a primordial time when humans lacked *phya* and animals lacked *g.yang*. The hero of the tale is a hunter, who must capture a miraculous deer, whose body parts serve as a "ground" (*gzhi*) for the life powers descending from the sky.

> As for the origin, it was at the beginning of the world age. As for the material, the material was the eternal deer. As for supporting, it supported the *phya* and *g.yang*. As for chanting [the rites], it was I, the human *gshen*, who chanted. Just as it was in the past for the *phya* of the Lord of Vitality, so this evening, too, will it be for our beneficent [ritual] patron. As for the descent, it is *phya* and *g.yang* that will descend. The descent of *phya* is not bad; the descent of *phya* is fine. Call *khu ye* for the fine descent of *phya*![45] (Huber 2020, vol I: 51)

This story allows us to pinpoint the most obvious element of the quest for life associated with animals like deer and sheep, namely that it reinforces the logic of a vertical vitality, which is said to descend to earth. Let us now turn to another story relating the mythical quest for vitality. A similar Bönpo text titled *The Ultimate Vitality: The Celestial Head-Ornament* was published by Samten Karmay in a collection of works from Dolpo under the name *The Call of the Blue Cuckoo*. In this text, we gather that people were deprived of the ground of vitality because of the activity of demons. In response, a prince by the name of Gampo is sent on a quest to Mt. Meru, where he meets a white deer with crystal antlers at a crystal cliff. The deer is reluctant to accompany the young leader back to his home country to bring his people *phya* and *g.yang*. As the animal tries to escape, the prince catches it with a miraculous lasso. Bringing the deer back to his country, he gives him to the Lord of Vitality, who then produces a number of ritual implements out of his various body parts. At the end of the story, the texts make an enigmatic prediction by stating that the deer will become a sheep.

From this story, we learn another trait of the cult of the sky-deer, namely that the definition of the deer appears to be rather open and flexible. In the Tibetan world, for instance, the curious reference to the deer that turns into a sheep points to a certain parallelism between those two species. Charles Ramble notes that while the deer appear to be the paradigmatic animals in these stories, they were frequently equated with sheep. More specifically, he speaks of "interchangeability" of the two animals and notes that in contemporary fortune-summoning rituals, the sheep can be used as a substitute for the ideal animal, the deer (Ramble 2015, 513–14).[46] Despite the recent disappearance of sheep from certain regions on the Tibetan plateau—largely attributed to the caterpillar fungus that serves as a new economic source—Tibetan sheep have long been the most popular domestic animals of the pastoralists (Sulek 2019). This interchangeability seems to be a more general trait of the sky-deer cult in Eurasia, where deer is a general term used for the Cervidae family, which consists of fifty-one individual species that are semantically exchangeable. Mykhailova and Garfinkel, for example, note that "the term *bugu* in the languages of many Northern and Central Asian peoples means reindeer, elk, and horse, and simultaneously, supreme being, god, nature, and heaven" (2018, 5).

Another key trait of the early mythology of vitality is that the narratives serve as antecedent tales for the performance of rituals. These practices are generally oriented at worldly goals such as divination, the curing of illnesses, or the summoning of fortune, and were therefore quite different from the perfectibilism of Indo-Tibetan tantric traditions. Brandon Dotson, in his study of early Tibetan dice divination, shows that these animals were believed to be repositories of vitality, which the ritualist could draw to himself, his clients, or his natural environment through his actions (Dotson 2019). Similarly, Bellezza notes that contemporary vitality-summoning rituals (*g.yang 'gugs*) he observed in Tibet reproduce the cosmogonic descent of vitality from the sky by invoking a variety of deer- or sheep-like deities, such as the Divine Sheep of the Emergence of Existence, the Divine Sheep of the Emergence of the First Epoch, the White Conch Spiraling Tips of the Horns, the Conch White Sheep with a Smooth Coat of Wool, or the Sheep with a Spreading White Tail (Bellezza 2018, 12). This close association between cosmogonic myths and mundane rites is also a trait of the larger cult of the sky-deer, where the worship of the mythical deer is the foundation for rituals of hunting, regeneration, reproduction, and fertility (Martynov 1988; Mykhailova 2015).[47] Roberte Hamayon, an expert on the history of shamanism in the Siberian context, also suggested that the hunting for animals like deer was at the heart of archaic shamanism. "Obtaining the promise of game or good luck for the hunters of his community," so she writes, "is the shaman's main function in the most archaic Siberian societies, a function much more basic than curing" (1996, 61).

Let us now look at another text of this same genre, namely *Remedying the Lords of the Soil and Subjugating the Evil Forces of Creation through the Ground of Vitality*. Here, the myth opens up by explaining that there is a white deer at the slopes of the White Conch Shell Mountain before narrating the cosmogonic story of the creation of eggs. It then proceeds to set the stage for the quest for vitality by introducing a land that is disturbed because of demonic activity. In an attempt to overcome the crisis, the priests decide to perform a ransom offering. The story then recounts the hunt, explaining that the main protagonist kills a series of animals, including a conch shell deer with antlers as sharp as iron. At the behest of the gods, he and seven companions then proceed to the conch shell mountain, carrying with them a miraculous lasso, a silk snare, as well as bow and arrow. The hunters miss the target with their arrows but catch the deer's neck with the miraculous lasso. As it is time to return to the priest's kingdom, the deer inquires about his own origins. The priest answers and says that the miraculous deer is the offspring of his father, who is the White Conch Shell Mountain, and his mother, who is the Crystal Demoness. This story provides us with another constant in the quest for vitality stories, namely the credence that vitality is particularly concentrated within certain locations, both in the natural landscape where the topography of the hunt transmits cognate features (conch shell mountains, etc.) and in the body of the sky-animal (deer's antlers, sheep's coat, etc.) that is hunted.

The fact that the life-sustaining energy is concentrated in these physical attributes is clearly the reason why the deer are hunted and their body parts—frequently said to consist of precious substances like crystals or conch shell—are used to manufacture ritual implements, which are frequently described as made of precious substances like crystals or conch shell. This tendency is also part of the larger cult of the sky-deer, where parts of the body are particularly potent. As Maja Pasarić elaborates, "deer head and antlers are specific parts of the animal body embedded with complex symbolic implications and as *pars pro toto* represent the entire animal" (Pasarić 2018, 217). Based on the prehistoric art found in various places throughout Norther and Central Asia, Siberia, and Europe, it is quite apparent that the antlers played a particularly important role in the wider deer-cult. One reason for the prominence of this particular structure in the mythical-ritual imagination of Eurasian people might be that antlers are shed every year and then regrown. It is quite possible that this trait led to their association with vitality, fertility, and reproduction. Looking at the drawings and carvings, it is noticeable that the antlers are hypertrophied, frequently represented as much larger than the body and legs of the animals.[48] This is very likely a symbolic representation of one of the key functions of the deer, namely the vertical movement between the realm of the heavens and the realm of the earth. In fact, since "in the history of Northern Asia, hunting and herding always had primary significance," these regions developed "a cult of animal fertility equivalent to the cult of the 'tree of life'" (Martynov 1988, 13). The antlers—marked by their yearly regeneration, their vertical growth, and their branching like a tree—represent an alternative to the fertility cults that dominated other regions in the world. In this sense, it could also be that the antlers fulfilled a similar function as the "tree of life," which fulfills the role of connecting the earth and the sky in a series of cultures.

While some of the rock paintings found in Tibet also feature prominent antlers,[49] the messenger function of the deer obviously becomes apparent in the mythical narratives of indigenous traditions. If we already saw that the kings used sheep and deer as mounts to travel to earth during the initial descent of vitality, some later mythical-ritual texts ascribe them similar functions. In this context, it is worth discussing an anonymous text that I decided to translate as *Deer Way-Stations*.[50] First published in 2013, we are dealing here with a spectacular manuscript that has been carbon-dated to the eleventh century.[51] The text describes two different mundane rites, the *ste'u* and the *sha slungs*. If the former is concerned with "post-mortem procedures for conducting new human lives into the world from a realm of *lha* ancestors who are up the vertical cosmic axis," the latter "describes invocation of a range of living beings to protect new lives as they come down to the terrestrial realm" (Huber 2020, vol. I: 39).[52] This text is of central importance, not only because it is one of the earliest written documents proving the centrality of the movement between the realms of the earth and the heavens that will resurface repeatedly throughout this study, but it also reinforces the emphasis on deer-like animals as conveying agents of vitality. The manuscript is also marked by unique illustrations consisting of small color paintings of various animals, particularly various deer-like beings. On an illustrated page depicting what looks like three different types of deer, we read that these three animals belong to the precious deer way-station. They are described as a stag with antlers, resembling thorn-like horns (standing on the right side), a doe with its eyelashes sticking upward (on the left), and a young deer with richly patterned fur (in the middle).[53] Most importantly, the manuscripts tell us that these animals serve as messengers (*pho nya*) who are swift and act as mounts (*chibs*) to various spirits (Huber 2020, vol. II: 65).

Based on this brief and by no means comprehensive survey of texts of this nature, I believe that the pervasiveness of the motif of a deer in the quest for vitality could potentially make it a subcategory of a larger Eurasian cult of the sky-deer. I will have more to say about these myths and about the cult of the sky-deer in Chapter 3. However, what is more important is that the idea of the sky as the source of life and the role of sheep and deer as messenger animals remained constant traits in the Great Perfection and deeply influenced tradition. Indeed, although this chapter's account of pre-Buddhist cosmologies might seem far removed from the meditative practice of Skullward Leap—particularly if we follow the dominant reading of Dzogchen as a tradition operative under the aegis of Buddhist monocentrism and its doctrine of perfectibilism—their symbolism suggests that they might be watered by the same cultural reservoir. These narrations therefore should be regarded not only as the prehistory of Tibet, but also as a sort of "unofficial" prehistory of the Great Perfection. In the remaining chapters of the first part of this study, we will encounter a series of temporal and social ruptures that undermined the pre-Buddhist beliefs and practices associated with the heavenly descent and maintenance of vitality, decisively contributing to the crystallization of the Great Perfection tradition and its meditative techniques.

Chapter 2

THE TIBETAN EMPIRE AND THE (INCOMPLETE) BUDDHICIZATION OF VITALITY

If the opening chapter explored the indigenous Tibetan conception of vitality as a vertical descent of life from the sky to the earth by means of animals like sheep or deer, the second chapter turns its attention to the introduction of Buddhism to Tibet in the seventh century by demonstrating that it advanced a new model of vitality. With the arrival of a South Asian worldview, more specifically, Tibetans were exposed to a mythical cosmogony based on a "spherical" model of vitality that leads energy from the inside toward the outside. In accordance with our understanding of myth as something real, this juxtaposition of competing flows of life will be interpreted in light of the particular historical circumstances during this period, which included the conversion of Tibet to Buddhism, as well as the rise and fall of the Tibetan great empire.[1] The spherical model of vitality, in particular, gained relevance as it lays the foundation for two central religious phenomena of the Ancient School, namely its teachings (i.e., the cosmogony of the ground's manifestation) and its scriptural creativity (i.e., the development of a robust institution of revealing so called treasures). At the same time, however, this alternative model of vitality did not simply replace the indigenous Tibetan version as Dzogchen continued to be animated by the earliest Tibetan motifs even as the tradition changed throughout its history. The buddhicization of Tibet, in other words, was incomplete. Or, put differently, the buddhicization of Tibet was accompanied by equally strong trends toward the Tibetanization of Buddhism as the new "Buddhist" emergence of vitality out of the ground maintained the logic of the earlier vertical descent of life-giving energy from the sky-realm.

The Spherical Vitality of Buddhism

Although the introduction of Buddhism in the seventh century was the determining factor in the history of Tibet, it has not been a positive experience for all people on the plateau. Bönpos describe the conversion of Tibet as a forceful process, a veritable catastrophe for the proponents of indigenous traditions and the Zhangzhung polity, leading to a series of new developments in the mythical conception of vitality.[2] Many of these stories revolve around a single mythological figure, namely the emperor known as Trigum Tsenpo (gri gum btsan po/dri gum btsan po).³ If the early kings were adherents of Bön and lived in a state of harmony and prosperity, it was during the reign of the eighth king, Trigum Tsenpo, that the empire started to deteriorate. In fact, according to the tradition, Trigum was the first king to suppress Bön for political reasons by exiling priests and repressing its clergy.⁴ While the details of this story are not historically verifiable, the conversion of Tibet to Buddhism was no smooth process as the plateau consisted of various political and religious communities that competed for power. This state of affairs, furthermore, finds not only expression in Bön sources but is equally documented in certain Tibetan historical records. *The Old Tibetan Annals*, composed of two manuscripts written in old Tibetan language found in the early twentieth century in the Dunhuang caves, reveal an almost permanent tension between various forces, especially the Tsenpos and the leadership of indigenous clans.⁵

Trigum Tsenpo's mythological life-story represents a worthwhile illustration of these early times of Tibetan history. He is most famous for being the protagonist in another story, which offers a mythical counterpart to his historical association with Buddhism and the suppression of indigenous Tibetan religion. In the first chapter of *The Old Tibetan Chronicle*, we read that Trigum unintentionally cut through his celestial cord during a fight. While his predecessors were able to return to heaven upon the end of their reigns, Trigum and his successors were confined to a purely earthly existence.⁶ As a consequence, Tibetans started to build tombs to enshrine the bodies of the kings. As the kings continued to be seen as divine figures, their burial mounds, such as the ones constructed between the seventh and ninth centuries in Chonggye ('Phyong rgyas) in Central Tibet, soon became places of sacred importance. There is no doubt that these stories surrounding Trigum's life identify the introduction of Buddhism with a traumatic rupture of cosmic proportions as it interrupted the natural flow of the vitality from the realm of the sky. Even more, the mythical-historical narrative of the cutting of the sky-cord expresses a shift in priorities from the pre-Buddhist fascination with the sky to an emphasis on the earth, a transition from the vertical vitality of the sky to the spherical vitality of the ground.⁷

If the pre-Buddhist valorization of the heavenly realm as primordial locus of vitality was accompanied by a commensurately negative conception of the ground below,⁸ the Buddhist conception of vitality finds expression in several aspects of the Great Perfection. Consider, for instance, that the spherical model of vitality is epitomized in the Dzogchen cosmology's most famous cosmogonic myth, the so-called manifestation of the ground.⁹ As you might recall, this myth imagines the cosmogony as the radiating expression of a ground that moves from the inside toward the outside. More specifically, it centers on a youthful body in a vase of light, which breaks open to shine forth rainbow-colored lights. After the manifestation of mandalic shapes of luminosity, the radiation gradually loses its transparency, solidifying more and more, until one path leads it to take on the form of living beings and the universe of material objects as we know it. In a recent article, I have argued that the spherical myth of the cosmology should be considered as a parallel development to the rise of what is one of the spectacular modes of textual production found anywhere in the world, namely the so-called treasure tradition,[10] which plays a central role in the Bön and the Nyingma traditions. According to this fascinating religious phenomenon, the so-called treasure revealers, unearth teachings from various places, oftentimes from the Tibetan ground.[11] These "earth treasures" (*sa gter*) fit exceedingly well with the narratives that announce Tibet's gradual transition from heavenly vitality to earthly powers. If the indigenous Tibetan tradition embraced rituals oriented toward the heavenly realm surrounding sky-dwelling animals like sheep and deer to increase their numbers, the introduction of Buddhism led to a transplanting of this reproductive fertility into the Tibetan ground. The earth, indeed, became a source of unceasing spiritual vitality and ever-multiplying scriptural revelation. It is hardly a coincidence that the literary genre of treasure revelations is only attributed to the Bön tradition and the Nyingma School of Buddhism as both of them shared a similar fate within Tibetan history (Martin and Bentor 1997, 14).

The spherical myth of the body-in-a-vase is also marked by a particular "ontology of interiority," which extends into a specific conception of nature, itself of central importance to the revelation of treasures. Indeed, the natural world forms part of a larger network that extends into the cultural-religious realm where the interdependence between human beings, their environment, and the divine beings residing in there all form part of the ecosystem of treasure revelation. Jacoby notes:

> The treasure revealers calibrated this equilibrium through the exchange of precious substances into and out of the earth at key locations. Most scholarship on the treasure tradition has focused on the scriptures and artifacts that revealers claim to have withdrawn from the Tibetan earth and sky, but Treasure revealers also often inserted sacred substances back into the earth and water called "Treasure substitutes" (*gter tshab*) or "Treasure vases" (*gter 'bum*) filled with precious materials. (2014, 103).[12]

This conception of nature as alive and filled with agency reveals an indigenous understanding of the cosmos. Indeed, just like the Great Perfection, the treasure tradition is a profoundly Tibetan phenomenon that draws extensively on pre-Buddhist ideas and practices. In her long-standing exploration of this phenomenon, Janet Gyatso has emphasized that it is a practice with an essentially "Tibetan character, or thrust," noting that "whether drawn out of the Tibetan ground or a Tibetan mind, the Treasure stands as a Tibetan product" (1996, 152–3). Consequently, it is hardly surprising that treasures are also related to notions of "vitality" (*g.yang/phya*). For instance, we find many attempts at "compensating" the natural environment for our appropriation of vitality in so-called rituals of "fortune-summoning" (*g.yang 'gug/ 'gugs*). Since the ritual is successful if the human side gains fortune—or, in the case of revelation, new scriptures—by removing it from somewhere else, it is not surprising that we find rituals of compensation. Indeed, *g.yang*-summoning rituals on behalf of mountain gods, or the burying of "fortune vases" (*g.yang 'bum*) in such locations are commonplace in Tibetan culture.¹³

Antonio Terrone invokes the example of the treasure revealer Tashi Gyeltsen (b. 1957) and his consort Khandro Pelchen Lhamo (b. 1964). He notes that "when it is time to perform the revelation they typically prepare a small vase of precious substances (bum rdzas) properly consecrated that Tashi Gyeltsen then inserts in the Treasure door (gter sgo) immediately after extracting the sacred object before sealing the opening" (Terrone 2014, 471). Of course, the terms *gter bum*, *g.yang 'bum*, and *bum rdzas* bring to mind the Dzogchen myth, which puts the "youthful body in a vase" at the center of its cosmogonic account as it identifies it explicitly with the powerful ground.¹⁴ In other words, the treasure tradition's endorsement of the Tibetan ground as the land of a continued revealing radiance parallels the spherical narrative of the youthful body in a vase, it too representing a pure interiority out of which all the vital energies of the universe radiate. Like the treasure—in its pre-revelatory state—the youthful body is invisible, formless, and self-contained. Both the treasures of the royal period and the ground embody potential rather than actualization, interiority rather than exteriorization, hiddenness rather than manifestness.

It is likely that the revelation of treasures was not only building on the spherical metaphor of the cosmogony of the ground but also on the practice of burying the kings in earthly tombs. This association is not only due to the fact that they both participate in the ideology of spherical vitality, but also due to the historical circumstances that befell Tibet after the fall of the empire. Indeed, it is possible that the looting of the royal tombs contributed to the initial emergence of the treasure tradition (Hazod 2013). The kings' tombs were usually filled with funeral treasures; a link that is further reinforced by the etymology of the word for royal "tombs" (*bang so*), clearly derived from *bang ba* or *bang mdzod* meaning "store-room," "store-house," "repository," or "treasury" (Jäschke 1995). Another powerful indicator for the association between the connection of royal burials and treasure revelation is another reference to king Trigum. In fact, Bön sources point out that the treasure tradition originated during the reign of Trigum, the king whose sky-cord was cut in battle. They further specify that the reason for its institution was that this specific king persecuted Bön and that the tradition's scriptures had to be hidden away and preserved for future generations because they would have been lost otherwise.¹⁵ For Bönpos, in other words, the introduction of Buddhism led to the rise of a new model of spherical vitality—accompanied by religious phenomena like the cosmogony of the ground and the revelation of treasures—and a marginalization of their teachings, all of which is contained in the story of the singularly momentous figure of emperor Trigum.

Buddhist accounts of the treasures, unlike the Bön counterparts' focus on the introduction of Buddhism, emphasize the collapse of the empire as the crucial moment for the institution of revelation. The tradition suggests that *The Seventeen Tantras* came into being with the Buddha Samantabhadra, who passed the teachings on to Vajrasattva, before they entered into the world of human beings in the country of Oḍḍiyāna, which is usually identified with the Swat

Valley in present-day Pakistan. Even after they penetrated history, however, the teachings remain located somewhere in between myth and history as scriptures represent a group of writings, which came to be considered as part of the treasure tradition.[16] More specifically, after having entered Tibet during the empire's most powerful moment, the Dzogchen scriptures were then transmitted to Nyang Tingzin Zangpo (myang ban ting 'dzin bzang po), who chose to not disseminate but to conceal them in the late eighth century at the famous meditation center association with Samye (*bsam yas*) monastery, known as Chimphu (*mchims phu*). According to the colophon of the longest of the scriptures—*The Tantra of Self-Arisen Awareness*—after they have been hidden in the eighth century—the tantras were discovered as Termas in the late tenth century by Dangma Lhungyi Gyaltsen (ldang ma lhun rgyal) at the Hat Temple (*zhwa'i lha khang*) in central Tibet. After that, the texts were again continuously transmitted and passed along to Chetsün Senge Wangchuk (lce btsun seng ge dbang phyug, eleventh to 1twelfh centuries) and Zhangtön Tashi Dorje (zhang ston bkra shis rdo rje, c. 1097–1167). Both secondary scholarship,[17] as well as indigenous Tibetan critics of the Ancient School[18] have suggested that these two figures were not only responsible for the reinsertion of the scriptures into the human world, but even for their composition.

Besides the suggestive nexus converging on the mythological life of Trigum, there is further evidence that the spherical model of vitality was introduced to Tibet from India. Not only are Buddhist models of the cosmogony, such as the classical variants found in the *abhidharma*, frequently spherical in nature, but the treasure tradition has also been largely attributed to Indian influences (Davidson 2005, 212–19). An element that has not been noticed by scholarship in support of an Indian origin of the tradition is the prevalence of gold in the funerary treasures of the kings. Unlike the precious substances associated with the cult of the sky and the animalistic messengers, such as conch shell and crystal, the royal cult focused on other material objects. The funerary cult of the kings, indeed, seems to have been primarily associated with the precious metal of gold, which appears in most accounts about the funerary treasures. In *The Chronicle of the Kings*, for instance, we read that his body was inserted into a copper vessel together with a golden representation of the monarch and that this whole arrangement was accompanied by gold and silver, the "king's treasures" (*rgyal po'i dkor nor*) (Sehnalova 2022, 227).

As per Esther Jacobson, who has extensively studied the solarization of the deer-cult in Eurasia, the association between the solar symbolism and the cult of royalty and warriordom did not emerge in the regions of the Central and North Asian steppes, but rather in Indo-European or Indo-Persian contexts (2018, 39–41). I believe not only that her assessment is correct, but that her argument regarding the clear differentiation between the sky-deer and the solar cult points to a fundamentally different conception of vitality in the Tibetosphere, on the one hand, and South Asia, on the other. If the vertical quests for the primordial source of vitality in the steppes of Eurasia was part of a larger cult of the sky and the descent of the life-sustaining energy in the form of emissary animals, the agricultural context of the land to the South of Tibet embraced a model of vitality that included not only the sun but also the fertility of the ground. In fact, it is well known that the early agricultural zones like India endorsed a vegetative fertility cult centered on solar deities and a fascination with the underground world (Martynov 1988, 27). Like the religious transformations after the arrival of Indian Buddhism in Tibet, this South Asian model of vitality displays a striking proclivity for all things "spherical," such as the fascination with circular representations of the sun, the life-sustaining powers of the earth, both of which were used to symbolize a fascination with cyclical processes like the change of seasons, the stages of life, or the ever-repeating cycle between life and death. While the final verdict on the true origin of the spherical model of vitality will have to wait for more research, I am fairly certain that it represented an alternative to the vertical model that dominated the conception of life of the sky-worshipping pre-Buddhist Tibetans.

As Above, So Below

The competition between two forms of vitality—one vertical coming from the sky and the other spherical emerging from the ground—points to the paradoxical nature of the Ancient School in particular and Tibetan Buddhism as a whole. Caught somewhere in between a pre-Buddhist worldview and Buddhist teachings imported from other lands, the tradition tries to satisfy its need to maintain its own heritage while finding legitimacy within a nation converted to Buddhism. In other words, while the spherical conception of vitality can be understood as a Buddhist innovation, marking a decisive mythical rupture from pre-Buddhist reality in which the vertical model of the descent of the kings was dominant, this new model was simultaneously infused with specifically Tibetan conceptions of the universe. The spherical model of the vitalization of our cosmos is the product of complex processes involved in the acculturation of Buddhism, consisting of "two asymmetrical sides of a single operation with distinct ramifications" (Halkias 2016, 130), namely the "buddhicization of Tibet," on the one hand, and the "tibetanization of Buddhism," on the other. The spherical conception of revelation did not simply erase the pre-Buddhist tendencies of the Ancient School. Rather, the tradition found ways to maintain its teachings of the vertical vitality and subtly change it to reflect the priorities of the new religion. Indeed, in many ways, the apparent shift from a vertical to a spherical emergence of the universe was never completed and the proponents of the Ancient School lived in a dual reality that moves both from top to bottom and from the inside to the outside. In the remainder of this chapter, I will show that key dimensions of the spherical vitality—such as the ground, the mountain, the tomb, or the treasure—should be regarded as "liminal concepts" that allowed Tibetans to maintain their connection to the sky despite the cutting of the sky-cord, the increasing distance from the vertical vitality of pre-Buddhist culture.

A first way to describe the Tibetanizing thrust of Dzogchen is by relying on the term *snang ba* (Skt. *pratibhā*), which can be variously illustrated as "epiphany," "vision," or "disclosure."[19] Liberation, for the Dzogchen practitioner, is not effortful transformation but rather based on simplicity, spontaneity, and inherent perfection. In *The Seventeen Tantras*, the energy of awareness is furthermore qualified as "spontaneously productive" (*lhun grub*) and frequently expressed through metaphors of light. The ground is marked by "(dis)play" (*rol pa*), "radiance" (*gdangs*), "effulgence" (*ye gdangs*), and "radiant light" (*'od gsal*). The myth of origin of the Great Perfection, in fact, is not only concerned with the ground in its primordial interiority but also in the "way in which the ground manifests in spontaneous presence." In *The Tantra of Great Beauty and Auspiciousness*, this spontaneity of the ground is construed as follows: "Unceasing (*ma 'gags pa*) space manifests as energy. Unceasing epiphany arises as lights. Unceasing enjoyment dawns as wisdom. Unceasing essence emerges as bodies" (214,4).[20] There is no doubt that the centrality of the symbolism of light represents an important continuity between the myth of the ground's manifestation and the indigenous Tibetan beliefs regarding the descent of primordial vitality.

Indeed, the early Tibetan understanding of vitality was profoundly suffused by the idea of luminosity. Of course, it is quite intuitive that in a location where we witness up to 330 days of sunshine a year, the sky is not only a familiar backdrop but also intimately linked to light. The gods of the Tibetosphere are overwhelmingly associated with both the heavens and with light. In Sherpa and Khumbo myths, for instance, the ancestral gods frequently descend from the sky-realm in the form of white light or rainbows, and Huber even suggested that the bodies of the kings "consist of light" (Huber 2020, vol. II: 382). Although the Tibetan fascination with light—or, as Tucci once called it, its "photism"—flows throughout much of Tibetan history, it is particularly prevalent in indigenous religion and the Great Perfection. (Tucci 1980, 63–4). In another text recounting the descent of the first Yarlung emperor, we also read that the *phywa* progenitor kings "supported by the *rmu* ladder and the *rmu* cord, departed to the sky in view of all the people and the bodies of the gods dissolved into light (*'od du yal*) without a corpse [being left behind] (*The Great History of Buddhism*, 22).[21] Similarly, in the *Mirror of Royal Genealogies*, a fourteenth-century historical work composed by Sönam Gyaltsen (bsod nams rgyal mtshan, 1312–1375), we read of the "seven kings of the sky," who would disappear like a rainbow upon ascending to the sky through the *mu* cord. (55.15). In early Tibet, the kings were believed to be connected to the sky-realm by means of a so-called sky-cord (*dmu thag*), which was itself said to be in the form of light. Upon the king's death, his body would gradually—and from the feet upward—dissolve into light, join with the sky-rope, and merge with the heavenly realm of the *mu*.[22] Kapstein translates a relevant passage from the twelfth-century *Pillar Testament* as follows;

> With reference to those seven, they possessed, on their crowns, the so-called "divine daemon-cord" (*mutak*). This was a ray of white light. When those seven passed from suffering and journeyed to the realm of the gods, they dissolved into light from their feet upwards, and after the light faded into the sky they left no corpses behind. So it is said that the mausoleums of the seven thrones were planted in space. Translation in (Kapstein 2006, 37)

Not only do these divine kings return to the heaven by means of the *dmu* rope, leaving behind no corpses, but the rope itself is said to start at the top of the head. From there, it would form into a sort of rainbow and the king's sinciput, also known as the cleft of Brahma, is described as the gate to heaven.[23] Furthermore, vitality itself is said to be luminous in nature. Very much like the external radiance of rainbow-colored lights in the wake of the breaking of the youthful body in a vase, in indigenous origin myths, vitality is linked to the radiation of beams of light, which "emanated to the ten directions and surrounding countries of Tibet, bringing *g.yang* from them." As we saw, the notion of *g.yang* is also part of the spherical conception of vitality as *g.yang*-summoning rituals are performed until today in moments when the wild natural environment is disturbed by humans by either making it into habitable space (through construction) or robbed of some of its vitality (through mining, etc.). In this sense, *g.yang* is a liminal concept that allowed for the continuity between vertical and spherical conceptions of vitality: Once vitality descends from the heavens and circulates the earthly realm, it has to be regulated and maintained in this new realm.

A second locus where we find an abundance of pre-Buddhist motifs is in the emphasis on mountains and the ancestor cults associated with them.[24] The indigenous tradition of Tibet has frequently been described as shamanistic or animistic because it is premised on the belief that the world—the sky, the mountains, the soil, and the lakes—is inhabited by spirits.[25] Indeed, not only are these regions inhabited by beings, but the spirits are furthermore said to be the ancestors of political leaders from the past.[26] Gyatso links the "thorough-going Tibetanness of the eidos of Treasure" to the diachronic link between the moment of the treasure's revelation and the Tibetan empire: "It was concealed during the period of the Tibetan nation's apogee of military might and golden age of Buddhist practice; it was formulated specifically for this particular moment in Tibetan history; its prophecies in fact describe this moment pointedly; and now this particular Tibetan master has revealed it to Tibet at the proper time" (1996, 152–3).[27]

While Herbert Guenther has called the Great Perfection tantras "forgotten" tales (1994, xvii), they must also be understood in their function as exercises at *anamnesis*, texts of remembrance. Indeed, it is precisely because of the fragmentation caused by the collective trauma that the Ancient School can reclaim their past in new ways. The rupture in the fabric of time allows for the stitching of a new pattern. The Great Perfection myth of cosmogony, of course, plays a central role in this as it prioritizes the past over the present. Of particular importance, in this context, is the emphasis put on a state of being before the birth of the universe as we know it. As something that has been there "before" the rupture, the depiction of the ground prioritizes what is ancient over what is modern. Indeed, the ground is frequently also called the "original ground" (*gdod ma'i gzhi*), "primordial ground" (*ye gzhi*), "initial ground" (*thog ma'i gzhi*), "original state" (*gdod ma'i ngang*), and "the way of original being" (*thog ma'i gnas lugs*), and described as "originally pure" (*ka dag*). Although scholars are correct in pointing out that this expression should not be regarded simply as a temporal definition of the ground,[28] there is no doubt that a priority for what is past is central to the concept.[29] The only commentator noting this peculiarity is Arguillère, who clarified that "even though it has been too rarely highlighted until now, this temporal connotation, present everywhere in Dzogchen, to speak about realities—of which it incidentally puts forth an eternal nature—is very remarkable" (2007, 337).[30]

Although it might seem that the memory of the Great Perfection and the memory of ancestors in the mountain-cults of Tibet belong to the spherical model of vitality, this is not necessarily the case. Here, it might be useful to invoke the cautioning words of Toni Huber, who has recently addressed an "analytical blindness" among scholars of Tibet, who are "by now so strongly conditioned to accept that the mountain is a topographical and cosmological reference *par excellence* in all contexts that it goes without question."[31] Instead, he shifts his readers' emphasis from mountains toward the sky by noting that the ritual "solutions" proposed by the long-standing cults he encountered in his research, "whether ancient or present-day, are to be found up in the sky, or sometimes up and down the courses of river valleys," but not in the mountains (Huber 2020, vol. II: 82). He also remarks that while "the *Srid-pa'i lha* often complete their descent to earth at a specific arrival point associated with a mountain or hill … this does not deify the peak or summit in question in any way, nor reify it somehow as a special territory or 'sacred place.'" On the contrary, in the shamanic cults, the importance of mountains is rather pragmatic in nature, it is a "logical choice for the mythmaker since peaks are closest to the sky" (Huber 2020, vol. I: 404). In other words, the mountain is the place where the ancestors of humans first landed when they brought with them the source of vitality from the sky above.

The idea of the "genealogical" connection between humanity and the sky brings us to the third liminal concept, namely the tomb and its continued association with the realm of the sky. In the treasure tradition, the ontology of interiority is not purely synchronic, but also diachronic in nature. As Davidson propositioned, both Dzogchen and the treasure tradition draw their identity from the "tomb and ancestral cults of the royal house" (2005, 242). However, what Davidson did not emphasize enough is that Tibetans continued to operate according to a logic where "that which is above is like to that which is below, and that which is below is like to that which is above."[32] This Hermetic reference, sometimes summed up with the axiom "as above, so below," seems appropriate because the shift from the sky to the earthly tombs with the legendary cutting of the sky-cord and the subsequent burial of Trigum did not only fail to eliminate the centrality of the sky. On the contrary, the burial sites themselves might—quite paradoxically—reinforce the primacy of the sky. There is some clear evidence that suggests that the importance of the ground ultimately stemmed from the skies above. Consider, the early archeological sites in Tibet, where we find "monolithic / megalithic arrays" consisting of thousands of large standing stones that seem to be laid out in rows so as to form quadrangular shapes. These formations of stones, intentionally arranged from east to west, point to an astrological and astronomic concern, as well as a continued relevance of the celestial deities. As Bellezza, in commenting on such structures, concludes, "Early Tibetans were keen sky watchers" (2000, 14).

The true consequences of such an approach, of course, are radical as the spherical vitality of later Dzogchen would be subordinate to a much more dominant vertical model. As Guntram Hazod, in a paper presented at the fourteenth Seminar of the International Association for Tibetan Studies in Bergen, once suggested, "This would imply an image of the universe where the sky is not above but below, here recalling the notion of a reversal of the vertical order, or the (shamanistic) aspect of mirroring the sky in the landscape" (2016, 5). Indeed, the idea of the mirror-world is not only a prominent theme in Tibetan religions, but it also points to the fundamentally relational nature of these cosmological conceptions of the universe. Along the same lines, Ramble suggests that while the "vertical ordering of the world and the wider cosmos" has been extensively studied by scholarship, the idea of perspectivism has been underestimated. Drawing on a broad anthropological literature, he suggests that "a given perspective is not rooted in a particular ontology but in a position, and that a position, unlike an ontology, can be changed; what appear to be ontological identities are actually 'relational notions.'" Based on this relational approach, he shows evidence from various textual sources to delineate "a vertical mirror-imagery in Tibetan representations of the cosmos" (Ramble 2013, 81).

For us, another location of particular relevance to reconstruct this Tibetan mirror-world is the royal necropolis in Chonggye, particularly a place known as Mu ra "where the largest mounds of the emperors are arranged in an almost straight line across the valley and up the slopes of mount Mu ra ri" (Vogliotti 2019, 571). It is likely that these impressive burial sites in Central Tibet played a role in geomantic practices as early as the seventh century.[33] Even though the term "geomancy"—a method of divination that interprets markings on the ground—emphasizes the importance of the earthly dimension in the connection to the royal tombs, the original power of these places came from above. William Romain, who is specializing in archaeo-astronomy, uses the term "geomancy" to indicate "the practice of situating a structure such as temple or tomb in an auspicious, favorable, or harmonious location relative to celestial and/or terrestrial influences" (2018). Finally, Hazod has recently suggested that the association between sky and earth was not a one-way street, but rather one of mutual influence: Not only did the earth give access to the heavens, but the earth also allowed for the return to the sky. He explains this reciprocity by discussing the Mu ra burial mounds and the heavenly realm of the *dmu*:

> Not only *mu* but also the name part *ra* is documented as a Tibetan-Burmese root, with the meaning of "to come," "to get to" .... Mu ra, which is usually read as the "enclosure of (D)mu," may thus originally have meant something like "arrival in heaven"—a suitable description of the place where in the course of the tumulus burial the kings and other members of the royal family went to heaven or were ritually taken to the heavenly paradise. Although not documented in Old Tibetan sources, this term, *mu ra*, could actually be of a quite old, possibly

pre-imperial history, with the roots in southern Tibet, the region where also the Spu rgyal kingship originated. (Hazod 2020, 297)

If we transport this hermetic logic into the seeming split between treasure revelation and Dzogchen meditation, it could even be argued that the revelation of treasures is paradoxically rooted in the vertical vitality and the sky. In a fourteenth-century treasure text revealed by Orgyen Lingpa (o rgyan gling pa, 1323–1360?), we read that one enters into the lower world by "windows of heaven" in order to get a treasure text (*The Chronicle of the Kings*, 96a). Stein summarizes the passage as follows:

> In a site described earlier was found a plaque. It was to be lifted and underneath would be found a "gate of Heaven," covered by another plaque. That was penetrated by means of a cleft in it. There one finds, "in the direction of the gate of Heaven," a window. By breaking it, one creates a path of light. Going through it, one finds a mandala. Below this circle, there is another "window" containing skulls. After an obscure description, the text mentions yet again the "gate of Heaven" of the cave, where one finds a turquoise talisman. (Stein 1990, 163–4)

This passage is interesting not only because it links the revelation of treasures out of the earth with the sky, but also because it combines the two models of vitality. Since the earth offers an access to the heavens as the breaking open of the ground reveals a "path of white [light]" (*dkar lam*), it is quite clear that we are dealing here with a liminal myth that perfectly illustrates the continued interpenetration of the vertical and the spherical models of vitality.

Indeed, the "manifestation of the ground" that culminates in the liberation of Buddha Samantabhadra is directly associated with the heavenly vitality as the latter is not always described in terms of a descent, but sometimes also involves the tearing open of the sky. Just as the Dzogchen cosmogony is imaged as the tearing of a youthful body in a vase and Samantabhadra's enlightenment is seen as his return within this unity, we find early Tibetan texts using the same vocabulary to speak about the sky. In a Dunhuang manuscript, for instance, we read about a king and a minister who manifest as gods. While the minister is responsible for the sowing up of a crevice in the earth, it is the majesty of the king that leads to the sowing up of a "tear in the sky" (*gnam ral ba*) (IOL Tib J 751, 41.2).[34]

Of course, the most important element of the lengthy passage cited above— and this brings us to the fourth and final liminal concept under scrutiny in this chapter—is that the sky seems to play a crucial role in some practices of treasure revelation. This might even be true throughout the history of this phenomenon. Treasures, indeed, are sometimes said to fall from the sky. In other cases, treasure revealers recover the vital teachings themselves by journeying into the sky. One illustration of this can be found in the life of Guru Chöwang (gu ru chos dbang, 1212–1270), a great treasure revealer and instrumental figure in the standardization of the treasure-revealing process. Indeed, before revealing his first major treasure at a place known as "Sky Ladder Rock" (*gnam skas brag*), Chöwang traveled to the thirteenth level of the sky where he met Vajrasattva inside a tent of light and received a vase of elixir (*The Autobiography of Guru Chöwang*, 12a, 3–4.)

Sometimes, the treasure revealers rely on visionary processes that resemble Tögal even from a phenomenological perspective as they lead from primordial atemporality into human history and language. This is particularly obvious in the so-called mind treasure (*dgongs gter*). In fact, there exist two primary modes of treasure discovery: The first one is known as "earth treasure" (*sa gter*) and involves the unearthing of textual fragments buried in the ground, a statue, or a monastery wall; the second one, known as "mind treasure," involves a mental process during which a text that is buried in the discoverer's mind is revealed. The revelation of mind treasures can be depicted as a process of "un-minding": The texts were buried in the revealer's most fundamental level of mind in the past, encoded in the "genuine awareness of radiant light," and recovered in the present through a process of "pure vision" (*dag snang*).[35] This visionary process gives access to the memory of this pristine state of radiant light, with the mechanism of perceiving the treasure text closely reproducing the rhythm of the appearance of the visionary manifestations during Tögal (discussed in more detail in Chapter 5). In both cases, the manifestations move gradually from an initial dawning in the form of unclear appearances that are changing and shaking randomly to increased clarity and stability. In the treasure-revelation process, this ultimately culminates in the spontaneous translation of visionary texts into Tibetan (Gyatso 1998, 159–73).

The treasures are initially appearing in a "symbolic script of the *ḍākinīs*" (*mkha' 'gro brda yig*), which the revealer has to "break" in order to "meet" the literal encoded treasure. While there are several options of how this decoding works—such as a "key" with one-one-one correspondences of letters or clues in the environment, which allow for the translation of the code—there exists also a method known as the "face value of letters" by means of which "the encoded Treasure text can simply become clear to the discoverer, 'without regard for either (an alphabet or external circumstances).'" This third case is particularly relevant for our discussion because here "the medium is a spontaneous vision or some other internal prompting, which results either in a direct perception of the encoded Treasure text, or consists in a gradual process, in which repetition of the internal clue or image finally evokes a perception of the text" (Gyatso 1986, 19). Similarly, the content of the encoded text can take on various forms and corresponds in different degrees to the actual treasure that is to be revealed. Sometimes, the code is "just an appearance," in which case "there will appear a single symbol, or a character or two, not necessarily completing a phrase or even a word." Gyatso rightly points out that these "appearances," just like the ones perceived during Skullward Leap, are intimately linked to memory: "We might understand this mode as a mnemonic cue of sorts; the discoverer is given the opening letters of the Treasure, which serve to evoke in his memory the full text" (1986, 19).

While we will explore the exact nature of the visionary appearances of Skullward Leap in a later chapter, the present discussion has shown that since meditation cannot be separated neither from the mythical horizon that founds the practitioner's worldview, nor from the historical context that gave rise to the practice, contemplation is about much more than just present-centeredness; even more, the site of the present only comes into relief if it is stretched out over a more expansive temporal territory, which, in the case of Tibet, accounts for its particular mix between a vertical type of vitality descending from the sky, on the one hand, and a spherical type of vitality that emerges out of the ground, on the other.

Chapter 3

THE RISE OF THE NEW SCHOOLS AND THE CIRCULARITY OF VITALITY

Based on the previous chapter's addition of a Buddhist spherical model of vitality that entered into competition with the vertical descent of primordial energy that was indigenous to Tibet—and possibly even part of a larger Eurasian cult of the sky-deer—this chapter explores a further development precipitated by the introduction of Buddhism, namely the promotion of a tantric model of vitality. With the rise of the New Schools (*gsar ma*, Sarma), which received their religious energies through a direct link with Buddhist teachers living in India, the ground of Tibet was fertilized with new streams of vitality. Relying on the most powerful transformative exercises that tantric Buddhism has to offer, the proponents of the New Schools soon rose to become the indisputable rulers over the Tibetan realm, further marginalizing the social groups that embraced the Dzogchen teachings. The Great Perfection scriptures, composed during those very same years, feature a set of intriguing narratives centered on the struggle for life-sustaining substances that catapult us back into the depths of indigenous culture on the plateau. Although the adherents of the Ancient School experienced new historical circumstances throughout the centuries, they frequently interpreted their struggles for survival by means of older indigenous models of vitality. Through a comparative reading of the Dzogchen riddles and the corpus of mythical-ritual texts introduced earlier, we quickly realize that they likely come from the same cultural substratum. Indeed, both sets of stories are marked by the same identical structure: a crisis moment disrupts an otherwise idyllic context, a youthful heroic figure emerges, and authority figures instruct him to embark on a mission to recover precious substances associated with a heavenly realm. Furthermore, the Dzogchen stories also help us refine our understanding of these narratives by emphasizing that vitality is susceptible to being lost or even stolen by other forces.

Tantric Vitality

The sociocultural ground upon which the Dzogchen tradition proceeded to construct its identity during the Renaissance of Tibetan culture during the eleventh and twelfth centuries is just as diverse as its geographical features. Although the

Tibetan plateau is the highest in the world with an average elevation of over 5,000 meters, it is also a place of unique topographic variability, featuring both the barrenness of the highest peaks on earth and deep valleys with fertile ecologies. In this same spirit, the spherical ground of vitality in Tibet was contested, conflicted, and fragmented, and therefore best imagined as consisting of a series of tectonic plates that push and pull in various directions rather than as a single homogenous surface.

Consequently, I have recently suggested that the narrative of the fragmentation of the youthful body in a vase should be read as a mythical representation of the historical circumstances involved in the collapse of the Tibetan empire in the middle of the ninth century (Geisshuesler 2019c; 2020b). Ü Dumtsen (*'u'i dum btsan*)—the successor of the third Dharma king—was to become the last king of the Yarlung Dynasty. Shortly before the middle of the ninth century, a civil war broke out and the Tibetan empire fell. What followed the collapse of the empire was a period marked by conflicts between warring groups as a civil war broke out as two sons of Ü Dumtsen competed for power. Tride Yumtän (*khri lde yum brtan*), the son of his first wife, ruled over the central kingdom of Ü (*dbus*), and Namde Ösung (*gnam lde 'od srung*), the son of his second wife, ruled probably in the eastern territories (Shakabpa 2009, 173).[1] Regardless of the details, the fall of the empire, only two short centuries after its emergence as one of Asia's great powers, led Tibet into a period that has been described as one of anarchy and religious degradation.[2] After the contested initial conversion of Tibet to Buddhism, the collapse of the kingdom was in many ways the second trauma affecting the Tibetan people. The period was, without a doubt, characterized by the disintegration of the empire's political centralization, rebellions against the inheritors of imperial Tibet, and the rise of a series of regional warlords (Van Schaik and Galambos 2012, 4). Lasting roughly one hundred and fifty years, Tibetans speak of the period following the collapse of Great Tibet as a "time of fragments" (*sil bu'i dus*).

The collective memory of the Tibetan people was forged out of the need to make sense of the overwhelming historical problem of the loss of the empire. Being degraded from the rulers of much of Asia to a loosely organized set of clans without unified center, Tibetan leaders were searching for new ways to assert their power and develop a stable reign; a process that culminated in the so-called Tibetan Renaissance around the eleventh century.[3] While the Ancient School built their identity by soliciting answers from the mythical-religious ground—and, more implicitly, from the sky—of imperial and pre-imperial Tibet, the New Schools rose to the status of political power because they were nourished by a fresh stream of life in the form of new teachings from a land to the south, namely India. In a land where Buddhism served as the lingua franca since its introduction in the seventh century, the access to new teachings during the so-called later spread of the teachings (*bstan pa phyi dar*) turned out to be the decisive advantage for the neo-conservatives. During this period, the prioritization of Indian materials did not emerge in a vacuum but was rather the result of a complex constellation that included both the disappearance of

Buddhism from India and the rise of Yuan or Mongol dynasty in China. On the one hand, the Indianizing ideology became crucial to preserve Indian Buddhist traditions; on the other hand, Yuan power was more easily swayed by a Buddhism of supposedly pure Indian pedigree.

Be that as it may, the New Schools were not only directly attached to the umbilical cord of Indian Buddhism, but also fed by the very powerful energy of what could be described as "tantric vitality." Although Indo-Tibetan tantric systems are complex and consist of a motley variety of theories and practices,[4] the New Schools categorized tantric materials into four different classes,[5] with the tantras of the *anuttarayoga* class being the most sophisticated and intended for the yogis with the highest ability.[6] In these texts, we find new teachings from the homeland of Buddhism, which decisively shaped the identity of the New Schools. Many of these more extreme forms of tantra—involving violent as well as sexual teachings—emerged in India from the ninth century onward and quickly became immensely popular.[7] The life-giving dimension of these practices is not only connected to their bodily performance—as they involve the manipulation of physical energies regulated by our breath—but also contained important political dimensions that are best summed up in the notion of "power;"[8] a key concern for tantric systems of thought and practice. Indeed, the new systems introduced from India operated by means of "initiations" or "empowerments" (Skt. *abhiṣeka*, Tib. *dbang bskur ba*), which transferred the authority to practice meditation from the teacher to the disciple. Ronald Davidson has highlighted the centrality of "power" in tantric Buddhism, clearly demonstrating that it played off the political transmission of royal authority in India.[9] Of course, this political dimension of power was intimately linked to tantric practice as the exertion of power went hand in hand with the transformation of mind and body through yogic exercises. In the Tibetan universe, this close link between the techniques of sensory manipulation and the exertion of power (*dbang*), is even reflected in the etymology of the term used to describe the senses as "that which has power" (*dbang po*). By offering extensive instructions for breathing patterns, bodily postures, hand gestures, verbal utterances, and so forth, the tantric texts aim at transforming the very identity of the meditator.

Consider, for instance, the practice of "deity yoga" (Skt. *devatā yoga*, Tib. *lha'i rnal byor*), which involves the visualization of oneself as a divine figure and starts with the "vivid appearance of the god," during which the meditators develop focused attention on attributes of the "personal deity" they are visualizing.[10] After vividly calling to mind the attributes of the god, the practice continues with the so-called recollection of purity, which stands for a profound identification of one's self with that of a supremely reigning deity. The visualizations are implemented by following a standardized protocol, a so-called *sādhana* (Tib. *sgrub thabs*, lit. "means of achievement"), whose goal is to elucidate the specific symbolic meanings of each individual attribute of the deity. Finally, the practitioners are instructed "to assume the ego of the deity" as they engage in "divine pride." Scholarship has rightly declared that deity yoga practice essentially corresponds to the "transformation of personality" (Davidson 2002, 164).[11] Quite literally vitalized by the identification with life-giving power itself, the practitioners then engage in various physical exercises that allow them to manipulate this energy within their bodies. This becomes particularly apparent in *anuttarayoga,* which is characterized by a second, much more physical, group of practices.[12] These techniques capitalize on the newfound divine identity to engage in various bodily practices, to explore the soteriological potential of extreme experiences such as sexuality, violence, and death, and aim at generating great bliss.[13]

Overall, the tantric model of vitality offers a super-charging of the spherical model introduced in Chapter 2. The Ancient School's spherical vitality, as I have shown, was premised on life-giving powers of a radiating ground that manifested its productivity both in a cosmological force, as well as in a scriptural originality. In the Indo-Tibetan tantric context, which was likely already imbued with a spherical model through the pan-Buddhist *abhidharmic* cosmology, the spherical vitality receives another twist as it is imagined as an inward flow of external energies. Put differently, if the indigenous Tibetan model can be summed up by the axiom of "as above, so below," the new tantric model of vitality embraced another dictum: "As without, so within." This is apparent in the production of texts, which are not pulled out of the earth, but rather directly transmitted from India into Tibet. Similarly, this inward flowing vitality becomes apparent in the subtle body (Skt. *sūkṣma śarīra,* Tib. *lus 'phra, phra ba'i lus*), which can be seen as a microcosmic universe model of the macrocosmic universe. In his discussion of the role of the body in the *Cakrasaṃvara Tantra,* for example, David Gray observed that it is premised on the idea that "Śrī Heruka, the buddha with whom the meditator in this tradition will identify in deity yoga practices, pervades the entire universe, collapsing the distinction between self and other, the subjective and the objective." Not only that, Gray also notes "the contemplation is to be internalized, via what came to be known as the body mandala practices," which "included mapping the twenty-four sacred sites to various internal bodily sites (*sthāna*) and the male deities to various bodily constituents (*dhatu*)" as well as "the mapping of the female deities to subtle body channels (*nāḍī*) connected with the twenty-four internal sites" (Gray 2021, 8).

If the flooding of Tibet with new sources of vitality in the form of tantric systems of practice empowered certain Tibetan schools to increase their influence, this act of vitalization undermined the influence of others. While the new translators of Buddhism quickly rose to prominence and became celebrated feudal lords upon their return to Tibet, the power, prestige, and authenticity of the aristocratic clans of the Ancient School, which already suffered previously, were radically challenged. "With each new translation," so Adam Lobel recently put it, "the older Tibetan translations came to seem less genuinely Indic; and some claimed that the previous tantras were indigenous fabrications, especially without access to the Sanskrit originals" (2018, 56).[14] We could say that the rise to power of the New Schools represents a third trauma—after the introduction of Buddhism and the collapse of the empire—affecting the adherents of the Great Perfection within a few centuries. As with these earlier transformations, the

Ancient School sought to process this sense of disempowerment through their mythical narratives.

Dzogchen Riddles

This brings us to one element of the classical Dzogchen myth of the manifestation of the ground that we have not yet discussed, namely its strikingly strong interpersonal dimension. In fact, the emphasis on the early moments of existence is ultimately an expression of the Great Perfection's larger inquiries into the creation of its own self; or, as the tradition itself would call it, the "epiphany of the self" (*rang snang*). The Dzogchen myth suggests that as the ground manifests, we witness the birth of selfhood: "From within this abiding ground, the seed of straying and its causes are the aspect of lucidity that has slipped outward [to] suddenly epiphanize objectively as the mind that holds to a self … In this way, the objective sphere is apprehended as a self" (*Treasury of Words and Meanings* 45.6).[15] The ground's manifestation, the breaking and opening up of the vase, its slipping outward, its projecting into a vast "expanse," rather paradoxically, leads into the "capturing" of the "self." The birth of the "self," so Germano argues, is the result of a "proliferation of 'frames' [that] generates a complex web of intellectual and emotion fabrications that we call our 'world'" (1992, 402). In *The Tantra of Unimpeded Sound*, we read:

> The ground and cognition become sullied and the revolving process of apprehended objects and sensory faculties sets in. The conditions are that, through the objective sphere and the apprehension factor, there come to be individual distinctions based upon their respective boundaries. … The psychic energy in question involves subjective apprehensions that are flickering, subsiding, and prolific. The pollution lies in its apprehension in a stained fashion, such that your own self-identity is fettered by this way of comprehending. Even though that which is comprehended is not what it seems, you become tightly bound by clinging to its veracity (142.6).[16]

The dynamism of acceptance and rejection, the "adopting" of certain things, and the simultaneous "discarding" of others, serves as a sort of membrane through which human beings establish the homoeostatic balance that we call "self." Thus, the Great Perfection advocates for a conspicuously parallel conception of how human existence is marked by suffering due to mental dysregulation. The mind of humans is predisposed to a painful existence because it forms its "self" through interpersonal relationships, which can be illustrated as a "boundary making" with what is "other." These attempts to articulate the Dzogchen self as the result of interpersonal relationships is even more evident in another set of myths that accompany the cosmogony of the ground. In these anthropomorphized stories, described as "allegories," "riddles," or "symbolic codes" (*lde'u*), we find young children forced to leave their mothers and fathers, before being imprisoned in deep ravines by old women and grandmothers, who are helped by friendly and warring soldiers. The most prominent example is found in *The Tantra of Self-Arisen Awareness*, where the scene is set by introducing an intelligent child and his dull-minded grandmother:

> In the past, in a country known as "thoroughly pure awareness buddha field," there stood a castle with eight doors. On the top of this castle there lived a little boy whose name was "Performing the Awareness of Epiphany" and his grandmother known as "Cataract." In the lower part of this country, there lived a wicked king named "famous lord," who had five children. As the five princes went to amuse themselves and the grandmother Cataract appeared down in the lower part for some rest, they put her into prison. Just imagine! Then, when her son went after his grandmother, he too was arrested and put into shackles. Just imagine! (579.4–580.5) [17]

The child's name, Performing the Awareness of Epiphany (*snang ba'i rig byed*), points to his productive and energetic qualities that he shares with the "ground." Guenther has meaningfully translated the son's name as "the inspiring youngster," emphasizing his vitality as the most differentiating characteristic.[18] Even more relevantly, he points to the uneasy relationship between the child and his caretakers as it is his vitality that distinguishes him from the sluggishness of his grandmother Cataract (*ling tog can*) (Guenther 2005, 124–5). The same tantra narrates the early life of little children, which is filled with hardship as they suffer at the hands of the older generation. In the thirty-ninth chapter, for example, the scripture recounts two children's story as a dramatic abduction by figures standing close to them.

> In the past, in a country known as "vastness," there existed a teacher by the name of "dispenser of light." He had two children, who had been imprisoned in a barren and deep ravine. Just imagine! Then, five soldiers appeared and conquered the stone castle from the top. Just imagine! After the two children had been thrown into a deep pit, grandmother Cataract shut the door. Just imagine! (560.6)[19]

This narrative, short and abrupt—and consistently punctuated with the interjection "just imagine" (*zer te ya cha*)—represents yet another anthropomorphization of the myth of cosmogony. The two children are reified figures that contrast sharply with both the teacher and the kingdom in which they are born. Understood to be the siblings of a single mother, they stand for the manifestation of the ground, the rupture in the original unity of the primordial foundation, and the source of vitality that would ultimately form the universe as we know it. Finally, their imprisonment stands for humanity's straying as it mistakes its own identity and enters into the captivity of *saṃsāra*, as if living a life bereft of true sustenance. Even more, read as mythical-historical documents, these stories point to the sociopolitical realities that gave rise to them. It is striking that the children are quite literally "being framed" as they are betrayed by various figures standing close to them. In his commentary, written in the fourteenth century, the revealer of the Northern Treasures (*byang gter*), Rigdzin Gödem Ngödrup Gyaltsen (rig 'dzin rgod ldem dngos grub rgyal mtshan, 1337–1408) specifies that the soldiers were closely associated with the children, noting that they were originally jailed by "four disloyal friends" (*The Tantra on the Difference between Mind and Awareness According to the Great Perfection*, 633–50).

In the fortieth chapter of *The Tantra of Self-Arisen Awareness*, we read about a mother and a father, who conceived two children, a girl and a boy. As the parents send the children away to the country of a demon to retrieve fire and flowers, the son refuses to go out of fear of being imprisoned by the demon. In response, the parents argue: "Son, don't say this. In the country of the demon, there lives an old woman called Cataract. She is your grandmother, ask her for fire" (*The Tantra of Self-Arisen Awareness*, 570.4).[20] After requesting the support of five companions, the boy sets out to the country of the demon. Of course, as expected, the two children are found by their grandmother Cataract. So far so good, but now there comes a surprising twist in the story. While we do encounter the aforementioned grandmother, her demeanor toward her grandchildren is quite contrary to the parents' prediction.

> Grandmother Cataract locked the doors and told the attendants: "Because they killed my children in the past, do not let them escape." The servants responded: "It will be done so." There was no opportunity for them to leave. Then, the child spoke as follows: "Grandmother, my two [parents] told me that my grandmother by the name of Cataract lives in the country of the demon and they told me to ask for fire. Therefore, let me go without holding me [prisoner]." The old woman answered: "I will not let you go. I will not set you free because your father has killed my children." Then the boy responded: "If you don't let me go, I will raise an army." The woman responded: "Raise an army, I will not let you go." At that point, the youth passed along the following message to three visitors: "Friends, in the country "jewel heap," there are four outcasts. Your little child "intelligence of epiphany" has been imprisoned there. Swiftly bring a big army." The visitors, saying that they would do so, left. (*The Tantra of Self-Arisen Awareness*, 572.2) [21]

This episode not only revisits previously encountered themes (such as the imprisonment of young children) and familiar characters (such as the little child Intelligence of Epiphany, or the grandmother Cataract), but it also offers new details about the incarceration and the contact between the jailors and the captives. If I already set down that the trauma in Great Perfection narratives is personal and frequently grounded in family relationships, the plot gradually thickens as it becomes clear that the suffering is a phenomenon that crosses generations. The grandmother not only imprisons her two grandchildren, but she also accuses them and their father of killing her own children. These anthropomorphic stories add an important layer to the social reality of marginalization, political struggle, and competition for power. They offer yet another mythic representation of historical circumstances.

Crisis and Crisis Management

These anthropomorphized myths of little children and their quest for life in situations of persecution also offer us a powerful illustration of the fundamental tension underlying the formative years of Dzogchen Buddhism, namely that between an increasing buddhicization of the realm of Tibet and a continued reliance on an indigenous Tibetan worldview. We see this in a larger mythological theme of the vertical descent of vitality; it too testifies to a tension between an unceasing stream of life descending from the heavenly realm and an unpredictable rupture of this vital flow. While this already became apparent in the myth of Trigum, who cut his sky-cord and thus lost his connection to the heavenly world, the message of the fragility of our intimate connection with heavenly vitality is further reinforced by the anthropomorphized riddles introduced in this chapter. Here, kingdoms are bereft of their vitality, and various social actors fight each other for the access to life-sustaining energies. The dialogue between the children and the grandmother, who insists that she will not let them go despite their pleading, for instance, shares certain traits with a famous passage describing the destiny of Bönpo priests during the rise to power of the Tibetan empire. In a Bönpo treasure text attributed to Drenpa Namkha (dran pa nam mkha')—an "eclectic" Tibetan, who is said to have converted from Bön to Buddhism during the eighth century—entitled *The One Hundred Thousand Tantras of Eternal Bön*, we read about how the priests were exiled by the Tibetan kings out of fear of their power. In response to being asked to leave, one of the priests, Gyimbo Lentsa, responded in terms that are quite reminiscent of the young boy's interpellation in the Dzogchen myth: " If the four series of divine Bön flourish, the temples will maintain its vitality. I will not leave, but surely remain. Divine Bön must not disappear." As a result, so the text reports, the priest "carrying with him the Thimar [text] to protect the king, was confined in the palace as if in a prison" (26.3–6).

This tension between changing historical circumstances and the persistence of older mythical models for interpreting them, of course, leads to a rather paradoxical situation according to which the Ancient School makes the cause of its marginalization into a virtue for its continued survival. The tradition struggled to find legitimacy during the Tibetan Renaissance because it actively promoted the controversial practice of the revelation of treasures to maintain its scriptural vitality—implicitly carrying within it the heritage of godly vitality descending from the sky. Nonetheless, this did not deter the Nyingmapas from reinforcing their link with this indigenous source of life. While the parables of the little children and their grandmother Cataract are clearly rooted within the canon of the Buddhist Great Perfection scriptures, it has so far been overlooked that likely emerged out of the Bönpo quest for vitality narratives studied in the first chapter. As we remember, these stories told adventurous tales of the descent of royal kings, bringing vitality on flying sheep and deer, the hunt for such animals in a quest for their precious body parts like conch shell coats and crystalline antlers, and long chases during which the young hunter follows an injured animal throughout the whole land.

While we can already intuit that the Dzogchen parables of the little children share certain key traits with these myths, such as the quest for precious substances,[22] they are actually helping us stitch together a richer tapestry of early indigenous mythology. More specifically, the stories point to a series of traits that I have not yet highlighted, the most important of which is the idea that vitality is liable to being lost or stolen and therefore requires heroic emissaries that allow not only for its recovery but also for its protection. Hank Blezer, who extensively studied the mythical texts of Bönpos, uses the expression "crisis and crisis management" paradigm to identify such plotlines as the stories usually open with a moment of crisis—something is either lacking or stolen from the world of humans—before recounting a primordial search to obtain what is needed (2008, 423).[23] In the following pages, I will not only further refine our understanding of the Bönpo "crisis and crisis management" paradigm, but I will also argue that the Dzogchen myths found in the heart of *The Seventeen Tantras of the Ancient School* manifest strikingly similar characteristics.

The first thing that is striking across many of these mythical narratives is that they open with what Dotson described as a "family scene" (Dotson 2022, 49), which involves a father and a mother conceiving a son or multiple children. Both Nyingma and Bönpo myths that accompanied us throughout this first part of the book display an overwhelming fascination with family origins. The scene frequently opens with a mother and a father, who start their own lineage by conceiving children. Just as the Dzogchen myths speak of a "youthful body in a vase" (*gzhon nu bum pa'i sku*), "youth" (*khye'u*), "children" (*bu*), or "siblings from the same parents" (*bu spun*), Bönpo narratives feature "little men" (*mi chung*), "little humans" (*mi'u*), or "small little humans" (*mi'u chung*) as their protagonists. Similarly, in the ancient Dunhuang text titled *The Age of Decline*, the main protagonist is described as "son" (*bu, bu chung, sras*). That these figures are primogenitors directly connected to the cosmogonic myths becomes particularly apparent in *Extensive Elimination and Offering Rites*, where a couple of heavenly gods beget two children from which the "Four Groups of Little Humans" descend (*Extensive Elimination and Offering Rites for the Gods of the Four Groups of Little Humans*, 1). In the *Deer Wild Stations* and the closely related *Methods of Subduing Crisis-Spirits* (the latter text has recently been discovered in the Gathang Bumpa in Southern Tibet[24]), ritual texts likely stemming from the eleventh century, we find almost identical procreation myths involving little humans that stand at the origin of life on earth; here variously designated as "small gods" (*lhe'u*), "young ones" (*ne'u zhon*), or "small gods offspring who are brother and sister" (*lhe'u sras lcam dral*).[25] Nyingma and Bönpo myths that accompanied us throughout this first part of the book display an overwhelming fascination with family origins and the principal *dramatis personae* seem to continue even into the myths of the sky-deer. Here, the prey frequently engages in dialogues with their hunter in order to inquire about their place of birth as well as their parents' names.[26] Similarly, thinking back at the illustrated page of the *Deer Way-Stations*, we remember seeing a scene of a stag-father, a doe-mother, and a young deer-offspring. While these ideas have not yet been raised by scholarship on Tibetan myths surrounding the quest for vitality, we are gleaning at an earlier version of the more expansive "indigenous" substratum, the wider Eurasian sky-cult. In fact, the hunting for sheep and deer has been identified as an integral part of coming-of-age rites in several of these cultural contexts. It is therefore not implausible that the young males in charge of the quest for vitality in the mythical narratives in the Tibetan context are also on a journey to adulthood and that one of the functions of the cult of the sky-deer might have been that of a rite of passage (Myers 1997; Steward 1941, 318).

Be that as it may, the descent of vitality is associated with genealogical descent of families. This trans-generational dimension of the cosmogony takes the form of human descendance from the heavenly gods, and is frequently evoked in the term *rgyud*, which can be variously translated as "continuum," "string," "lineage," or "descent." "*rGyud* and its synonyms (*skye rgyud, rus rgyud, pha rgyud*, etc.)," so Huber elaborates, "strongly emphasize the continuities in relatedness, and hence the common transmission shared across and running between generations" (2020, vol. I: 49). The tantric adepts of the Ancient School, the *ngag pa* practitioners of the mantra, passed their mythical-ritual teachings within family lineages from father to son throughout the dark period and felt the need for faithful continuity with the tradition of their forefathers (or -mothers). This trans-generational transmission of knowledge practiced by the Nyingma mantrins might very well be a custom inherited from the non-Buddhist traditions of Tibet. Spirit-mediumship, for instance, "has been kept alive by lineages of practitioners, nearly all of which are hereditary [and] the most prominent spirit-mediums are thought to be heirs to lineages many generations old" (Bellezza 2005, 19). Similarly, invocations of kin terms (such as father, mother, or son) in Bönpo sources, so Huber suggests, "are best understood as expressions of a particular form of 'ancestral' genealogical thinking":

> The terms themselves reference perceived descent links between ritual specialists and the auxiliary beings who are also their ancestors, and ultimately, as well, a genealogical connection back to the ancestral realm of apical progenitor deities from whom the source of life can be traced, and with whom the designated specialist stands in a relation as intermediary. In fundamental respects, the older Tibetan royal cult encapsulates the same genealogical thinking and may even be closely related to its occurrence in the realm of ritual specialists. (Huber 2020, vol. I: 177)

It could even be argued that the ideology of genealogical descent, flowing in a vertical direction as in the cosmology of indigenous Tibetans, was already a feature of the very early phase of Tibetan history, where the kings themselves were exalted as the "sons of god" (*lha sras*).[27] The idea of royalty brings us a bit closer to the setting of these stories. Indeed, most myths under consideration here involve a heroic youth, who is charged with the task of finding precious substances endowed with fortune-bringing qualities. In *The Ultimate Vitality*, for instance, we read about a castle known as "Beautiful Jewel" and a king, who laments the absence of the *phya* because of demons. As in other stories, it is the king's son, the prince, who is sent to a foreign land to retrieve a precious deer. In *The Great Main Text of the Vitality Ritual of the Lord of the Vitality*, which also documents the cosmogony from eggs and the descent of *g.yang* from the sky, we read about parents and their son named "Man of the Emanation," who live in a great palace. The text explains that "when the father, the mother, and the son were there, humans had no *phya*, and there was much illness; beasts had no *g.yang*, and deadly epidemics were rife; food had no nutrition, and gave little strength." Thus, the three of them hold a council and invite the "Bön God White Turban," who suggests that the son go out of his country to search for the *phya* requisites (224).[28] The son then sets out on his exploratory expedition, traveling from one place to the next until he finally comes upon a jewel deer: "Casting his sun-ray noose, he lassoes the jewel deer, and the deer speaks to him in a human voice: 'I am the stable base of *phya* and *g.yang*; the nine *phya* items are fully present in me; Man, I am your deer.'"[29] Having found the precious substances he needed to recover, he takes the jewel deer and returns home (525).

Stories such as these point to another key trait of the early Tibetan conception of vitality, namely that the continuous flow of life-sustaining energy is anything but guaranteed. In fact, most—if not all—stories are marked by a moment of crisis during which vitality is at risk of being lost. If we have already seen several examples of the loss of vitality, such as the little children who are imprisoned by their grandmother in the land of the demon, the most extreme illustration might come from another passage of The Tantra of Self-Arisen Awareness. Here, we read of an old woman possessing a precious jewel, which is stolen by five thieves.[30] The story then takes a more gruesome turn as her son by the name of "White Fire God," asking about the whereabouts of the jewel, is told: "The jewel has not been lost, but you must kill your mother, the old woman. If you do not kill your mother, you will not get your jewel."[31] According to the parable, the son proceeds not only to kill his mother, but he also "eats her flesh, drinks her blood, sucks her bones, and completely obliterates her." In turn, "the thieves give him the jewel" (581.1-3).[32] In an allegory contained in *The Symbol of the Secret Seminal Nuclei Tantra*, another locus classicus for anthropomorphized stories in the Dzogchen tradition, we read about a king, who possesses a "precious jewel chest filled with inconceivable many smaller gems."[33] While he is talking to the Old Lady Cataract, five thieves steal his chest of jewels, which he is then able to retrieve and return to his kingdom thanks to the help of the Little Child of the Inconceivable Epiphany (53). The persona of Old Lady Cataract might also be part of a more general trait of many Tibetan antecedent tales of this sort as figures like the stepmother and other maternal relatives are frequently considered to be wicked and dangerous (Dotson 2022, 50).

The motif of the loss of vitality due to malignant forces takes on strikingly similar forms in other narratives under discussion. Let us consider the example of the previously mentioned Gathang manuscript titled *Methods of Subduing Crisis-Spirits*, which describes rites addressed at the post-mortem well-being of miscarried infants and mothers who died during childbirth. I have decided to translate the term *rnal dri* (sometimes also *dri, dri ma, ba dri*) as "crisis-spirits" because their primary function in these antecedent tales seems to wreak havoc by creating crisis in the world of the humans by posthumously possessing the living in the wake of culturally problematic deaths.[34] Similarly, we have seen that the *Remedying the Lords of the Soil and Subjugating the Evil Forces of Creation through the Ground of Vitality* takes place in a country that has been disturbed because of demonic activity, requiring the hunting of the deer and the performance of a ransom offering (*glud*). Berounský comments on this text, noting that here, the "ground of *g.yang*" is not intended to bring "some good fortune, but it is used tin order to pacify the evil forces" (2014, 61). In other instances, the hunt itself seems to be problematic as the activity of hunting is oftentimes associated with illness. In fact, both the hunting for deer as well as the dangers associating with it are so widespread in indigenous culture that they can even be found in the oldest strata of Tibetan manuscripts found at Dunhuang. In *The Age of Decline*, for instance, we find another young man who is going into the wilderness to hunt animals. After unsuccessfully shooting arrows at three different stags, he finally wounds a deer that is specified to have antlers of conch. Although hurt, the deer manages to flee and the hunter pursues it across the whole country until it finally succumbs to its injuries and dies. As he is butchering the animal, a demon arrives and steals his own "vitality" (*bla*). He falls into a comatose state and priests arrive to perform various rituals to restore his health.

Although the term *bla* has an "ambiguous existence and polysemous nature" (Gerke 2012, 138),[35] it forms part of the semantic field of what I describe as "vitality" and Huber recently proposes to translate it as "mobile vitality principle" (Huber 2020, vol. I: 70).[36] Indeed, it is likely that one of the sources of the term cascades from the same mythical reservoir of heavenly vitality as other terms that we have encountered in the first two chapters, particularly, *lha*, *g.yang*, and *phya*. Like these notions, the *bla* seems to have originally been associated with the luminous vitality that descends from the sky (Karmay 1998c, 315).[37] In the context of Tibetan Buddhism, the *bla* is also intimately linked to another early Buddhist concept, namely the "five protective spirits" (*'go ba'i lha*), which play a crucial role in the maintenance of vitality indigenous to Tibetan world. Although the texts are not explicit about this, it is quite possible that these deities play an important role in the Dzogchen myths. In fact, it is here that we find "five companions," "five soldiers," or "five thieves," which serve to move the stories along by either liberating, imprisoning, or stealing. It is likely that we are dealing here with a reference to the "five protective spirits." According to Tibetan folk religion, these spirits are crucial for human existence as they accompany individual beings on their entire life journey.[38] Their function is closely associated with the sustaining of life as they are said to "live with each person, follow him like his shadow and increase his well-being" (Norbu 1995, 65). They are, furthermore, central to practices like "fortune-summoning," as they are regarded as private gods governing health, wealth, luck, and good fortune for all individuals.[39]

Consequently, it is likely that both the *bla* and the *'go ba'i lha* were transformed through the buddhicization of Tibet. In fact, in indigenous culture, these concepts are not person-specific as if attached to individuals for their entire lifespan, but rather mobile, divisible, communal, and cosmic. This trend is not only clearly visible in the extensive discussions of the close relationship between the *lha* and the *bla* among Tibetologists,[40] but also surfaces in an article by Brandon Dotson. Discussing the role of protective deities in Dunhuang texts dating from the period of the Tibetan empire, Dotson recently argued that the verb *'go* is primarily describing "the proper and improper relationships between humans and gods" as "*'go* is performed by gods for humans, usually following offerings that humans have made to the gods." Importantly, Dotson adds that the gods seem to hold a lot of power in this dynamic of exchange as their favor is conditional and, at least in some instances, "the gods' act of *'go ba* can also be withheld from undeserving supplicants" (2017, 529, 536). In one of these texts (PT 1194, 21–2), which describes a non-Buddhist funeral rite, Dotson cites a passage that catapults us back into earlier discussions surrounding the role of fortune and its connection to the heavenly realm: "When his parents ... were offering to the gods, the required gods did not *'gos*, and the white *dmu* cord was indeed cut" (2017, 534).[41] Although Dotson himself does not entertain the "thorny question" of whether this helps us to "imagine pre-Buddhist beliefs and rituals in Tibet," it appears nonetheless clear that their association to heavenly vitality matches the earliest layer of Tibetan culture available to us.

Ambiguity and Circularity

Based on the stories looked at in this chapter, we could say that early Tibetan culture was pervaded by a dual orientation: On the one hand, we find the symbolism of the abundance of vitality, which includes the ideas of well-being, fortune, and life-force; on the other hand, there is the symbolism of the fragility of vitality, which includes notions of hunting, stealing, retribution, and protection.[42] This same tension emerges in the scholarly approach to the relationship between *bla* and *lha*, where it has been discovered that these life-sustaining energies take on the form of ambivalent beings as they can be both positive and negative. This duplicity, of course, would help us explain one of the most perplexing dimensions of the Dzogchen myths studied in this chapter, namely that the "five" seem to take on both protective (companions, princes) and harming roles (thieves, soldiers). As Norbu notes, "all the energies or 'deities' that live in symbiosis with the individual, such as the Five Deities of the Individual (*'go ba'i lha lnga*), ... can also be contaminated or weakened through man's deeds. When this happens the person's ascendancy-capacity or power dwindles and he becomes like a magnet that attracts all sorts of misfortune and negativity" (Norbu 1995, 116). Dotson, similarly, reminds his readers that "the *'go ba'i lha* also come into play in tantric rituals for harming or killing one's enemies. In order to make one's victim most vulnerable to attack, one must first carry out rituals to remove his or her *'go ba'i lha lnga*" (2017, 526).

Indeed, if the mobile vitality principle can be protected, it is also susceptible to being stolen by unfriendly forces. This belief was likely an integral part of early Tibetan religion as we find a reference in ancient Dunhuang manuscript on divination, where we read: "*Kye*! To the heaven of the gods and that of the wild sheep (*gnyan*), would he happily go! But the demon of the ground, Dun 'phyam, cuts off the path [and] leads away the wool of his body to [the land] sDig dgu sngon dgu. As his *phyva* flees, his *g.yang* equally fades, [bringing with it] a calamity with each subtle breath" (PT 1051, 19–20).[43] The *bla*, indeed, is vulnerable to being seduced by all sorts of forces that can take it hostage. Interestingly, here our mythical narratives surrounding the Old Lady capturing the lively youngsters might even have pointed to the stealing of souls through witchcraft.

The dual nature of vitality as something that not only sustains but also holds the potential to cause harm is still common in the contemporary religious context of the Himalayas. It is particularly apparent in the logic that underlying a popular practice among Tibetan communities, namely witchcraft. Consider, for instance, the ritual of soul-calling (*bla 'gugs*) during which the *snags pas* tie

> a thread around each finger of the patient's left hand and links one finger to each of the effigies. These strings represent the lassos thrown by the soul-stealers onto the patient and describe their intentions towards him. Since they already possess his *bla*, it is only a matter of time before the spirits gain complete control and capture the ultimate price, the *rnam shes* or eternal soul. (Calkowski 1985, 227)[44]

This being said, "the lasso tied to a finger" not only symbolizes "the power of the soul-stealers over the patient's *bla*" but also serves to restrict the movement of a witch. Indeed, unlike most people, the *bla* leaves the witch's body while she sleeps and "wanders about attempting to possess someone and, in so doing, control that person's *rnam shes*."[45] Calkowski reports a case where the relatives of a possessed man "tied the third finger of each of his hands to prevent the witch's *bla* from escaping and then beat the man until they had extracted a promise from the witch never to return to him" (1985, 231).[46]

This example leads us to another key characteristic of the crisis and crisis management stories, namely their dialogical nature. In fact, one of the effects of the ambivalence of good and evil forces is that it opens up the potential for redemption in light of a loss of vitality. Even more importantly, it is in this context of recovery that the deer come to play out one of their primary roles within the larger Eurasian sky-deer cult, namely that of a mediator (Mykhailova 2008). It is striking that already in the *Pillar Testament*, deer or stags have been described as an animal that knows how to speak (255). In *Remedying the Lords of the Soil and Subjugating the Evil Forces of Creation through the Ground of Vitality*, for instance, the hunter tells the deer that it is now time to return to his home country, but the deer refuses to accompany him. Insisting on asking the hunter series of questions—particularly related to his origin—it only agrees to be used as a ransom offering after a sort of negotiation with his capturer. An even more striking instance can be found in *The Narrative of the Deer*, where the deer tells the hunter that he is not the animal that he is looking for. The deer even engages in some sort of ruse as he tells the hunter that the footprints of the specific deer, which he was seeking were spotted elsewhere a few days earlier. Despite the pleading, however, the hunter does not change his mind and shoots the stag with an arrow. Just like in the other stories of this kind, the animal–human dialogue is not over at this point. On the contrary, the wounded deer explores various options as to the best place to die. After another short chat with the hunter, the deer finally decides to pass away in a high region of his land, fleeing from the hunter through various regions before finally dying on the boundary between the meadow and the forest.

In conclusion, while it is currently not possible to prove that the Dzogchen parables of the little children emerged with certainty out of the same context as the Bönpo quests for vitality, the similarities outlined in this chapter suggest that the mythical stories of Dzogchen Buddhism participated in an indigenously Tibetan conception of reality where life-giving energy was a precious good that was constantly at risk of being lost. In many ways, the stories are not only dialogical but also dialectical in nature. The ambiguity of vitality allows for the recovery of energy in moments of crisis; furthermore, the seemingly prosperous moments endowed with plenty of vitality can end in an instance as its presence is inherently precarious. It is certainly for this reason that the mythical antecedent tales are frequently repeating themselves as well as contained in multiple versions in the same manuscript. Without a doubt, the eternal return of crisis and the circularity of loss and recovery allowed the Dzogchen myth-makers to develop a proven model of the vitality-quest where it was the task of heroic youths to recover the sustaining materials—usually shiny objects with luminous qualities associated with the realm of the sky—by departing from their place into some other realm.

While the reconstruction of the indigenous worldview of the Heart-Essence Great Perfection is no easy task—particularly in light of the success at expurgating by Buddhist monocentrism—the mythical narratives of the quest for vitality will play a prominent role in a series of later chapters, where the activity of hunting (Chapter 5), the preciousness of coats and antlers (Chapter 6), the inherently ambivalent status of vitality (Chapter 8), and the redemptive potential of animalistic attributes (Chapter 9) will help us make sense of some of the most perplexing dimensions of the Dzogchen contemplative system in its visionary, physical, and material dimensions. I therefore reiterate that the ventures into the mythical-ritual world of indigenous Tibetan culture, although not immediately concerned with Skullward Leap, will prove invaluable in the chapters to come. The conversion to Buddhism, the rise and collapse of the empire, the fragmentation of Tibet, and the subsequent marginalization on the hands of the New School established the horizons not only for the Great Perfection's mythical stories—which frequently appear to reflect and process the tumultuous historical circumstances in which they were redacted—but also for meditation practice. Just as the first part of this study looked at mythical-historical narratives to demonstrate that the Ancient School was fed through the umbilical cord of indigenous Tibetan culture and profoundly troubled by a series of temporal and social ruptures that threatened their identity—leading to a curious mix between various models of vitality—the second part of this study explores Skullward Leap to show how it relies on complex psychophysical networks used to effectively channel life-sustaining energy in its multiple forms.

Part II

THE EMBODIED-TECHNICAL CIRCULATION OF VITALITY

It is now time to build upon the mythical-historical background underlying the Great Perfection system by turning our attention to the key theme of this study, namely the meditation practice known as Skullward Leap. As I mentioned, we are dealing here with a technique during which the meditators gaze into the open skies until they start to perceive flickers of light that are described in rich phenomenological details as a gradual increase in patterns and images. The technical details of the practice are furthermore anchored in an elaborate spiritual anatomy as the radiant energy is said to move out of our hearts, circulate through light-channels, and shoot out through the gateways of the eyes before being perceived in the form of visions. Although the tradition frequently portrays Skullward Leap as a culturally neutral practice under the monocentric Buddhist aegis of freedom, it will soon become apparent that the exercise is profoundly rooted in the mythical universe of indigenous Tibetan culture. Based on its visionary, technical, and anatomical details, Skullward Leap can be regarded as an indigenous Tibetan practice that offered a sort of contemplative enactment of the mythical narratives surrounding the quest for vitality. In other words, just as the mythical search narratives served as antecedent tales for ritual practices performed throughout the Tibetan world, the stories function as charter myths that provide a blueprint for the contemplative performance of Tögal. Exploiting the powers of the sky as source of life, participating in the movement in between earthly and heavenly realms through luminous cord-like structures, and relying on the nomadic qualities of animals like sheep and deer, the yogi mimetically takes on the role of the hunter of precious life-sustaining energies. At the same time, however, this central part of the book continues to investigate how the quest for vitality and the sky-deer transformed throughout the history of the Great Perfection. Indeed, the practice dramatically alters the cosmological quest for life by transposing the drama of (re-)vitalization from the macrocosmic realm of the universe into the microcosm of the "subtle body." This tendency becomes particularly evident in some of the most extraordinary anatomical structures found in the Dzogchen body, such as the "deer-lamp *tsitta*," the "far-reaching lasso," "white silk thread," "crystal tube," or "buffalo horns." These traits, entirely foreign to tantric systems of Indian provenance, only make sense if they are interpreted against the elaborate backdrop of the quest for life and the mythical narratives involving the hunt for precious substances.

Chapter 4

THE FOUR VISIONS AND THE MEANING OF VITALITY

This chapter offers a systematic analysis of the most famous aspect of Skullward Leap meditation, namely the luminous apparitions known as the "four visions" (*snang ba bzhi*). The writings, both original scriptures and later commentaries, describe this display in great phenomenological detail and explain that it represents a gradual unfurling of enlightened energy from within the meditators' bodies. Symbolically described as "naked vision" (*cer mthong*), the yogi-scholars promote their visionary approach as an effortless, nonconstructive, and spontaneous process during which their inborn nature manifests itself. By means of an interdisciplinary approach that draws heavily on the latest findings from the cognitive sciences, the chapter explores this idea of naked vision and shows that it is marked by an inherent tensions.[1] On the one hand, I provide examples from a series of cognitive theories about perception—specifically, meaning-making, enactive approaches to cognition, the constructive nature of perception and emotion, or the Theory of Mind—to demonstrate how it is indeed possible for the meditators to spontaneously start perceiving all sorts of visions while they are staring at a seemingly empty space like the sky. In short, because the human mind has a natural proclivity to generate meaning, seeing is just as much an internal process of conceiving, creating, and forming, as it is receiving stimuli from the outside. On the other hand, the construction of meaning in cognitive processes like perception is not neutral, but rather premised on experiences and expectations that are decisively shaped by our cultural context. In the case of Tögal, this embedded dimension of cognition becomes nowhere as apparent as in the visionary display, which is characterized by a series of prominent motifs—such as the sky, luminosity, or deer/sheep—that are highly reminiscent of the quest for vitality introduced in the first part of this study. Ultimately, the presumed perceptional nakedness of Skullward Leap is clothed in a series of garments that have been woven from the threads formed during the ancient—largely pre-Buddhist—period of Tibet.

An Experimental Study of Perception

Skullward Leap functions by significantly restricting environmental stimulation, particularly visual input. Indeed, the yogi—who awaits in a state of complete concentration and calm for the emergence of visions that naturally and spontaneously populate his field of visions—meditates during the day not only by gazing into the open sky, the rays of the sun, a lamp, a reflective pool, or a crystal, but also with the framework of a completely dark chamber. I am speaking here, of course, of a particular style of practicing Skullward Leap, namely the so-called dark retreat (*mun mtshams*) practice.[2] In this meditation, which is sometimes also known as the "nighttime practice" (Lobel 2018, 221), the yogi spends time in complete isolation and darkness within a special cave, room, or hut (*mun khang*) that hinders light penetrating from the outside. The standard time of such dark retreats is forty-nine days, but it has been claimed that Dzogchen masters have spent several years in dark retreat (Wangyal 2000, 166).

Techniques of "sensory deprivation," in which "darkness, silence, isolation, bodily stillness," are used to restrict "the subject's visual, auditory, social, and kinesthetic experience," are not only popular in Buddhism (Lindahl et al. 2014, 7), but they also a standard staple in experimental research (Suedfeld 1980). It is no coincidence that researchers, who have extensively studied how sensory deprivation contributes to neuroplasticity (Boroojerdi et al. 2000; Fierro et al. 2005; Pitskel et al. 2007; Maffei and Turrigiano 2008, 3) and visual manifestations (Zubek et al. 1961; Merabet et al. 2004; Mason and Brady 2009), did so by putting them in contexts that closely resemble those found in the Tibetan tradition: Subjects are exposed either to specifically designed chambers (Zubek, Hughes, and Shephard 1971), to flotation tanks (Lilly 1977; Kjellgren, Lyden, and Norlander 2008), or to ganzfeld imagery, which creates an unstructured and homogenized visual field (Avant 1965; Wackermann et al. 2002). Especially the ganzfeld experiments rely on the typically Dzogchen topos of the uniform sky as the ideal backdrop for sensory deprivation (Wackermann, Pütz, and Allefeld 2008).

In this sense, Skullward Leap, providing ideal conditions to explore the subtlest activities of mentation, can be understood as an experimental practice dedicated to the study of consciousness. It is a type of technique that Alan Richardson finds to be "recognizing and breaking through the illusory or virtual character of human cognitive experience" (2010, 23). "The aim of the Buddhist enterprise," says another commentator strikes a similar tone, "is therefore not just to show that all things are like illusions because the way they appear is different from the way they are," but rather "to bring about a complete change in how we perceive and conceptualize phenomena" (Westerhoff 2010, 7). Finally, Janet Gyatso makes this same point, specifically discussing the Skullward Leap visions, as she states that "the point is not simply to have more meditative experiences but to achieve 'realization' (*rtogs pa*) or understanding of the nature of such experiences" (1998, 191).

The Dzogchen discussions surrounding the four visions take the form of detailed phenomenological descriptions of what meditators see during the practice.[3] The "four visions" unfold over time, gradually intensifying as they progress from one stage to the next, before reaching their denouement in the dissolution of any manifestation during the final vision. Within the sequence of appearances, the "seminal nuclei" (*thig le*), drop-like specks of light that one translator pertinently describes as "pixels" (Dowman 2013b), take a privileged position. As they are ordered in a progressive sequence that follows the manifestation of the four visions (*The Treasury of Words and Meanings*, 257.5) and conceptualized as specific "signs" that mark the progress of the practitioner's meditative practice (*The Treasury of the Supreme Vehicle*, vol. II: 372.2), the seminal nuclei are a useful heuristic category to reconstruct the modus operandi of awareness as it radiates through and emerges out of our bodies, and is perceived by our eyes.

The first vision is known as "the vision of reality's immediacy" (*chos nyid mngon sum gyi snang ba*), which is described as follows: "Initially you see something that resembles smoke, then white wafting clouds, mirages, stars, fire sparks, butter lamps, and the great pervading blue light in the form a black *naro*. Eventually, light rays, seminal nuclei, and immeasurable empty forms of the wisdom-expanse (*dbyings rig*) will shine forth" (*The Treasury of Words and Meanings*, 283.2).[4] The visions start with the manifestation of luminous and foggy appearances of low intensity that may or may not develop into sequences of "seminal nuclei," specks of light that can vary in size. The opening vision is generally characterized by a lot of movement and instability as the seminal nuclei never remain still in one place. They are described as "minute and linked," manifest fluttering and undulating, appearing and disappearing, coming and going, and become steady only after extended periods of contemplation. Contemporary teachers compare the nuclei to a waterfall coming off a high mountain or drops of quicksilver (Wangyal 2000, 196–9).

The second vision is known as "the vision of contemplative experience's intensification" (*nyams gong 'phel gyi snang ba*). This vision is characterized by an intensification of the appearances in terms of their number, shape, and size. At first, the perception of light that was present in the inaugural vision intensifies radically and its manifestation becomes more balanced so that it now includes five colors. The seminal nuclei increase in number and size and there is a gradual appearance and multiplication of "linked vajra sheep" (*rdo rje lu gu rgyud*). These resemble lights that are strung together like a garland of pearls appearing within the seminal nuclei. Besides the seminal nuclei and the linked sheep, the practitioner perceives a vast array of additional luminous configurations, such as cloudbanks; smoke; background patterns of the light at dawn, dusk, or the sky in the fall, sunset or shooting stars,;checkered geometric forms; lace-work designs; vertical lines; wheels; round rainbows; lotus flowers; fireflies; or large *stūpas*. Like before, these appearances fluctuate greatly in intensity and stability.

The investigation of such perceptual phenomena has become an indispensable theme of investigation, especially as the field of meditation research moves beyond the study of mindfulness. Exemplary for this revolution is the research conducted by Willoughby Britton and Jared Lindahl in the Clinical and Affective Neuroscience Laboratory at Brown University. They focus on meditation experiences described as lights or as having luminous characteristics, showing that they are characterized by a noteworthy continuity across various Buddhist traditions and geographical contexts. Like the Great Perfection phenomenology of visions, they illustrate the prevalence of various isolated light manifestations in the early phase of contemplation, which meditators define as "globes," "white spots," "little stars," or "ropes of shimmering," and specified as "very distinct," like "Christmas tree lights hanging out in space except they were round," or "float[ing] together in a wave, like a group of birds migrating." There appears to be some cross-traditional stability to the manifestations in those first two visions, as the pattern of crystallization is found in other meditative experiences across the Buddhist universe, particularly the Theravāda literature.[5]

The simplest physiological explanation for this perceptual spectacle is that we are dealing here with entoptic phenomena, visual effects that are created by the eye itself, without external stimulus. The so-called floaters, also known as *muscae volitantes* or "flying flies," manifest as spots, threads, or fragments of "cobwebs," which usually float slowly before the eyes (Johnson and Hollands 2012). However, this seems not enough to account for what is happening to the Skullward Leap yogis as their perception is much richer in detail and fundamentally meaningful to the practitioner. Invoking an English expression, we could say that the yogis make sense of their perceptive experience during Tögal by "connecting the dots," gradually allowing the specks of light into more elaborate patterns and motifs. In this context, the recently emerging research into the phenomenology of perceptual processes might be useful. Analogous to the Dzogchen insistence that the visions are occurring spontaneously, experts emphasize the tremendous impact of unconscious, implicit, and automatic processes in human perception (Goodale and Milner 2004; Jacob and Jeannerod 2006). Mario Sigman, for example, observed that

> from a stream of light, our visual system manages to identify shapes and emotions in a tiny fraction of a second, and what is even more extraordinary is that it happens without any sort of effort or conscious realization that something must be done. But converting light into shapes is so difficult that we have yet to create machines that can do it. (2017, 193)

Much of the insight into the miracles of perception comes from various experimental phenomena (Crick 1994; Eagleman 2011; Dehaene 2014), such as binocular rivalry (Alais and Blake 2005; Cosmelli et al. 2004; Ooi and He 1999; 2006; Williams et al. 2004; Carter et al. 2005), visual masking (Loftus, Hanna, and Lester 1988; Breitmeyer 2007; Ansorge et al. 2008; Bachmann and Francis 2014; Rey et al. 2015), or attentional blinks (Shapiro, Raymond, and Arnell 1997; Jolicœur, Dell'Acqua, and Crebolder 2001; Vul, Hanus, and Kanwisher 2008; Dux and Marois 2009; Nieuwenstein, Potter, and Theeuwes 2009; Martens and Wyble 2010; Griffiths, Herwig, and Schneider 2013). These experiments, as Shaun Gallagher and Dan Zahavi assert, show that we "are often incapable of seeing things happen right before our eyes" (2008, 108). Similarly, phenomena like poor peripheral vision, the continuous eye movements known as saccades, and blind spots demonstrate that our perception—despite its seeming coherence—is not very accurate, stable, or clear. The images we receive through our retinas are distorted, discrete, tiny, upside down, and marked by absences. The fact that our experience is nonetheless characterized by a great degree of constancy is largely due to our brain's capacity to fill in the gaps.

Vilayanur Ramachandran, the foremost expert on a phenomenon known as "gap filling," launched a series of experiments in order to probe the brain's capacity for filling in perceptual gaps. In one case, studying a particular type of blind spot known as scotoma—typical in sufferers of migraine—he projected a series of numbers and letters in front of a patient. Despite the presence of a blind spot in the middle of his field of vision, the subject did not just perceive a black spot without visual information but rather a continuous column of numbers without gap. However, when Ramachandran asked him to read the numbers, the patient said: "Um, one, two, three, um, seven, eight, nine. Hey, that's very strange. I can see the numbers but I don't know what they are. ... They don't look blurred. They kind of look strange. I can't tell what they are—like hieroglyphics or something" (Ramachandran and Blakeslee 1998, 101).

Perception, of course, is part of a larger human need for sense-making. As Ramachandran puts it, the ultimate reason for our gap filling is that the mind "abhors a vacuum," propelling it to "supply whatever information is required to complete the scene" (Ramachandran and Blakeslee 1998, 89). According to such enactive approaches to cognition, all living organisms are "sense-making" or "seeking" because they are both autonomous yet adaptive to their environment. According to the cognitive sciences, life is inherently precarious and living organisms strive to maintain themselves through self-regulation and exchange with the environment (Varela 1979; Thompson 2007), with the seeking system allowing them to meet their basic biological and emotional needs (Panksepp 2007).

Attempting to unify all cognitive functions under one model, enactive approaches to perceptual awareness also argue that much of what we "see" depends not primarily on our eyes, but on the much larger sensorimotor apparatus of our bodies. In Skullward Leap, of course, this is most apparent in the "six key points" (*gnad drug*), according to which the practitioner should adjust his gaze, posture, and breathing pattern in order to induce the visions.[6] It could be argued that they perform what Alva Noë suggested to be our basic mode of establishing perceptual "presence." Taking a mundane example, such as the desire to see the back of a tomato, he insists that "we peer, and squint, and move, and adjust ourselves, nearly continuously, in order to come near to, achieve access to and stabilize our contact with the world around us" (Noë 2012, 40). In the Great Perfection, the dynamic sensorimotor system that pervades the entire human body is described in terms of four "divine palaces" that represent the central foci of enlightened awareness, namely the heart, the channels, the skull, and the eyes. From an enactivist perspective, meditation is best understood as an emerging procession of our innermost essence through these four hot spots: It abides in the heart (*tsitta*), overflows through the luminous channels (*'od rtsa*) that serve as pathways, spreads inside of the skull (*dung khang*), and is finally released through the eyes (*tsakshu/ briguta*).

Furthermore, the seminal nuclei are not only visual phenomena that appear to our eyes in the form of luminous displays but also scintillas of energy located in our bodies. If the channels are seen as "sanctuaries" for our enlightened energy and the winds as the "moving" force that propels awareness throughout our bodies, the seminal nuclei are described as "arrayed" (*bkod pa*) throughout our bodies (*The Treasury of Words and Meanings*, 210.2).⁷ In their dual function as both internal drops of energies and external visionary flashes, the seminal nuclei are consequently both "arrayed" within the luminous channels of our bodies and also "arraying" our visionary experience. As Germano aptly put it, the seminal nuclei are "the in-forming intelligence that 'arrays' or 'organizes' our energy into meaningful complex patterns that are integrated to form a functioning *gestalt*" (1992, 523). In accordance with the nexus of meanings of the term *'god pa*—the present form of the word *bkod pa*—we could say that enaction is marked by a "framed freedom": The seminal nuclei are both "arranged" and "placed," as well as "transferred," "displayed," and "manifested"; they are both confined within structures and freely moving within space.

The tension between confinement and freedom is not only present in the dual nature of the seminal nuclei as something that is both stabilized by structure within our bodies and dynamically displaying externally in our field of vision but also present in the visual (re)-presentation of the seminal nuclei: On the one hand, they are imaged in the form of enframing structures, such as fences, corrals, walled cities, or lassos. On the other hand, the visionary display of seminal nuclei is also said to be naturally disclosing itself in the sky. "The move from the inside to the outside," so Hatchell reminds his readers, "is in fact one of the main features of these visionary *thig-le*, which not only function as containers—of bodies, Buddhas, ideas, energies, and so forth—but also put those contents on display so they can be seen, recognized, and function in the external world" (2014, 144).

The seminal nuclei form part of a larger visionary anatomy of the Great Perfection, which ultimately allows for the concretization of the flow of energy out of its latency into the world. Here, the body acts as a parallel to the ground's manifestation, while giving it a more ordered and structured form of flowing that is contained within intentional pathways. A key concept during the cognitive process of awareness manifestation is the "lamps," which indicate the externalization of the internal wisdom in the form of visionary manifestations. One of the most interesting of those lamps is the so-called water lamp of the far-reaching lasso. This particular lamp stands not only for the totality of luminous pathways and gateways, but for our inner luminosity radiating outward. As such, it plays a stellar role in the process of blurring the boundaries between internal imagination and external reality. It has rightly been explained that this lamp's designation as a "far-reaching lasso" points to the particular trait of the sensory faculty of vision, which has the ability to apprehend objects of external reality that are quite distant from us (Germano 1992, 104). Skullward Leap, consequently, "involves a radically active mode of perception, as instead of the mere passive registering of incoming sensory data or even the semi-active filtering and manipulation of that data, the 'sensory data' (i.e. the lights) itself … issues outwards from our own interiority via the eyes" (Germano 1992, 98). The darkness of the hut and the monochromatic background of the cloudless sky, of course, reduce external stimuli and provide us with a screen for the performance of a largely internal theater of our minds.

In its emphasis on the externalization of the interior, the imposition of what is "imagined" over that which is a "real" stimulus from the exterior world, Skullward Leap could be construed as a type of hallucination. Oftentimes, the central mark of a hallucinating person as well as a schizophrenic is that they cannot distinguish between what is truly experienced because of an external stimulus and what is imagined in the form of an internally generated thought. This being said, the association of Skullward Leap with pathological or hallucinatory phenomena is not as simple as one might think. Consider, for instance, the following reflections by Ann Taves, who recovers the value of internally manufactured visionary worlds in the study of religion, noting that "the pejorative (and presumptively pathological) definition of hallucinations as false perceptions artificially divides the class of phenomena that arise from internal sources and completely ignores visions that occur (remarkably frequently) in the normal population" (Taves 2009, 78).

The notion that the vividness of imagination "bleeds" into the world (Luhrmann 2013, 159) is even compatible with a neurological perspective, where hallucinatory visions are in many respects just as real as the perception of "real" external stimuli.[8] The Great Perfection conceives of the visionary manifestations displayed during Skullward Leap in a parallel way, namely as an interplay between the mental and the physical eye. Herbert Guenther, for instance observed:

> It would be extremely helpful if one could understand "awareness" in a verbal sense as an "awaring" inasmuch as this pristine awareness is not only a process (a "way") of understanding, but also a certain manner of seeing which for all practical purposes has as its starting-point the eye. The eye that "sees" does not exist apart from its cognitive domain: light and eye codetermine each other and what we call the eye is therefore nothing solid, but a dynamic regime. As such a dynamic regime the eye is termed *spyan*—the eye that "sees" in contradistinction to *mig*—the eye as an object removed from its living context.[9] (Guenther 1992, 81)

In the cognitive sciences, such an active understanding of perception reminds us not only of the theories of meaning-making and enactive cognition discussed earlier, but also relates to studies on imagery and imagination. Researchers are gradually gaining awareness of a continuity between quotidian perception and meditative visions, or between the physical eye and the mental eye (Ffytche et al. 1998; Lloyd et al. 2012). The neurobiology of perceptual hallucinations and veridical perceptions, for example, have been found to be closely related to one another (Ffytche, Blom, and Catani 2010; Lloyd et al. 2012). Experiments have illustrated that visual perception and creative imagination have more in common than usually thought as ordinary perception is itself "creative" in nature. Already in the 1970s, James J. Gibson established what he called an "ecological psychology," claiming that what we see in our head is not just a passive representation of the external world but rather the result of our embodied actions in the world that surrounds us (Gibson 1986; Heft 2001). According to the so-called perceptual activity theory (Ellis 1995; Ramachandran and Hirstein 1996; Noë 2004;

Thompson 2007) the mind plays an active role in constructing its apprehended objects, thus not only blurring "the boundary between indirect perception and imagination" but also suggesting "that imagery should in fact be viewed as a process of perceptual projection" (Coseru 2012). Neuroscientific data confirming this imagist presupposition has led Steven Kosslyn to conclude that the same neural processes "underlie [both] perception and depictive imagery" (2000) and Donald Hoffmann to propose that "to experience is to construct" (1998, 48).

In the Great Perfection, the constructivist nature of perception is expressed as a dialectical movement between freedom and enframement. As before, the seminal nuclei serve as the primary metaphor to articulate this tension: On the one hand, the nuclei change their form from that of an enclosure into an extended chain of interconnected dots as they move out of the frame of the body into the practitioner's visual field. On the other hand, as they take on the shape of long ropes, they swiftly reclaim their potential to be flung through the air as lassos. Perception is a grasping, constructing, and ultimately enframing process that imposes separations, division, and structure on the surrounding environment. Imaged as a lasso, Dzogchen vision is not only a freeing activity that opens up the containment of the human body but also a projective operation, an active process through which the meditators impose themselves onto the material universe surrounding them.

As I protocoled, the first two stages of the four visions are characterized by a gradual growth in size, a steady increase in complexity, an intensification in vividness, and a strengthening in stability of the manifestations. The climax of Skullward Leap is characterized by the manifestation of vast *maṇḍalas*, divine palaces filled with richly adorned Buddhas and their retinues in the third vision in the *scala contemplationis*, named "the vision of awareness reaching its limit" (*rig pa tshad phebs kyi snang ba*). As its designation already indicates, this is the moment when "awareness" reaches its limit, the moment when the visionary manifestations appear in their greatest clarity and crystallize in their most structured form. The meditators confirm that this is the high point of transforming the initial chaos into order as they report seeing the *maṇḍala* of 100 peaceful and wrathful deities, buddhafields, and palaces.

Again, like in the previous visions, the seminal nuclei remain central to this process. The circle-shaped seminal nuclei and the linked chains are said to "mature into spiritual bodies" (*The Treasury of Words and Meanings*, 247.3) and to "ripen into the Spiritual Bodies and wisdom" (*The Treasury of Words and Meanings*, 211.5). Longchenpa specifies that there are six stages over the course of which the *maṇḍala* of deities gradually takes shape. First, only half of a Buddha's body is seen, then single bodies, then the Buddha in sexual union with his consort, then the five Buddhas with their retinues, then the five Buddhas arranged in their *maṇḍala*, and finally the "great *maṇḍala*," which represents all the 100 peaceful and wrathful deities and the climax of the Tögal visions (*The Treasury of Words and Meanings*, 258.3; *The Treasury of the Supreme Vehicle*, vol. II: 83.5).

Although such a natural evolution of a rich mixture of living beings in their own inhabitable spaces might sound extravagant, the fact that visions are populated in such ways is not entirely surprising from a cognitive perspective. Researchers, in speaking about this human tendency to attribute mental or soul-like presence to our environment, have coined the term "Theory of Mind" (Bloom 2004; Lillard and Skibbe 2005; Mar and Macrae 2007). This field of investigation is concerned with the "folk psychology" of social cognition, specifically with how humans identify mental states of others in order to predict, understand, or explain their actions (Premack and Woodruff 1978, 515). As Tooby and Cosmides phrase it, "normal humans everywhere not only 'paint' their world with color, they also 'paint' beliefs, intentions, feelings, hopes, desires, and pretenses onto agents in their social world. They do this despite the fact that no human has ever seen a thought, a belief, or an intention" (1995, xvii).

Cognitive scientists of religion, in particular, have combined this biosocial view of meaning-making with an evolutionary perspective. They speak of a "hyperactive agency detection device" when trying to explain the human tendency to make mentalistic inferences. Specifically, they suggest that our tendency to attribute agency to our environment, not only other humans, but also animals, nature, and other "hard-to-identify" phenomena, offers evolutionary benefits to humanity (Guthrie et al. 1980; Barrett and Keil 1996; Boyer 2001; Atran and Norenzayan 2004; Barrett 2004; Epley, Waytz, and Cacioppo 2007). Jesper Sørensen, for instance, suggests that "religion" can be seen as "a by-product of an evolved ability to scan an ambiguous perceptual environment for agents." Indeed, from an evolutionary perspective, according to which our life on earth is inherently precarious, this makes a lot of sense: "Since false positives are relatively cheap (seeing a stone as a bear) in contrast to a false negative. Not perceiving a potentially dangerous agent (seeing a bear as a stone) is most likely to be fatal." In short, so Sørensen summarizes his position, "the popularity of culturally transmitted concepts of religious agents might be conceived as the result of human tendency to infer the actions of intentional agent from scarce an ambivalent perceptual cues" (2007, 288). Something similar appears to be happening in the later stages of the unfurling of visions as the yogi multiplies actualizations of gods, spirits, and other anthropomorphized figures in light of unclear visual stimuli.

Seeing the Mythical Self

We have seen that since it observes perceptual processes in detail, the Dzogchen phenomenology of visions can make a meaningful contribution to our understanding of cognition. The visionary appearances, however, can also point to a particular strength of an interdisciplinary study of meditation that includes both universal psychological cognitive mechanisms and idiographic historical-cultural contexts of cognition. Indeed, this chapter reveals a fundamental tension between two types of knowledge generation achieved during Skullward Leap meditation, namely that of the "minimal self" stripped of its social and developmental conditioning, on the one hand, and a culturally embedded social self, on the other. As for the first, Skullward Leap fits well with the priorities of recent research on contemplation, which combines insights from traditional Buddhist sources with studies from phenomenology, philosophy of mind, and neuroscience to better understand the nature of the self. These different disciplinary fields, in fact, started to converge on a similar conception of our identity: While Buddhist sources argue for the lack of an inherent self and propose meditative practices used to observe the constant flow of consciousness, the other fields of investigation come to similar conclusions. Specifically, all of them point to a parallel discrepancy between the common conception of a bounded identity, on the one hand, and evidence from experimentation that points to a less-than-reified selfhood, on the other. These discourses also share in the belief that the self is made up of varying "degrees" of selfhood. This idea is pertinently described by Evan Thompson, who summarizes the Buddhist perspective as follows:

> The first aspect is awareness, which is often likened to a light that reveals whatever it shines upon. The second aspect is whatever the light illuminates, that is, whatever we happen to be aware of from moment to moment. The third aspect is how we experience some of these contents of awareness as "I" or "Me" or "Mine." To understand how we enact a self, therefore, we need to understand three things—the nature of awareness as distinct from its sensory and mental contents, the mind-body processes that produce these contents, and how some of these contents come to be experienced as the self. (Thompson 2015, xxxii)[10]

Contemplative scientists, such as Richard Davidson or Antoine Lutz, similarly suggest that Buddhist meditation is such a compelling phenomenon precisely because it gives access to dimensions of our being that are usually hidden to our conscious minds. The embodied and pre-reflexive level of subjectivity experienced during meditation, so they argue, familiarizes us with the core and minimal selves, effectively bypassing the full-blown narrative self (Lutz, Dunne, and Davidson 2007; Dreyfus 2011; Dambrun and Ricard 2011; Austin 2009; Coseru 2012; Arnold 2012; Metzinger 2009). Scholarship has rightly acknowledged that meditation involves the "uprooting [of] this illusory sense of an extended self—perhaps similar to the phenomenological notion of narrative self—and uncovering [of] a profoundly embodied, intimate meeting with experience—perhaps akin to the contemporary concept of minimal self" (Lifshitz, Cusumano, and Raz 2014, 220).

This being said, cognition is always colored by our expectations, which are themselves conditioned by prior experiences. Consider, for instance, the example of Ramachandran's reports on a subject, who automatically filled in numbers without receiving such a visual stimulus. Most fundamentally, what happened in this fascinating experiment can be linked to the practice of Skullward Leap because both cases demonstrate to what extent the human brain abhors the vacuum of seeing something that has no meaning. As a technique scrutinizing the unconscious processing mechanisms involved in human perception, Tögal shows that human mentation—whether it be conscious or unconscious—can never be truly naked. On the contrary, it is always clothed since it tends to make meaning, to create order, and to impose structure in its thirst for understanding.

Even more importantly, however, is a second parallel: Just as the experimental subject automatically fills the black spot in his visionary field with information that makes sense to him, a series of consecutive modern numbers—which themselves originated in India in the sixth century before being introduced to Europe by Arabic mathematicians—that extend on what he sees outside of his black spot, the yogi fills the blank space with meaning that makes sense to him and his cultural background. While it is true that some elements of the visionary apparitions during Tögal are found cross-culturally, from Ayahuasca-séances to Kabbalistic meditations (Beyer 2010, 227–8; Garb 2011, 12; de Araujo et al. 2012), it is quite evident that the subtle perceptual clothing of the Tögal visions is stitched from the spatiotemporal fabric made up of the mythical narratives introduced in the earlier chapters.

In the exploration of the relationship between this rich mythical background and the practice of Skullward Leap, scholars of meditation might benefit from drawing on the famous "ritual repetition of myth" theory, which has received plenty of attention, both in the discipline of religious studies (Eliade 1949) and in the field of Buddhist studies (Karmay 1998c; Huber 1999, 40; Mayer and Cantwell 2010, 76). In Tibet, more specifically, it has been argued that myth and ritual operate according to a unified "model" (*dpe srol*), with the ritual reenacting the mythical account as a sort of "antecedent tale" (variously known as *smrang, rabs, lo rgyus*) (Karmay 1998c, 288–9).[11] While scholarship on Dzogchen has recognized this reality to some extent inasmuch as it applied to the cosmogonic myth of the youthful body in a vase by noting that the story of Samantabhadra offers an alternative way to deal with the inevitable epiphany of the ground and the swirling play of rainbow-colored light-displays,[12] it has so far neglected the important parallels between the practice and the narratives surrounding the quest for vitality. In other words, the visions should not be considered as an encounter with one's self, but rather with a very particular type of selfhood, namely one that is profoundly infused by the cultural background that is unique to Tibet. It is in this sense that I suggest that ancient Tibetan myths should be considered as real because they serve as a blueprint for what reality should be like. More specifically, the mythical narratives are records of ritual-contemplative practices directed at sustaining vitality performed in the Dzogchen contemplative system.[13] The stories are not merely a literary exercise, an expression of a primitive worldview dominated by superstition, or simple entertainment, but much rather a description of what takes place during contemplative practices.[14] Thus, while these first chapters make only marginal references to Skullward Leap, the terminology introduced, and the themes discussed will resurface in the latter parts of this investigation and are pervasive throughout the meditation practice.

If the following chapters will offer a more detailed discussion of the morphology and function of the practice, showing how it draws heavily on the hunt for deer known from the mythical narratives, I will limit the present discussion to a very short overview of three key motifs that surface in the contemplative enactment of cosmological myths, namely the correlated ideas of sky, light, and animals. The first and most obvious trait connecting the sky-gazing practice to the indigenous Tibetan culture studied in the first part of this study is their shared valorization of the sky. The sky, of course, represents the most fundamental motif of Skullward Leap, where it serves as the canvass against which the meditating yogis perceive "awareness" (*rig pa*). The liberating visions, indeed, are disclosed in the unstructured space, preferably the cloudless sky, which represents—in a location where we witness up to 330 days of sunshine a year—a familiar backdrop (Bellezza 2014, 34). Within the Bön tradition, Samantabhadra is also known as the "sky divinity" and is even invoked as the "Sky Guide" (*dran pa nam mkha'*) (Snellgrove 1961, 46–7).

The second element that is closely associated with the sky and the destiny of Samantabhadra is the emphasis on light. In Chapter 2, indeed, we have seen that luminosity was one of primary organizing principles of early Tibetan myths, dominant both in the conception of *g.yang*, as well as the sky-cord. Consequently, it is hardly a coincidence that the "seminal nuclei," which in the world of tantra are generally filled with reproductive fluids, are understood to be kernels of light. In the Great Perfection, light is something that transcends the mythical realm to enter into our physical anatomy in the form of nodes of light energy before manifesting during the contemplative experience of the meditators, whose visions are premised on the same sort of photism.[15]

This brings to a third and final core motif pointing to a deeper indigenous background of the Skullward Leap meditation, namely the fact that the seminal nuclei, which could also be called "drops of vitality," manifest in the form of animals, particularly sheep. While the perception of certain geometric forms (dots, lines, pearls, faces, and so forth) is found across many cultural contexts,[16] their definition as sheep-like appears to be specific to the Tibetan context of the Great Perfection. Similar to the myths that can be found in the very early strata of Tibetan culture, where early kings are not only connected to the sky through cord-like structures of light but also ride upon sheep in order to descend from the heavenly realm to reach the earth, the linked sheep take a prominent form in the visionary practice. The embodiment of vitality itself, the itinerant animals form a procession and flicker in between the realms of heaven and the earth. While more details of this intimate association between Tögal and ancient Buddhist mythology will be further substantiated in the coming chapters, we have already seen that effective perception is not only vital for survival, but that—in the case of the Great Perfection—the very efficacy of seeing is premised on vitalistic impulses that inform the mythical universe of the early Tibetan religion.

Chapter 5

THE PRELIMINARY PRACTICES AND THE DOMESTICATION OF VITALITY

One of the most distinctive attributes of Dzogchen meditation is that it is said to be largely effortless, spontaneous, and natural.[1] However, not unlike the claim to a neutral type of perception that we deconstructed in the previous chapter, this self-description of the practice is somewhat misleading, especially if we consider that the quest for life-giving energy has been at the heart of the tradition since its very inception. The technical instructions for the practice show that Skullward Leap is a powerful method that involves various modes of engaging our bodies' somatic energy, ranging anywhere from complete immobility to extreme exertion leading to states of physical exhaustion. This spectrum becomes nowhere as apparent as when we compare the serene scene of the yogi sitting quietly on top of the mountain to the so-called preliminary practices (Tib. *sngon 'gro*) that precede the main practice. Many of these exercises are far from relaxing in nature, but rather exhilarated by intense moments of stimulation and function by arousing the energies residing in our bodies. Invoking the root meaning of *Buddha*—the "awakened one" (from the root *budh-*)—we could say that "awakening" is not simply a metaphor, but rather an actual process premised on the arousing of vital energies. In trying to make sense of the "paradoxical wildness" of Skullward Leap, oscillating between arousal and relaxation, this chapter capitalizes on our previous inquiries into the primordial search narratives. More specifically, the discussion shows that Dzogchen not only drew on isolated mythical motifs, such as the sky, light, or deer, but also remained anchored within an indigenous logic surrounding the quest for life. By interpreting the performance of Skullward Leap side by side with the mythical narratives, it becomes apparent that we are dealing with a technique that is reproducing the domestication of wildness that is at the core of the indigenous Tibetan quest for life. More specifically, the meditating yogis imitate the two prototypical behaviors that marked the exploits of the mythical protagonists of yore, namely hunting and herding.

The Activation of Vitality

A discussion about vitality and meditation, quite naturally, brings to mind the human body, the cornerstone of our lives on earth. Particularly tantric forms of meditation, which I already introduced in Chapter 3, celebrate the body as an "indispensable aid to awakening, the innately pure basis for the awakening process" (Gray 2021, 1). Unlike earlier forms of Buddhism, tantric traditions elevate the movement of the body, the circulation of energy, and the activation of vitality to eminent positions in their practices.[2] However, just as the mythical crisis-narratives have shown that vitality is susceptible to being lost, stolen, or imprisoned, the yogis' psychophysical energy is oftentimes both present and at the same time limited in its range of movement. As a consequence, the luminous display of energy during Skullward Leap practice does not appear immediately because it is obstructed within the depths of our bodies. In one of the early Great Perfection texts, *The Heap of Jewels Tantra*, we find a passage that depicts human beings as suffering from a type of sensory paralysis that prevents vitality from manifesting. The scripture opens by noting a tragic situation of confusion:

> From the very beginning, the self as well as the objects of attachment are reality, which is entirely self-appearing through itself. Although it is primordially manifest, this has previously not been understood. The five passions, which bind you to you to your concept of "self," although they are primordially self-arising awareness, abiding together, this has not been recognized. (79.3)[3]

The text then continues to address several other confusions, which are all due to the "blocking of the gateways to the various faculties" (81.1). The "eyes," for example, are said to be dull because they do not see that "the four elements of earth, water, fire, and wind are primordially the body of our self" (79.4).[4] Similarly, the tantra wonders whether their "auditory faculty" might be missing because humans do not hear that the teachings are "self-resonating without interruption" (79.4–5),[5] or whether their "noses are blocked" because humans appear to be incapable of smelling the "scent of the self-abiding expanse and wisdom" (79.5–6).[6] In a delightful passage from *The Mirror of the Heart of Vajrasattva*, we read about the human body in a more positive light:

> Ah ho! Listen up, you who have realized the vast expanse! The essence of the One Thus Gone abides within all sentient beings of this world, just like oil permeates a sesame seed. Furthermore, its support is based in the aggregate of form. As for its residence, in the center of the heart, it is called "Samantabhadra's amulet of the wisdom intent" and resembles a closed amulet of red-gold enamel. Within that, in the center of five-colored light, are the peaceful spiritual bodies about the size of a mustard seed, abiding in home of light. That is the residence of awareness, which resembles a body in a vase. (334.1)[7]

According to the Great Perfection, the most energetically charged spot of our human body is the heart. Known as *tsitta*, a word derived from the Sanskrit term for "mind" (Skt. *citta*), the heart is considered the principal locus of enlightened power and the residence of awareness. Not unlike the passages on the blocked or dull nature of our senses, this scripture describes awareness as contained within our hearts with a decisively constrictive undertone.[8] To illustrate the latency and obstruction of our vital energies within our bodies, it suffices to look at the nomenclature used to identify the heart, most of which points to its enclosed nature: the amulet of the wisdom, the crystal palace of five lights, the divine palace of the precious *tsitta*, the tent of brown carnelian, the precious palace, or the precious envelope.

In light of this heavy emphasis on interiority, it is not surprising that Skullward Leap meditation—aiming at the vivification within our bodily vitality—reprises the cosmogonic myth of the initial stirring of spherical vitality from within the ground.[9] Of particular relevance, in this context, is the identification of the heart with the "youthful body in a vase" (*The Tantra of Self-Arisen Awareness*, 536.1), which is sometimes even specified as being "in the manner of a body within a vase is replete with faces and arms" (*The Tantra of Unimpeded Sound*, 126.5). The terminology makes it clear that the Dzogchen body is the stage upon which the meditators replay the startling myth of the cosmogony in order to activate the dormant vitality within. Parallel to the "ground's manifestation," imaged as a youthful body in a vase that is ripped open (*ral*) after the mysterious stirring of the cosmic vitality wind, the "four visions" emerge only after the "seal" (*rgya ma*) of our hearts is "torn open" (*ral*) in the early stages of Skullward Leap meditation.[10]

The most powerful means for mobilizing our internal energies are the so-called preliminary practices. In the Great Perfection, the standard Buddhist territory of seven preliminaries (such as the meditations on impermanence, the Vajrasattva purifications, guru yoga, contemplations on the law of karma, and so on) are complemented by unique techniques not shared by other traditions. Specifically, in the Nyingthig tradition, the preliminaries consist of a threefold series of practices, namely the yoga of the four elements' sounds, the conduct of differentiating between the domains of *saṃsāra* and *nirvāṇa*, and the preliminaries of body, speech, and mind.[11] As for the final set of exercises, the preliminaries of body, speech, and mind, they seem quite similar to more standard forms of meditation practice, consisting of simple visualizations and analytical types of meditation on the nature of the mind. The other two techniques, by contrast, appear quite unlike standard Buddhist meditation and are rather distinctive for the Great Perfection tradition.

For our purposes, particularly the "Preliminaries of Differentiating between the Domains of *Saṃsāra* and *Nirvāṇa*" (*'khor 'das ru shan*) are relevant as they operate by embracing the wilder dimensions of meditation practice.[12] The preliminaries of differentiation are divided into three stages aiming at the training body, speech, and mind.[13] "In terms of the body," *The Tantra of The Self-Emergent Teaching* encourages meditation practitioners to "run, lay down, stand up, shake the limbs, circumambulate, prostrate, whirl the limbs, or roll the head." The preliminaries involve the performance of "whatever action comes to memory, dancing, performing *mudrās*, changing position, whatever action imaginable" (*The Treasury of Words and Meanings*, 372.6).[14] We find an analogous description of the behavior surrounding the body in *The Tantra of Unimpeded Sound*, where the yogi is encouraged to "move, sit, twist, or extend and contract limbs" (*The

Tantra of Unimpeded Sound, 92.2). Rather than activating the parasympathetic nervous system and relaxing the body, the Great Perfection preliminaries consist of techniques of sensory stimulation

As for the preliminaries of speech in the differentiating between the domains of *saṃsāra* and *nirvāṇa*, their most striking feature is the repeated insistence that practitioners should intersperse their meditation with unexpected verbal utterances, particularly the syllable "*phat*," which the meditators shout in a fierce tone in between the enactments of savage identities.[15] Returning to the preliminaries of speech, *The Tantra of Unimpeded Sound* explains the practitioner's behavior as follows:

> Since verbal expressions are the nature of conceptual thoughts, through a variety of languages, say whatever comes to mind without repressing anything. In the languages of the gods, the serpent spirits, the demons of the earth, the scent eaters, the vampire ghouls, and Viṣṇu, verbalize different kinds of good and bad things. In short, the languages of the six classes of beings are mnemonically envisioned and verbally expressed. (92.4)[16]

From a functional perspective, the logic of these techniques of speech seems to closely reflect that of the practices involving the body. Not unlike the alteration that is produced by the sensory overload that results from abrupt and uncontrolled physical movements, the verbal exclamations also jolt the meditator out of his ordinary frame of mind and arouse the nervous system.

As for the third dimension of the preliminaries of differentiation, in the section on the mind, *The Tantra of the Self-Emergent Teaching* introduces them as follows: "Act out various discursive thoughts: likes, dislikes, happiness, sorrow, permanence, impermanence, views, meditation, and conduct, dharma, non-dharma, virtue, non-virtue, desire, hatred, delusion, and so forth" (*The Treasury of Words and Meanings*, 373.2).[17] Like its physical and vocal counterparts, the preliminary of the mind plays with the malleability as human beings and our states of consciousness. In the preliminaries, Dzogchen practitioners experience the good, the bad, and the ugly of their existence. Thus, they are encouraged to break out of their ordinary behavior to embrace every type of energy contained within their bodies. In *The Tantra of Unimpeded Sound*, the meditator is instructed to "practice mindful attentiveness" of anything that emerges, particularly emotions, such as happiness and sorrow, and so forth (93.3).

Since the role of the preliminaries in the contemplative itinerary is akin to the breaking open of the vase of life to give rise to vitality, it is no surprise that the early stages of Skullward Leap are also making frequent use of alterations in breathing. One of the most important motifs of the "subtle body," indeed, is the "breath" or "wind" (*rlung*). In ways that are strikingly similar to the body in a vase, where the stirring of the wind leads to the breaking open of the luminous container, the Dzogchen meditators rely on the activating force of the breath to mobilize "vitality" and to circulate it throughout their bodies.[18] Just like in the myth, the movement of the nuclei is dependent on the porousness of our bodies, especially their ability to breathe as "the linked chains' movement and pulsating, coming and going, increasing and decreasing, as well as their potential to appear externally is due to the circumstance of the five winds" (*The Treasury of Words and Meanings*, 378.4).[19] "The key to winds," Germano summarized the Dzogchen position, "is movement, and therefore life on all dimensions—life is essentially dynamism, whether physical or psychic; what is inert is dead" (1992, 687). The primary function of the winds, at least in the Skullward Leap preliminaries, is that of activating the latently dormant energies. If Longchenpa speaks of the need to "revitalize" and "coil up" to stimulate the flowing of the winds, we find similar ideas already in the earliest Dzogchen scriptures. In one text, the meditator is exhorted to "draw the winds upwards" (*The Tantra of Unimpeded Sound*, 96.4), to "draw them in" (112.3), to "spur them" (112.2, 167.6), or to make them oscillate by "propelling-away and gathering-in" (112.4). Similarly, in *The Blazing Lamp Tantra*, it is spelled out that it is the hyperactive rhythm of the wind—described with adjectives like "moving, shaking, wavering, lightened, and agitated" (295.2)[20]— which allows practitioners to rouse dormant energies.

> When temporarily it is itself bound by wind, cognition is without memory and lazy. ... When the dynamic strength of insight is activated through the winds, even things that have not previously been heard will be remembered by the mind and shine forth. This capacity of having clarity or unclarity emerges because of the movements of winds, which abide in the channels in the center of the body. (295.2–3)[21]

If the heart is the locus of awareness, the breath is the mobilizing force that makes sure that awareness radiates throughout our bodies and beyond. Human cognition is regarded to be the result of the mixing of these two dimensions as the Dzogchen texts specify that the mind abides "in between the heart and lungs" (*The Tantra of Self-Arisen Awareness*, 528.4).[22] In the interstices between the lung and the heart, the subtle anatomy of Dzogchen locates a slender channel into which awareness enters from the heart and the wind penetrates from the lungs. The mind is then said to flow through a passageway that "moves upward" where our affective states— such as the five poisons, anger, and emotional afflictions—use it to "mount the horse of the breath to flow out through the mouth and nose."[23] The terminology for the pneumatic dimensions of the body points to the overwhelming prioritization of "vitality" (*srog*) over both relaxation and insight. The pathway between the heart and the lungs is called the "red vitality-channel" (*srog rtsa dmar po*) (*The Mirror of the Heart of Vajrasattva*, 335.6), and the mind is specified to "emerge in the pathway of the vitality-channel," which runs into cranial region (*The Tantra of Self-Arisen Awareness*, 528.4).[24]

Even though the vocabulary underwent a change—moving from pre-Buddhist terms like *g.yang* and *phya* to the notion of *srog*—the emphasis on vitality lived on in the Great Perfection's new incarnation as a practice within the tantric landscape of Tibet.[25] Not unlike the mythical quests for vitality, which involved the extraction of certain body parts to appropriate the wildness of the divine animal realm, the meditators' engagement with vitality can sometimes take on a visceral dimension. Specifically, they are instructed to engage the material dimension of their bodies in order to release blockages of energy. For instance, the manuals clarify that during the first moments of the actual practice of Tögal, the practitioner should "press the eyeballs, using only two fingers rather than three" in order to give rise to visual appearances (*The Treasury of Words and Meanings,* 283.3).[26] Although the text specifies that "after three or four days, phenomena will arise even without applying any pressure,"[27] it is apparent that meditation frequently opens with an impelling force. This also becomes clear in other passages that detail practices that directly stimulate the vitality-channel, which is frequently identified with the aorta, the main and largest artery in the human body.[28] In *The Mirror of the Heart of Vajrasattva*, we read: "By turning the eyes up towards the sky and by applying pressure to this channel, the sky will be filled with luminous appearances of wisdom" (334.1).[29] The idea of applying physical force also surfaces in the writings of Longchenpa, who explains repeatedly that the practitioner should start his practice by "pressing" on the vitality-channel if he is struggling to make the visions arise naturally (*The Treasury of Words and Meanings,* 284.7; *The Treasury of the Supreme Vehicle,* vol. I: 407.6; *The Treasury of the Supreme Vehicle,* vol. II: 19.7; *The Heart-Essence of Vimalamitra,* vol. I: 373.1).[30]

The Yogi as Hunter and Herder

While the pressing of this vitality channel—just like the shouting of the syllable *phat*—accentuates the need to wake up the energies that lie dormant within the yogic body, the contemplative quest for life is not a simple process of arousal. This becomes nowhere as apparent as in the main practice of Tögal, which is performed by relying on the so-called six key points (*gnad drug*). These exceedingly simple teachings, generally divided into two sets of three, correspond quite closely to what we would imagine as a technique of relaxation. The most characteristic trait of these practices is their ubiquitous emphasis on stability and immobility. While reading the opening paragraph of this book, where we grasped the first glimpses of the sky-gazing yogi sitting steadily on the side of the mountain until the visions effortlessly divulge themselves against the background of the deep blue sky, it was hard to imagine that he prepared himself for this revelation by means of an undertaking like the preparatory practices.

We are struck by a sort of "paradoxical wildness" that characterizes the discrepancy between the main practice of sky-gazing and the preparatory exercises: On the one hand, we enter a serene contemplative scene of a peaceful yogi sitting on a snow-capped mountain, effortlessly gazing at a symbolically rich display of luminosities that rises gradually against the backdrop of the cloudless Tibetan sky. On the other hand, we feel ourselves overstimulated even just taking stock of the hyperactive, sensory, and arousing nature of the complex matrix of preliminary practices that the yogi is said to perform leading up to Skullward Leap. Put differently, even though Dzogchen meditators need to undomesticate themselves in order to give rise to the luminous display, this does not mean that they engage the wildness of their life-energy in an uncontrollable manner. How can it be that a practice that is premised on stability and immobility is preceded by so much frenzied activity? One possible answer can be found in the following text composed by Longchenpa in the fourteenth century:

> Before this, in training with speech, in an unfamiliar place, you incessantly utter whatever comes to your mind from the past or the future like the words of a lunatic. When you become exhausted with such verbiage and your need to speak subsides, abide in a state of not-speaking. Occasionally, even though you do not have a desire to speak, go to an isolated valley, and shout aloud until exhausted and train in the speechless state. Then, avoiding any talk with others except for reciting spiritual discourses, mantras, and prayers, remain silent and stable. Then, having stopped all of these activities, determine not to say anything at all. (*The Treasury of Words and Meanings*, 406.2–3)[31]

This scene offers a replay of the sequence that we found in Skullward Leap, which moves from the stimulating techniques of the preliminaries to the controlled immobility of the six key points so characteristics of the main visionary practice. There is no doubt that this points to a simple yet profound truth about relaxation: Stimulating our bodies to the point of exhaustion is one way to enter a deeply relaxed natural state, which Dzogchen yogis call "settling into the state of naturalness" (*rnal du dbab*).

Based on the extensive explorations in the first part of this study, however, I would now like to propose an alternative explanation for this paradoxical wildness of vitality. Let us proceed by reinserting the practice within the indigenous Tibetan context that we encountered through its mythical narratives. Indeed, the vertical descent of life-giving energy from the sky is frequently imagined as an introduction of wildness into the human world. During their descent to earth, the deified kings rode on animals such as sheep and deer to land and be harmonized within the earthly realm. It is likely for the purpose of this gradual accommodation of wildness within the orderliness of the terrestrial world that some of the stories' most crucial moments—such as the landing of the deities or the passing away of the hunted deer—take place in a very specific location, namely on mountains,[32] and, even more specifically, in between the meadows and the forest.[33] In other words, the quest for life is frequently commensurate not only with a pursuit of wildness, but also an attempt to subdue, tame, and domesticate it in order to make it part of human culture. Just like the meditators perform the preliminaries within a strictly followed sequence that culminates on the slope of the mountain in a stable pose—rather than abandoning themselves to their wild impulses without any sort of predictable itinerary—the vitality we encounter in the mythical narratives is not simply given free reign, but rather subjected to an intentional process of domestication. As Dotson notes, the *g.yang* is brought "down from the high, wild repositories of fortune," to be integrated into "the domesticated spaces of lowland valleys and villages, to be incorporated into the fortunate bodies of the humans and the livestock dwelling there" (2019, 9).

More specifically, we can identify two mythical ideal types of how to best domesticate vitality, which are both useful in further contextualizing the practical details of Skullward Leap meditation, namely hunting and herding. As for the first, we already saw that the activity of hunting—deer or other animals—is not only pervasive in literature on divination and fortune-summoning but also a core theme in the primordial search for vitality.[34] Hunting seems to have been an integral part of the life of early Tibetans, and Bruneau and Bellezza note that "at least half of all anthropomorphs in Upper Tibet are hunters" (2013, 15). There is evidence from Siberia and Northern Europe, as well as other regions (such as North America) that traditional peoples hunted animals like deer by imitating their behavior in multiple ways. In order to stalk their prey, hunters would don frontlets on their heads, wear fur on their bodies, imitate their movements, or shout to reproduce their sounds (Sapir 2002, 212; Vander 1997, 221, 487; Birket-Smith 1929, 107; Kroeber 1970, 158). It is highly likely that this mimetic behavior, emerging from the activity of hunting, also turned into a ritual practice during which the shamans of the Eurasian steppes would increase their fortune and luck for the hunt of their community (Hamayon 1996, 61). This same mimetic behavior is also part of the mythical-ritual universe of indigenous Tibetans, possibly reaching back all the way to the early Tibetan emperors, who have been described as a "sort of berserker."[35] The mimicking of wild animals is also widespread in the "gods of procreation" rites studied by Huber. In one ritual, premised on a short myth titled *Narrative of Seeking the Peacock's Nest*—which is generally performed together with *The Narrative of the Deer*—the participants imitate the behavior of the peacock and the stag. In these moments, so Huber explains "ritual performers including bon shamans mimic both the act of hunting and the behaviour of wild animals" (2020, vol. I: 542).[36]

It is likely that some of the strange enactments found in the preliminaries of the Great Perfection emerged out of this type of hunting behavior. The manipulation of consciousness in these exercises is not only achieved through sudden and disruptive activities, but also through the imaginative endeavor of "othering" one's self, almost as if the practitioners were taking on another existence through their actions. As part of this practice, the meditator should "first imagine the behaviors of the beings of the six classes and then act them out with the body" (*The Tantra of Unimpeded Sound*, 92.3).[37] The preliminaries of speech in differentiating between the domains of *saṃsāra* and *nirvāṇa*, for instance, instruct the meditator to "repeat the sounds of mantras, recitations, preaching, express things that are non-existant, existant, and appearing, as well as verbalizations of mental analysis, the cries of different animals, and the various aspects of their languages" (*The Treasury of Words and Meanings*, 373.1).[38] Dominant scholarly interpretations have generally assumed that the preliminaries of Skullward Leap serve to de-habituate the meditators from their usual frame of mind. In encouraging the yogis to take on these unfamiliar identities, they can break their routines and blur the rigid boundary between wholesome and unwholesome actions.[39] While this is certainly true, I do not believe that this "Buddhist" interpretation fully captures the true spirit of these techniques.

Rather than motivated by an ethical impulse, these practices seem theatrical and performative in nature. This becomes particularly clear if we consider that the meditators are sometimes instructed to play out specific roles. In other instances, and here we start to grasp how profoundly the contemplative technique of Skullward Leap is embedded within indigenous Tibetan culture, the texts are even more specific as meditators are instructed to act in the manner of a deer. In *The Eleven Words and Meanings on the Great Perfection*, likely the earliest systematic exegetical work on *The Seventeen Trantras*, written by Zhang Nyima Bum (zhang nyi ma 'bum, 1158–1213),[40] the meditator is instructed to imitate specific behaviors: they should wander around like a beggar in humility, or behave like a bee that is testing holes of a cliff-face to create a nest, and so forth. The only behavior that is repeated twice throughout the text, however, concerns that of the deer (*ri dwags*). While the first instance has a very Buddhist undertone, instructing yogis to become like sheep inasmuch as they live in isolated places, stop talking, give up work, thus allowing their body, channels, and mind to relax; the second reference picks up a dominant mythical theme of ancient Tibet: the yogi should act like a wounded deer, fleeing alone into an isolated place!

Although the revelation that such narratives exerted a crucial influence on contemplative systems like the Great Perfection is certainly new, the wider context of indigenous Tibetan quests for vitality has been well studied. One of the most important contributions in this regard is Brandon Dotson's article "Hunting for Fortune," where he draws on old Dunhuang manuscripts to abstract the underlying functioning of these pursuits. He calls this strategy the "hunter dynamic" and explains that it is premised on a "dual perspective as hunter, mimetically as (imitator of) prey" (Dotson 2019, 17). In our inquiry into the quest for vitality and the hunting of the sky-deer, this dual nature of the hunter has been a constant undertone. Consider the narrative in *The Age of Decline*, where the hunter wounds a deer, which then flees to an isolated place where it passes away. As the hunter is starting to butcher the animal, a demon arrives and steals his vitality (*bla*), so that he is now facing death. More generally speaking, the dual nature of the hunter is also apparent in the fact that the hunters engage in lengthy conversations with the deer, develop a rapport with them, clarify their questions regarding their family history, and so forth. At the same time, however, the hunter in pursuit of his prey, mimetically acting as if he himself were a deer, does not lose his human identity. If the hunter wants to "successfully stalk and kill animals," so Dotson notes, "he must to some extent adopt the perspective of his or her prey while also retaining sufficient grasp of his or her own human identity as hunter" (2019, 17). The mimesis involved in a hunter's dual perspective has been effectively illustrated in the context of the Yukaghirs of Siberia:

> When a hunter mimics the elk to bring it into the open so that he can shoot at it, he acts simultaneously within two motivational spaces, which could be called "the space of predatory mastery" and "the space of animal imitation." The first has to do with the hunter's intention of killing the animal, the second with his

need to take on its identity in order to fulfill that intention. The hunter, we might say, acts with a dual nature: he is both hunter and animal.

Broz and Willerslev elaborate by remarking that "to act in between these two identities is a highly complex task." Indeed, just like the Dzogchen yogi, who engages in wild behavior and takes on the identity of animals, he does not lose his human identity in this process of "un-domestication." If the yogi imitates the behavior of animals while remaining relentlessly self-aware of his greater goal of domesticating his energies, "the hunter ... needs to be aware not only of the prey animal, but also of himself being aware of the prey, in order to make sure that his perspective is neither that of a hunter nor that of the animal, but instead somewhere in between or both at once. In other words, the success of the hunter depends upon his ability to keep up a double perspective, or act as a mimetic agent" (Broz and Willerslev 2012, 96–7). Like the hunter, who is a mimetic agent playing a dual role, becoming part animal to subdue it, Skullward Leap practitioners know that the domestication of our wild vitality is only possible if we are willing to actively engage it. In this light, meditation becomes a mimetic practice marked by alterations in consciousness, change in rhythms, dynamism in intensities, and fluctuations in control that might have once been inspired by the hunting behavior of the ancient inhabitants of the Eurasian steppe.

In this same part of the world, we also find another prototypical activity surrounding the domestication of wild vitality, namely the corralling of animals. In the context of early Tibet, the domestication of what is animalistic, wild, and untamed is a prevalent theme in indigenous narratives, and the descent of the kings is already concerned with turning the wildness of what is a natural place into a cultivated and habitable space.[41] It is no surprise that deer and sheep, creatures that move in between wildness and domesticity, play a key role in those mythical stories. Several early Tibetan manuscripts describe the gods arriving on earth as the "masters" or "owners" of "maned animals," thus identifying them as domesticators of wild animals (PT 1038, 1.14–15). Studying divination texts found in Dunhuang, Dotson also relates how in one specific response, the *mu sman* goddess, the owner of the wild animals, declares:

> I The sky ... says: Above the soft meadows, to draw the deer (*sha*) and *'bri* (female yak) to the lower part, they chase deer thither and stalk seven gazelles hither. I appoint them as my livestock. I collect them and put them in a paddock (*ra bar stsol*). The paddock walls are encircled by snow mountains. The snow mountain walls are encircled by cliffs. You, human, who are beset by accusations, now you shall be free of them. (IOL Tib J 738, 1.39–42)[42]

"The image of the goddess corralling the wild animals and housing them in an enclosure or paddock," which Dotson interprets as "a wild corollary of the human domestication of animals" (Dotson 2019, 10), is actually another strategy employed by hunters in ancient societies. In communal hunts, for instance, the huntsmen would surround the sheep and drive them into enclosures (Stewart 1942, 242).

This behavior is also reproduced in the mythical-contemplative performance of Tögal, particularly the engagement of the luminous sheep. We find an explicit description of how the strung-together sheep manifest during Skullward Leap meditation and an outline of the techniques that can be used to stabilize their visionary appearance.

> The lamp of the pure expanse gathers the nature of awareness so that it appears in the enclosure of the linked sheep. For whomever is experientially familiar with this, it is an unchanging and self-radiant blue, abiding in the enclosure of an aura of encircling hoops. It appears as naturally radiant outer objective sphere, unfabricated in nature. (*Treasury of Words and Meanings*, 62.6)[43]

The meditator is instructed to engage these "strings of sheep" in a very particular way, specifically aimed at domesticating their spontaneous vitality. During the visionary practice, the linked chains and the seminal nuclei are complemented by a third element, namely the patches of dark blue color, the so-called "expanse." Already in the early scriptures, we find countless examples in which the Skullward Leap practitioner is taught to stabilize the manifestation of the linked chains and the nuclei by containing them within the blue expanse, which serves as a sort of canvas on which the intricate details of the visions are painted during contemplation. In a passage from *The Blazing Lamp Tantra*, the yogi is guided to "place the linked chains within the prison of the expanse, where they will continuously appear without dependency and in a non-grasping and non-abiding manner" (307.4).[44] Elsewhere, it is written that the practitioner "should train" by means of the "key points of binding, capturing, transforming faculties, and severing the root" (*The Tantra of Unimpeded Sound*, 118.2).[45] Later, in Longchenpa's *Treasury of Words and Meanings*, we read: "The key point of awareness is to keep the eyes unwavering and the mind undistracted. Based on that, when the appearance of the expanse along with the linked sheep dawns, subdue the chained sheep so that they do not flutter and apprehend them within the enclosure of the expanse" (377.4).[46]

If we look at the domestication performed by the Dzogchen yogis in light of the mythical narratives surrounding the imprisonment of young children found in *The Tantra of Self-Arisen Awareness*, we could say that by apprehending the sheep within the expanse, they replay the original drama while giving it a new outcome. This becomes even more unambiguous if we consider that Longchenpa wields the same terms to image the imprisonment of the little children and the fencing in of the luminous chains of light. In another section from the same masterpiece, we read:

> Without separating from the target [the appearances], always abide in the thought of the buddhas. By inserting awareness into the prison of the expanse, fundamental nature of things will not be lost. Continually remaining within that, it is certain that the four visions will reach optimization. If there is movement, by reifying the conceptual, you accumulate the karma of *saṃsāra*. By controlling the key point of the support of those movements, that is, the channels and winds,

the flow of reifying conceptuality is severed. This is an extremely important point. (*The Treasury of Words and Meanings*, 406.4)[47]

It appears, in this section, that the contemplator explores another dual nature. Because he is both mythical child and contemplative herder, we witness the dramatic metamorphosis of the contemplators from the status of prisoners—as we encountered them in the mythical-historical reality—into that of a jailor. This emancipation, of course, is already implicit in the narratives themselves. The story of the two blood-related boys—whose adventure we left as they were captured by five soldiers and the Old Lady—takes a dramatic turn toward liberation: "Just imagine! Then four persons pursued and captures the five riders and unhorsed them. Just imagine! The two boys liberated themselves and killed their prison guards. Just imagine! They immediately escaped to the Sun Castle in the distance, where they collected the taxes from the people" (*The Tantra of Self-Arisen Awareness*, 563–7).[48] Just as the little children activate their own resources, violently overcoming their jailors, and breaking out of the prison, it can be said that the yogis activate the energies that are latently trapped within their bodies.

It is imperative to stipulate, however, that the type of incarceration we talked about in the first part and the techniques of "fencing in" of sheep discussed here differ in significant respects. Chiefly, the little sheep are not detained within a narrow and confined space, such as the prison or the ravine in which the children were held captive in the mythic account, but rather in an area that is open and spacious. What happens during the meditation, indeed, might be more akin to the behavior of the little children, who travel to a foreign land, suffer imprisonment, and then escape the prison to return to their home (*The Tantra of Self-Arisen Awareness*, 567).[49] In reading the phenomenological accounts of the visions, one gets the distinct impression that the contemplative journey leads to a sort of return to one's origins. In this sense, the "fence" into which the sheep are being transplanted could also be described as their "home." Like sheep that are free to roam on a patch of grass, the linked chains appear in the practitioner's vision against the background of an enormous field known as "the expanse" (*dbyings*), which the scriptures refer to as something akin to a "home of awareness" in which the nuclei are put into (*The Six Spaces Tantra*, 126.4). Interestingly, the expanse is also called *yul*, a term that means as much as "home" or "home region" in colloquial Tibetan. In the early Tibetan mythology, similarly, *yul* is identified as "domestic space characterized by cultivation and by lowland valleys," and thus contrasted to *ri*, "wild space, imagined as being high" (Dotson 2019, 9). Finally, we might also recall that Hazod, in his remarks on the burial mounds of the early Tibetan kings, speculated that the original meaning of the term *mu ra* might have not been related to an enclosure, but much rather to the arrival of the royal family within a heavenly paradise. Just like sheep, who are corralled in a fence, or kings who return to their home in the sky-realm, the scholars of Tögal have compared the final vision to a sort of homecoming: "The expanse," so Hatchell put it, "is thus the place where at the end of the day things settle down, where the chaotic motion of the sheep is finally contained, and into which visions finally dissolve" (2014, 68).

Chapter 6

THE DZOGCHEN BODY AND THE INTERNALIZATION OF VITALITY

Although the Great Perfection tradition portrays the climax of the practice as a dissolutive moment that culminates in the so-called rainbow body (*'ja' lus*), or rainbow body of the great transference (*'ja' lus 'pho ba chen po*), it is useful to remember that the Skullward Leap practitioner does not just float off into the ephemeral realm of air. On the contrary, he engages in some highly physical exercises during the preliminaries and inhabits a human body made of flesh and bones, blood and veins, hormones and chemicals. Rather than resting in unobstructed "space," Dzogchen texts emphasize that vitality, after the initial manifestation during the epiphany of the ground, continues to abide (*gnas*) in our bodies.[1] Thus, the yogis' physical constitution is not simply biological, but rather a cultural construct as the Great Perfection gradually transplanted the vitality of the mythical narratives within the visceral realm of the body. The subtle anatomy of Dzogchen amplifies the concurrent processes of buddhicization and Tibetanization that we have already encountered in earlier parts of this study. In a series of highly idiosyncratic traits, particularly the vitalistic nomenclature applied to the subtle body's luminous channels, Dzogchen takes the Indian tantric body and lavishly ornaments it with non-Buddhist Tibetan motifs. Finally, the yogi's physical basis is not only imbued with subtle vitality that resides in various nodal points throughout his body and flows through a complex network of channels, but it even extends into the surrounding environment. This vertical projection of internal energies into the sky is more than just a metaphorical or perceptual process, but it must be regarded as a contemplative extension of the indigenous Tibetan conception of vitality as something that is imbued with the ability to circulate in between the earthly realm inhabited by our bodies and the heavenly realm of the gods.[2] Skullward Leap can therefore be understood as a technique of redemption or reparation. Developed against the mythical-historical background of the ruptured vertical connection with the realm of the sky, the practice aims at reestablishing the flow of vitality between heaven and earth for the benefit of humanity.

The Six Key Points

A good place to start an inquiry into the status of the body in the Great Perfection is a discussion of the "six key points" (*gnad drug*), instructions regarding the physical performance of Tögal. As I previously noted, these exceedingly simple teachings, generally divided into two sets of three, are marked by their ubiquitous emphasis on stability and immobility. The "three key points" (*gnad gsum*), for one, follow the standard Buddhist categorization of body, speech, and mind; all of which "must be thoroughly controlled (*rab tu bcun*)" (*The Treasury of Words and Meanings*, 373.5).[3] The key point of the body (*lus kyi gnad*) consists not only of applying three distinct physical postures—namely that of a "lion" (*seng ge*), an "elephant" (*glang chen*), and a "sage" (Tib. *drang srong*, Skt. *ṛṣi*)—but also emphasizes a lack of movement (*The Treasury of Words and Meanings*, 243, 275–7).[4] Longchenpa, in his *Treasury of Words and Meanings*, elaborates that the "body remains still without taking part in physical activities," that "the body's limbs remain still without movements to and fro," and that "one remains still without exertion as one brings actions down to the ground" (406.2-3).[5] The key point of speech (*ngag gi gnad*) is essentially a quieting down into increasing silence and calm. In *The Tantra of Unimpeded Sound*, it is explained that speech "must be trained, remain abiding, determined, and stabilized" (91.1).[6] Elsewhere, we read that "speech, like a mute, should be cut off in such a way that … one is not speaking to anyone even with mere symbols, naturally (*rang*) cutting off one's mental projections and contractions" (*The Treasury of Words and Meanings*, 375.6).[7] Furthermore, Longchenpa offers his readers a threefold definition of how the "speech is kept unwavering": one has to "not speak with others," "cut off the forth and back of words," and "stop expressing all of one's own verbalizations" (*The Treasury of Words and Meanings*, 406.1–2). Finally, the key point of the mind (*sems kyi gnad*) consists in the concentration on the sky, both through the conceptual faculty of the mind and the perceptual faculty of the eyes.

If the first three key points already illustrate the necessity for the restriction of sensory input, the second set, known as the "three unwavering states" (*mi 'gul gsum*), only reinforces this impression. The term "unwavering" (*mi gul ba, mi g.yo ba*) stands for a physical type of stability, and the three states are intimately associated with the body of the meditation practitioner. In short, we could speak of the three unwavering states as techniques that focus on the centering of the practitioner's body. The key point of the gates (*sgo'i gnad*), for example, consists in adopting three distinct gazes with one's eyes, looking upward, downward, and sideways, while leaving the pupils immobile and steady.[8] The key point of the object (*yul gyi gnad*), similarly, consists in centering one's perceptual focus on the luminous display emerging in the pure cloudless sky. Finally, the key point of the wind (*rlung gyi gnad*) consists of breathing slowly and naturally through the mouth, letting the breath and vital energies be natural, without altering them in any way.

To truly appreciate the body in Skullward Leap, it might be useful to recall a few details of the "subtle body." Known as the "adamantine body" (*rdo rje'i lus*), the tantric body serves as the basis of contemplative practice and represents an attempt to establish correspondences between the material and the spiritual or the ordinary and the enlightened dimensions of our being. The subtle body generally consists of a triad of basic elements: Channels (T. *rtsa*, S. *nāḍī*), winds (T. *rlung*, S. *vāyu*), and seminal nuclei (T. *thig le*, S. *bindu*). In the Great Perfection, just as in Buddhism more generally, the human body is not primarily relevant for its materiality, but rather for how it functions.[9] The three core elements of our subtle bodies form part of a system, within which they are profoundly interconnected: The channels serve as pathways by means of which the winds move through our body to transport the seminal nuclei, which can be seen as the intelligent kernels of our vital energy. Relationally speaking, the channels are defined as the "sanctuaries" (*gnas pa rtsa*) of the spatially arrayed seminal nuclei (*bkod pa thig le*) and the dynamically moving winds (*g.yo ba rlung*). Ordinarily, the channels and the seminal nuclei are identified as stationary and "non-moving," while the wind currents transporting the energies are said to be moving. Indeed, the bodily practices—particularly in the anuyoga tantras—are largely centered on the gaining of mastery of the vital energy of the body through the controlling, manipulating, and developing of the "wind" or *prāṇa*.

In the key points of Skullward Leap, by contrast, even the movement of the breath is interrupted. In *The Tantra of Unimpeded Sound*, for example, it says that "by settling the winds as much as possible and by sending them out thoroughly, the connection between body and mind is severed without returning to the three realms" (61.1–2).[10] Longchenpa elaborates on how to control one's breath, arguing that the winds have to "remain still in three ways": "they don't go externally," "they don't fill up internally," and "they don't go and come externally or internally" (*The Treasury of Words and Meanings*, 407.1–2).[11] The efficacy of the six key points is premised on the stabilization of the various levels of our bodies, including coarse dimensions like our posture or our eyes, and more subtle dimensions, such as the internal winds. Together with the preliminary practices, the six points form part of a larger Great Perfection project of embodiment. Just as *gzugs/rūpa* is not just materiality but also sensation, the human body is not just a physical *Körper*, but rather the first-person experience grounded in a *Leib*. As Sue Hamilton puts it, it is "lived body rather than simply its flesh" (2000, 29). The starting point of enaction, precisely because it is premised on the relationship that we establish with the world that surrounds us, is our own body and our own position in the world.[12] Holding one's body and gaze intentionally in a very precise and stable way enables the practitioners to strengthen their vantage point, to reinforce their position, to increase their stature and status.

Embodying Myths

While this phenomenology of embodiment could be understood as a universal trait that is shared by contemplative traditions attuned to subtle unconscious processes underlying our physical existence, the Dzogchen body is also imbued with a particularistic tendency that can best be explained by relating it to the ancient mythical-ritual substratum of vitality in Tibet. Indeed, just as the previous chapter demonstrated how the quest for life was transmitted from the realm of myth into the visionary contemplation—accounting for the yogis' identities as hunters and herders of divine energy—so the powerful substances acquired during the pursuits of the sky-deer were transplanted into their yogic bodies. Although remarkable in its details, the mechanism of somatization of this mythical reality is not altogether surprising if we consider that early Tibetans regarded concepts like *lha, bla, phya* or *g.yang* in a vitalistic sense as the essence of life itself. Quite logically, it can also be argued that these indigenous notions had a physical dimension to them, linking vitality directly to the visceral experience of the human body.[13] More specifically, such a comparative undertaking is warranted because the Dzogchen anatomy is marked by idiosyncratic traits that are hard to account for in a purely Buddhist universe. Since the origins of this anatomical system have received very little attention to date and the details are highly technical, the present account will have to remain somewhat speculative. Nonetheless, the unique terminology designating the most energetically charged points of the subtle body give away a series of clues to the system's likely provenance, namely the pre-Buddhist religion of Tibet as it comes to us through mythical antecedent tales involving the quest for vitality and precious substances.

Dzogchen texts explain that the vitality, which courses through and beyond our bodies during meditation practice, is particularly concentrated within four hot spots: it pumps out of the heart (*tsitta*), flows through the luminous channels (*'od rtsa*), spreads inside of the skull (*dung khang/ dung khang dkar*), and is finally released through the eyes (*tsakshu/ briguta*). As we now review each one of these abodes of vitality, it will become apparent that the Great Perfection subtle body operated an internalization of the precious substances that were the focal point of the indigenous Tibetan quests for vitality. A first indication of this embodiment of mythical searches comes to us through the curious designation of the four focal points themselves. Indeed, just like in the mythical quests for vitality, where the hunters are frequently identified as young sons of divine and royal descent living in palaces or castles (e.g., *The Great Main Text of the Vitality Ritual of the Lord of the Vitality, The Tantra of Self-Arisen Awareness*), the centers of vitality in the Dzogchen body are known as the four "divine palaces" (*zhal yas khang*).

The first locus of vitality in the subtle body is the heart, which is designated by some rather idiosyncratic terminology: the amulet of the wisdom, the crystal palace of five lights, the divine palace of the precious *tsitta*, the tent of brown carnelian, the precious palace, or the precious envelope. The most interesting designation, however, is the "deer-lamp of the *tsitta*" (*tsitta sha'i sgron ma*). While existing scholarship has always translated the term *sha'i sgron ma* as the "flesh lamp," I believe that it is much more likely that we are dealing with a lost reference to the sky-deer of the indigenous Tibetan world. Indeed, just as the deer is the primary source of vitality, the container of precious substances that encapsulated divine vitality in their essence, the deer-lamp of the *tsitta* is the place where the quintessence of the yogis' enlightened energy is concentrated.

I would also suggest that this centrality of the heart as the center of vitality might be the original reason for the tradition's nomenclature as the Heart-Essence Great Perfection.

The association between the precious substances of indigenous Tibetan culture and the Dzogchen body becomes even more apparent if we look at the second palace, namely the luminous channels, whose main purpose is the circulation of the vital energy contained in the heart. The system of luminous channels is so central to the tradition that we find elaborate lists and extensive discussions of their designation, physical appearance, and function throughout the early scriptures and the commentarial tradition, particularly in Longchenpa's work.[14] Oftentimes the main channels are described as fourfold, which is why they are also known as "the four principal channels." This list of four serves to distinguish the three "standard" tantric Buddhist channels—the flavor channel, the solitary channel, and the all-encompassing channel—from the truly innovative Dzogchen channel of light known as "the crystal tube" or "the kati crystal tube" (*The Tantra of Unimpeded Sound*, 126.6; *The Blazing Lamp Tantra*, 295.2). In other instances, the texts focus exclusively on the luminous channels and describe them as "four especially great channels," which are said to serve as the pathways for our awareness: the great golden *kati*, the crystal tube, the white silk thread, and the slender coil (*The Tantra of Self-Arisen Awareness*, 526.2).

Taking a closer look at the nomenclature used for the luminous channels, it is quite apparent that they reproduce the precious substances associated with the mythical quest for vitality, particularly silk and crystals. The most important and innovative Dzogchen channels is the "the crystal tube" (*shel bug can*) or "the *kati* crystal tube" (*ka ti shel gyi sbu gu can*), which Longchenpa specifies to "connect the heart with the eyes," thus "supporting innumerable appearances of the chained sheep (*Treasury of Philosophical Positions*, 377).[15] Thinking back at earlier parts of this study, particularly the designation of the heart containing enlightened awareness ("crystal palace of five lights") or the nomenclature of the courageous youth of the parables ("little child crystal," "thoroughly radiating," "little child of the inconceivable epiphany," etc.), it becomes apparent that crystals are closely associated to light and that both of these notions hold a noteworthy status throughout the Great Perfection. As we saw in earlier chapter, crystals also play a prominent role in the mythical-ritual stories surrounding the quest for vitality. *The Great Main Text of the Vitality Ritual of the Lord of the Vitality*, for instance, tells the story of cosmogony out of eggs and the establishment of the "ground of *phya/g. yang*" by searching and hunting for a jeweled deer. Indeed, before the Man of the Emanation sets out to lasso the precious animal, he is told that the deer's parents are called "Sky-Deer with Long Antlers" (*gnam sha ru ring*) and "*Mu Doe*" (*dmu sha yu mo*) and that he should find a deer by the name "Conch Shell Deer with Crystal Antlers" (*dung sha shel ru*) (525). While the animal's parents' names—recalling the trope of the sky-deer—remind us of the divine origins of vitality in the celestial realm, the name of the offspring introduces the idea of the "crystal antlers" (*shel ru*) as the main source of vitality.[16] Just like the deer-lamp of the *tsitta* serves as an implantation of the quintessence of the sky-deer's vitality within our hearts, the crystal tube channel are an embodiment of the deer's life-giving crystal antlers.

To see how closely the mythical quest for life became incarnated within the yogic body, we only need to take a more detailed look at the name of the "Conch Shell Deer with Crystal Antlers" (*dung sha shel ru*). In fact, the deer's name leads us directly to the third node of vitality in our dissection of the subtle body, namely the "skull." Indeed, this anatomical structure is just as puzzling as the deer-lamp heart or the silken and crystal channels as it is idiosyncratically labeled as the "Conch Shell House" (*dung khang*) or the "White Conch Shell House" (*dung khang dkar*). The conch shell is not only one of the most frequently appearing precious substances in indigenous search narratives, but it is also in association with cosmogonic vitality itself. Reviewing the texts discussed in this study, the precious substance of conch shell is associated with cosmogonic eggs (*The Great Main Text of the Vitality Ritual of the Lord of the Vitality, The Extensive Elimination and Offering Rites for the Gods of the Four Groups of Little Humans*), the emissaries bringing vitality to earth (*Extensive Elimination and Offering Rites for the Gods of the Four Groups of Little Humans*), and locations where vitality is especially concentrated, particularly mountains. (*Remedying the Lords of the Soil and Subjugating the Evil Forces of Creation through the Ground of Vitality*). Let us take a look at another text in which the Conch Shell Deer with Crystal Antlers crops up as a major protagonist in the moment of the cosmogony, namely *Extracting Vitality in Nine Sections*. As Charles Ramble reports, it is used by Lama Tshultrim of Lubrak, a remote place in Mustang (Nepal), during "fortune-summoning" (*g.yang 'gug*) performances, where the narrative establishes an explicit nexus between the body of the mythological deer (*dung sha dkar mo shel ru can*) and the cosmogony:

> Homage to the presence of the *phywa bön* and the *g.yang bön*. First, as for the spreading of the ground for the *phya* of the phenomenal world, [recite as follows]: *Kyai!* When the sky first came into existence, at the beginning of the world-ages, at the boundary of being and non-being, there came into being a white conch-shell deer with crystal antlers. As for what came into existence, it was the first world-age that came into existence. As for what descended, it was *phya* and *g.yang* that descended. Call "*khu'i*" to summon that *phya* undefeated; call "*khu'i*" to summon the *g.yang* undefeated! There was an emanation from that deer's heart, and dependent on the head of that emanation there came into existence the *phywa* castle and the *g.yang* heart.[17]

In this cosmogonic myth, describing the ground of vitality as a white conch-shell deer with crystal antlers, we find a nexus of rich symbols that do not only reverberate back into the mythical-historical narratives of indigenous Tibet, but also bring to life the body of the yogic meditators. Just like the hunters in the previous chapter take on a dual identity, becoming both deerstalker and deer, the meditator uses his anatomy to become re-embodied into the sky-deer: its emanation is implanted in the yogi's heart, and its crystal antlers flow within the walls of his channels, the conch shell forms his skull.

Lassoing Vitality

While I have no guarantee that all these correspondences between the Dzogchen subtle body and the mythical narratives regarding the descent of vitality hold up to scrutiny, the theory of the embodiment of mythical content within the physiology of the contemplative system opens up new avenues for understanding the meditative practice itself. More specifically, I propose that the subtle body serves not only as a static replication of indigenous energies, but much rather as a stage upon which the mythical quest can be played out during the performance of Skullward Leap. In order to substantiate this claim, we now move on to the fourth and final divine palace in the Dzogchen system, namely the eyes. The texts emphasize that the pure energy within our bodies—after pulsating out of our hearts and through the luminous channels to reach the skull—naturally radiate from the conch shell house to the eyes, where it is projected outward to be seen in the sky in the form of various visionary displays.

This preeminence of verticality in the quest for vitality did not limit itself to the mythical realm, but it also resurfaces in Skullward Leap practice. Frequently the embodiment of indigenous motifs has a performative dimension to it as the peculiar attributes function in ways that are strikingly similar to their mythical archetypes. Tendencies of this trend can already be found in the concept of the luminous conduits, such as the crystal tube channel. It is likely that the crystal antlers within the meditator's anatomy replicate the function that they enact in the mythical worldview of pre-Buddhist Tibet, namely their ability to connect the realm of the earth with the world of the sky. We have seen that the antlers' capacity to move vertically led to their depiction as a sort of tree of life that climbs into the sky. The luminous channel of the crystal tube clearly mirrors this vertical movement of the tree. In *The Heart-Essence of the Ḍākinīs*, we read that it branches into two smaller channels of luminosity connecting the skull with the eyes and that these light channels resemble horns of the *ba men* buffalo (*ba men gyi rwa*) (503). Unlike the horns of the buffalo, which are gradually narrowing, the luminous channels are said to be tapered in a reverse direction: They are narrow at their base in the skull, then expand in diameter as they move towards the tips, which are the eyes. Functionally, indeed, the crystal tube channel is crucial for the flowing of vitality, not only of the yogi's body but also the surrounding world that he encounters during his meditation practice. The channel, indeed, represents the major vertical artery for the yogi's enlightened energy: It leads from the heart to the eyes, extends beyond the frame of the physical body, and quite literally shoots into the sky, giving rise to the luminous visions that are populated by chained sheep moving in between the world of men and that of the gods.

Evidence that the vertical mobility of vitality was transplanted from the mythical substratum of early Tibet into the body of the meditators is abundant. Besides the channels of crystal and buffalo horn, we also encounter many references to the "white silk thread" (*dar dkar snal ma*) channel. This conduit is certainly one of the main luminous channels in the Dzogchen body and provides yet another illustration of this embodiment of the mythical quest for life. Here, the idea of a white silk thread curving through the yogi's body while transporting a steady stream of luminous energy within it not only brings to mind associations with the "chained sheep" appearing as part of the visions, but also reminds of the mythical "sky-cord." Again, the presence of silken channels within the yogi's bodies offers an embodied parallel to the sky-cord, which also served as a luminous passageway that connected the gods and kings (as well as humans more generally) to the sky.

Finally, the bodily enactment of a vertical journey toward the sky becomes perhaps nowhere as apparent as one of the tradition's most animated ways to illustrate this projective tendency of energy, namely "water lamp of the far-reaching lasso" (*rgyang zhags chu'i sgron ma*). The lamp stands for the totality of luminous pathways and gateways, that is, the channels as well as the eyes. Just like with the other bodily idiosyncrasies, it is likely that the peculiar designation of the far-reaching lasso channel represents an embodiment of indigenous Tibetan narrative materials. The motif of the lasso, indeed, reinforces the impression that the mythical drama of the deer-hunt offers a sort of screen play for the embodied reenactment of vitality's journey throughout the yogic body and the visionary apparitions of Tögal. The lasso is not only a prominent motif in the rock art of Upper Tibet, where the hunters are depicted using them to catch deer (Bruneau and Bellezza 2013, 15), but they are also a popular motif in the four visions, where sheep that are roped together are sometimes said to resemble lassos of light. We have also seen that the meditators are instructed to gather up these chained sheep by corralling them in a fence-like structure as if domesticating the wild energy of heavenly life. Indeed, in Tibet, the lasso plays a central role as a device for catching vitality.

The most prominent location for lassos, however, is likely to be found in the mythical quests for vitality. Let us return to the search narrative as it is recorded in *Extracting Vitality in Nine Sections*. The story of the mythological deer-hunt proceeds by explaining that because the prince wants to use the body of the crystal deer to craft his ritual implements, he must take it with him. However, this turns out to be challenging because the deer is, quite naturally, reluctant to accompany him voluntarily. It is for this reason that the youth uses a special instrument, namely a magical sun-rays lasso (*nyi zer 'phrul zhags*), to hook the animal and take it with him. Finally, after having caught the Conch Shell Deer with Crystal Antlers, he proceeds to make an enigmatic prediction and tells the deer that it will become a sheep in the future.[18] The archetypical story of the deer-hunt, thus, allows us to illustrate the pervasiveness of the transplantation of mythical narratives into the yogic body. In fact, in its totality, the narrative of the hunt for the primordial deer allows us to make some sense of what are likely the four most elusive motifs of the Dzogchen body, namely the crystals (the deer's antlers), silk (the deer, who is becoming a sheep in the future, possibly as the prince makes silken ritual implements out of the sheep), the conch (the body of the deer), and the luminous lasso (the tool used by the young hunter to finally capture the deer).

Before concluding the discussion of the embodied technical dimension of the Dzogchen contemplative system, I would like to point to one final element worthy of discussion in regard to the status of the lasso in Tibetan culture, namely that it points to the profoundly ambivalent position of vitality. It cannot be overlooked that the lasso is used for a rather violent purpose, namely to subdue the deer and to strip it of its animating vitality. Vitality, as we have seen in previous chapters, can be both acquired and stolen, beneficial and harmful, domesticated and uncontrollable.[19] Remember, for instance, that the lasso serves Tibetan witches and healers to steal or safeguard the life energy of ordinary people. We have also seen that indigenous culture frequently expresses this ambiguity of life energy by invoking the term *bla*, another classical Tibetan term belonging to the larger semantic field of vitality.[20] While later Buddhist interpretations of this notion translated it into a person-specific consciousness oftentimes translated as a "soul,"[21] we have seen in Chapter 3 that early Tibetans regarded *bla* as a vitality that is divisible and multiple, bodily and cosmic, mobile and distributable.[22]

Since the early Dzogchen tradition emerged on the fringes of Buddhism, in a profoundly Tibetan world, it is likely that its own understanding of vitality was quite similar. While texts do contain references to *bla* as roaming sheep that leave our bodies[23]—inviting a comparison with earlier references to the sheep roaming their homeland that is the sky—there is more solid evidence for this mobile conception of vitality in the Dzogchen system. Consider, for instance, the narratives related to the Old Lady capturing the little children because they are in search for precious substances, where the competitive nature of a struggle for a mobile vitality principle seems to be the driving impulse. The loss of vitality, more importantly, harkens back at the narrative of King Trigum, which we identified as one of the decisive episodes in the history of vitality in Tibet. It is in this moment that the direct connection to the heavenly realm of life-giving energy is abruptly ruptured, and the descent of vitality reveals its precariousness most vehemently. Although the Tibetans developed alternative ways to assert their vitality, particularly through the spherical model adopted from Buddhism and promoted in cosmogonic myths and in the practice of treasure revelation, there is little doubt that the vertical model of vitality remained a dominant theme in indigenous Tibetan culture. We have unearthed evidence of this persistence of the quest for life in its vertical dimension by showing that the sky remained the determining factor in practices like mountain worship, treasure revelation, or burial practices.

Similarly, the lasso is not only limited to the yogic body but also extends the vertically arranged channels coursing through the yogi's body to the eyes, the apex of the sky-gazing yogi's physical anatomy, and thus initiates the projection of visionary apparitions into the sky above the meditator. By extending beyond the body, it is almost as if the lasso reversed the process of embodiment of the drama by allowing the practitioner to finally disembody the myth by living it out in contemplative visions. Just as the mythical-historical narratives tell the tale of early Tibetan kings returning to their heavenly abode to sleep at night and after their death on earth, leaving behind nothing but light, Tögal culminates in the dissolution of the body of the meditator. Calling this the attainment of the "rainbow body of the great transference," Dzogchen teachers claim that upon successful meditation, the five gross elements composing the physical body dissolve back into their essences, manifesting as five-colored light. Like with the silk thread and the crystal tube channels, it might even be possible to relate the rainbow body to the "chained sheep" (*lu gu rgyud*). Not only are they functionally related as they both transmute from the physical dimension of our bodies into ephemeral luminosities, but the two phenomena display a striking phonetic parallel and the term *lu gu rgyud* might even be the result of a corruption of the Zhangzhung term for "rainbow" (*dmu ru rgyud*) (Martin 2010, 175).

Although these speculations about the original performance of Skullward Leap might strike the reader as somewhat fanciful, it is important to remember that the projection of life energy from within the body into the world of the sky would have made perfect sense according to the indigenous conception of vitality. Indeed, vitality is "fundamentally distributive in nature" (Gentry 2017, 343) and therefore frequently connects the energies flowing through internal and external realities. On the one hand, the *bla* is located within our bodies, particularly within the heart; although it can also move from part of the body to another (Karmay 1998c, 314).[24] Particularly, in Himalayan folk traditions, the *bla* can live outside of our bodies and take residence in "a place of vitality" (*bla gnas*) located close by in our environment, such as a stone, a tree, a mountain, or an animal. In this sense, it is very conceivable that the Dzogchen practitioner's projection into the sky, operated on the basis of the crystal tube channel, the white silk channel, and the water lamp of the far-reaching lasso, was originally much more than just a predictive process.

While the final chapters of this study will provide some intriguing evidence from later writings, such as Longchenpa's commentaries, to suggest that such a projective understanding of Skullward Leap as a practice of transference of vitality into another realm remained present in Tibet until the fourteenth century, I would like to conclude this discussion with another observation. The indigenous ambivalence of the mobile vitality principle as something that can be found and lost, protected and harmed, gifted and stolen allowed the Dzogchen contemplative system a way to redeem older models of vitality, particularly the vertical type of vitality that connects the realm of humans to that of the gods. Skullward Leap also offer a re-instantiation of the Tibetan cult of royalty, where the early kings were connected to the heavenly realm through the sky-cord,[25] as well as the custom according to which leaders of the country had the ability to project their vitality into the natural environment as a means to offer protection for their realm.[26] Ultimately, then, Skullward Leap can be understood as a redemptive practice aimed at overcoming the traumatic loss of vitality provoked by the cutting of the sky-cord of Emperor Trigum by repairing the meditators' tie to the heavenly realm. In the advanced stages of the practice, the embodied vitality is externalized and reestablished in the place where it belongs. The entire visionary field transmogrifies into a buddhafield, the energy flowing through the four embodied palaces is restored in the form of "inestimable mansions" in the sky, and the chained-together sheep take on the form of a *maṇḍala* of 100 peaceful and wrathful deities.

Part III

THE INSTITUTIONAL-MATERIAL CRYSTALLIZATION
OF VITALITY

In the final part of the study, we explore the contemplative system of Dzogchen in its institutional-material aspects and turn our attention to the crystallization of the tradition as an independent and powerful religious school during the fourteenth century. While the Heart-Essence Great Perfection was a relatively minor tradition in the centuries before, it burst onto the scene of Tibetan Buddhism during this period as the third Karmapa Rangjung Dorje (rang 'byung rdo rje, 1284–1339) and others started to draw attention to its teachings. The rise of Dzogchen, however, is most intimately associated with the life and work of a singular scholar-yogi, namely Longchen Rabjam. Indeed, it is the merit of Longchenpa that the previously loosely associated teachings were organized into a coherent system on par with that of other schools on the Tibetan plateau. In light of the dominance of the vitalistic thrust and the overwhelming presence of indigenous Tibetan motifs in the Dzogchen tantras, Longchenpa's project was spectacularly successful. Indeed, contemporary practitioners of Dzogchen as well as the dominant scholarship on the tradition—who access the beliefs and practices of the tradition frequently through the interpretation of Longchenpa or one of his successors—are not only convinced that the tradition is deeply anchored in Mahāyāna and Vajrayāna teachings, but also celebrate freedom as its primary ethos. This being said, a more careful look at Longchenpa's writings reveals that they are fraught by an internal tension between two opposing trends: On the one hand, the crystallization of Dzogchen teachings appears to harden the tradition, setting its teachings in stone, and cutting it off from the dialectical circularity of the quest for vitality. Quite appropriately, Longchenpa frequently uses the image of a crystal that is "primordially pure" (*ka dag*) to defend his tradition's doctrine of freedom. On the other hand, even in its crystalized form, the Dzogchen teachings continue to be driven by the hunt for precious life-sustaining energy below the surface. The crystal, although adamantine, upholds its vitality as a powerful substance that reveals a richly dynamic display as soon as light shines through its prism. This tendency is particularly evident in the so-called "introductions" (*ngo sprod pa*), during which a teacher uses various means—frequently both metaphorical and material crystals—to show their students the nature of their mind. Exploring such performative techniques in their linguistic, material, and psychological dimensions, this final part provides substantial evidence for Dzogchen's surprising parallels with other religious traditions, not only the indigenous substratum that has concerned us so far, but also its closest living relative in the wider Tibetosphere, namely shamanism.

Chapter 7

VITALITY AND THE BUDDHIST PATH

We have seen that *The Seventeen Tantras* delineate an elaborate contemplative system, fully equipped with its own collection of cosmogonic myths, a rich visionary phenomenology, varying techniques for arousing and domesticating the body's energies, as well as an extraordinarily ornate subtle body anatomy. In all these dimensions, the tradition demonstrates too many idiosyncrasies to be attributed to any other Buddhist system found in India or Tibet, or to be a new tradition that pops up suddenly in late tenth-century Tibet. Instead, I have provided substantial evidence that the vocabulary, morphology, and function of the Dzogchen system point to its origins in a substratum of pre-Buddhist thought and practice that centered on the quest for vitality. Despite its initial status as an indigenous practice, however, Dzogchen gradually became recognized as a Buddhist teaching, allowing it to boost its status to one of the most important traditions of Tibetan Buddhism. This chapter introduces the life and work of Longchen Rabjam, arguably one of the Ancient School's most brilliant teachers, whose systematization radically transformed the Great Perfection in the fourteenth century. As a typical product of Buddhist scholasticism that rose to unprecedented strength during the lifetime of Longchenpa, he employs various strategies in order to assert Dzogchen within the larger Buddhist world, particularly personal experience, philosophical polemic, and commentarial emendations. Furthermore, Longchenpa also had to address two specific indigenous beliefs of the early Great Perfection in order to successfully align it with Buddhist priorities, namely the idea that the quest for vitality was a cyclical process that is based on repeated moments of crisis and recovery, on the one hand, and the closely related idea that vitality constantly oscillates in between different realms, on the other. In response to these challenges, the great scholar invoked the idea of the Buddhist path that leads from *saṃsāra* to *nirvāṇa*, thus dramatically altering the nature of the Dzogchen contemplative system.

Longchenpa and the Systematization of Dzogchen Buddhism

Taking a short look at Longchenpa's biography leaves no doubt that he was a central figure not only in the Dzogchen tradition but also in the history of the Ancient School as a whole.[1] He was born into an aristocratic family that enjoyed a prestigious religious heritage in the valley of Dra (*grwa*) in the eastern part of Central Tibet in 1308. His father, Tänpa Sung (bstan pa srung), was a non-monastic tantric yogi and part of a Nyingma family lineage called Rog, which traced its origins all the way to one of Padmasambhava's twenty-five direct disciples and one of the original seven monks ordained by Śāntarakṣita (Tib. zhi ba 'tsho, 725–788). Longchenpa's lineage from his mother's side, by contrast, was related to Dromtönpa Gyelwa Chungne ('brom ston rgyal ba 'byung gnas, 1005–1064), who was the main disciple of Atiśa Dīpaṃkara Śrījñāna (982–1054) and the founder of the Kadam school. These impressive genealogical affiliations were only buttressed by his early education. After displaying signs of extraordinary intellectual potential, he began his studies at age five under the tutelage of his father. At age twelve, after losing both his parents early in life, he decided to become a monk at Samye, Tibet's oldest monastery. Based on this background and on his studies at Samye, Longchenpa sought for the rest of his existence to express and give voice to the Nyingma vision of Buddhist enlightenment, which—for him—was ultimately rooted in the Great Perfection teachings.

He wrote extensive and systematic commentaries on the previously loosely associated tantras. If the early scriptures read like an assemblage of texts stemming from various authors, composed over decades, and reaching back into an oral tradition stemming from the pre-history of the Tibetan people, the philosophical masterpieces written by Longchenpa strike the reader because of their unprecedented coherence. Consider, for instance, the mythical narratives of cosmogony. The earliest versions of the myth of the Buddha Samantabhadra and the allegories of the little children were abrupt and disjointed in nature, and their true narrativization only took place in the work of Longchenpa.[2] While this thrust toward systematic construction is apparent in many of his writings,[3] it is particularly conspicuous in *The Treasury of the Supreme Vehicle* and *The Treasury of Words and Meanings*,[4] which are entirely devoted to provide a philosophical grasp of the Heart-Essence Great Perfection; with the former being a tightly structured journey through eleven key points, and the latter representing an encyclopedic summary of all philosophical topics conceivable within Dzogchen.[5]

The process of the buddhicization of the Great Perfection, it must be remembered, started much earlier than the fourteenth century. We have seen glimpses of it in the earliest scriptures. Composed in the tenth century, they contain a mixture of Buddhist and indigenous teachings that coexisted simultaneously. The tradition became increasingly Buddhist in the following centuries as scholars started to write exegetical works to elucidate the beliefs and practices in the scriptures, providing the teachings more structure and direction. We have already encountered the name of Zhang Nyima Bum, the twelfth-century teacher, who wrote what is likely the first compressive synthesis of the Heart-Essence Great Perfection. The text, titled *The Eleven Words and Meanings on the Great Perfection*, offers an exegesis of the teachings contained in the tantras and structures them according to eleven themes that are originally mentioned in the root tantra of the Great Perfection, *The Tantra of Unimpeded Sound*. More importantly, Nyima Bum aligns the topics in a sequence intended to offer a comprehensive roadmap to awakening, beginning with the moment of the cosmogony, proceeding with the separation of the ground into the realms of *nirvāṇa* and *saṃsāra*, expanding significantly on the details regarding various practices required for a return, and concluding with the final moment of enlightenment.

There is no doubt that this work—and its outline of a path toward enlightenment—had a significant impact on the later development of the Great Perfection tradition as Longchenpa not only copies his work's elevenfold structure, but also incorporates large portions of his treatise into his own compositions. Since Longchenpa, in his *Treasury of Words and Meanings*, directly appropriates Nyima Bum's path-structure to elaborate his own systematization of the tradition, these two texts offer a thought-provoking opportunity to explore the evolution of the Great Perfection teachings over time.[6] If Nyima Bum was particularly interested in weaving together early scriptures, dynamically molding the teachings so as to bring a coherent structure into them, Longchenpa's writings reveal a different prerogative, namely the harmonization of the Dzogchen teachings with other Buddhist traditions in Tibet. As Yeshi and Dalton recently put it, "by the fourteenth century, Klong chen pa appears to have been less concerned with making the sNying thig tradition cohere with the *Seventeen Tantras* and more with bringing it into line with wider Buddhist norms" (2018, 269).

Longchenpa's systematization must be understood within the context of his age, which was marked by a further intensification of the move toward Buddhist monocentrism in Tibet, manifesting in the rise of a scholastic approach to Buddhism: a movement that was concerned with issues like canonization, standardization, and orthodoxy. After the collapse of the Yarlung dynasty in the mid-ninth century, Tibet was divided into different factions consisting of noble families and clans vying for power. Particularly after Buddhism resurged with full force in the eleventh century, these groups developed a series of different Buddhist schools, frequently in monastic centers that sprung up throughout the Tibetan plateau. Although these large monasteries grew into formidable economic and political powerhouses,[7] they served primarily as centers of learning. While the applicability of this term to the Buddhist context has been debated,[8] there is no doubt that the rise of "scholasticism" during the age of Longchenpa allowed Tibetans to systematize individual traditions through terrific intellectual prowess.[9] The emergence of a self-confident Tibetan academic industry aimed at systematic presentations of the entire range of Indian Buddhist material can be illustrated in numerous near-contemporaries of Longchenpa: Butön Rinchen Drup (bu ston rin chen grub, 1290-1364) codified the Tibetan Buddhist canon, Dölpopa Sherap Gyeltsen (dol po pa shes rab rgyal mtshan, 1292-1361) founded the Jonang (*jo nang*) tradition based on his controversial "extrinsic emptiness" teaching, and Tsongkhapa (tsong kha pa blo bzang grags pa, 1357-1419) established the Gelug School (*dge lugs*) based on his vast learning and a rigorous standard of thought and practice. As the monastic institutions and sects started to define their teachings, the Tibetan religious landscape became less flexible and fluid than in previous centuries.

The fourteenth century was a decisive era in the history of Tibet because it marks the moment when the country took another major step in its monocentric journey toward becoming a thoroughly Buddhist culture. The catalogue of the Buddha's word (*bka' 'gyur*) and the commentaries (*bstan 'gyur*) of Butön—who was himself from a Nyingma background—excluded many core tantras of the Old School because they were judged to be inauthentic—compiled or composed in the Tibetan language in Tibet rather than in India.[10] The same, of course, is true of the other tradition embracing Dzogchen teachings, namely Bön. "The section of the clergy that adhered to apocryphal traditions above and beyond the commonly recognized canon, so Schwieger reminds us, was largely denied any social influence." Particularly the Bönpo, who "did not recognize the Buddhist canon as binding and produced their own canon in response to the canonization of Buddhist texts," were "socially marginalized" (Schwieger 2013, 67). The scholastic turn was part of a larger process of systematization of religious traditions that had profound consequences for the self-conception of Tibetan culture as fundamentally Buddhist. "Tibet evolved into a religion-centric culture unified by Mahāyāna Buddhism in its special form of Vajrayāna, perceived generally nowadays as a 'unique culture.' This view is enhanced by the fact that the clerical Tibetan elite began distinguishing themselves from others by narrating a coherent history of common origin, common fate, and a common project of salvation" (Schwieger 2015, 8).

In this sense, Longchenpa's lasting impact lies not only in his systematization of the Great Perfection teachings, but also in how he managed to integrate the teachings into self-aware and explicitly Buddhist religious tradition on par with the most powerful sects of Tibetan Buddhism. Giving it a public face, Longchenpa "was for the *Rdzogs chen* school what St. Thomas Aquinas was for Christian scholastic philosophy" (Smith 2001, 16). As van Schaik puts it,

> Longchenpa set down, in a coherent and systematic form, the miscellaneous and heterogenous doctrines and practices contained in the Heart-Essence collections. In lengthy discourses he attempted to place these materials in the context in which he felt they belonged, that is, as the supreme method of Buddhist practice, not only for the Nyingma, but for all of the Tibetan schools. He attempted to secure this place for the Heart-Essence by relating it to the Indian heritage (especially the Madhyamaka and Yogacara) and to the interpretations of the tantras found in the new schools, thus giving the Great Perfection an acceptable place in the Tibetan Buddhist milieu of the fourteenth century. (Van Schaik 2004b, 10)[11]

Besides being a uniquely gifted individual, Longchenpa was also able to perform this type of harmonization of his tradition with the larger Buddhist teachings because he cultivated extensive contact with other systems of thought and practice present on the plateau. In fact, the lifetime of the great yogi was not only a time in which scholastic philosophers rose to prominence, but also one that has been described as "peripatetic, as students travelled from monastery to monastery taking instruction in various topics from many different teachers, seeking out those renowned as having special expertise in a particular text or lineage of teaching" (Napper 2003, 5). Longchenpa's life displays his strong ties to other sectarian traditions populating the Tibetan plateau. A few years after receiving his ordination at Samye, Longchenpa entered Sangphu Neütok (gsang phu ne'u thog), one of the most famous monasteries of the New Schools and he clearly valued a variety of religious traditions and practices, such as "mind training" (*blo sbyong*), the "path and the result" (*lam 'bras*), Mahāmudrā (*phyag chen*), or the Shangpa Kagyü (*shangs pa bka' brgyud*). He maintained active correspondence with eminent figures belonging to other Buddhist systems, most prominently, the Karma Kagyü hierarch Rangjung Dorje (rang 'byung rdo rje, 1284–1339) and Sönam Gyaltsen, the Sakya Lama Dampa (bsod nams rgyal mtshan sa skya pa bla ma dam pa, 1312–1375).

Strategies for the Buddhicization of Dzogchen

Considering how profoundly indigenous the beliefs and practices of early Dzogchen presented themselves in *The Seventeen Tantra*, there is no doubt that Longchenpa's participation in the push toward a Buddhist monocentrism had many far-reaching consequences for the tradition and lastingly altered its interpretation. Many of these changes are a direct result of the scholastic age during which he composed his writings. Consider, for instance, the status of the scriptures, which changed dramatically in the time between Nyima Bum's exegesis in the twelfth century and Longchenpa's commentaries in the fourteenth century. While the former cites them with much flexibility, pulling lines from different parts of the various texts to create a sort of *bricolage*, Longchenpa's commentaries regard the scriptures as less open to reinterpretation and reorganization. In his commentaries, one gets the distinct sense that *The Seventeen Tantras* are a concrete entity, a closed collection of scriptures. Canonization, indeed, is one of the most marking traits of established Buddhist monocentrism in Tibet. "By committing themselves to its canon," so Schwieger remarks, "the members of the Buddhist clergy had finally cemented a monocentric culture in place" (2013, 67).

As a tradition with an uncertain historical pedigree, endowed with scriptural sources that claim antiquity despite having only been revealed during the late tenth century, Longchenpa needed to perform a paradoxical operation if he wanted to assert his tradition within the larger universe of Buddhist traditions in Tibet: On the one hand, he needed to establish the uniqueness of his tradition by distinguishing it from other schools on the plateau; on the other hand, he was forced to insert his rather idiosyncratic tradition within the canon of monocentric Buddhism that was further solidified by the rise of the scholastic tradition. Longchenpa accomplished this dual task by means of a series of strategies, with three specific techniques standing out in my own readings of his corpus: an appeal to personal experience (that can take on an aggressive tone toward his internal and external adversaries), the sparking of philosophical polemics (that frequently take on melodramatic moods), and commentarial emendations (that lack any sort of explicit acknowledgment).

While Longchenpa continued a trend that was present already in the early Dzogchen scriptures, where the rejection of the practices of the other vehicles was commonplace (Van Schaik 2004b, 76–7), he emblazoned his tradition's status with an unprecedented appeal to his own meditative and scholarly accomplishments. Despite the vastness of his work, Longchenpa has a peculiar way to bring up controversy in his writings, which manifests in the relentless wielding of a particular formula of gravitas, namely "this is an extremely important point" (*gnad 'di gal che ba, chings gal po che*) that is frequently tied to his own experience as scholar-yogi. In a particularly illustrative passage, he remarks that "while such key points (*gnad*) are explained in the Great Perfection, nowadays, I alone have clearly realized it, and thus understood how to interpret these tenets. This is an extremely important point" (*The Treasury of Words and Meanings*, 429.2).[12] Unlike *The Seventeen Tantras*, which are said to have been authored by transcendent Buddhas, Longchenpa embodies here the preceptor of perfection, who proclaims the truth based on his own meditative achievements and intellectual insights.[13] Imbued with the idea of primordial freedom, Longchenpa's compositions are particularly scolding toward any sort of goal-oriented, intentional, and dualistic mindset, whether it be practical, psychological, or epistemological. Longchenpa accuses all other approaches of relying on the construction by "architects" (*bzo bo*),[14] and warns Dzogchen practitioners against creating outlines for contemplative exercises, structures of doctrinal thinking, or elaborate systematic treatises.

By the time of Longchenpa, the Old School availed itself of Atiyoga practice, particularly Tögal, in order to assert its own vision of meditation in response to the techniques of the earlier tantric traditions. It is, indeed, legitimate to distinguish Skullward Leap from the practices of other tantric traditions,[15] as they operate according to a different logic. One central element of distinction is the Great Perfection's emphasis on naturalness in its teachings. For instance, in *The Seventeen Tantras* we find passages that associate esoteric tantric teachings with ordinary human activities. One example is the treatment of the classical tantric ritual practices involved in the so-called propitiation and accomplishment (Tib. *bsnyen sgrub*; Skt. *sevā-sādhana*). If "propitiation" generally involves the making of offerings and the recitation of mantras aiming at the empowerment of the practitioner and "accomplishment" means the directing of this power toward a specific goal of the ritual activity, *The Pearl Necklace Tantra* correlates them to prosaic activities. Here, the "approach" and the "evocation" correspond to "eating and drinking" as well as "sleeping and sitting" (*The Pearl Necklace Tantra*, 445.5). In other words, in the early Heart-Essence scriptures, the ritualistic practices like the recitation of the mantra of the *yidam* and the visualization according to the *sādhana* are transformed into the most ordinary of our activities, such as eating and sitting. In the same tantra, we find a passage that identifies ordinary human movement with regulated tantric activities: "The paths of wanderers are visualized as the great lines of visualization, their footprints are the designs of colored powders (of the *maṇḍala*), the urge to move is the posture (of the deity), while the movements of the bodily limbs are the *mudrās*" (*The Pearl Necklace Tantra*, 446.5).[16] Here too, exercises that are usually esoteric, ritualistic, and complicated in nature are identified with our ability to walk, one of the most ordinary and fundamental of all human activities.[17]

Moreover, in contradistinction to deity yoga, which focuses on the generation of buddhas and their body images, the Great Perfection proffers its very own form of visionary encounters with deities. Instead of basing themselves on *sādhanas* that involve the intentional, painstaking, and repetitive visualization of specifically chosen deities with their particular characteristics,[18] Tögal visions are said to manifest spontaneously as the Buddha-nature is already present within the practitioner's body. Longchenpa explicitly distinguishes Skullward Leap from the "contrived" (*bcos ma*) visualizations of the "generation phase" practices by his repeated call for procedures and visualizations that are "spontaneous" (*lhun grub*), "free from action" (*bya bral*), and "without elaboration" (*spros med*). Thus, while the generation phase visualization is controlled and patterned, the vision of deities in Skullward Leap discloses themselves spontaneously. Dzogchen meditation also differs dramatically from perfection phase practices.[19] Longchenpa differentiates between the visual appearances of seminal nuclei, which form the core of the practice of Skullward Leap, on the one hand, and analogous manifestations of light that present themselves in the context of other Tibetan Buddhist tantric practices, on the other (*The Treasury of the Supreme Vehicle*, vol. II: 103). These tantric techniques—which can be found both in the *anuttarayoga* of the New Schools and the *anuyoga* texts of the Old School—emphasize the role of the *ḍākinī*, the various blisses, and the channels, drops, and winds, and rely on forceful techniques, such as vase breathing.[20] From a Dzogchen perspective, these "lower vehicles" embrace a model of practice that could be defined as "executive" as the transformation of the meditator happens in a top-down fashion through the manipulation of the subtle body.[21] Meditation, in this sense, is largely a process of habituation with the conscious mind gradually transforming the operation of the unconscious mind.

By contrast, Longchenpa presents Skullward Leap as a spontaneous technique that involves no effort, no repetition, and physical manipulation beyond the preliminary practices and the exceedingly simple key points. In his critique of other tantric techniques, Longchenpa speaks once again of "an extremely important point," noting that some people, "in training on the conventional [seminal nuclei], advocate many strenuous yogic exercises and binding visualizations practices, while asserting that the fruit of such training is the bliss and emptiness of depth-contemplation within the coarse body" (*The Treasury of Words and Meanings*, 259.3).[22] In *The Treasury of the Supreme Vehicle*, he makes a very similar distinction, noting that while the "direct path of the Mantrayāna (*gsang sngags*) is a method that is strenuous, elaborate, and in agreement with the key points of the channels, winds, and seminal nuclei," Skullward Leap is "effortless and free from elaboration" (*The Treasury of the Supreme Vehicle*, vol. I: 407.2).[23]

Besides his occasional personal critiques, largely premised on his claim to superior experiential access to the truth through contemplative practice, Longchenpa also relied on a second strategy, namely the reference to philosophical polemics. One such debate is the axiomatic distinction between the "ordinary mind" (*sems*) and "wisdom" (*ye shes*). Accordingly, this distinction has been identified as the central organizing trope by David Higgins, who claims that "an assessment of Klong chen pa's extant corpus reveals the mind/primordial knowing distinction to be a central and unifying theme in the author's rDzogs chen writings" (2013, 21). Higgins also notes that Longchenpa not only returned "again and again" to this matter, but also characterized it as "extremely important" (21–2). While "mind" designates the neurotic and dualistic way of thinking of non-enlightened human beings, "primordial wisdom" stands for an ever-present (*ye*) type of intelligence. In a passage from Longchenpa's *Treasury of Words and Meanings*, we read:

> The illusory appearances of the mind's objects are the phenomena of *saṃsāra* and summarized into six aspects: form, sound, smell, taste, touch, and phenomena. All of these manifest from the mind's karmic propensities like various strands of hair (i.e. optical illusions). If one wonders why they appear, they manifest because of the confused mind. Conversely, the object of wisdom is the sky-like pure reality of vast and luminous appearances of pure-land presences of spiritual bodies and wisdom. (239.1)[24]

Another one of Longchenpa's most effective ways to assert his tradition's distinctiveness within the canon of Buddhist teachings was the comparison between a simultaneist approach that promises immediate enlightenment based on already perfected qualities, on the one hand, and a gradualist approach based on the step-by-step cultivation that culminates in enlightenment, on the other.[25] Scholarship has rightly noted that Longchenpa's portrayal of Dzogchen has strong simultaneist impulses.[26] Exemplified by the open blue sky, Longchenpa's Great Perfection styles itself as beyond conceptualization and systematization ("see the view of no viewing"), beyond meditation and practice ("train in the meditation with nothing meditated upon"), and beyond morality and ethics ("carry out the conduct of nondoing").[27] This simultaneist tendency is also present in the common translation of *thod rgal* as "Direct Transcendence," clearly implying that the practice offers some sort of shortcut, a direct access to enlightenment without having to follow a long path of transformation. According to the Dzogchen master, Skullward Leap is a meditation that values contemplative experience (*nyams su len pa*) rather than blindly following the standardized itinerary laid out by the "tenet system" of religious schools and institutions (*The Treasury of Words and Meanings*, 163.2). Longchenpa speaks of the highest Dzogchen practice as the falling away of any "frame of reference" (*gtad so med*) and specifies that it is the moment when "ordered gradual steps of 'things to do' do no longer exist," and "only openness, relaxation, and vastness exist" (*Relaxation in the Nature of the Mind*, vol. II: 167.2).[28]

It is because of such challenges that Longchenpa's work operates under a "dual logic": On the one hand, it embraces primordial freedom and celebrates it as its primary innovation; on the other hand, it has to immediately raise protective walls around it, not only from challenges raised by other traditions but also because of the very logic contained in primordial freedom. Consider, for instance, the paragraph from *The Treasury of Words and Meanings* cited above. Reading passages such as this one, it is undeniable that the radical emphasis on "appearances" (*snang ba*) as something that is "free"—in the sense that it can either be the cause for straying or for enlightenment—entails a fundamental risk for the Great Perfection tradition. Just as with the idea that one can construct a religious tradition without outlines and architecture, or that one can practice meditation without applying effort, the emphasis on naturally manifesting appearances could ultimately lead to the dissipation of the Dzogchen tradition. Longchenpa himself is acutely aware of this dilemma. He cerebrates on this problem, commenting that while many people claim that "since these appearances manifest as illusions, it would follow that radiant light is an illusionary appearance." He explains that "since these appearances commonly manifest in the minds of ordinary sentient beings, it would follow that clear light also commonly manifests." "However," he elaborates, "if you believe that, then it would follow that all beings are freed just like great practitioners." (*The Treasury of Words and Meanings*, 239.4)[29] A few lines below, Longchenpa's writing takes on a more aggressive tone, leaving no doubt to what extent he was willing to defend the ethos of freedom from potential distortions.

> To expand on this, these days common fools say: "Appearances are your own mind!" Visions are the Reality Body! Primordial wisdom (*ye shes*) is the mind (*sems*)! There is no difference between such people and the lunatics, who say whatever comes to their mind: "My head is my butt! Fire is water! Darkness is illumination." (240.6)[30]

Longchenpa, in some instances, even invokes the language of incarceration reminiscent of the mythical substratum studied in the first part of this book to impugn his opponents. "In brief," he concludes his tirade against anyone questioning the preeminence of wisdom and its appearances, "those who make these absurd claims resemble a herd of bulls that should be put into a single corral, since they are not even worthy to be defeated through scriptural citation or logical reasoning" (242.1).[31] Through such examples it becomes apparent that Longchenpa succeeded in systematizing his tradition through a paradoxical operation, which sets itself apart from other schools by rejecting any sort of structure, while simultaneously proposing a sequential path toward enlightenment. Despite his radical repudiation of any sort of architectonic effort, Longchenpa himself became his tradition's greatest architect.

While the polemics raised by Longchenpa generally address legitimate issues in his attempt to grapple with his tradition and its place within the Buddhist universe, I must confess that all this high-flung philosophical discourse seems at times theatrical to me, particularly if we consider that the texts that he is interpreting are filled with more flamboyantly non-Buddhist elements. In fact, even though Longchenpa himself never expresses such thoughts, the idea that whatever "appears" next in our journey through life can be either good or bad, requiring us to remain ever-vigilant in light of new challenges despite moments of peace and prosperity, is clearly a core principle of the cyclical and dialectical worldview of pre-Buddhist Tibetans. Consequently, I would like to propose that some of these controversial philosophical debates might have served as a sort of distraction.

Couldn't it be that this rather melodramatic defense of a self-constructed fortress of freedom might also represent a tactical move that served to distract from the presence of non-Buddhist tendencies in his tradition? In fact, it is not only striking that the issue of the overwhelmingly present indigenous motifs found throughout the earlier parts of this study finds no place within Longchenpa's discussions, but it is equally suspect that some of the controversies he raises seem to be self-fulfilling prophesies.

Let us look at another example of this, namely the discrepancy between Longchenpa's extensive writing campaign, which is fundamentally exploited for a single purpose: to tout the benefits of non-conceptual experience. Indeed, Atiyoga claims its place on top of the Buddhist hierarchy by explicitly distinguishing itself from the eight earlier vehicles with the assertion that true understanding is not gained through study and reflection, but rather through direct realization of the nature of the mind itself. Awareness, according to the Great Perfection, is "non-conceptual" (Skt. *nirvikalpa;* Tib. *rnam par mi rtog pa*), which means that it lies beyond the discursive intellect.[32] Lonchenpa reprimands anyone who performs the function of the architect of any sort while clearly being the most constructive exponent of his entire tradition. Sometimes, this polemical style takes on bizarre forms as in *The Adamantine Song of Definitive Examples and Meaning*, where he compares "philosophical positions" (*grub mtha'*) to the "spittle of worms" (*srin gyi kha chu*), reasoning that they lead us "to ensnare our very own existence" (223.1). The assertion is grotesque, of course, because he is the famed redactor of a text entitled *The Treasury of Philosophical Systems*. Germano even suggests that "the Heart-Essence literature is clearly a genre of philosophical tantra that is systematic, complex and extremely architectonic" (1994, 297). This "genre of literature," so he continues, "is scholastic not only in its clear love for language and thought for its own sake, but also in its intense structuration with analytical internal outlines" (298). While Longchenpa embraces a rhetoric of open and unstructured space, his most decisive legacy is his extremely structured treatises, which make him the unquestioned architect of the Great Perfection tradition.

In this same vein, we could consider that the repeated discussion regarding the gradualist and simultaneist paths to enlightenment might be part of a similar strategy. In fact, is there a better way to distract from the fact that we are dealing with a tradition with a non-Buddhist origin than by reproducing an older Tibetan debate where a seemingly unorthodox tradition (the simultaneist) became part of the canon of Buddhism (even if it might have been defeated during the debate by the Buddhist orthodoxy from India)? I believe that it might be more than a coincidence that Longchenpa's writings rehash the eighth-century debate held at Samye, the monastery where he received his education as a young monk. The episode at Samye is a crucial moment in the introduction of Buddhism to Tibet. During the deabte, the possibility of an "instantaneous" form of enlightenment proposed by the Chinese monk Heshang Moheyan was opposed by the proponents of the "gradualist" approach expressed by the Indian master, Kamalaśīla. Even though most Tibetan sources, basing their accounts on *The Testament of Ba*, pronounced Kamalaśīla the victor, it might be more relevant to remark on the fact that this debate provided religious traditions on the margins, such as Longchenpa's Heart-Essence Great Perfection, a model to articulate their place within the Buddhist world of Tibet. If Gidi Ifergan even goes as far as to contend that Longchenpa established a liaison between Dzogchen and the teachings of Heshang Moheyan,[33] I believe that what really matters is not his position or even who won the debate, but rather that the mere invocation of the polemic associated with the debate at the oldest Tibetan monastery inserts Longchenpa's controversial tradition within the fold of Buddhism. I think it is fair to say that at least some of the discussion surrounding the issue of primordial freedom takes on melodramatic tones in the sense that it creates an exaggerated drama that likely serves to distract from more fundamental challenges. Longchenpa defends primordial freedom at all costs, while simultaneously knowing that it leads to an untenable teaching from the point of view of a religious tradition that insists on the existence of a linear path of transformation culminating in a state of enlightenment. Put differently, I suggest that the explicit polemic regarding instantaneous versus gradualist forms of enlightenment might have received such an eminent position within the development of the Great Perfection because it served as a sort of distraction from much more problematic issues regarding its teachings.

Let us now look at a third type of strategy employed in Longchenpa's writings, which points to the possibility that he had not tried to distract from certain issues, but actively suppressed—or at least altered—them. A pertinent example of this type of strategy can be found in his discussion of the physical pressing of the eyes to stimulate the initial appearance of the visions, which I discussed in some detail in Chapter 5. Longchenpa, without acknowledging this emendation, offers his meditative instructions with a slight modification regarding the textual citation from an old tantra that he uses to bolster his argument. In commenting on a portion of *The Absence of Letters Tantra*, where the practitioner is instructed to "press the eyes firmly" in order to stimulate the manifestation of the linked sheep, Longchenpa writes: "The esoteric precept of the placement of awareness involves a slight pressing of the eyes while gazing to the side" (*The Treasury of Words and Meanings*, 386.2). The ever so subtle substitution of the adverb preceding the term "to press" from "firmly" (*rab tu*) to "slightly" (*rtsam*) is likely not due to a lapse of attention but rather an assertion of Longchenpa's very own priorities over the scriptural materials at his disposal. The amended adverbial qualification tones down the activist and vitalizing stance of the original scripture and gives the instruction a more "naturalist" connotation.[34]

Another example of this strategy can be found in Longchenpa's discussion of the contemplative practices. As in Nyima Bum's *Eleven Words and Meanings on The Great Perfection*, Longchenpa dedicates the entire eighth chapter to his presentation of the various practices available to the Dzogchen meditator. In both texts, furthermore, the contemplative chapter is by far the largest of the eleven topics discussed. While Longchenpa reproduces many of the elements—not only the overall structure of his work, but also many textual citations and his overall discussion—from his predecessor, he obfuscates one of the most glaringly indigenous references in Nyima Bum's work. In fact, if the twelfth-century exegete makes two references to the behavior of deer and explains how the early tantras instruct the yogi to imitate the behavior of a wounded deer, fleeing alone into an isolated place, Longchenpa makes no reference to such animals in his commentaries. While we have no way of knowing whether Longchenpa's emendations were intentional, it is quite apparent that both the pressing of the eyes and the acting out of deer-like behavior—both of which have shown to be of central importance to the conception of vitality in the early tradition—gradually lost importance as the tradition became more and more assimilated to Buddhism.

It is for this reason that my discussion of certain "strategies" employed by Longchenpa needs to be put into a wider perspective. It is tempting to attribute individual historical actors, particularly those of the stature of Longchenpa, with unlimited agency, However, it is important to remember that they are always part of a larger epoch that determines their own range of expression. While the idea that the Dzogchen tradition might have exaggerated certain polemical debates in order to distract from more substantial objections is certainly intriguing and likely holds some truth, it should also not be overlooked that the Great Perfection tradition also has simply forgotten certain elements of its past by the fourteenth century. Peter Schwieger points to this possibility by commenting on the combination between the rise of Buddhist monocentrism, the canonization of orthodox beliefs, and the falling into oblivion of indigenous influences:

> Just as the various clans vied with each other to gain new esoteric Buddhist teachings from India, various distinct Buddhist traditions were established in Tibet. However, unlike the European Renaissance, the Tibetan "rebirth process" did not result in a liberation from traditional and religious fetters but in an increasing canonization of beliefs and views. Compared to the period of the Tibetan kingdom, the horizon became narrow and closed. Whole segments of the world, once part of the Tibetan sphere of interaction, were simply forgotten. (Schwieger 2015, 7–8).

Traces of the Quest for Vitality

As these examples show, Longchenpa never directly mentions the pre-Buddhist heritage of his tradition, and the polemics he raises frequently seem far removed from an early Tibetan world so deeply imbued by the quest for vitality. Nonetheless, a careful analysis of his writings reveals that traces of this earlier worldview likely persisted into the fourteenth century. In light of the unstoppable rise of Buddhist monocentrism, Longchenpa apparently felt compelled to deal with two specific issues that arise out of the pre-Buddhist heritage of his tradition, namely the question whether the Dzogchen path can be circular or whether it must lead to the definitive goal of *nirvāṇa*, on the one hand, and the dispute about whether our mobile vitality principle is divisible or not, on the other. As for the first issue, Khenpo Yeshi and Jacob Dalton have recently pointed to a fundamental tension in Longchenpa's discussion of the final moment of enlightenment. They note that

Nyima Bum's discussion of the eleven topics is circular in nature as the state of enlightenment leads the practitioner back to the initial moment of the ground before its manifestation. In an important passage in Longchenpa's *Treasury of the Supreme Vehicle*, we read:

> Saying that [Samantabhadra] liberates right within the ground is clumsy. He is liberated when the ground's manifestation dawns out of the ground. He is liberated at the moment of raising up from the ground. Where is he liberated? Saying he is liberated back into the ground is also clumsy. He is liberated in the place of spontaneously present completion. If he were liberated back into the ground, he might relapse [back into to *saṃsāra*], because that ground has been posited as that within which confusion can occur, that is, because it is the ground of both *saṃsāra* and *nirvāṇa*. Suppose one says, "in the line, 'the place of liberation itself is the beginning,' isn't this ground the beginning [ground]?" One can explain the way of abiding as the beginning, but it is not the ground of the first [topic]. In short, when one recognizes one's own face (rang ngo shes), one completes the good qualities of the sphere, whereby one is liberated into fruition through being devoid of obscurations. (*The Treasury of the Supreme Vehicle*, translated in Yeshi and Dalton [2018, 266])

If Nyima Bum is amenable to the idea that the final moment is not that final—in the sense that it leaves open a door for a renewed descent into the world of *saṃsāra*—Longchenpa defends a different and much more orthodox model of Buddhahood. According to his understanding, enlightenment cannot be identical to the ground because this would allow for the possibility that a Buddha could stray back into the world of *saṃsāra*. Longchenpa's problem can be rearticulated as a need for a Buddhist path. In fact, if the end is just like the beginning, then why would one even become a Buddhist? Longchenpa's linear view, however, does not necessarily reflect the priorities of Nyima Bum or the teachings contained in *The Seventeen Tantras*. As Yeshi and Dalton put it, "In many respects, this more linear view does not fit comfortably with the overall narrative of the eleven words and meanings, which were originally intended as a history of buddhas that never really goes anywhere. Nyi ma 'bum's history that ends where it begins is a narrative non-event, and as such it threatens to undo the entire rationale for the Buddhist path" (2018, 268–9).

While it might not be compatible with a Buddhist approach to enlightenment, the idea of circularity is a core principle in the indigenous worldview of Tibetans. Let us remember that the mythical quests for vitality are fundamentally repetitive in nature. These narratives are frequently packaged within each other so that one begins where the last one left off; moreover, the stories oftentimes culminate in the same identical setting in which they started. Thus, although the quest for vitality was successful, inasmuch as a kingdom that was once prosperous and then lost its vitality is restored to its old glory because of the endeavors of the young adventurers, the story remains fundamentally unfinished. This same tension, of course, is reinforced in the ritual-contemplative practices. Not only are these practices reproducing the logic of circularity by perpetually replaying the quest for vitality outlined in the mythical narratives, but they are also themselves culminating in a state of ambiguity. We have encountered this ambiguity in the constant precariousness of vitality as something that can be gained and lost, protected and stolen, pursued and struggled for. Although Skullward Leap repairs the lost connection between the realm of the earth and the heavens by means of a visionary journey that externalizes the embodied substances from within the yogic body into their original "home" in the sky, this conduit is not secured for perpetuity, but requires repetitive moments of revitalization. In its indigenous incarnation, the goal of Tögal practice was not the reaching of a final state of liberation. Just as a hunter does not return home to retire but to temporarily feed his family before embarking on his next mission, the meditator's adventurous quest for vitality would only be a short episode in an ever-repeating cycle—the perpetual process of overcoming moments of crisis and searching for solutions.

The persistence of a pre-Buddhist logic in the Great Perfection also surfaces in other passages of Longchenpa's expansive writings, most prominently in the question whether the mobile vitality principle is divisible. This would allow the yogis to temporarily project themselves into a heavenly realm before returning fully into their bodies. He engages this controversial issue in passages dedicated to a minor detail of the Dzogchen subtle body, namely the eyes. Longchenpa, in *The Treasury of Words and Meanings*, mentions that "some claim that the eyes are bigger than the body, and that the roots [of the eyes] are slender and their tops are vast." In light of the description of the luminous channels resembling the horns of sheep leading to the sky explored in the previous chapter, this interpretation does not sound all that far-fetched. Longchenpa, however, derides these opponents by stating that such people are "not well-versed in orthography" and that their comments consist of "words uttered without thinking, inconsiderate talk without rhyme or reason!" (248.5–249.1).[35]

Longchenpa's outrage seems to be particularly focused on an enigmatic expression used to describe the eyes, namely *phul thag*. Indeed, in one of the early scriptures, *The Mirror of the Heart of Vajrasattva*, we find a mysterious sentence, which explains that while the body is "the size of a mustard seed, … the eyes are the size of a *phul thag*" (334.5). Although we have no way of knowing for certain what this term originally meant, it is significant to note that Longchenpa's attitude toward this notion is rather bizarre: He discusses it repeatedly in a virulent tone while simultaneously offering a banal answer to elucidate the seemingly "true" meaning of the term. He proposes that the term *phul thag* is "an old local term (*yul skad rnying pa*) meaning proportionate (*'tshams pa*)" (248.5–249.1).[36] Even though Germano rightly observes that we are dealing here with a "controversial term" (1992, 922), scholarship has generally just accepted Longchenpa's translation at face value,[37] ignoring the fact that this term points quite possibly to the pre-Buddhist heritage of the tradition.

Although the term has multiple possible translations, I believe that *phul* invokes the meaning of something that is conceived to be "highest."[38] The term, indeed, likely has this same role in a series of other mysterious early Tibetan notions, such as *phul med* (a term used to indicate the pinnacle of royal tombs)[39] or *mthong phul* (an expression connected to the view of the sky).[40] In accordance with this terminology, the word can be deciphered as a reference to the "highest" part of the human body that is closest to the realm of the sky, namely the eyes. Just like in Dzogchen anatomy, where the eyes represented the "top" of the body, the Tibetan fascination with the sky also involved a prioritization of the top of architectural structures, particularly the top opening of buildings. The sky—and its close association with light—led Tibetans to an isomorphism between the macrocosm of dwellings and the microcosm of the human body. The architectural structures like windows and roof holes fulfilled a parallel function to the eyes and the sinciput of the yogis. Light, quite intuitively, is essential not only for our perceptual processes as photoreceptors in our retinas detect light, but also for architectural reasons as the sky allowed for the penetration of light and the exiting of smoke in ancient Tibetan dwellings.

This likely meaning of the word *phul* as a sort of gateway to the luminous and ethereal realm of the sky is further cemented by another significance of the term that has been pointed out by Dan Martin, namely "expelling or driving out."[41] It seems that this interpretation of the term was prominent during the time of Longchenpa as the Buddhist master continues his critical commentary on the scriptural passage on *phul thag* as follows: "If they claim that the eyes are like that, [meaning] that they diffuse out from the body, this would have the faulty consequence that the eyes would be unrelated to the body, or that the eyes would become detached" (*The Treasury of Words and Meanings*, 249.1).[42] Collectively, these allusions suggest that the term *phul thag* was associated with a form of teleportation or transference of consciousness into the sky that seems to have been propagated by some early practitioners of Skullward Leap.[43] Elsewhere in the same text, we find a passage in which he chooses to expand on the expression phul thag. This is without a doubt a rather remarkable moment in his commentarial work as the scriptural passage he analyzes does not even mention the term; highlighitng just how controversial this issue must have been for Longchenpa. He writes:

> As for the explanation that the body is the size of a mustard seed and the eyes the size of a *phul thag*, *phul thag* should be understood as an ancient term meaning "proportionate." When explaining this term, some say that wisdom undergoes transference (*'pho ba*), such as increasing through the wind. If consciousness were to be ejected, then body and mind would be rent apart. (*Treasury of Words and Meanings*, 232.5–6)[44]

Longchenpa's claim to a linguistically superior translation based on an "old local term" might at first seem rather puzzling. However, upon closer analysis, his intervention repeats the modus operandi of examples found in this chapter. Just as previously, where Longchenpa's commentaries struck us with dual-logic of his attempts at defending the boundaries of freedom, his reinforcement of the Buddhist nature of Dzogchen is marked by a profound paradox: He defends his tradition as Buddhist and rejects its indigenous pre-Buddhist heritage by invoking an old and local linguistic knowledge to which he claims to have access.

What Longchenpa—as an eminent exponent of Buddhist monocentrism—does and cannot address in his analysis is that the term can be recognized as an old local term for an entirely different reason: The underlying logic of the pre-Buddhist religion of Tibet would allow for the ejection and projection of our consciousness without "body and mind being rent apart." Unlike the dominant Buddhist traditions on the Tibetan plateau, where the soul is emphasized as being singular, with one consciousness belonging to each individual being, the indigenous conception of vitality allows for multiplicity and mobility. As Huber puts it in the case of the Himalayan highland populations, humans have "multiple souls–nine, seven, six, five and three are the more common enumerations—or a soul that is a divisible entity and which can thus exist simultaneously in different locations as 'divisibles'" (Huber 2020, vol. II: 71). It is precisely this multiplicity of the mobile vitality principle that allows the shamans—as well as the forgotten yogis of Dzogchen—to undertake a journey while their bodies remain stationary (Huber 2020, vol. I: 257). If we add to this multiplicity of vitality everything that we have heard so far about the Great Perfection body, its understanding of perception, and the mythical-ritual topos of the vertical vitality descending and ascending through the sky-cord, then the term *phul thag* most definitely does not mean that the eyes are "proportionate" to the overall size of the yogi's body. Instead, the expression *phul thag* points to a pre-Buddhist belief in a cord-like structure made of light—think back at the kings' sky-rope (*rmu thag*)—which was not only associated with the culminating point of our bodily limits (the eyes and head), but also carried within it the potential to expel some parts of the meditators into the higher reality of a sky-realm, the heavenly homes of their ancestors.

In the context of indigenous Tibetan religion, Longchenpa's objection that a teleportation of consciousness would necessarily lead to the death of the practitioner is no more valid than his objection to the spiritual path being circular. According to pre-Buddhist Tibetan beliefs, vitality is not only marked by an inherent ambiguity that makes a final passing into some state beyond ambiguity a non sequitur, but it is also marked by an inherent multiplicity, divisibility, and distributiveness. In the indigenous quest for vitality, emissaries leave their own realms to search for vitality, hunt its most powerful properties, and appropriate its precious substances to distribute their life-sustaining energies within the realm of humans. Based on this plurality of vitality, the indigenous Tibetan religion could be described as an immanentist tradition according to which a loss of consciousness, or a projection of parts of oneself into another realm does not represent a radical ontological break, but rather a minor alteration within a much larger flow of cosmic vitality. Longchenpa's Buddhist conception, by contrast, is much more akin to a transcendentalist understanding of religion according to which such a "temporary teleportation" is simply not possible because it would represent a fundamental rupture (i.e., death) as "consciousness" departs the body.[45]

Regardless of the details, many of which will have to remain a mystery without new textual evidence, Longchenpa's interpretative maneuverings surrounding the term *phul thag* point toward the Great Perfection's struggles to maintain a Buddhist identity in light of the overwhelming presence of pre-Buddhist ideas and practices. Indeed, it is highly probable that the indigenous Tibetan anthro-cosmology as well as the practice of projecting one's consciousness into the sky were still present many centuries after the conversion of Dzogchen to Buddhism as this is the most plausible reason for the great master's repeated wrangling with a term that simply means "proportionate." While it is by no means clear whether Longchenpa's interpretations are innocent "re-readings" or intentional "mis-readings" of earlier scriptures, there is no doubt that his exegesis exerted some form of textual violence onto the *Seventeen Tantras*. It is also certain that while Longchenpa was "responsible for the revitalization of the Heart-Essence tradition" (Van Schaik 2004b, 9), his reinforcing of the bulwark of freedom brought with it the risk of harming the integrity of the tradition.[46] Put differently, Longchenpa's systematizing activity had critical intra-sectarian consequences as it redefined the tradition itself, curbing some of the indigenous vitality that nourished the tradition from the inception. By staking out the boundaries of freedom to protect his tradition from the competing forces on the plateau, the architect of the Great Perfection pinned the openness of the indigenous Tibetan sky onto the ground of a very Buddhist reality. Crafting blueprints out of the playfulness of light, he turned luminous formations that once carried life-sustaining energies in between distant worlds into solid walls imbued with ontological rigidity.

Chapter 8

THE INTRODUCTIONS BETWEEN LANGUAGE AND VITALITY

If the previous chapter has shown that Longchenpa's scholastic systematization of the Dzogchen system was a success inasmuch as it transformed it into a widely celebrated teaching on the Tibetan plateau, whose status as an expression of Indian Buddhist thought was less exposed to serious debate, his endeavors simultaneously cut off some of the religious tradition's vitality. At the same time, however, we have seen how many pre-Buddhist themes—such as the circularity of the spiritual path, or the mobility of our vitality—continued to be widespread in the tradition until at least the fourteenth century. This chapter takes a closer look at the Great Perfection's use of language—also that of the great scholar Longchenpa—and shows that it immortalizes the fundamental dialectical nature within the contemplative system, even in its most Buddhist instantiation. Whether the language is used for systematic treatises on Dzogchen doctrines, mythical narratives, poetic musings, simple metaphors, or apparently meaningless syllables, it carries a dual function within it: On the one hand, it sets up a wall between text and experience; on the other hand, it functions like a ledge, a launchpad from which readers can catapult themselves out of the text to dive into more expansive experiences. This becomes particularly evident in my discussion of what is likely the Great Perfection's most effective tool to revitalize contemplative experiences out of linguistic concepts, namely the "introductions" (*ngo sprod pa*). Describing the process of pointing out the nature of mind, the "introductions" perfectly illustrate the liminal nature of Dzogchen language that allows for a fluid movement between linguistic concept and meditative experience. Since the introductions can be interpreted as a re-evocation of previously attained meditative experience, either by the teacher offering the instruction or even by the disciples themselves, they also point to a fundamentally circular nature of the Dzogchen path itself.

Experience and Language in Dzogchen Buddhism

Language has a paradoxical status in Buddhism. On the one hand, Buddhists are critical of language because ultimate reality is ineffable and therefore beyond concepts. Words are not only inadequate for representing reality, but their nature is even more problematic because they reify experience in such a way that they might become a hindrance to achieve awakening.[1] On the other hand, Buddhists—particularly in Tibet[2]—celebrate language, as scripture, exegesis, and commentary, as a necessary instrument on the path toward enlightenment. Particularly during such periods like the scholastic age of Longchenpa, understanding words and their meaning serves as a preparation and complement to meditative experience.[3] It is little surprising that this same tension finds its expression also in the Dzogchen tradition of Longchenpa. Scholarship has rightly noted that Dzogchen Buddhism is particularly critical of conceptuality in its approach to contemplative practice, and this trend is definitely central to Longchenpa's work.[4] Speaking of deviations that a mediator can fall prey to during his practice, he warns his readers about yet another "extremely important point," namely the danger of forming any sort of reified view of reality: "If there is attachment to words in your conduct, you deviate into reified views, and thus it is crucial to remain unfettered by systematizations of philosophical views and meditative practices" (*The Treasury of Words and Meanings*, 389.2).[5] It might be constructive to clarify that even the early scriptures themselves already contain a critique of the architectonic-structuring mood of language. Consider, for example, *The Pearl Necklace Tantra*, where we find a passage discussing the "five emotional afflictions" (*nyon mongs lgna*) in terms of binding and constraint:

> If you know that the emotional afflictions are stainless, self-arisen, and natural, then how are human beings bound. Concerning this, if you cling to the truth, then even Buddha himself will be bound. Which human being could not be bound? If you know that there is no truth and no inherent existence, then the defilements are naturally purified like the naturally cleared dirt of water. … If you are clinging to dualistic fixations, you will be stuck in cyclical existence for a long time. In the house of the three realms, you'll be locked into the prison of names and forms, restrained by the chains of karma and ignorance. Separated from the self-arisen lamp, you'll be covered in the dense darkness of cyclical existence. (487.3)[6]

The scripture continues by associating the various afflictions to "being bound," "one's head wrapped," "being surrounded by armies," "one's neck being tied with a lasso," and so forth. The highest point of this rhetoric of restriction, of course, is the recurrent theme of "imprisonment" as it is specified that human beings are locked into a particular type of prison, namely that of "names" and "forms." Readers familiar with Buddhist philosophy and Abhidharma literature will have recognized that "name and form" (Skt. *nāma rūpa*; Tib. *ming dang gzugs*) is the designation used for the fourth of the twelve links of dependent arising. More specifically, it stands for the five-aggregate model of the mind (Skt. *skandha*, Tib. *phung po*), according to which our mind operates as follows: *Form* arises before we feel a *sensation*, then we witness the manifestation of *perception*, then of *activity*, and finally of *consciousness*. Without going into an unnecessarily detailed discussion of this matter, the doctrine of the five aggregates explains how the human self constitutes itself due to our senses and our minds. Eleanor Rosch, who links the early Buddhist teachings of the *skandhas* directly to the enactive conception of the mind in the cognitive sciences, chronicles the process as follows:

> It begins with a living body with its dualistic senses; develops through that living being's perception of the world through the filter of what is felt to be good, bad, or indifferent for the subject pole of the dualism; develops yet further into habits based on actions to get the good, shun the bad, and ignore the indifferent; and ends with birth into a moment of consciousness already situated in a complete inner and outer "world" stemming from whichever of the basic impulses (desire, aversion, or indifference) of the subject towards its objects predominates. (Rosch 2016, xxxxiv)[7]

Buddhism is aware that the human mind, particularly because of its inherent tendency to attribute "names" (*ming*) to experience, is always setting up frames. As another commentator put it, the "*skandhas* are simply mechanisms for presenting stimuli to the human mind, and allowing it to form representations of phenomena." The "consciousness," which emerges in this process, "can often come between us and a more immediate representation of outer reality by virtue of our ingrained tendency to attach concepts to all sense experience" (Fontana 2013, 36). In *The Tantra of Unimpeded Sound*, we find strikingly similar reflections on the workings of the human mind and its tendency to "represent" reality through language: "By the distinctive proliferation of secondary implications, everything is [labeled] with a specific name and the objects of bewilderment come to have two aspects" (141.6).[8] The "two aspects" is not only a reference to how our application of language contributes to dualistic grasping, but it is also an indication of how the experience and its linguistic representation are two different things. As David Germano observes, "because of the extensive discursiveness or 'naming' which comes to dominate our experience, a fissure develops between the immediate presence of that which presents itself to us, and their images which we create in fantasy and history, private and public" (1992, 437).

As Longchenpa embraced interpretation, definition, and categorization—the fundamental operations of the philosophical turn in the fourteenth century—he himself risked falling prey to the human mind's inherent trend to close itself off from lived experience. Acutely aware of this hazard, Longchenpa decided to leave his classical scholastic training at Sangphu Neütok because he was not satisfied with this monastic environment. In autobiographical poems, such as *The Joyful Tale of Potala* or *The Swan's Questions and Answers*, he tells of his religious journeys, in which he leaves the spiritually corrupted atmosphere of monastic institutions in search of contexts that were more conducive to his religion of inherent perfection, "a mythical haven of peace and liberation" (Higgins 2013, 44). Similarly, in *The Forest Delight*, Longchenpa describes a hero-saint "who lives a life of contemplation and who, although materialistically deficient, possesses the real wealth of religious discipline, knowledge and wisdom, but who is also not acknowledged for these attributes" (Ifergan 2014, 60). Leaving the monastery in

1334, he took up a peripatetic life in the wilderness of the Tibetan plateau and started following a teacher by the name of Kumārādza[9] (*rig 'dzin ku ma ra dza*, sometimes also *Kumārarādza*; alternative name: Shönnu Gyalpo, *gzhon nu rgyal po*, 1266–1343). This *Ngagpa* practitioner, a renowned yet mysterious figure, became the most stimulating muse for his thinking, motivating "the entire course of Longchenpa's later career" (Kapstein 2000, 165). By abandoning his scholastic education and embracing the teachings of Kumārādza—the tantric yogi who was not only an expert meditator but also an artist known for his painting—Longchenpa enacted a move that we also find in his writings, namely that of using language in order to return to a contemplative experience.[10]

After leaving Kumārādza, Longchenpa spent extended periods of time in isolated caves, frequently around Chimphu (*mchims phu*), a hermitage above the monastery of Samye founded during the reign of king Trisong Detsen in the eighth century. During one of his retreats, Longchenpa experienced a vision of two founding figures of his tradition in the form of Padmasambhava and his consort Yeshe Tsogyal (*ye shes mtsho rgyal*). Empowering Longchenpa as a future teacher of Dzogchen, they conferred a name on him, which he would henceforth adopt to redact his most sophisticated compositions, namely Drime Özer (lit: "Stainless Rays of Light," *dri med 'od zer*). It is in these writings that the Great Perfection reached its highest philosophical expression, and the system became increasingly encapsulated in the strictures and structures of language—thus, once again risking losing the very ethos it was intended to promote. With the mental framework being fixed and the boundaries between the Great Perfection and all other traditions being drawn, the great master's language threatened to transform his visionary philosophy. A type of "thinking" that grew out of the dynamic visions of Skullward Leap was gradually turned into a tedious endeavor, far removed from the contemplative experience that originally nourished its vitality.

What are we to make of Longchenpa's autobiographical itineration between contemplative experience and linguistic conceptuality? Matthew Kapstein once remarked that "the distinction between visionary and scholastic approaches to the interpretation of Buddhist teaching was ... by no means an impermeable one, and to recognize this is one of the ways in which our conception of Tibetan scholasticism needs to become more nuanced" (2000, 87). Indeed, even though the integration of the substance of experience with the form of language represents the Buddhist ideal type of the "scholar adept," who is both intellectually learned (*mkhas*) and contemplatively accomplished (*grub*), the means to achieve this varies in different traditions. If Cabezón characterizes the "philosophical enterprise" of the Gelugpa School as "an attempt to maintain [the] balance between scripture as a necessary means but insufficient end" (Cabezón 1994, 51), I suggest that we think of Dzogchen philosophy as a more dialectical undertaking. This is reflected in Longchenpa's lifelong oscillation between scholastic and contemplative endeavors.[11] Put differently, we are not dealing with a balancing-act, but rather a dynamic movement in between language and experience, reasoning and disclosure, logic and spirituality. In a passage found in *The Treasury of Words and Meanings*, where Longchenpa describes the fourth and final vision of Skullward

Leap, he highlights the intimate association between words, speech, and syllables, on the one hand, and meditative experience, on the other:

> At the time of seeing the vision of reality's exhaustion, your body becomes like a sky-faring bird freed from a trap through your mind entering into the matrix of radiant light. This is the merging with the Great Perfection's view of natural freedom, such that panic and anxiety, expectation and disappointment, hope and terror disappear. Purifying physical karma through the word-empowerment, exceedingly unelaborate wisdom will arise self-emergently. Your speech, like an echo, will be free from expression and apprehension through the syllables abiding within the channels re-entering into the seminal nuclei of the wind. This is the meaning of "the ineffable Great Perfection merging with the resonance of speech," bringing mastery with exceedingly unelaborate wisdom transcendent of verbalization. (408.6)[12]

In this quotation, we are first of all reminded that Dzogchen grows out of meditative experiences during Skullward Leap. Settling at White Skull Mountain (*gangs ri thod dkar*), Longchenpa lived in the famous hermitage of Orgyen Dzong (*o rgyan rdzong*), an ideal place to engage in extended periods of meditative practice while becoming a famous writer and teachers in his own right. To get a sense of how meditative experience came together with his philosophical teachings, we only need to recall the detailed accounts of the four visions. Through these descriptions, we can appreciate that the texts composed by Stainless Rays of Light—full of such phenomenological reports of lived experience—are infused with something that once stood outside of the text. At the same time, this passage demonstrates that Longchenpa's appreciation of the relationship between experience and language is dialectical in nature: Even if experience risks losing its spontaneous vitality when being enframed in the strictures of language, the freedom of experience can be recovered from within the framework of speech.

Longchenpa explores syllables and submits that "contemplation … is syllables, lights, and colors, the radiation and reabsorption of emanations" (*The Treasury of Words and Meanings*, 317.1). We could, with a certain degree of interpretative freedom, reframe this sentence as follows: "Just as the letters are externalized onto a piece of paper in the process of writing, they are again internalized when the practitioner reads them." Indeed, it seems that the fundamental pulsating movement of emanating and absorbing of the human mind is happening in an isomorphic manner across various (maybe all) domains of human existence: the display of luminous radiance and the reintegration into the vase of light during cosmogony, the gradual amplification of visionary displays and the reabsorption into emptiness during Skullward Leap, and the literary exposition of meditative experiences and their reinvocation during the process of reading.[13]

In accordance with the dual logic of his framework, Stainless Rays of Light delineates the analytical mind as a sort of *phármakon*, as it is both a medicine and a poison: "Since all views and meditations will become mental obscurations of the analytical mind if you don't nakedly identify this originally pure and unimpeded awareness, the antidote becomes a poison, such as a medicinal overdose" (*The Treasury of Words and Meanings*, 292.6).[14] Applying this homeopathic logic, Longchenpa inserts language within our bodies in the form of syllables that reside in our vital channels because he not only considers language to be the outgrowth of religious experience but—rather paradoxically—also one of the means for recovering experience.[15] Dan Martin, in an article to Padampa Sangye, speaks of "counterintuitive methods in dealing with negative mental states," describing the homeopathic logic with a simple example: "We could say that the best method to avoid slicing your thumb when slicing a banana is to draw the blade toward your thumb." Martin explains that the "psychological counterintuitive methods" used in Buddhism "might be defined as techniques for the principled interference in problematic mental patterns that make use of those same problematic patterns" (Martin 2017, 194).[16] In *The Pearl Necklace Tantra*, we find a passage that shows that this type of logic was already at work in the early Dzogchen scriptures:

> Similar to how a stain is cleansed through dirt, through purity there is pure liberation. Through poison that cures different poisons, iron that cuts through iron, stone that crushes stones, and wood that burns up wood, the nemesis of each is none other than itself. Liberation will not occur through conflicting natures. (466.6)[17]

Applied to Longchenpa's counterintuitive use of language, we could say that concepts—the very symptom of the distancing from contemplative experience—can equally transport us back into meditative experience. Like breaking the chains and opening up the gate for a caged animal, he uses language to crack open conceptual frames and to invite the reader to roam the wildness of a primordial experience. Germano points to this inherent tension within Great Perfection literature: On the one hand, "it tricks one into expecting closure, the definitive take, the master narrative that will finally bring the uncomfortable ambiguity of this long human journey to an end," while on the other, it "is in many ways a complete deconstruction of the structures one brought to the text, an opening up to the process ambiguity of life-in-formation" (Germano 1994, 300). Longchenpa's genius resides in his use of language to move in between these two tendencies: On the one hand, the sculpting of a scholastic text that can fulfill the public need for order and structure; on the other hand, simultaneously allowing for the breaking out of conceptual thought and into the realm of intimate contemplative experience.

The Introductions and the Quest for Vitality

One of the Great Perfection's most characteristic means of using language to revivify a vibrant and fresh experience out of petrified texts is through meditative techniques known as "introductions" (*ngo sprod pa*). In Indian and Tibetan forms of Buddhism, particularly in tantric lineages, this term describes the introduction to the nature of mind, which is generally performed by a spiritual master to a qualified disciple. Scholarship has remarked that the verb *ngo sprod pa* means to "indicate, identify, point out, introduce, or recognize" (Jackson 2019, 91), to "encounter" (Guenther 1993), "direct confrontation" (Achard 1999), or "coming face to face with" (Guenther 1996, 159). While "the practice of bestowing such instruction has a long, yet unchartered, history in tantric forms of Indian Buddhism" (Apple 2020, 170),[18] it is particularly popular in the Nyingma and Kagyü (*bka' rgyud*) lineages.[19] The encounter with ultimate reality can theoretically happen at any moment, but as a formal practice, the introduction frequently takes the form of reading or listening to religious teachings. In the Nyingthig texts, they are frequently aesthetically mediated meditation practices, which are premised on a creative use of a language that is rich in symbols, metaphors, and images.[20] Providing so-called examples that express/point to (the highest reality) (*mtshon pa'i dpe*), the introductions perfectly illustrate how language facilitates the dialectical movement between representation and experience.[21]

Dzogchen language does not only fulfill a synchronic function, but also retraces the itinerary of contemplative practice to reconnect the yogis to a previous visionary experience. Although they offer a fresh meditative moment, the pointing-out instructions are ultimately premised on the idea of a re-evocation of an earlier experience. Franz-Karl Ehrhard, in his discussion of this religious phenomenon, convincingly argued that the "examples" used in the introductions aim at "the *reactivation or reinforcement* of a previous spiritual experience" (1990, 80). This idea of revitalization raises a few questions regarding the position of the pointing-out instructions within the Dzogchen contemplative system as a whole. We could ask ourselves, for instance, whether the introductions form part of Skullward Leap itself? It could be said that when the yogi reads and performs the introductions after he returns from the mountain, he is led back into a meditative experience that he first achieved on the side of the mountain through Tögal. Generally speaking, however, the confrontations with the mind are not associated with Skullward Leap but rather with the other famous Dzogchen practice, namely Breakthrough. Breakthrough is a meditative technique that presents itself as firmly anchored within the essence of relaxation as it operates through the invocation of poetic imagery of naturalness, purity, un-fabricatedness, and freedom. The practice is famous for being predicated on effortlessness, which is assumed to give access to the mind's emptiness and primordial purity (*ka dag*).

In his commentaries, Longchenpa cites a series of passages from *The Tantra of Unimpeded Sound* to explicitly critique Breakthrough for being not "experiential" enough and for relying too much on discursive thinking. In the original tantra, we find a typical articulation of the centrality of "visionary experiences" as the text speaks of "wisdom's key point is that it emerges from the eyes" (158.3),[22] of the "ceasing of the flickering memories of conceptuality through nakedly seeing the linked chains" (177.4),[23] and of the "special feature of reality's immediacy," through which "all sentient beings are residing nowhere else than in Buddhahood" (137.1).[24] Stainless Rays of Light, however, far from simply collecting these spread-out textual references and weaving them together into a tight narrative, also appropriates them for his own purposes. He proceeds to make a much stronger plea, not only asserting the importance of sensory liberation in Skullward Leap, but also arguing that this is the reason for its ascendency over any other form of meditation. Specifically, he relies on these scriptural quotations to propose a series of seven "particularities" (*khyad par*) to differentiate the two main Dzogchen practices. Obviously, he gives Tögal priority in virtually every category, thus minimizing Breakthrough as a secondary technique.

To start, Longchenpa points out that while "in Breakthrough, one seeks wisdom from out of the conceptual radiation in the gateway of the mind," Skullward Leap "is superior to this because it involves the luminous radiation of non-conceptual awareness as it shines forth from the eyes."[25] In the same vein, he argues that while Breakthrough is marked by the "uninterrupted arising of various conceptual thoughts," during Skullward Leap, "when nakedly seeing the linked chains in vision through the faculty of the luminous channels' brightness, all conceptual thoughts cease instantaneously and wisdom appearances shine forth boundlessly."[26] Conversely, describing Breakthrough as a meditation centered on conceptuality, in which "wisdom is not directly looked at," he concludes that Skullward Leap is "superior in its greatness" because it is "directly seen."[27] In other words, what Longchenpa implies is that while Breakthrough might be giving rise to visions, there are no "manifestations" other than confused appearances and thus the mind, which fixates upon confused appearances will become deluded cognition (*The Treasury of Words and Meanings*, 366).[28] In his concluding annotations, Longchenpa summarizes the upper hand of Skullward Leap in the following terms:

> Furthermore, [Skullward Leap] is superior as it involves seeing through the faculties, which are independent of the words of mental analysis and insight. There is no difference between faculties as sharp versus dull or karma as good versus bad because the three Buddha bodies manifest on the path. (368.5)[29]

What does this deprioritization of Breakthrough mean for the status of the closely related phenomenon of the introductions? Like the introductions, Breakthrough is described as a technique that operates by overcoming dualistic modes of thinking by allowing the practitioner to recognize the very nature of reality. Franz-Karl Ehrhard, for instance, translates the term *ngo sprod pa* with "confrontation" and argues that this direct encounter with the nature of our mind is indicative of its association with Breakthrough. He also comments that the introductions, which are intended to offer us an "in-sight," or "inward look" (*Innenschau*), is frequently labeled as a process of "thoroughly investigating." Since this term could literally be translated as "cutting at the root," and Breakthrough itself is dedicated to both the "investigation and the cutting through of the mind," he enjoins that the pointing-out instructions are closely associated with this second type of Great Perfection practice (Ehrhard 1990, 82).

Upon final analysis, I uphold that the introductions should not be ascribed to either one of these major techniques of meditation but should rather be imagined as a sort of entredeux operating in between Breakthrough and Skullward Leap.

This in-betweenness becomes apparent if we realize that the introductions do not only rely on language, but also on other, more practical, means. For instance, let us consider introductions involving crystals. On one hand, conceptually speaking, the crystal stands for specific philosophical assumption of Dzogchen Buddhism, namely non-duality and primordial perfection. In this role, the symbolism of the crystal is inseparably linked to Breakthrough, where it represents the "primordially pure" dimension that is inherent in the "ground" (Ehrhard 1990, 81).[30] On the other hand, if we think back at the earlier chapters of this book, the reference to the crystal has the capacity to catapult us into a very different reality, namely that of Skullward Leap as a contemplative enactment of the quest for vitality.

From an even broader perspective, it could be argued that the crystal stands as an entredeux in the development of the Great Perfection tradition overall. As we have seen in the previous chapter, the emphasis on the primordial purity in the ground is a primary argument of Longchenpa's linear approach to the Buddhist path as something that leads from a state of *saṃsāra* to *nirvāṇa*. In fact, the ground of *nirvāṇa* must be primordially pure in order to avoid the pitfall of Buddhas falling back into the world of *saṃsāra*. In the mythical antecedent tales, by contrast, the crystal stands for something entirely different, namely the hunt for vitality. Recalling the various stories retelling the physical hunt for the Conch Shell Deer with Crystal Antlers or the elaborate subtle anatomy that is dominated by the *kati* crystal tube running though the yogi's entire body, it is incontrovertible that we are dealing here not simply with a world of metaphors, but rather an exceedingly visceral and material reality centered on the quest for vitality-giving substances. In short, and here we might be summing up one of the crucial differences between the two instantiations of the Great Perfection, according to the indigenous roots, the Dzogchen crystal does not primarily stand for purity and permanence. On the contrary, it points to the vicissitudes of the spiritual journey, the continued search for vitality, the quest for life itself. Even though the crystal might have received a new meaning in the process of increasing buddhicization under the leadership of masters like Nyima Bum and Longchenpa, it is likely that its older significance was not simply eradicated, but rather continued to resonate—even if just below the surface.[31]

In the case of the introductions, the metaphors come to life within the experience of the meditators through physical enactment in the form of what is perhaps best described as "contemplative paraphernalia." The crystal is not only an image for our inborn purity, but it is also used as a physical object by teachers and students during the introductions. Thus, the precious substance sought during the quest for vitality manifests its function as a "power object," which Gentry defines as an "object believed to have the power, or capacity to exact transformations in the state of being of persons and environments" (Gentry 2017, 7). This cathexis of the crystal, more specifically, gets channeled in practical ways during the introductions, where they can shape the meditator's perceptual experience. In one example, the practitioners are instructed to take "a stainless crystal, to hold it up into the appearance of the window and look into it so that lights of five colors arise abundantly" (*The Tantra of the Introductions*, 338.1).[32] As the crystal refracts the radiance of light sources behind it, it is apparent that the meditators attempt to reintroduce the type of visionary experiences they had during Skullward Leap when they were gazing into the rays of the sun. The crystal is both a philosophical symbol of primordial purity and a practical tool to manipulate the perceptual apparatus of the yogi. In other words, the introductions move not only between Skullward Leap and Breakthrough, but they also bridge a series of other gaps by means of a dialectical movement, including those between philosophy and practice, intellectual insight and sensory knowledge, and metaphor and material.[33]

Despite there being two different modalities to the crystals, the underlying mechanism of the introductions remains the same regardless of whether they are aesthetic-linguistic or practical-gestural in nature. Both of these phenomena allow for new insight as a result of seeking meaning in dynamic situations that are marked by multifariousness. Contemplative paraphernalia employed during the introductions, such as crystals, create an effect of ambiguity and uncertainty in a visceral sense. In the case introduced above, the rays of the sun shining through the crystal bring forth a multitude of images depending on the angle, the perspective, the lighting, or the space upon which the light is projected. This logic is blatantly obvious in the third introduction, which resembles certain techniques associated with the early stages of the sky-gazing meditation. The meditators are instructed to "press the eyes with their fingers" so that "the seminal nuclei of Tibet arise like fish-eyes" (*The Mirror of the Heart of Vajrasattva*, 338.5). It seems that the pressing of the eyes, a physical and almost violent engagement with one's body leading to the appearance of disorganized perceptual flashes, gives the impetus for the introduction to the state of mind that is sought. Now, just as the yogi's play with physical crystals or the pressing of the eyes with one's fingers produces a dynamic ambiguity by refracting the light arriving at our retinas into a kaleidoscopic multiplicity, the language of the introductions—filled with imagery, metaphors, and symbols—open up a linguistic space and populate it with a "glorious indefiniteness" (Klein and Wangyal 2006, 68).

The Great Perfection relies on the term "dynamic display" (*rtsal*) to describe this energy of playfulness and spontaneity, ambiguity and indefiniteness, plurality and potential. As Klein and Wangyal put it, unlike other forms of philosophy, "structured to take the measure of specific phenomena," which fail "to ascertain the multifarious whole," Dzogchen reasoning is "itself an instance of dynamic display" (Klein and Wangyal 2006, 66). This interpretation of the introductions as techniques aimed at inducing states of participation makes perfect sense in light of my previous discussion of Tögal as a meaning-making technique. As I have concluded in Chapter 4, one way to understand the cognitive efficacy of the practice is by interpreting the gradual assembling of the initially chaotic perceptive phenomena into coherent images of great complexity as an expression of the inherent human tendency to create meaning. This same logic can also be applied to the introductions: By leading the practitioner back to the dynamic display that they encountered in the form of the flickering lights in the visionary meditation, these techniques aim at increasing cognitive participation by activating our inborn meaning-seeking mechanism.

This association between the generation of "dynamic displays" and "meaning-seeking" is potentially of pre-Buddhist origins. While not explicitly articulated in Dzogchen texts, the connection between them is implicitly enclosed in the search narratives studied by the first part of this book.[34] In *The Great Main Text of the Vitality Ritual of the Lord of the Vitality*, for instance, the young prince is instructed by "Bön God White Turban" to hunt for the Conch Shell Deer with Crystal Antlers in order to bring *g.yang* and *phya* to his kingdom. Donning a white turban on his head and carrying a magic sun-ray lasso in his right hand, he travels to the center of Mount Meru, where he finds a deer with white foreparts made of conch shell, a golden middle part, agate hind parts, and iron hooves. Its antlers are clear white and made of crystal, its tongue made of heavenly lightening, and its multicolored eyes were made of *gzi* (a brightly shining precious stone). After catching the deer and before returning home to let Bön God White Turban perform the rituals for summoning the *phya* and the *g.yang*, the youth speaks as follows: "I have obtained the substances we wanted [and] I have found the precious items we sought" (525).[35] This story, saturated with indigenous motifs, is equally pervaded by both dynamism and meaning-seeking: If the dynamism manifests in the shininess of the deer's various body parts—such as the tongue made of heavenly lightening, antlers made of crystals, or the multicolored eyes—the seeking is implicit in the youth's quest to find the precious substances. Even more, the two traits are intimately interconnected as the prince seems to search precisely these objects that manifest the radiant dynamic qualities. Linguistically, this confluence between the two operations is epitomized in the expression the "precious items we sought" (*rtsal ba'i nor rdzas*) as the term "to search" is slightly misspelled as *rtsal* instead of *btsal*. Regardless of whether this is intentional or not, the close link between the ideas of the dynamism (*rtsal*) of precious substances and the seeking (*btsal*) by those looking for these vitality-giving attributes is more than evident in the crisis and crisis management narratives.

Fleshing out this comparison with the early Tibetan quests for vitality, we could even argue that if the introduction's dynamic display—engendering a situation a state of epistemological plurality, ambiguity, and confusion—manufactures a cognitive crisis and loss of certainty, the seeking for meaning provides the students with the necessary answers to manage this crisis and make sense of their reality.[36] Consider, for instance, that the transporting efficacy of the introductions, their ability to lead the meditator back to contemplative experience, frequently presupposes a startling moment of surprise or confusion. This mechanism becomes particularly apparent if we consider the contemporary manifestation of the religious phenomenon of the introductions. Today, the spiritual teacher not only uses linguistic concepts or symbols, but also performs physical gestures that can take extreme forms in combative and even assaultive behavior, such as shouts and blows. This means that the state of crisis, the confusion, the loss experienced by the disciple, is not purely intellectual in nature, but can also take on affective, sensory, and somatic forms. Oftentimes, the master shocks his disciples gathering around him into a state that is said to allow them to break through their ordinary way of thinking and to gain access to a deeper level of selfhood. Lama Surya Das, an American Buddhist teacher, notes that one of his Tibetan masters would offer teachings during which he "used to pound on a table or clap his hands loudly at a crucial moment to introduce us to the intrinsic nature of mind," asking "Who is hearing? Who is experiencing?" Another one, so he continues, used to "wake up disciples with provocative words and symbolic gestures," before asking them to "look directly into this immediate moment to see what color, what shape, what size was their mind, and in what location the heart-mind was to be found" (Surya Das 2005, 30).

Just as the myths of the primordial search for precious substances usually start in a kingdom that was once imbued with these forms of vitality, the crisis induced by the Dzogchen introductions is not one-dimensional. It is not marked by the simple absence (of insight, awareness, consciousness, etc.), but rather by a sudden loss, a rupture of a previously wholesome state. Consequently, it might be best to think about the crisis as a result of a dialectical movement between predictability, on the one hand, and confusion, on the other. It is, indeed, questionable whether introductions could even shatter our frames of reference without first setting them up. The introductions, in fact, are frequently characterized by the beauty of rich imagery, the serenity of poetic musings, the flowing of narratives, and the acting out of predetermined roles. In the case of Surya Das, for instance, we read that "the breakthrough or spiritual epiphany," which passes "from the parentlike guru to the childlike disciple," takes place "amidst an elaborate Tantric ritual" that is highly structured and predetermined (Surya Das 2005, 29).[37] Dzogchen teachers initially set up a structured scene in which the participants find themselves comfortable and at ease, before then shocking them by introducing some sort of ambiguity and uncertainty.

This tension between comfort and its disruption is so fundamental to the Dzogchen contemplative system as a whole that it is already engraved within the mythical narratives of the tradition. Consider, for instance, the epiphanic moment of the breaking open of the vase of luminosity, which stands out in its suddenness precisely because of the serenity of the initial situation. Much of the power of the moment of confusion and "error" that offered Samantabhadra the opportunity to realize his true nature and achieve instantaneous enlightenment stems precisely from the stability out of which he emerges. Similarly, in the contemporary phenomenon of the introductions, the poetic lectures, aphoristic verses, and aesthetic gestures strategically create an elaborate literary context, a mise en scène, which serves as the stage upon which the surprise moment is played out. It is the discrepancy between spontaneous intervention and the state of calm, created by the harmonious and aesthetically pleasing presentations of the teacher, which makes the moment of revelation stand out.[38]

Here, it might be useful to switch our cultural frame of reference to introduce two German terms: If representation is *Dar-stellung*, showing us something that is already there in its concreteness, *Vor-stellung* means "idea" and "image," as well as "introduction." Like a *Vorstellung*, introductions are performative, transformative, and generative as they create something that wasn't apparent before. This more nuanced conception of the introductions has important consequences for our understanding of freedom and spontaneity in Dzogchen Buddhism. Lobel recently argued that for Longchenpa, "spontaneous presence means that something exists without coming into being through causes and effects. It is just there—suddenly, naturally, freely, and completely" (Lobel 2018, 6). In the "framework for spontaneity" that I outlined here, by contrast, we find a more dialectical mechanism as spontaneous insight is—even in Dzogchen—embedded in exceedingly stable structures. Set forth more radically, the spontaneity of the contemplative phenomenon of the introduction is only efficient if it is embedded in more deliberate types of thinking that involve planning. Dzogchen language is not simply grounded in a logic of *reprise* of experience, but more significantly in a project of an *enterprise* of *reprise*: Contemplative language, even though frequently aiming at reviving spontaneous experience, is premised on a complex plan that needs to be executed with much commitment, effort, and persistence.[39] In this sense, the conclusion that Longchenpa rejects many practices as "intentional attempts to create the causes and conditions for freedom become an obstacle to that very freedom" (Lobel 2018, 6), should be reconsidered. In the Great Perfection, whether it be in Skullward Leap, in the introductions, or in the philosophical writings of Longchenpa, spontaneity is planned inasmuch as the flow of images is cultivated and the implicit insight is explicitly primed. Ultimately, it is not only questionable whether meaning can ever jump out from a book or painting if there is no frame, but also whether it is ever possible to truly seek meaning without shattering one's framework first.

Chapter 9

DZOGCHEN YOGIS AND THE FORGOTTEN SHAMANS

Thanks to the proliferous writing of Longchenpa, one of the most brilliant teachers of the Nyingma lineage, the Dzogchen teachings became a powerful contender in the religious arena of Tibet. Some four hundred years later, in the eighteenth century, when Jigme Lingpa ('jigs med gling pa, 1730–1798) revealed the Longchen Nyingthik (*klong chen snying thig*) teachings in the form of a mind treasure, he would claim to have received them through a series of visions from his master, Longchenpa. Today, the Longchen Nyingthig is one of the most widely practiced traditions in all of Tibetan Buddhism, and particularly popular among Western Buddhists. By then, the traces of the earlier substratum of indigenous Tibetan culture have largely been lost—either because they were simply forgotten or due to being actively suppressed. However, we have also discovered that certain ancient Tibetan elements remained alive even after the more progressive stages of the buddhicization of the tradition. If the previous chapter explored how language crystallized surprising messages of life-sustaining experience within its symbolism, this chapter turns its attention to the material culture and the performative aspects of Skullward Leap meditation. This maneuver allows us to compare the practice to what is likely the most "living" indigenous tradition in Tibet, namely shamanism. Although the contemporary Great Perfection might look unrecognizably different from shamanistic traditions found in the Tibetosphere, this chapter not only grounds them within the same pre-Buddhist cultural complex but also points to continued parallels between the two religious traditions.

For one, a brief comparison between the profiles of the Dzogchen guru and the shaman reveals striking similarities in terms of the setting for their respective "teachings," their behavior, as well as the physical instruments employed. At the same time, the contrasting part of my comparison will highlight the significant differences between the two phenomena, allowing us to further refine our understanding of the Dzogchen tradition qua Buddhist teaching. A closer look at the material culture of the two traditions clearly confirms that while both of them continue to play out the mythical hunt for vitality, they do so in opposed directions: While the Dzogchen tradition insisted on internalizing the dramatic search for life-sustaining substances into an embodied reality, the shamans do so in a much more externalized and physical manner, employing an elaborate outfit consisting of drums, mirrors, and a decorated headdress. Finally, we must assess the most fundamental rupture between Tögal and the shamanic visionary journey, namely that the former introduces a dimension of linearity that is absent in the indigenous Tibetan worldview. If the shamanic practitioner completes his exploration of the sky-world to return fully within his human body on earth to then embark on new adventures when the need arises, Skullward Leap comes to a definitive resolution as the yogi's material body dissolves into light.

Playing with the Mirror of the Shaman

My suggestion that the contemplative system of Great Perfection Buddhism might share important traits with long-standing shamanic traditions in the Himalayas and beyond is not new in scholarship on Tibetan religion.[1] Anthropologists like Stan Mumford and Sherry Ortner, for instance, have studied the complex intermingling between Tibetan Buddhism and shamanism in the context of Himalayan regions, particularly in Nepal (Mumford 1989; Ortner 1995). Geoffrey Samuel, similarly, famously describes Tibetan Buddhists as "civilized shamans," offering innumerable examples of how the religion in this region of the world consists of an amalgamation of indigenous (and larger Eurasian) and Indian or Chinese Buddhist orientations (Samuel 1993).[2] Hildegard Diemberger, finally, argues that origins of spirit-mediumship are related to the embodiment of pre-Buddhist deities, which are also involved in Buddhist tantric practices. She suggests that shamanic and tantric practices—although separate traditions—formed part of a twofold assimilate process that started with the introduction of Buddhism in Tibet (Diemberger 2006, 146–8). During my own ethnographic experiences visiting Buddhist teachers as well as shamanic ritualists—in various regions in Nepal—it was oftentimes not clear whether I was witnessing a shamanic ritual or a Buddhist guru's teaching; nor did it seem to matter to any of the attendees. Like many of my predecessors, I suggest that we are dealing with two parallel systems of practice that not only emerged out of the same cultural substratum but continue—despite their seeming distance—to share certain characteristics.

A good way to expose some of these lasting resemblances is by scrutinizing the profiles of the two main protagonists of their respective traditions, namely the shaman and the Dzogchen guru. First of all, we know already that they both participate in ritual-contemplative reenactment of mythical antecedent tales. If we have seen that the Dzogchen meditators emulate the mythical quests for vitality through their visionary journey—turning their focus to the latent energies within their bodies, letting them course through a complex network of luminosity consisting of deer, silk, crystal, or lassos, and finally engaging them in their perceptual field by domesticating them in the form of chained sheep—the shamanic performances reproduce these antecedent tales in a more explicit manner. Shamans are individuals that, usually in their youth, undergo a crisis that initiates them into the world of the gods. Learning to communicate with various spiritual beings, many of which are animalistic in nature, they become themselves messengers in quests for vitality as they move in between the divine and the human worlds. Upon completing this process of apprenticeship, the shamans then become reintegrated into society where they take on their communal role as managers of crisis; their help being requested for a wide variety of purposes like healing, divination, hunting, or funerals.

The Dzogchen guru, at least in his contemporary Buddhist variant, performs his role for salvific rather than such pragmatic reasons.[3] However, he nonetheless undergoes a strikingly similar process of maturation as a spiritual leader of his community. After having performed Skullward Leap meditation on the slope of the mountain, he returns to his community, where he becomes a teacher capable of transmitting what he experienced during his own visionary journey. This communal function of the meditator becomes nowhere as apparent as during the introductions to the nature of the mind, where the guru takes the disciple onto a similar type of journey by reevoking meditative experiences acquired during Tögal. In the contemporary context, the introductions are intense moments with a strong performative dimension. As we saw, the "introductions to the nature of the mind" are frequently physical in nature and can culminate in assaultive behavior, such as shouts and blows. Surya Das retells his revelatory experience with Dilgo Khyentse (dil mgo mkhyen brtse, 1910–1991), one of the most revered Tibetan Lamas of the past century and head of the Ancient School from 1987 to 1991, as follows:

> One day in the 1980s, Khyentse Rinpoche directly introduced me to the intrinsic nature of mind or mind essence by holding up a radiant crystal, gesturing toward it menacingly and symbolically with one large gold ring finger, and suddenly exclaiming in a shockingly loud voice, "What is mind?" With this, he shocked me into another way of being and seeing in which his buddha heart-mind, the Buddha's heart-mind, and my heart-mind were obviously not two, not three, but one and inseparable. (Surya Das 2005, 29)

It is not altogether surprising that such scenes have a theatrical dimension to them as the impulse for "play" or "playfulness" (*rol pa*) holds a preeminent position in the Dzogchen contemplative system overall. Consider, for instance, the centrality of playfulness in the moment of the cosmogony where Samantabhadra himself is presented as a sort of cosmic play,[4] or its resurfacing as a term used to describe the initial meditative experience on the slopes of the mountain where the flickering lights playfully populate the perceptual field of the meditators.[5] The playful dimension of the introductions becomes palpable if we appraise that they tend to employ various power objects that take on the function of a sort of stage prop.[6] Consider, for instance, the fifth introduction during which the practitioners are instructed to "place the statue of a buddha in front of themselves and to put cotton clothes on it, before looking into the sky while putting crystal-glasses on top [of their eyes]." The result of this scenario is that the practitioners "will not only see the Enjoyment Body of the Buddha—including his mouth, eyes, and nose—but also the respective Pure Land" (*The Mirror of the Heart of Vajrasattva*, 339.1).[7]

A closer look at the material culture of shamanic and Dzogchen practitioners offers us another fruitful avenue to explore the abiding similarities between the two traditions. One such item is the mirror. In Dzogchen, mirrors hold an eminent status during the introduction to the nature of the mind. Here, it might be worthwhile to finish the odyssey of the two blood-related boys found in *The Tantra of Self-Arisen Awareness*, which we tracked over the course of this study. Having been captured by five soldiers and the Old Lady before killing their prison guard and liberating themselves, we left the story as the children returned to their home, the Sun Castle. The allegorical account then concludes by alluding to the central theme of this chapter, namely the introductions, which are here referenced by means of twenty-one queens, who are said to counsel the children:

> After having been counseled by twenty-one queens, they ran to an incredibly beautiful temple guarded by five gate keepers wearing shields so that nobody could enter. Just imagine! Then, the four persons looked at their faces in four mirrors and recognized themselves. Just imagine! When they saw that the one house had eight doors, they broke out in laughter at themselves. (563)[8]

While this tale's conclusion is just as mystifying as the entire narrative, it communicates an unambiguous fact about the introductions, namely their performative nature. Like the Buddhist teachers of today, who carefully embed the moments of affective shock within a narrative arch, the protagonists of this story are counseled by twenty-one queens before looking at their faces in "four mirrors," ultimately "breaking out in laughter at themselves" as they recognize their true nature. While mirrors are prominent in Buddhism in general,[9] in Dzogchen they perform a dual role as they act both as symbols and as contemplative paraphernalia. They function as a metaphorical description of ultimate reality, reflecting everything while remaining themselves untainted.[10] Yet, the mirror is much more than merely a metaphorical concept. As a matter of fact, it is also a technical tool used in many introductory practices, and the exercising with mirrors is so central that one of the main tantras dedicated to these meditation exercises is titled *The Mirror of the Heart of Vajrasattva*. In the so-called mirror-like wisdom introduction, for instance, the meditators are guided to "paint a *maṇḍala* out of colorful dust between two mirrors." After that, they should "plant the two mirrors by moving them from side to side and look at them until two visions arise" (342.4).[11]

In strikingly parallel ways, mirrors are used throughout many shamanic practices. Known as *me long*, they are generally made from metal, circular in shape, and serve as "one of the most important ritual implements of the Upper Tibetan shamans" (Bellezza 2014, 290). Spirit-mediums (*lha pa*), in particular, have been relying on mirrors to perform their rituals, especially those related to healing demon possession (Waddell 1895, 482–3) and divination (Nebesky-Wojkowitz 1956, 462–3) for centuries. They set up mirrors on the altar, wear them around the neck (Peters 2016, 21), attach them to their headdress or hats (Bellezza 2014,

263), affix them to the chest, or sometimes even wear a miniature version on the ring finger (Bellezza 2005, 125). Mirrors play a particularly crucial role during the shaman's visionary journey,[12] and they are said to be the residence both of the spirits and of the ritualist's consciousness when he journeys into the divine world.[13]

Although the Great Perfection's metaphorical and symbolical meaning attributed to mirrors is firmly anchored within a Buddhist worldview, their performative manipulation can be fruitfully compared to shamanic séances of Tibetan spirit-mediums. The two traditions share an emphasis on the meeting between two individuals (student/patient and teacher/healer) that operate by means of a similar set of ritual or contemplative paraphernalia—such as mirrors, but also crystals, feathers, and so forth—that accompany certain bodily gestures performed by the teacher/healer. To take this comparison a bit further, we could even propose that the climax of the trance-ceremony, when the deities colonize the mind of the spirit-medium, is not all that different from the "merging of two minds," which is a commonly used expression to explain what is happening during the Dzogchen introductions to the nature of the mind.

It can also be remarked the terms *khelnā* (Hindi) and *khelnu* (Nepali), both meaning "to play," are used to describe states of possession.[14] While my conjecture that the psychological processes involved in such a mental fusion could also be described as a "playing" of one mind with the other has to wait for a future research project, there is little doubt that the interactions between the shaman and the spirit world resemble the Dzogchen visionary journey in their endorsement of a "playful" attitude. Roberte Hamayon's extensive research in Siberia has not only emphasized the centrality of dramaturgic games in shamanism, but has also demonstrated that these shamanic roles are premised on a mythical background that closely resembles the quest for vitality in Tibetan communities (Hamayon 1996, 2007). Specifically, she notes that they consist of cosmological perspectives involving a divine spiritual world of ancestors, a mobile vitality principle that can move in between these realms, and the shaman as a mediator in between worlds operating by "play-acting" various roles. Furthermore, the playfulness in both traditions is related to the quality of light. Accounts reporting the moment of the deity's entrance into the shaman speak of the manifestation of luminosity and its diffusion within the shaman's body. The deities are said to descend from heaven in a luminous form, to enter the mirrors, and then to gradually populate the shaman's body in the form of light rays. Not unlike the Dzogchen subtle body, which distinguishes itself from other tantric systems of meditation by its emphasis on light that led to the contouring of an elaborate system of luminous conduits, the shamanic mediums explain that the light rays of the deities occupy their bodily channels, with a particular emphasis on the vitality-channel.[15]

The Interiorization of the Shaman's Headdress

Like many of the motifs discussed in this book, the earliest *me long* date to the pre-imperial and pre-Buddhist period.[16] Although an inquiry into the historical origins of these mirrors is beyond the scope of this work, they nonetheless tempt me to offer a brief diachronic intermezzo that allows us to revisit one of this study's most pivotal contributions regarding the maturation of Tibetan religion. Indeed, I suspect that mirrors offer an illustrative example of the complex intermingling between spherical and vertical models of vitality that is typical of early Tibetan culture. On the one hand, they are likely rooted in a spherical model associated with the solar and vegetative fertility cults pervasive in locations like ancient India or Persia.[17] This impression is reinforced if we consider that the solar cult of these regions was also part and parcel of a culture surrounding royalty and warriorship. Mirrors, in fact, appear prominently during the imperial period, where they served as the breast plates, or cuirasses of the emperors.[18] This martial dimension of mirrors remained preeminent into the modern period as Tibetan soldiers wore cuirasses known as the "four mirrors" (*me long bzhi*)—mainly for symbolic reasons and during official occasions—into the twentieth century (LaRocca et al. 2006, 6; Walter 2009b, 260).[19] On the other hand, the mirrors perpetuate the earlier Tibetan logic of the vertical descent of vitality. Not only are the deities taking residence in the mirrors descending from the heavenly realm, but the mirrors themselves are believed to have initially fallen from the sky (Bellezza 2005, 23).

This brings us to another theme in our advancing search for continuities between the religious traditions of shamanism and Dzogchen, namely their shared emphasis on the vertical flow of vitality.[20] Let us first, however, look at another detailed report about the performance of a shamanic trance ritual, this time by a young spirit-medium interviewed by Bellezza in Upper Tibet:

> For the séance, Lha-klu uses a single antique brass *me-long* discovered by his paternal uncle many decades ago in the sands of Ma-pham g.yu-mtsho. It is thought to have fallen from the sky. He employs his *me-long* in the usual way, as an assembly point for the deities of the trance. … For the trance, he wears a mantle, apron and *rigs-lnga* ornamented with the five rGyal-ba rigs-lnga. Above the central diadem of the *rigs-lnga* there is a lammergeier plume, which is said to have a therapeutic function for the entire ceremony and its participants. It is thought to emanate healing rays of light. Lha-klu also observes that the plume symbolizes that after death the great spirit-mediums will reside in the palaces of the mountain gods. The eyes on the *snyan-gshog* (rainbow flaps) of Lha-klu's headdress represent the eyes of the *gza'* (planetary gods) who destroy harming forces and demons, and help cure patients. (Bellezza 2005, 108–9)

This passage, rich in ethnographic detail, provides us with a series of shared tropes between spirit-mediumship and Tögal, such as the descent of precious substances from the sky, the centrality of the mirror during the visionary journey, the emanation of healing rays of light, and so forth. The passage also shows that the primacy of the heavens is directly associated with another key attribute of Lha klu's costume, namely his rainbow-colored headdress, likely the most important element of his entire attire.[21] Although the headgear's nomenclature points to a certain degree of buddhicization as the "five families" (*rigs lnga*) represents a direct reference to the five Buddha families (*rgyal ba rigs lnga*) of tantric Buddhism, the headdress takes on a fundamentally indigenous function. It serves as a conduit allowing the shaman and the spirits associated with him to move in between the realms of the sky and the earth. As the deities descend from the sky-world to enter into the realm of humans, they usually first land on the head of the shaman by holding onto his headgear.[22] The head, as the highest point of the human body, has long been associated with vitality and its descent from the sky-world. Dunhuang manuscripts suggest that the belief in the direct link between the sky and the head was likely a feature of the earliest Tibetan religion (Stein 1990, 204). As a matter of fact, we have seen suggestions that the emperors' sky-cord was attached to the top of their heads. Similarly, throughout the wider Tibetosphere, the uppermost parts of the human body—the head, shoulders, and armpits—are the abodes of the "five protective spirits" (*'go ba'i lha*).[23]

Furthermore, the feathers attached to the shaman's headdress carry the peculiar name "birdhorns" (*bya ru*).[24] They fulfil a crucial role in shamanic practices— particularly for the safeguarding of the mobile vitality principle—and their main function is to host the auxiliary beings, which protect the shamans during their rites.[25] Like the mirrors, the birdhorns extend deeply into the material culture of imperial Tibet as they represent a key attribute of the early Tibetan royalty. The term does not appear frequently in religious texts.[26] However, Bön sources offer extensive lists of the so-called *bya ru can* kings.[27] While Martin rightly notes that "royal ornaments are traditionally used in the portrayal of Bodhisattvas and other Buddhist *lha*" (Martin 2005, 132), and Vitali dedicates his inquiry into the *bya ru* by looking at the "ancient kings of the Indo-Iranic borderlands," showing "that various monarchs had zoomorphic crowns" (Vitali 2008, 389), it is possible that these references to horns rising into the sky form part of the wider Eurasian cult of heavenly vitality. Put differently, just like the spherical shape of the human head adorned by vertically rising feathers, the headdress represents the blending of two distinct cults of vitality, namely a spherical one that is likely of Indo-Iranian origin and a vertical one stemming from the Eurasian steppes (Martynov 1988, 17).[28]

It is in this larger cultural substratum that we find numerous depictions of antlered figures in rock art of prehistoric times, with many of them having been interpreted as individuals wearing an animal headdress (Mykhailova and Garfinkel 2018, 5). Furthermore, the idea that horns can serve as a flying instrument of the shaman is widespread throughout the Himalayas as well as Siberia.[29] The turban's capacity to transport the shaman to the realm of the gods is also related to its material. Most prominently described as a "white turban" (*thod dkar*), they are traditionally crafted from wool.[30] Of course, wool is also linked to another core trait of the early Tibetan mythology, namely sheep. Based on the previously cited death rite contained in PT 1194, we know that sheep have long been depicted as psychopomp animals, as a sort of guide that leads a person's soul back to his home in the sky. Huber therefore concludes that "the psychopomp sheep and the flying sheep representing 'soul travel' are symbolically equivalent to the woolen turban that the bon shaman wears to engage in the same activity when undertaking a verbal ritual journey to the sky. Both shaman and sheep are also *g.yang* bearing because they are associated with the source of life in the sky world" (2020, vol. I: 186).[31]

Ultimately, it is likely that the Dzogchen system and the shamanic tradition complex are nourished by the same pre-Buddhist substratum, which might have once extended throughout a vast area of Eurasia. However, over time they clearly drifted apart. The transcendent-salvific objectives of the Dzogchen yogi are quite different from the worldly pragmatic goals, such as healing sicknesses, addressed by the shaman. But the Skullward Leap meditators do not usually wear a headdress during their practice. In this sense, one of the most effective ways to conceptualize this gradual rift between the shamanism and Dzogchen might be by speaking of an externalization versus an internalization of the quest for vitality. Indeed, while shamanic traditions maintained quite overt references to the quest for vitality and the activity of hunting as an endeavor involving an exchange and engagement with animal spirits—epitomized in the wearing of a headdress that imitates the appearance of sky-faring animals—the Dzogchen tradition's rootedness in this cultural matrix has been largely internalized.[32] Consider, for instance, the subtle body's emphasis on the skull, the so-called Conch Shell House or White Conch Shell House. Just as the "skull" (*thod pa*) is the residence of the fifty-eight wrathful deities that the meditator encounter during his visionary journey, the shaman's turban (*thod*, *lha thod*, or *thod dkar*) is considered to be the seat of the deities, allowing him to move in between the earthly realm of humans and the heavenly home of the gods.[33] Thus, although the yogis themselves do not wear headgear akin to that of the shaman, the subtle body system maintains the logic of verticality and the primacy of the uppermost part of our human bodies. Similar processes of interiorization appear to be at work in other elements of the headgear. Not only is the shamanic identification of the feathers as horns reminiscent of the most striking details of the subtle anatomy of the yogis, namely the description of the luminous channels leading to their eyes as "horns of the *ba men* buffalo," but this shared emphasis on horns could be grounded in the pre-Buddhist cosmological myths of the sky-dwelling deer with "crystal antlers" (*shel ru*).[34] This process of interiorization is also apparent in another trait of the Dzogchen body, namely the so-called white silk thread channel, which represents a vitality that moves along a vertical axis throughout the practitioner's body, from the heart to the eyes, from where it then projects—like a lasso—into the sky.

The Indigenous Tibetan Practice of Transference

So far, the evidence for continuities and ruptures between Dzogchen and shamanism has dealt with the roles of the main protagonists, the material culture underlying their interventions in the social realm, as well as the increasing interiorization of the quest for vitality in the Great Perfection. The final part of this chapter is dedicated to what is likely the most intriguing parallel between these two religious traditions, namely the vertical journey toward the sky-world. Let us look at a classical example of the cult of the gods of the phenomenal world studied by Huber. During his "verbal ritual journey" as part of the Aheylha Festival of Changmadung, the shaman takes on the identity of the Priest-God White Turban (*gshen lha thod dkar*) by "meditating" or "visualizing" (*bsgom*) his odyssey through the various stages of the itinerary toward the sky.[35] Being "seated still and silent in the corner of the room at his small altar," the shaman's "vision" consists of "a ritual journey through the local landscape and eventually up to the sky world" (Huber 2020, vol. I: 399). The story then continues to list the names of the thirteen gods of the phenomenal world that the Bön po encounters once he reaches the thirteenth level of the sky. As we have seen, this idea of the ascent to the realm of the sky has a long-standing tradition in Tibet.[36] *Showing the Way to the Deer with Antlers*, an eleventh-century manuscript discovered in the Gathang Bumba stupa,[37] tells the story of a deer that travels to his homeland in the thirteenth level of the sky-world, where it returns to his parents and his brother.[38] The deer is also the protagonist in another Bönpo text, namely *Remedying the Lords of the Soil and Subjugating the Evil Forces of Creation through the Ground of Vitality*. Here, the cosmological prelude moves into a situation where the world of humans is disturbed by demonic activity, requiring them to perform a ransom offering consisting in a deer with precious antlers that is to be hunted. After the priest engages in his dialogue with the deer, trying to persuade it to come with him, the animal is led through a rather detailed list of thirteen levels of the sky-realm until it reaches the highest point and is ultimately accepted as a ransom offering (488–95).[39]

While this vertical ascent, sometimes described as "soul-flight," has been seen as a defining trait of shamanic practice at least since the work of Mircea Eliade (Eliade 1964),[40] it is rarely considered in connection with Buddhist meditation. Eliade himself notes that many of the archaic pre-Buddhist beliefs and practices were incorporated into Tantric Buddhism and then changed in the process and emphasizes that since Buddhist meditation puts an emphasis on "embodiment," its philosophy rejects the reality of the soul and techniques of ecstatic soul-flight (Eliade 1964, 436–41, 506–7). However, such a strict separation between shamanic techniques and Dzogchen meditation is problematic, not only because they likely emerged out of the same mythical-historical context but also because they have much in common in terms of their motifs, vocabulary, symbolisms, and even their overall functioning. While it might be a coincidence that one of the thirteen deities that the shaman/Priest-God White Turban encounters is called "Sky Embryo" (*nam mkha'i snying po*), thus carrying the precise same name as one of the children in the Dzogchen myths of the quest for vitality studied in Chapter 3,[41] it is incontrovertible that the vertical propulsion from the realm of the earth to the realm of the sky is operative in Skullward Leap meditation. We have already discussed how this verticality is encapsulated in the first half of the practice's name as the syllable *thod* (or *thod pa*) stands not only literally for the "skull," but also carries within the direct associations with the turban (*thod dkar*), as well as the sheep and deer animal spirits that enable for the ascent to the realm of the sky. The chanted ritual journeys of the shamans might also assist us in unearthing the original meaning of the second syllable of the expression *thod rgal*. The chants that accompany the shaman's soul-journeys into the realm of the sky make frequent use of the term "to leap" (*rgal*). More specifically, they use this particular term to account for how the ritualist's vertical itinerary leads along a cosmic axis through a series of specific topographical level that he has "to pass" or to "step over" one by one. In the *Methods of Subduing Crisis-Spirits*, for instance, we read about nine such levels that are frequently identified with "doors" or "thresholds," carrying idiosyncratic names such as the "bamboo door of the sheep" (33). I consider it to be quite plausible that Skullward Leap reproduces this upward vertical journey of the shamanic practitioner. While it lost some of the details regarding the journey, such as the individual levels and the various particularities with each topography (doors, wood, animals, etc.), the idea of the departure point of the skull as the uppermost part of the body, as well as the process of "leaping" upward from there toward the sky were maintained in the Buddhist practice. Just as *The Methods of Subduing Crisis-Spirits* instructs the shaman to "step (*rgal*) upwards over the first doorsill and depart" (33–4),[42] the Dzogchen yogi is instructed to mobilize the latent vital energy within his heart, make it rise through body, and, once it reaches the skull, project it out through the eyes to leap upward into the sky where it is perceived in the form of luminous visions.

The term to "depart" (*gshegs*), which appears together with the notion of "leaping" (*rgal*), reinforces this idea of an ascent to the sky-world. As Nathan Hill has shown, in *The Old Tibetan Annals*, this particular verb is utilized exclusively for describing the death of emperors in the standardized expression "went to the sky" (*dgung du gshegs*), whereas other verbs are used for describing the deaths of ordinary persons (Hill 2008).[43] It is plausible that this indigenous belief in the return to the ancestors withstood the test of time to become inscribed in the fundamental goal of the Tögal practice. In fact, the upward journey into the realm of the sky gained a much more significant meaning in the Dzogchen tradition, where the practice of Skullward Leap became associated with the reaching of enlightenment before the moment of death. In the case of the most accomplished practitioners, so it is said, the practice culminates in a dissolution of the physical body as the practitioners achieve the "Rainbow Body of the Great Transferance" (*'ja' lus 'pho ba chen po*). Longchenpa describes this final moment as follows: "When [in the practice] of Tögal, the atoms dissolve, through the radiance of light, there will be mastery over birth and entrance and the ability to arise (*bzhengs*) again in the transference body (*'pho ba'i skur*)" (*The Treasury of Words and Meanings*, 429.4).[44] In another passage, he elaborates as follows:

> The manner of arising as the transference body (*'pho ba'i skur bzhengs lugs*) is that, when the visions gradually become exhausted, occasionally the five fingers of the hands will vividly appear in the midst of light. By focusing on that, those visions will transform into the appearances of the six classes, like a moon in water or a dream, and even the body will look to be like the moon's reflection in water—self-appearing as utterly unimpeded. Others will only be able to see the [practitioner's] previous body. (*The Treasury of Words and Meanings*, 401.2)[45]

The practice of the transference of consciousness at the time of death is widespread among all tantric schools and generally attributed to Indian sources as these techniques are described both in Hindu and Buddhist tantras of Sanskrit provenance. This being said, while transference has become a widespread phenomenon in Tibetan Buddhism, with most schools accepting it as part of their practical repertoire in post-imperial times, scholarship has also commented on the fact that there are "allegedly earlier references to a unique Dzogchen procedure that leads the superior practitioner to bypass the process of dying and realize the 'Rainbow Body of the Great Transfer'" (Halkias 2019, 76).[46] It is quite possible that this type of transcendence emerged not out of the Indian sources regarding such practices, but rather out of the indigenous Tibetan cult of the quest for vitality and the sky-deer. There even exists a further subtle linguistic hint that this association with non-Buddhist beliefs and practices could persist until today. In fact, the term "to rise" or "to manifest" (*bzhengs*), which—as the examples cited above show—is Longchenpa's preferred way of expressing the arising of the rainbow body, is pervasive throughout contemporary Tibetan shamanism (Huber 2020, vol. I: 150, 154, 246, 261, 338, 368, 483; vol. II: 13–19). Indeed, the word *bzhengs* is so intimately associated with pre-Buddhist soul-journeys that Huber even declares it to be "one of the most important and frequent verbs occurring in *Srid-pa'i lha* rites" (368).[47] The shamanic "soul-flight" is a fundamentally "aerial activity" during which the shaman takes on the identity of a "soaring bird looking out over the surroundings." Akin to the Dzogchen case, the idea of this bird's eye perspective during the soul-flight "appears directly derived from, or related to, very old pre- and early post-11th century Tibetan cosmographic images of the multi-levelled sky world in ritual antecedent narratives" (Huber 2020, vol. I: 261).[48]

The term plays a strikingly analogous function in the Great Perfection tradition. Nourished by the same indigenous infatuation with the vertical ascent to the sky-world, Dzogchen relies on the exact same word in other aspects of its contemplative system. Consider, for instance, a powerful passage in *The Pearl Necklace Tantra*, where the moment of cosmogony, the birth of the universe, is described as follows: "Phenomenal existence rising (*bzhengs*) from the ground, how lofty in height! Effortless self-liberation, how vast in its extent! A great primordial beginning, how wise in its domain!" (470.2).[49] The myth that tells us of the "rise" of phenomenal existence from within the ground should be understood as an antecedent tale for Skullward Leap as the yogi stares into the sky as if he were soaring above the ground. As Germano puts it, the rise of these phenomena from the ground is not only "used in discussing contemplative practice," but also itself "imaged as a display of light viewed by a nameless viewer standing on a cliff (the 'ground'), with original purity the cloudless sky above him/her, the Bodies of Enjoyment in the sky in front on the horizon and so on down to the six impure worlds stretching across the plains below" (Germano 1992, 372). While the evidence available to us does not allow for a final verdict on this matter, the vertical trajectory of Skullward Leap practice, as well as more concrete linguistic associations with ancient Tibetan notions like "leaping" (*rgal*), "departing" (*gshegs*), or "rising" (*bzhengs*) suggest that the indigenous Skullward Leap practice provided an alternative model for the transference of consciousness to the one imported from South Asia.

This chapter has gathered significant evidence to show that Tögal meditation and shamanic soul-flights, two seemingly far removed religious phenomena, share an impressive amount of traits. Some of the most prominent features include: the personal meeting between a guiding figure and an aspirant (who is either a patient or a disciple), the manipulation of similar paraphernalia (such as mirrors, crystals, or feathers) involving a "play" (*rol pa*) that is both metaphorical and performative in nature, similar visionary phenomenologies (specifically, the vertical upward movement that allows for a more expansive view), and analogous anatomical depictions (both of which are centered on rays of light leaving and penetrating the subtle body). This being said, we cannot overlook that any direct identification of these two traditions would be simplistic and unrealistic. Concretely, there is little doubt that the contemporary manifestations of shamanism and Dzogchen display more differences than similarities. While the interiorization already offered one dimension where the buddhization of the Great Perfection led to an innovation over the indigenous system, this final part of the book discusses what is likely the tradition's most important rupture from the shamanic system, namely the absence of the descent to the earthly world of humans after the yogi's successful mission in the ethereal realm.

Indeed, if the ideal type of the Dzogchen yogi reaches a state of enlightenment during the practice of Tögal that culminates in the dissolution of his body into light, the shaman does not just float off into the sky. On the contrary, his journey is not a one-way street but rather a dialectical process that leads in both directions along the vertical axis connecting the realms of the earth and the sky. Let us look at the second part of the verbal ritual journey during the Aheylha Festival of Changmadung, where the shaman travels upward in the identity of the Priest-God White Turban. After "passing" over the thresholds of the eight earlier levels of the sky-world, the shaman finally "leaps" into the supreme level and addresses the deities living there as follows:

> Now, in our human world there is no *lha*. Grant us your coming as the diligent *lha*! In our human world, there is no *g.yang*. Come to bestow *g.yang*! Our food lacks nourishment. Come to give us nourishing food! Our clothing lacks warmth. Come to give us warmth! Our bodies are lacklustre. Come to give us lustre! Our arrows lack [rear] notches. Come to give them notches! Our [bamboo] bows lack nodes [for strength]. Come to give them nodes. Our knives are not sharp. Come to give them sharpness! (Huber 2020, vol. I: 402)

Rising up to the realm of the sky and inviting the ancestral gods to descend to earth, the shaman's journey consists of a two-way vertical movement, where the descent of the gods is the key moment in the ritual procedure as it brings about the revitalization of the realm of humans. Beliefs about the sky-journey's harmony between anabasis and katabasis, that is the upward ascent and the downward descent, likely form part of the pre-Buddhist Tibetan world as we find this proposition already in early Dunhuang manuscripts.[50] Dotson, in his study of PT 1285, has shown that ancient Tibet rituals performed by *gshen* and *bön* priests followed specific territories that can be plotted along a vertical axis that moves both ways: an upward movement from East to West, upstream along the Tsanpo River, associated with recovering something, on the one hand; and a downstream movement from West to East, intended to abandon something (Dotson 2008, 56). We find a similar reciprocity between the worlds of the heavens and the earth in another ancient Bönpo text, namely *The Extensive Elimination and Offering Rites for the Gods of the Four Groups of Little Humans*. Here, we read not only the antecedent narratives involving the birth of humans from eggs and the original descent of the gods from the sky, but we also encounter a detailed guided enticement journey during which the shaman sends his animal-assistants up to the heavenly realm to supplicate the gods to descend to earth. Among the shamans of today, such mythical antecedent tales are still foundational in ceremonies surrounding liminal moments of human existence, such as marriage (Karmay 1998c, 150–2, 252, 418), and death (Huber 2020, vol. II: 22). Tibetans still rely on threads, strings, or ribbons—ritual paraphernalia made from silk in order to invite the descent of fortune and good luck.[51]

As we are looking for the reason for this discrepancy between the dialectical journey of the shaman and the linear mission of the Dzogchen yogi, it might be useful to briefly return to Longchenpa's role as the systematizer of the Great Perfection as a Buddhist tradition. More specifically, his discussion of the arising of the rainbow body and the dissolution of the yogi's physical substratum reproduces certain patters of his thinking that offer us an overture to further expand on his role within the buddhicization of the tradition. As in other examples, Longchenpa's defense of Buddhism over and against the pre-Buddhist heritage that so deeply saturates his tradition is rather paradoxical in nature. Just as the discussion of the term *phul thag* leads him to oppose the idea of a teleportation into sky during Skullward Leap and buttress his Buddhist position with the invocation of an "old local term," his defense of the Buddhist conception of transference relies on a profoundly indigenous notion, namely the idea that yogis can leap vertically into the realm of the sky. At the same time, however, he leaves the practice bereft of what is certainly the most essential aspect of the shamanic journey to the sky, namely the transmission of "productive, fertilising life power *g.yang* and the life force *srog*" (Huber 2020, vol. I: 47).

Dzogchen's schism from the indigenous Tibetan substratum is radical. The arising of the rainbow body of the great transference, the final dissolution of the physical body upon the completion of the yogi's visionary journey, allowed the Great Perfection to become fully Buddhist. However, the break with certain core beliefs of ancient Tibet, particularly the multiplicity of the mobile vitality principle and the dialectics of the upward and downward movements of life-sustaining energy, came at a costly price. Although necessary for the conversion of the tradition to Buddhism, it ultimately robbed Skullward Leap of its fundamental logic. The pre-Buddhist journey is premised on a continuous circulation of vitality in between the earthly realm of humans and the heavenly world of the gods. Unlike the Buddhist understanding of *nirvāṇa*, which Longchenpa insists is a permanent state of liberation, the indigenous ascent to the world of the gods is never permanent but marked by an eventual return into the world of humans that revitalizes our realm with divine energy. I leave up to others to debate what this loss of the oscillation between ascent and descent, as well as the linearity of the religious endeavor more generally meant for the Great Perfection tradition, in particular, and Tibetan Buddhism, more generally.

CONCLUSION: MEDITATION AND THE ADVENTURE OF LIFE

Although this study opened with a scene of a meditating yogi gazing into the open blue sky while sitting quietly on a serene mountainside in Tibet, our exploration of the Dzogchen contemplative system led us across a variegated terrain that was carved over the course of many centuries by the powerful currents of vitality. The ancient pre-Buddhist cosmology of Tibet could have very well emerged out of a larger Eurasian substratum premised on the descent of divine vitality from the celestial world and the worship of "vitality sheep" (*g.yang mo lug*) and "deer" (*sha ba, ri dwags*)—animal spirits that have the unique capacity to migrate between the realms of the sky and the earth. With the rise and fall of the Tibetan empire and the waves of Buddhist teachings flooding the Tibetan plateau, the model of vertical vitality was increasingly challenged by alternative conceptions of life-sustaining energy, primarily the spherical model encapsulated in the ground of the treasure tradition, or the tantric model incarnated in the enlightened energies coursing through the yogis' subtle anatomy.

Nonetheless, the Dzogchen contemplative system configured in *The Seventeen Tantras* in the tenth century remained profoundly nourished by the pre-Buddhist quest for vitality and the vertical movement of animalistic energies: Our story started with the mythical accounts of cosmogony of the little children and young princes on the hunt for vitality in the form of precious substances like "conch shell" or "crystal antlers;" it then proceeded to recount the appearance of the luminous apparitions of "linked sheep," which are to be domesticated during the four visions or the practice of mimicking a wounded deer by running into a place of isolation; and it culminated in the embodiment of the quest for vital energies in the form of luminous palaces and vertically aligned conduits designated as "deer-lamp of the *tsitta*," "white silk threads," "crystal tubes," or "far-reaching lassos."

Although the philosophical articulation of the major Buddhist schools and the systematization of the Great Perfection by Longchenpa during the scholastic period curbed the thrust of the indigenous ethos of vitality—putting an end to the spiritual journeys into other worlds and disrupting the dialectical movement in between heaven and earth—contemporary masters still gaze into the sky, perceive flickering lights as chained sheep emerging out of silken channels before corralling them into fence-like structures, and rely on crystals, feathers, or mirrors as precious substances for contemplative purposes.

I thus reassert the claim I made in the introduction: the present study represents a watershed moment in the reception history of Dzogchen Buddhism. It not only compiles a large collection of seemingly non-Buddhist motifs, but also makes a compelling argument that the morphology and function of the Great Perfection contemplative system was originally modeled according to indigenous priorities, particularly the cult of the sky-deer and the quest for vitality that was widespread throughout Eurasia long before the introduction of Buddhism to Tibet. Even if not all of my claims will withstand the test of time and some of my arguments will have to be corrected or overthrown, it is my genuine hope that the shift from an focus on the ethos of freedom—epitomized in the image of the cloudless sky on top of the world—toward the many puzzling dimensions of the contemplative system of Dzogchen, brings fresh energy into scholarship on this fascinating religious tradition. In other words, regardless of whether my explanation for the complexity, the richness, and the idiosyncrasy of Dzogchen is correct or not, it is incontrovertible that these dimensions deserve more attention in the years to come.[1]

The consequences of this work for the wider discipline of Tibetan studies are hard to predict. I believe, however, that today's scholarship on Tibet benefits from interdisciplinary projects such as this one as they allow us to gain an increased appreciation for just how deeply religious traditions are entangled. While the presence of non-Buddhist elements has been studied in Bönpo or shamanic currents in the wider Tibetosphere, this approach implicitly reproduces a long-standing Tibetan custom where a catch-all "alterity" serves as a foil to protect seemingly Buddhist teachings from critical scrutiny. I believe that the recurring debate surrounding simultaneist versus gradualist forms of enlightenment, emphasized in the third part of this study, serves as an illustrative example of how apparently intra-Buddhist controversies might hide much more fundamental questions regarding religious worldviews. Finally, I also hope that the partial reconstruction of the vertical quest for vitality as a central organizing principle of the indigenous substratum might animate scholars of other Tibetan Buddhist schools to embark on their own hunt for (dis-)continuities with this fascinating universe, whether they be thematic, structural, or functional in nature.

Despite the exhilarating itineraries afforded by the geographical richness of the indigenous Tibetan landscape, the cloudless blue sky has come to monopolize contemporary debates surrounding Dzogchen meditation. The rise of the ethos of freedom, while impacted by our own culture's priorities and the rise of Buddhist modernism, can now also be located on the historical trajectory of the Great Perfection tradition. In many ways, it is a by-product of the increasing buddhicization of Skullward Leap, particularly under the leadership and penmanship of Longchenpa. By submitting Dzogchen to a linear path directed toward the single goal of enlightenment, the great scholar-yogi flattened the variegated topography of the indigenous quests for vitality. He turned a ceaseless process of facing and overcoming moments of crisis into a one-way journey from *saṃsāra* to *nirvāṇa*, a linear path of liberation that culminates in the dissolution of the physical body and the transformation into a rainbow body.

As the Great Perfection fully embraced this ethos of freedom, it is no wonder that it became increasingly popular among Western practitioners.[2] Meditation, in fact, has become a spectacularly popular phenomenon in our times. Mindfulness meditation, in particular, is now practiced by all strata of society and applied in many different settings that range anywhere from schools and hospitals to prisons and board rooms. Talking to friends and family, teaching in classrooms across the world, or browsing through the self-help sections on Amazon, it has frequently surprised me that meditation is not only on everybody's mind, but that it is described as a rather simple practice. It involves sitting with a straight back and closed eyes while focusing one's attention on an object—such as the natural movement of one's breath and the rising and falling of one's belly in the process. In this way, mindfulness invites the meditators to disattend from their ordinary discursive thoughts, resulting in a more present and calm state of mind that allows them to see things as they really are.

Amid this enthusiasm, it is quite easy to forget that this seeming familiarity with meditation is hiding a surprising fact, namely that our culture's appreciation of contemplative practices *in loco* is rather superficial. In concluding this book, I propose a brief imaginatory exercise during which we envision how a practice like Skullward Leap, in its indigenous origination as part of the quest for vitality, could enrich our contemporary understanding of meditation. Far removed from the open blue sky and the ethos of freedom, the indigenous conception of Tögal is rich in narratives, which open with a moment of crisis, before following the lives of mythical figures—such as hunters and shamans, witches and princes, or deer and sheep—through their adventurous exploits in search for a remedy. Although the cultural context seems far removed from the world that we live in, the spectacle of Skullward Leap is eminently familiar to all of us because it is the drama of life itself. Meditation is about living life and facing the challenges it throws at us; it requires us to take responsibility when things have gone wrong and to embark on an uncertain and dangerous journey of recovery; during such a quest, we not only venture outside our comfort zones by exploring new locations, but also adopt unfamiliar identities that allow us to enter into contact with other forms of being; the expedition is, furthermore, driven by an urgency reserved for eminently personal dramas, as if we were hunting for something that is absolutely necessary for our very existence; upon the conclusion of this exploit, carrying with us a precious new attribute that was acquired during the arduous journey, we return to our familiar place and role; although we return to a seemingly identical situation, we are better equipped to face the next crisis, which is likely fast approaching.

I wonder whether such a model of meditation, premised on a courageous, committed, and intentional embarking on the adventure of life, would offer contemporary civilization new impulses to deal with the radical challenges we are facing. Put differently, I ponder whether sitting in our rooms, closing our eyes, watching our breaths, being in the present moment, and cultivating a nonjudgmental attitude is truly the most effective way to "manage" today's stress.

What makes Skullward Leap relevant for our world is that it recognizes—and even actively embraces—the fundamental challenges of life. The truly liberating power of meditation, according to this model, stems from increasing our awareness of the various limitations that make up human existence: Present-centeredness requires us to be aware of our pasts and to envision our future, relaxation involves an appreciation of all our bodily energies, and a nonjudgmental attitude calls for an understanding of how our brains are inherently geared toward structure and meaning-making. More radically, Skullward Leap puts crisis, which frequently manifest on an ecological and cosmic scale, at the heart of practice and turns it into an opportunity for growth. Following the inherent human drive to create meaning out of ambiguity, it encourages us to make our lives count, to write own story with courage and curiosity, imagination and creativity, playfulness and excitement. Although the quest for vitality concludes where it first started, with the meditators returning to their home to await the next adventure that life throws at them, the circumstances are not quite the same. An open-ended process, meditation does not provide us with specific solutions for our problems, but rather helps us cultivate resilience as it guides us through a process of finding meaning in crisis and teaches us to adjust with flexibility to ever-changing circumstances.

NOTES

Introduction: Skullward Leap Meditation and the Quest for Vitality

1 Tögal, a word consisting of the Tibetan words *rgal* ("to leap over") and *thod* ("above," "over," but also "head wrapper," "turban," "skull"), has usually been translated as "Direct Transcendence" or "Leap-Over." I consider these translations to be anachronistic inasmuch as they are basing themselves on a Buddhist reinterpretation of a practice that was originally shaped by indigenous Tibetan priorities. It is because of this association with pre-Buddhist culture that I propose a more literal translation as "Skullward Leap." For a more detailed analysis of my reasoning, see my comments later in the introduction.

2 The Great Perfection, which is also known as "Utmost Yoga" (Skt. *Atiyoga*, Tib. *shin tu rnal 'byor, gdod ma'i rnal 'byor*), intentionally—as if trying to pierce the sky—styles itself as the pinnacle of Buddhist religion. On a side note, it might be important to address the issue of secrecy. I am, of course, well aware of the ethical issues involved in making public what Dzogchen masters wish to keep secret. However, as a historian of religion, I embrace a critical approach that combines insider and outsider stances (Geisshuesler 2021). Thus, although I am revealing certain hidden instructions regarding the Dzogchen contemplative system, I am not claiming to reveal the true nature of our minds—as most Dzogchen teachers would. To some extent this position is in line with the emic tradition's understanding of secrecy. The term "secrecy," indeed, has multiple meanings with the non-revelation of the teachings being only the most superficial layer. Equally important is the idea that most readers of these materials have no access to the teachings because of linguistic or psychological barriers that prevent them from grasping their true meaning. I hope that the study is of value not only to academic scholarship on Dzogchen, but also to practitioners.

3 The Dzogchen tradition consists of a complex amalgamation of teachings, lineages, and orientations. Unless otherwise indicated, I use the terms Great Perfection (*rdzogs chen*) and Heart-Essence (*snying thig*) interchangeably in this study. This is not only a result of my focus on the latter, but also because the Heart-Essence tradition itself self-identifies as the Great Perfection, even if there are, in fact, many other variants. The most prominent method of separation is the division into three "series": the "mind series" (*sems sde*), the "space series" (*klong sde*), and the "instruction series" (*man ngag sde*, lit. "secret oral instruction series"), which corresponds to the Heart-Essence tradition. For a discussion, see Geisshuesler (2020b).

4 For more information on Bön and its relationship to Buddhism, particularly the Ancient School, see later comments in the introduction.

5 Both the early scriptures and the later exegetes of Dzogchen offer extensive discussions on freedom, even going as far as distinguishing five different types of freedom: (1) natural freedom (*rang grol*), (2) primordial freedom (*ye grol*), (3) naked freedom (*cer grol*), (4) unbounded freedom (*mtha' grol*), and (5) unique freedom (*gcig*

grol) (*The Pearl Necklace Tantra*, 465.5; *The Tantra of Unimpeded Sound*, 178.6; *The Treasury of the Supreme Vehicle*, vol. II: 1614.4).

6 While the relationship between Skullward Leap and Breakthrough will be discussed in more detail in Chapter 8, it is useful to note that the tradition itself sometimes articulates the difference between them based how effortful they are. When compared to Breakthrough, Skullward Leap is described as "involving effort" (Germano 1992, 124). From an etic perspective, however, even though the esoteric visionary method is more involved than the technique-free relaxation in the "nature of the mind," it is nonetheless grounded in the logic of the effortless expression of primordial freedom. This is particularly apparent in the repeated insistence—especially by later commentators like Longchenpa—that the lower tantric vehicles engage in practices that are unlike Skullward Leap because they are "effortful" (*rtsol ba can*) (Lobel 2018, 191–5; Sur 2017, 31). By contrast, as Klein and Wangyal put it, "effortlessness … is a crucial ontological and soteriological feature of Dzogchen" (Klein and Wangyal 2006, 115).

7 For a discussion of Longchenpa's life and work, as well as his crucial role in the systematization of the Dzogchen teachings, see Chapter 7.

8 *grol ni bkrol ba lta bu ma yin pas/ lta sgom gyis 'bad mi dgos/ grol zhes rang lugs su gnas pa las/ bcas bcos med pa'i don no/ de ltar yin pas lus ngag yid gsum rang lugs la lhod chags shing/ sems nyid rnal du phebs pa la grol zhes bya/ de yang gtan du de ltar gnas pas theg pa thun mong pa las 'phags pa'o.* For an alternative translation, see Higgins (2013, 220).

9 It might even be more correct to speak of the "co-construction" of modern Buddhism. "The modernization of Buddhism," so McMahan put it, "has in no way been an exclusively western project or simply a representation of the eastern Other; many figures essential to this process have been Asian reformers educated in both western and Buddhist thought" (McMahan 2008, 6).

10 As McMahan notes, "While meditation has always been considered necessary to achieving awakening, only a small minority of Buddhists practice it in any serious way. The vast majority of Asian Buddhists have practiced the dharma through ethics, ritual, and service to the *sangha*" (McMahan 2008, 183).

11 The territory that we circumscribe as modernity is complex and the construction of Buddhism was fed by many different priorities. For my own analysis of modernity as a crisis that provided the ground for the academic discipline of religious studies, see Geisshuesler (2019a; 2021).

12 Bodhi once described modern definitions of mindfulness meditation as so "vague and elastic that it serves almost as a cipher into which one can read virtually anything we want" (Bodhi 2011, 22).

13 In this sense, the study is inspired by earlier research into the work of Ernesto de Martino (1908–1965), an Italian historian of religions, whose work was marked by a type of comparison that combined the pursuit of continuities across time and space with rigorous attention to historical change (Geisshuesler 2021).

14 Although it is classed as Atiyoga, the highest of the three supreme forms of yoga, the Great Perfection's texts are said to have grown out of the lower tantric vehicles, Anuyoga and, more specifically, Mahāyoga.

15 It is well known that the Great Perfection is marked by an advanced technical vocabulary, and it has been noted that many terms that were previously known in Buddhism became reformulated in unique ways (Rossi 1999, 38).

16 For a study of the very popular Mind Series texts, see Liljenberg (2012).

17 In my account of this underlying tension, I draw on Jean-Luc Achard's account. Cf. Achard (2018, 231).
18 For an overview of these sources and their recent discovery, see my comments later in the introduction as well as throughout. Since these texts were composed, stored, actively used, and discovered across a remarkably broad temporal and geographic range, I try to provide as much context about individual texts in the footnotes.
19 It is important to note that we are talking here about a world of the sky that is its own separate—yet connected—realm. As a consequence, I translate the Zhangzhung terms *mu/dmu/smu/rmu*, as well as the old and modern Tibetan words *nam/nam ka*, and *nam mkha'*, by using various expressions like "sky," "sky-world," "heaven," "heavenly world," "heavenly realm," and so forth. What is central, however, is that in the indigenous "cult of the sky" that we reconstruct here, the sky is understood to be a world inhabited by gods and other beings that is not only home to primordial life-sustaining energies, but that can also be periodically visited in order to reinvigorate the separate—but connected—world of human beings.
20 This is the argument of Dmitry Ermakov in an article at Bon, Zhang Zhung and Early Tibet Conference at SOAS in 2011, titled "Bön as a Multifaceted Phenomenon: Looking beyond Tibet to the Cultural and Religious Traditions of Eurasia."
21 If scholars have sometimes considered Bön as a form of plagiarism of Buddhism or a deviant form of the Ancient School, Karmay and Achard have found significant influences and borrowings in the opposite direction (Achard 1999, 215–39; Karmay 2007, 220–3). This is particularly true if we look at Bön in its noninstitutionalized form, where it designates "the entire corpus of non-Buddhist religious traditions in Tibet (Bellezza 2011, 4). In this study, the primary meaning of Bön is that of an "ancient pre-Buddhist as well as later non-Buddhist religious beliefs and practices in Tibet" (Kvaerne 2013, 184–5). Another meaning of *Bön*, or "Eternal *Bön*" (g. *yung drung bon*) points to "an institutionalized religious sect" a sort of "fifth sect" of Buddhism, which has "its origins in the 10th and 11th centuries" and its relationship to Buddhism is still a topic of debate (Dotson 2008, 41).
22 For a description of Skullward Leap in Bön, see Achard and Tapihritsa (2016).
23 In light of such claims, it is likely no coincidence that two fundamental Buddhist teachers associated with the early Dzogchen scriptures bore names Zhangtön Tashi Dorje (zhang ston bkra shis rdo rje, *c.* 1097–1167) and Zhang Nyima Bum (zhang nyi ma 'bum, 1158–1213); this father-son duo might well point to their tradition's profound association with this cultural realm. For more on treasuries and their role in the Ancient School and in Dzogchen, see Chapter 2.
24 With Berounský, we could therefore say that "the label indigenous might mean non-Buddhist, but it does not follow at the same time that it is indigenous in relation to something else" (Berounský 2014, 58).
25 See Martynov (1988) and Jacobson (2018). Mircea Eliade, one of the most important contributors to the scientific study of shamanism was likely influenced by materials from this corner of the world when he identified the sky myths across a wide range of religious traditions. For his overview of this archetypical journey of the spiritual adventurer to a supramundane world, see Eliade (1958, 99–111).
26 It must be noted that the literature on the sky-deer is dominated by Russian scholarship and more Western engagement with these materials would be a great benefit for future scholars interested in this cult. For an excellent introduction in English, see Jacobson (2018). For an attempt to insert the Mongolian religious context within a wider Eurasian sky-deer cult, see Fitzhugh (2009). It is therefore no surprise

that some of the most concrete ventures into the Eurasian origins of the deer-cult in Tibet have been undertaken by Tibetologists familiar with this cultural context, such as Ermakov (2008) and Berounský (2015). The comparative research undertaken by Dmitry Ermakov has recently suggested that the idea that animals like deer or sheep have the ability to mediate between different dimensions of the universe, bestowing prosperity and good luck in the process, is likely a universal trait throughout various cultures of Eurasia from Palaeolithic until now (Ermakov 2008, 367–88). I agree with Berounský, who notes that

> it would be premature to conclude that the bulk of Tibetan rituals connected with the deer have their origin in Central Asia and more evidence is required." However, I also follow in his footsteps by providing much evidence in support of such a wider connection. Referring to the connection between deer and camels in the text he studies, he notes that this "strengthens the possibility that other elements found in the deer-rituals might also have been inspired by Central Asian traditions. (Berounský 2015, 14)

27 Bruneau and Bellezza note that if deer account for 1 percent of zoomorphic images in Ladakh, they represent about 10 percent in Upper Tibet (Bruneau and Bellezza 2013, 15).
28 For a study, see Allen (1997).
29 For literature, see Lalou (1952), Haarh (1969), Stein (1971), Bellezza (2013), and Huber (2020).
30 See, for example, Heller (2018, 2022).
31 The pervasiveness of deer as a source of life in the mythical-ritual complex of Tibetan religion was first pointed out by Anne-Marie Blondeau and Samten Gyaltsen Karmay in the late 1980s (Blondeau and Karmay 1988). Their article offers an analysis of a Bönpo text entitled *Deer with Large Antlers* (*sha ba ru rgyas*), which contains a myth about a deer that serves as a ransom offering. For more recent scholarly treatments, see Ramble (2015) and Berounský (2015).
32 For an inspiring example of how comparative research that includes Siberian shamanism can provide new insight into Tibetan religion, see Oppitz (2013).
33 Although the deer seems to be the ideal animal of this cult, in Tibet, the deer was frequently replaced by another zoomorphic character, namely the sheep, which was regarded as his substitute in the mythical-ritual context. See Chapter 1 for a discussion of this parallelization of deer and sheep; likely a more general trait of the deer-cult throughout Eurasia.
34 These terms appear particularly in the *Prajñāpāramitā* (Ruegg 1989, 164–75).
35 From studies by scholars like Stein, Bialek, and Blezer, we know that vocabulary belonging to the ancient Tibetan universe frequently received a new meaning as it found application in another religious context. Cf. Stein (1971), Bialek (2015, 2018), and Blezer (2011a).
36 The Sanskrit terms *avaskandha, viṣkanda, vyutkrānta,* or *vyatikrāntaka,* which have variously been proposed as the Indian equivalents of *thod rgal* (Stein 1987, 51ff.; Germano 1992, 944), are generally used to indicate a religious phenomenon that allows practitioners to leap or skip over something, particularly steps in the meditative itinerary (Ruegg 1989, 164–75).
37 Although Huber's study does intend to offer some diachronic reflections on the development of the source of life, his understanding feels a bit more static than my analysis.

38 For some secondary literature on this type of text, see Stein (1971), Bellezza (2008), Cantwell and Mayer (2008), Karmay (2010), Berounský (2017), Dotson (2008, 2013, 2022).

39 These texts display a wide temporal range in terms of their redaction, ranging from the imperial period until out time. The imperial texts, which are usually indexed by the terms IOL (India Office Library) or PT (Pelliot Tibétain), represent the oldest textual records of Tibet and are therefore uniquely useful in reconstructing the indigenous Tibetan worldview. These texts have an adventurous history of their own. They were discovered in the early twentieth century but have originally been produced between the late fourth and early eleventh centuries, before having been sealed in Mogao Cave 17, also known as "Library Cave" (Chin. *Cangjing dong* 藏經洞) at Dunhuang in the eleventh century. The Tibetan empire ruled over Dunhuang from either the 750s or 760s, or787, until 848. See Horlemann (2021), Sørensen (2019), but even after the end of the political control of Tibet, "remained a Sino-Tibetan region [and] Tibetan remained one of the main languages in the region throughout the Guiyijun [(851–1036?] period" (Galambos 2020, 13). The area must have been a bustling center on the Silk Road with inhabitants of diverse ethnic background as the texts found—consisting of a variety of religious and secular documents—were written in Tibetan but also other languages like Chinese, Khotanese, Tangut, Sanskrit, Sogdian, Uyghur, and other languages (Takata 2000). They are now kept in the British Library and in the Bibliothèque nationale de France. Some texts referenced in this study are as follows: IOL Tib J 075, IOL J 734, IOL Tib J 738, IOL Tib J 751, PT 126, PT 1038, PT 1047, PT 1051, PT 1052, PT 1060, PT 1194, PT 1285, PT 1286, PT 1287.

40 This collection of texts forms part of this corpus are folkloric texts, most of which are associated with Tibetan Bön and contain mythical-ritual systems dealing with vitality and/or the deer-cult. Some of these texts are in private ownership by lamas spread throughout the wider Tibetosphere, including India, Nepal, or Bhutan (e.g. *Extracting Vitality in Nine Sections* and *The Great Main Text of the Vitality Ritual of the Lord of the Vitality*, which are both held by Lama Tshultrim of Lubrak in Mustang, or *The Ultimate Vitality: The Celestial Head-Ornament* and *Extensive Elimination and Offering Rites for the Gods of the Four Groups of Little Humans*, which are both located in a monastery in Dolanji, India). Other manuscripts have recently been discovered in the Gathang Bumba (*dga' thang bum pa*) stupa in Southern Tibet and seem to be of ancient origin, possibly dating to the eleventh century (*Showing the Way to the Deer with Antlers, Methods of Subduing Crisis-Spirits,* published in 2007). In 2013, a manuscript held by a private collector in New York has been published for the first time (*Deer Way-Stations*). Finally, there are some texts that are part of the so-called New Collection of Bonpo Katen Texts, which were collected by Tempai Nyima in Lhasa in 1998 (*Remedying the Lords of the Soil and Subjugating the Evil Forces of Creation through the Ground of Vitality, Inviting Vitality from the Four Directions, Remedying the Agitation of the Lords of the Soil*). These texts are also of varying origin and provenance, some of which likely of ancient origin or, at the very least, influenced by older strata of indigenous Tibetan lore. Whenever possible, I will offer brief introductions to the origins of most of these texts when I first make reference to their content.

41 Although Huber correctly warns that it is problematic to identify sources like *Methods of Subduing Crisis-Spirits* or *Deer Way-Stations* as Bönpo texts because we know very little about the communities in which they circulated in the eleventh century

(Huber 2020, vol. II: 71), I nonetheless describe them as such for the sake of my reconstruction about a widespread indigenous cult centered on the quest for life and the cult of the sky-deer.

42 These texts play an important role, not only in Dzogchen, but also in the Ancient School more generally and are therefore frequently also called the *Seventeen Tantras of the Ancients*. *The Seventeen Tantras*, which eventually came to constitute part of the standard collections of Nyingma Tantras (*The One Hundred Thousand Tantras of the Old School* or *rnying ma'i rgyud 'bum*), is sometimes also classified as eighteen or nineteen. The texts can be found in the edition of *The Collected Tantras of the Ancients*, such as *The Mtshams-brag Manuscript of the Rñiṅ ma rgyud 'bum*, vols. 11–12 (Thimphu, Bhutan: National Library, Royal Government of Bhutan, 1982) (abbreviation: TB). In my citations, however, I have relied on the separately published three-volume edition of these texts based on the Adzom Drukpa blocks: *Rñiṅ ma'i rgyud bcu bdun: Collected Nyingmapa Tantras of the Man ṅag sde Class of the A ti yo ga (Rdzogs chen)*, 3 vols. (New Delhi: Sanje Dorje, 1973).

43 You will also find some references to *The Heart-Essence of Vimalamitra* (*bi ma snying thig*), which is part of a collection of texts by miscellaneous authors, known as *The Heart-Essence in Four Parts* (*snying thig ya bzhi*). I reference the eleven-volume edition published by Trulku Tsewang, Jamyang, and L. Tashi in New Delhi (1971), with *The Heart-Essence of Vimalamitra* spanning volumes 7–9.

44 *The Seventeen Tantras* are a central part of *The Heart-Essence of Vimalamitra*. Tibetologists like David Germano and Christopher Hatchell hold that this entire corpus was likely composed by its Tibetan discoverer, Zhangtön Tashi Dorje, who lived in the early twelfth century (Germano and Gyatso 2000, 244; Hatchell 2014, 54).

45 While some tantras make references to other texts in the collections, most of them seem to stand entirely on their own. They also vary greatly in style and content. While the texts are by no means interchangeable and further research into the specifics of their composition is warranted, this study treats *The Seventeen Tantras* nonetheless as a unified corpus as these scriptures are generally accepted as the oldest existing textual sources of the Nyingthig Great Perfection.

46 His oeuvre consists of over 270 titles, including systematic treatises, polemical writings, and poems. Many of his texts were gathered in a series of collections, such as *The Resting at Ease Trilogy* (*ngal gso skor gsum*) and the *Natural Freedom Trilogy* (*rang grol skor gsum*), which offer introductions to Dzogchen; the *Dispelling of Darkness Trilogy* (*mun sel skor gsum*), which offer a commentary on the *Guhyagarbha Tantra*, or *The Heart-Essence in Four Parts* (*snying thig ya bzhi*), which consists of three of his own commentaries combined with their predecessors; *The Heart-Essence of the Ḍākinīs* (*mkha' 'gro snying thig*); and *The Heart-Essence of Vimalamitra* (*bi ma snying thig*). His most influential writings, however, are *The Seven Treasuries*, two of which will be at the heart of my discussion in the third part of this book. Indeed, in *The Treasury of the Supreme Vehicle* (*theg mchog mdzod*) and *The Treasury of Words and Meaning* (*tshig sdon mdzod*), Longchenpa offers his most comprehensive interpretations of Dzogchen thought and practice.

47 For Longchenpa's *Seven Treasuries*, I relied on the six-volume *mDzod bdun: The Famed Seven Treasuries of Vajrayāna Buddhist Philosophy* (Gangtok, Sikkim: Sherab Gyaltsen and Khyentse Labrang, 1983).

Chapter 1

1. While my inquiry into the Tibetan roots of the tradition will go further than any previous study to date, I am not the first to note indigenous influences in the formation of Dzogchen. If I noted that Higgins singles out the radical transformation of the ancient Indian understanding of freedom as one of the marking characteristics of Tibetan Dzogchen, Karmay states that Dzogchen "seems to be the product of purely Tibetan speculation, formed out of various Buddhist and non-Buddhist elements when monastic discipline had totally broken down, while other religious practices had become wide-spread and the country itself was in a state of political chaos" (Karmay 1998b, 98).
2. It is important to note that the Nyingma school was not a homogenous and monolithic entity. As van Schaik put it, "although there was never a coherent Nyingma school as such, it became useful to refer to the lineages and scriptures that derived from the first period of transmission of Buddhism into Tibet with the term Nyingma" (2004b, 7).
3. Note that Christopher Beckwith pointed out that we should translate the Tibetan term *btsan po* as "emperor" rather than "king" because the term implies that he is a ruler superior to all other, laying claim to the whole world (1987, 14–15).
4. While Buddhism may have had fragmentary transmissions in Tibet since the time of king Lha Thothori Nyantsen (*lha tho tho ri gnyan*, fifth century) (Richardson 2003, 159), it is only with Songtsen Gampo that we witness an expansion of Tibetan power through the unification of what was previously a series of kingdoms, the creation of the alphabet and the classical Tibetan language, and the systematic introduction of Buddhism to Tibet (Shakabpa 1967, 25).
5. The second Dharma King, Trisong Detsen, pushed the conversion of Tibet forward, establishing what is commonly thought to be the earliest Buddhist monastery on the plateau, Samye (*bsam yas*).
6. Ralpacen, referred to as the "son of god" in the *Testament of Ba* (Wangdu and Diemberger 2000, 17), was also a great supporter of Buddhism, inviting craftsmen from surrounding countries, promoting Buddhist literature and translation, building and restoring temples, and regulating donations for monks (Shakabpa 1967, 49–50; Yeshe De Project 1986, 296–7; Das 1970). Ralpacen died in 838 and while some accounts suggest that he might have accidentally slipped down a flight of stairs, it is likely that he was sick and possibly died as part of a larger feverish epidemic that struck the region around this time (Pelliot 1961, 133; Richardson 1981).
7. For an overview, see Kolmaš (1967), Beckwith (1987), Vitali (1990, 17), and McKay (2003).
8. Although this would require more research, I am wondering whether we could find the ultimate roots of these associations even earlier in the Buddhist tradition. Consider, for instance, that Upatissa's *Path of Freedom*, where the idea of visionary imagery culminating in a state of bliss that is designated by the term "perfection" seems to be already present: "If the yogin develops the image (*nimitta*) and increases it at the nose-tip, between the eyebrows, on the forehead or establishes it in several places, he feels as if his head were filled with air. Through increasing in this way his whole body is charged with bliss. This is called perfection" (Upatissa 1977, 157–8).
9. Interestingly, we can note that this model of perfectibilism is in line with the modern construction of Buddhism. As McMahan, in his discussion of meditation and modernity noted, "Buddhism gained entry into modern western culture in part

10 *rdzogs chen theg pa'i nges tshig ni/ rig pa bya bral ngang la ye shes rdzogs pas rdzogs/ bsgom pa rtog med ngang la ye shes dri med rdzogs pas rdzogs/ spyod pa bcos med ngang la ye shes brdal ba rdzogs pas rdzogs/ lta ba dgag bsgrub med med pa'i ngang la ye shes rtogs med rdzogs pas rdzogs/ 'bras bu dmigs med ngang la ye shes nyi shu rtsa lnga rdzogs pas rdzogs.*

11 Throughout Dzogchen teachings, there exist many different versions of this myth of creation. I am drawing particularly from its earliest versions in *The Seventeen Tantras* as well as Longchenpa's retelling in his *Treasury of Words and Meanings*. For secondary literature on this myth, see Achard (1999, 103–9), Bertrand (2011, 21–8), Arguillère (2007, 334–438), Kapstein (2000, 167–70), Germano (1992), Kongtrul (1995).

12 The later chapters of this book will highlight several episodes of this long-standing idealization of Dzogchen under the aegis of perfection.

13 The biographies of such early lineage holders can be found in the fourth volume of *The Heart-Essence of Vimalamitra (bi ma snying thig)*.

14 The mythical-historical description of the origins of the Dzogchen scriptures, of course, reaches further back in time. It narrates how the wisdom of the Great Perfection was transmitted through an unbroken lineage that started from Vajrapāṇi to the obscure Garab Dorje (*dga' rab rdo rje*, Skt. *Vajraprahe*), before moving through the hands of the no less enigmatic figures like Mañjuśrīmitra, Śrīsiṃha, Jñānasūtra, to finally make it all the way to Tibet, where it arrived in the eighth century thanks to the Indian masters Vimalamitra and Padmasmbhava.

15 See also Schwieger (2000). For another perspective on the intricate interwovenness of fiction and fact in early Tibetan writing, see Van der Kuijp (2013, 115).

16 Norbu also addresses this ambiguous attitude of Tibetans toward their own heritage by noting that while the myths "are of inestimable value for acquiring knowledge of the most authentic ... part of the ancient Tibetan culture," they are frequently "being neglected and despised by the Tibetans themselves" (1995, 123). While Norbu warns that the "original wisdom of the Tibetans, which has imbued all the cultural and religious aspects of Tibet ... today runs the risk of sinking into oblivion" (1995, xviii), it must also be noted that things are not that simple.

17 As Mark Aldenderfer and Zhang Yinong argue, "until the latter part of the twentieth century, there was no real sense of a Tibetan prehistory, and there was certainly no significant empirical basis upon to develop one" (2004, 2). Other two scholars have noted that it is challenging to determine the specifics of Tibetan culture during the pre-imperial period (Walter 2009a, xxiv; Von Fürer-Haimendorf 1978). In general, the old data is secular, fragmentary, and ambiguous, while the later data is highly anachronistic and based on a reconstruction that highlights the importance of Buddhism for the development of Tibetan culture.

18 *gzhi la gnas pa'i rig pa ni/ ye shes dbyings na sku gsung rdzogs/ dper na rma bya'i sgo nga bzhin/ nang 'od ye shes gsal bar bstan/ lam la 'char ba'i rig pa ni/ dper na 'ja' tshon lta bur bstan/ mtha' la skyol ba'i rig pa ni/ dper na rma bya'i phru gu sgo nga nas/ brdol te don pa lta bu'o.*

19 For a classical example of the Bön myth of the origin of existence (*srid pa'i grol phug*), which introduces two cosmic eggs (*srid pa'i sgong nga*) "one luminous and the other

dark, which give rise, respectively, to the dimensions of being and non being, of light and of darkness," see Norbu (1995, 165). According to Karmay, while "most of the sources ... agree that primeval man was born from an egg, ... there is no coherent systematization in the different sources in which it is cited [as] the number of eggs, their colour, shape and size, as well as the way in which they hatch are as varied as the texts" (Karmay 1998c, 248).

20 More generally, the periodization of Tibetan history has always been expressed in Buddhist terms, with the two diffusions of Buddhist teachings in Tibet being the periods of greatest importance. As Cuevas put it, "the rather minimal division of time, marked only by the birth, decline, and rebirth of Buddhist teachings in Tibet, overemphasizes the significance of Buddhist doctrine, oversimplifies the socio-political factors causing change, and imposes restrictions on any historian who wishes to articulate a more far-sighted and deeply textured historical narrative of Tibet's past" (Cuevas 2013, 53).

21 "The final creation of a central, imperial authority," Walter recently noted, was "the result of the superimposition of a small outside group, with a leadership structure built around an inspirational warrior leader, the *btsan-po*, on a set of tribal aristocracies brought under his often unsteady central control" (2009a, 23).

22 It appears that Stein borrowed this sentence from Sumpa Khenpo (sum pa mkhan po, 1709–1786), a Gelugpa master who used it in his Buddhist polemics against Bönpo opponents. As Kvaerne notes, Karmay pointed out that the same sentence also appears in the *Blue Annals* of Gö Lotsawa ('gos lo tsa wa, 1392–1481). See Kvaerne (1980, 42–3).

23 See, for instance, PT 1047, PT 1051, PT 1052, PT 1060.

24 For information on Nampar Gyalwa see Kvaerne 1(995, 33–4).

25 *dang po g.yang bab dbyings nas bab/ yum chen ba ga'i klong nas bab/ dmu thag g.yang thag dgung du bres/ gnam gyi 'ju thag de la bya/ nam mkha' lta bu kun la khyab/ rgya che dpang mtho gting zab g.yang/ dgung nas 'phur te sa bon tsam/ sa ma dog la g.yang du dril*. Translation by Berounský (2014, 63).

26 In a Katen text titled *Inviting Vitality from the Four Directions Phyogs*, it is said that vitality descended through a ladder of the *dmu*, with each individual among the Tibetan people—here described as the black-headed people—receiving one portion of vitality (*g.yang*). In another ancient Tibetan manuscript of uncertain origins, titled *The Ultimate Vitality: The Celestial Head-Ornament*, we find mythological narratives that describe how this quintessential vitality descended from the sky. *Phya* is intimately associated with *mu* as both of them are old Tibetan terms that designate the "sky" and the beings residing there.

27 *yab gcig srid brag rtse mtho dang/ yum nis rid mtsho 'phrul mo che/ de gnyis thugs kyis sprul ba las/ srid pa'i sgong nga brgyad du byung*. For an alternative translation and more detailed elaborations of these eight eggs and the various fortunes that they summon, see Bellezza (2005, 327–8). The manuscript has been found and partially translated by Charles Ramble. Certain passages have also been translated by Toni Huber (2020) and Bellezza (2005, 327).

28 Ramble explains that he found this text while "going through a private collection of manuscripts in Lubrak" (2015, 516).

29 *phya khu ye ma pham brtan/ 'o na phya gzhi g.yang gzhi gang nas rtsal/ phya rdzas g.yang rdzas gang nas rtsal/ kyai gnas snga bstod kyis dang po la/ zhes snga bskal pa'i thog ma la/ dang po ci yang ma srid par/ de la bag tsam brdul tsam srid/ de la zil tsam phra mo tsam srid/ de la rgya mtsho mer bar srid/ rgya mtsho de la sbu bar chags/ sbu*

ha la ni sgong du 'dril/ rin chen sgong nga dgu ru srid/ dung sgong gsum dang gser sgong gsum/ lcags sgong gsum dang dgu ru srid/ dung sgong gnam du yal ha la/ de la lha dkar rten gsum srid/ gser sgong bar du chags pa la/ de la mi smra gshen gsum srid/ lcags sgong mthur du bah pa la/ de la 'dre sring byur gsum srid. For alternative translation, see Ramble (2015, 518).

30 This figure's name is spelled in a variety of different ways, such as yab lha sde drug, yab lha bdal drug, yab bla brdal drug, yab bla bdag drug, etc. I have decided to translate his name just as "Lord of Vitality," since he is frequently identified as such in the texts.

31 The myth is extremely widespread and appears in a series of texts, such as the *rtsa rgyud nyi zer sdron ma, bsgrag pa rin chen gling drags* (both twelfth century), the *srid pa rgyud kyi kha byang*, or *The Chronicle of the Kings* (both fourteenth century).

32 This figure would deserve a more thorough study as he pops up both in many contemporary ritual texts throughout the Himalayan region, as well as old Tibetan manuscripts from Dunhuang, such as *The Age of Decline*.

33 According to traditional accounts, the initial introduction of Buddhism to Tibet and the conversion of the old Tibetan kings to the new religion dawned in the sky (Bu-ston 1931, 183). In this narrative, we read that the first Buddhist scriptures appeared in Tibet when they mysteriously fell from the sky in a basket, which landed on the roof of the palace during the reign of King Lha Thotori Nyentsen (lha tho tho ri gnyan btsan) (Dudjom Rinpoche Jikdrel Yeshe Dorje 1991, 507). It has been noted that this fundamental Tibetan association of Buddhism with the sky might even be expressed in the Tibetan term for Buddha *sangs rgyas*. Although the etymology of this term points to the Buddha as someone that "clears away" (*sangs*) ignorance and "expands" (*rgyas*) the enlightened qualities, Geoffrey Samuel not only noted that *sangs* is related to the term used in the "central purificatory ritual of the Tibetan folk religion (*sangs*)" but that it also had "the general meaning of 'sky' or 'heaven'" in Old Bön language (Samuel 1993, 611).

34 As Dotson has shown, our understanding of these basic principles of Tibetan kingship, according to which the emperor is life-sustaining, linked to ancestral spirits living in the sky, and in charge of ruling over the heavenly and earthly territories, is the merit of a single towering figure in Tibetan studies, namely Giuseppe Tucci (Dotson 2011).

35 In PT 1038, for instance, we find an account where the ancestor-god is said to descent from the thirteenth level of heaven (PT 1038, 12). A similar association is made in *The Age of Decline*, where we find a non-Buddhist narrative about "gods" (*lha*) in the sky (*gnam*).

36 We find this in the *Old Tibetan Chronicle* (PT 1287) and *The Envoy of Phywa to Dmu* (PT 126), as well as a twelfth-century Tibetan historiographical work known as *A History of Buddhism and Its Development in Tibet in the Royal Dynastic Period* (*chos 'byung me tog snying po sbrang rtsi'i bcud*). As Hugh Richardson noted, "Although that myth is not found in surviving early manuscripts, that does not necessarily imply that it was not current in the early centuries" (1989, 6).

37 Based on his analysis of *The Envoys of Phywa to Dmu* (PT 126), Stein suggests that "the country of the *dmu* ... seems to be situated in the sky, where the sun does neither rise nor set (which is to say somewhere, where it is always?)" (1959, 64). According to Hill, the idea of the descent of the kings from the realm of the sky is also prevalent in other Dunhuang texts, such as PT 1287, ll. 62–63, PT 1286, ll. 31–35, IOL Tib J 0751, l. Hazod notes that the *mu* indicates the "name of the heavenly bride-giver lineage

and at the same time of the place from where the progenitor king travelled to Earth" (2020, 297). Bellezza, finally, writes: "The *dmu* or *mu* are an ancient class of elemental beings with a semi-divine nature mentioned in at least one Tun-huang manuscript. … However, *dmu* is also the Zhang zhung word for *nam mkha'* (sky) with the meaning of a paradise or the universe" (Bellezza 1997, 69; Martin 2010, 164).

38 In a famous antecedent tale from Dunhuang, titled "The Tale of the Separation of Horse and Kiang," the gods descend on horses (Dotson 2022).

39 For instance, the Zhangzhung term *mu*, meaning as much as sky, maintains a stable meaning across several Tibeto-Burman languages. Cf. Stein (1959, 63–4), Coblin (1987), and Hill (2013). Elsewhere, Huber elaborates as follows: "The Tibetan words *rmu* (or *dmu*) and *phya* (or *phywa*) have close cognates in Qiang *mú pià* and *mu bya* meaning 'sky' and 'sky deity', while in Naxi pictographic language the word *muân* (or *mûn*, now pronounced *mee*) means 'sky' or 'heaven', and also refers to the ritual tree as an axis mundi linking earth with heaven which is the legendary sky cord's analogue" (Huber 2020, vol. I: 67). Karmay, similarly, explains that the *mu* "are seen as the ancestors of man in various countries such as Khotan (Li), Nepal, or Iran (Tazig) and as the ancestors of animal" (Karmay 1998c, 252). Ermakov suggests that the old religion of the Buriat Mongolians and the Tibetans shared a focus on the sky and that they were "essentially the same religion in the very remote past" (Ermakov 2008, 229). Dan Martin also indicated to me that the Nenets, a people living above the arctic circle in Russia, also venerate the sky and call it "num," but pronounce it like the Tibetans as *nam*. Alexander Berzin proposes that pre-Buddhist Tibetan postulations are part of a larger Central Asian belief in a "cosmic force linking earth with the infinite sky," which Mongolians and Old Turkic people designated as *qut* (Berzin 2010, 15). As Stein notes, *qut* designates meanings like "good omen, luck, grace," as well as "vital force, spirit, soul," both of which are contained in the term *g.yang* and the terms that we will see closely connected to it (*phya, bla, srog*, etc.) (1990, 194). Finally, a similar example can be found in tengrism, a religion that was widespread in Turco-Mongolic regions and originated in the Eurasian steppes. In this system, believers worship the sky deity Tengri and the shamanic practitioner is said to move in between the heavens and the earth on the back of a deer or a rainbow (Roux 1956; Kvaerne 1980, 42).

40 In *The Age of Decline*, for instance, we find another young man who is going into the wilderness to hunt animals. After unsuccessfully shooting arrows at three different stags, he finally wounds a deer that is specified to have antlers of conch. Although hurt, the deer manages to flee, and the hunter pursues it across the whole country until it finally succumbs to its injuries and dies.

41 *khyed ya mtshan can gi bya lnga yis/ lha dang mi'i 'phrin pa gyis/ mi ru lha rnams spyan 'dren mrdzad*. Alternative translations of this text are found in Bellezza (2005, 211–12) and Huber (2020, vol I: 267).

42 *de ska gsungs pa dang/ pha gi ni rtsos lan smras ba/ lha spyan 'dren byed par 'gro dgos na/ da ni bdag cag rnams la rta re 'tshal/ 'di don rtags dang 'jal gcig zhu zer/ de la zhon.*

43 *gtsug gi skos rgyal zhal na re/ ri gtshug drag sde pa'i kha shed na / shug pa gyag rnga 'dom tsam dang/ de'i rtsa bar lug dkar po dung gi ra can yod.*

44 *dung gi ra can lnga la ling gis zhon/ sha ltar 'grogs te thal/ rgod ltar lding ste thal/ gnam rim pa bcu gsum steng du byon/ mda' dar sna lnga gyas su khyer/ gyon du me long khyier/ spos mngad dud pas bsang.*

45 *srid ni skal pa'i dang po la/ rgyu ni g.yung (g.yung drung) sha ba'i rgyu/ brten ni phya dang g.yang gis brten/ gyer ni mi gshen bdagis gyer/ sngon tsam srid pa yab lha bdal*

drug phya/ do nub rgyud'or (rgyud sbyor) yon+g la/ babs ni phya dang g.yang du babs/ phya babs mi ngan phya bab bzang/ phya bab bzang ba'i khu ye gsung.

46 Huber also calls the sheep the "parallel of substitute" of the deer in the context of Tibet (Huber 2020, vol. I: 185). He also notes that in the *Deer Way-Stations*, there is a section on the deer way-station of the precious (*yin chen yi sha slungs*), which—although clearly centered on the deer-cult—also includes other wild animals like wild ass and wild goats (Huber 2020, vol. II: 61). This is the reason why Huber translates as Wildlife Way-Stations. The association between "vitality" (*g.yang*) and the sheep, so scholars have observed, might also be due to a linguistic connection with *yang* (羊), which means "sheep" in Chinese (Berounský 2014, 55–6). The term *g.yang* frequently appears in the epithet *g.yang-mo lug*, with the term *lug* being used for sheep in contemporary Tibetan language.

47 Many of these rituals rely on the collection and burial of antlers and bones of the deer. For an interesting parallel regarding animal regeneration and the ritual of burying bones of hunted animals in the Tibetan context, see Oppitz (1997, 525–6).

48 In this group of representations, we find a conventional, schematic portrayal of the body and a relatively hypertrophied horn-tree which are characteristic and carry the basic semantic message. The horns are formed variously, in the form of straight or bent branches, arches with branches, lightly bound spirals, or fir trees with many wavy or bushy branches. Such variability in the representation of animal horns is not accidental.

49 This is a dominant theme throughout the North Asian rock art and it can also be found in Upper Tibet. For an beautiful example, see Bruneau and Bellezza (2013, 123).

50 In reality, the text that I translated as Deer Way-Stations (*sha slungs*) is only one part of a two-part set of texts (*ste'u* and *sha slungs*) that describe separate but complementary rites with a common goal. For more on these rites, see Huber (2018; 2020, vol. II: 61–3).

51 The manuscript is in private ownership by a collector in New York City. High-resolution images of the manuscript exist at the Western Himalaya Archive Vienna (Department of Art History, University of Vienna) and facsimiles have been published in Bellezza (2013, 30–76), and Klimburg-Salter, Würzl, and Ramble (2013, 39–45).

52 For other accounts, see Dotson (2008, 61–3) and Bellezza (2013).

53 *rin cen sha slungs nes/ sha yur po ru zed dang/ yu mo rdzi bshor ma/ she'u cung ris bkra byung.* For translations of this passage, see Bellezza (2013, 58) and Dan Martin's blog.

Chapter 2

1 The Great Perfection can be compared to the Kālacakra Tantra in India or the Vipassanā in Burma as these contemplative systems have equally been shaped by dramatic historical transformations on a sociopolitical level. Indeed, the "Wheel of Time" must be recognized as an attempt to respond to the "barbarian threat" of Muslim invasion into India (Newman 1998, 328), and the rise of the Vipassanā movement in the nineteenth century can be understood as an answer to the pressures created by the arrival of the British and "the loss of the kingdom to non-Buddhist foreigners" (Braun 2013, 35).

2   More in detail, Bön historiography identifies two moments of persecution of their teachings; the latter being during the rise of the Tibetan empire and the former being the reign of king Trigum. As Achard notes, it is unclear whether there were really two different persecutions of this indigenous Tibetan religion. However, he also remarks that while the details of this first persecution "might be the remnants of a myth whose interpretation may in no way be connected to any historical event," this does "appear doubtful" (2008, xviii).

3   The story of Emperor Trigum is one of the best-known myths of Tibet and the figure will make several appearances throughout this study. Besides being rich in imagination and adventurous in its plotlines, the myth has played a significant role in various attempts of interpreting the introduction of Buddhism in Tibet. For studies and translations, see Haarh (1969, 401–6), Macdonald (1971), Cutler (1991), Karmay (1998a), Kapstein (2006, 38–42), Hill (2006), and Zeisler (2011).

4   For more details, see Norbu (1995, xvi–xvii) and Kvaerne (2013, 190).

5   Not only is it "dubious" that the first Tibetan kings "all embraced [Buddhism] with zeal" (Tucci 1955, 197), but evidence also suggests that the "influence of the old religion was still present, especially among the aristocracy" (Li and Coblin 2013, 128).

6   For more details on this epic story, see Beckwith (1987, 13), Karmay (2001, 62–4).

7   In his *Religions of Tibet*, Giuseppe Tucci already made a clear-cut distinction between "two religions," one where the heavens and the gods of the heavens stand at the center, and a second one, where the gods of the soil and the earth play a more dominant role. Tucci, furthermore, emphasizes the importance of Trigum, noting that he "personifies the memory of a transition of great significance in the history of Tibetan culture" as it was during his reign that the two traditions were first united (1980, 246).

8   As Stein puts it, if "the gate of Heaven is propitious" and should therefore be opened, "the gate of the Earth is unlucky," and should consequently be closed (1990, 200–1).

9   The same tendency will also be observable in Part II of this volume, where we discuss the notion that our innate awareness is contained within our bodies and needs to be released through our sense organs to manifest on the outside.

10 I have shown that the traditions can be fruitfully compared through their reliance of the metaphor of the "ground" (*gzhi/sa*) (Geisshuesler 2020a).

11 For some literature on the treasure tradition, see Gyatso (1996), Doctor (2005), Gyatso (1993), Ehrhard (1999), Martin (2001), and Almogi (2019). While this mode of scriptural production is particularly developed in Tibetan Buddhism, there are certain Indian antecedents in the concealment and retrieval of Buddhist scriptures, such as the *Perfection of Wisdom Sūtras* (*prajñāpāramitā sutras*). These were first "directly taught by Buddha Śākyamuni," then "disappeared from the earth for about four centuries … hav[ing] been hidden away by nāgas in the depth of the ocean until Nāgārjuna retrieved these texts from them" (Brunnholzl 2012, 34). For more examples, see Gyatso (1996, 152–3) and Lopez (1988, 5–6). Further, researchers have found that the revelation of treasures is a practice that can be found in many cultures and historical periods (Stewart 2012; Mayer 2019).

12 For more on the substitutes, see also Thondup (1986, 79–84) and Terrone (2014).

13 Dotson is careful to note that "this does not signify balance at the point of exchange," but nonetheless emphasizes that we are dealing here with a profoundly interdependent conception of the human-environment interaction as these compensatory rituals are aimed at "the redressing of imbalances produced at the point of exchange, and the restocking of depleted reserves" (Dotson 2019, 17). In

his ethnographic study of pre-Buddhist Bön religious practices in central Bhutan, Kelzang Tashi has recently detailed very similar practices (Tashi 2020).

14 As an anonymous reader pointed out, the burying of the so-called treasure vases are not the special domain of treasure revealers, but rather a ubiquitous popular ritual concerned with deities of the landscape, which are particularly pervasive in indigenous non-Buddhist cosmology. The burying of these treasure vases, so *The Handbook of Tibetan Buddhist Symbols* (2003) explains, takes place "in sacred geomantic sites, including mountain passes, pilgrimage places, springs, oceans, and streams" and is intended to "spread abundance to the environment, and to appease the indigenous spirits who dwell in these places" (Beer 2003, 202). This being said, it is clear that the two traditions participate in the same "ecology of revelation." Recent ethnographic evidence collected by Valentina Punzi shows that some contemporary tantric practitioners use the two terms interchangeably, "occasionally identifying *gter bum* as the vessel that contains *gter ma*" (Punzi 2021, 241).

15 For more detailed accounts of this story, see Achard (2008, xviii) and Kvaerne (2013, 190).

16 The Dzogchen doctrines, interestingly, belonged to the two kinds of transmissions known to the Old School: that of the continuous and direct "oral" transmission (*bka' ma*), which passed text from teacher to disciple, on the one hand, and that of the "treasures," the hidden scriptures, which were concealed in the past and then rediscovered by a treasure revealer (Orofino 1990, 26).

17 Germano and Gyatso (2000, 244) and Hatchell (2014, 54).

18 Karmay (2007, 210).

19 As Dominic Sur has recently noted, "the term is subtle and straddles the line between objective and subjective." If the term can be translated as "appearance" from an objective perspective, it can be described as "perception" in subjective terms (2017, 18).

20 *thugs rje ltar 'char ba'i go ma 'gags pa/ 'od ltar 'char ba'i snang ba ma 'gags pa/ ye shes ltar 'char ba'i longs spyod ma 'gags pa/ sku ltar 'char ba'i ngo bo ma 'gags pa.*

21 *rmu skas dang rmu 'breng gis brten nas skye bo thams cad kyis mthong par gung du gshegs te lha'i lus la ro med par 'od du yal.* For an attempt at dating this text, see Van der Kuijp (1992).

22 For earlier descriptions, see Haarh (1969, 119) and Karmay (1998c, 150).

23 For more details on this anatomical description, see Stein (1990, 204).

24 For a classical presentation of the centrality of mountains in early Tibet, see Karmay (1996). For an excellent overview of the literature on the role of mountains in ancient Tibet, see Walter (2009a, 270).

25 For an excellent overview of how this conception of Tibet was shaped by Western scholarship over the decades, see Samuel (1993, 11–12).

26 Jacoby notes that terma was intimately linked to ancestral worship since its inception as the treasure revealers "participated in an economy of relationships aimed at maintaining equilibrium among the mandates they received from enlightened imperial Tibetan figures, celestial and earthly demons and divinities, and their patrons, including ordinary laity as well as local leaders" (2014, 103).

27 For other interesting perspectives on this theme, see Schwieger (2013, 69–70) and Gayley (2007, 215).

28 For this perspective, see Kapstein (2000, 167–70).

29 The ground is also described as "atemporal" (*dus med*), "indeterminate" (*ma nges pa'i dus*), or a sort of "fourth time" (*dus bzhi pa*).

30 Translations from works in French and German are mine unless otherwise noted.
31 My argument for the primacy of the sky over the earth in the earliest stratum of Tibetan culture parallels not only the argument of Huber but also that of Walter, who suggests that while "there almost certainly was a certain status *connected with mountains* at that time," there exists "no clear evidence" for a mountain cult during the imperial period (Walter 2009b, 231). This being said, it is becoming increasingly possible that the mountain cult was not as widespread as previously thought. Huber, for instance, notes that mountains are "completely absent from the central ritual concerns expressed in any manuscript from dGa'-thang and the Ste'u and Sha slungs manuscript as well" (Huber 2020, vol. II: 82).
32 Readers familiar with Western esotericism might know this sentence from the second verse of the *Emerald Tablet*, a Hermetic from the late eighth or early ninth century (Kraus 1942, 54). In the Latin translation of this Arabic source, the sentence reads: "*quod est superius est sicut quod inferius, et quod inferius est sicut quod est superius.*"
33 Rolf Alfred Stein has pointed out that the Tibetan "systems of geomancy and divination" are deeply pervaded by the "ambiguity [that] hangs over the changing of an uninhabited and uncultivated place into an inhabited and built-up site. The gate of Heaven may be projected onto the earth, within the site, and opening it brings good fortune. The gate of the Earth, on the other hand, is often unlucky. It must remain closed" (Stein 1990, 198).
34 Stein mentions several other instances in later texts, where the gate of heaven is opened and closed in such a manner (1990, 200).
35 Although "pure vision" (*dag snang*) does not directly correspond to the "mind treasure" (*dgons gter*), they are closely associated. As van Schaik notes, they represent "a rubric for texts of visionary origin that in practice are closely associated with, and sometimes overlap, the mind treasure tradition" (2004b, 31).

Chapter 3

1 The two warring parties, emerging out of an unresolved question of royal succession and centered on the two sons of Ü Dumtsen, were furthermore embedded in a more complex sociopolitical web of powers, in which clans—such as the Dro, the Chog, or the Ba—played a key role (Petech 1994; Vitali 1997, 196–7; Davidson 2005, 67).
2 It appears that the Yarlung dynasty came to an end because of external pressures, notably the collapse of the Uyghur Khaganate to the north as a result of the revolt by the Yenisei Kirghiz in 840 (Stein 1972, 71–2).
3 The revival of Buddhism in Tibet was promoted by two main groups, monasteries in the east and the aristocratic house around Yeshe Ö in the west. Some of the schools that were established after the resurgence of Buddhism include the Kadam (*bka' gdams*), Sakya (*sa skya*), and Kagyü (*bka' brgyud*), from which there were several branches including the Phagmodru (*phag mo gru*), Karma (*ka rma*), and Drigung (*'bri gang*). The most powerful of the New Schools, the so-called Gelug (*dge lugs*) sect, emerged in the fourteenth century.
4 The Nyingma, as we shall see in Chapter 7, classified their tantras in a different way, with a classification into six different groups being the most prominent model.

5 Four different classes: "Action" (Skt. *kriyā*, Tib. *bya ba'i rgyud*), "Practice" (Skt. *caryā* Tib. *spyod pa'i rgyud*), "Union" (Skt. *yoga*; Tib. *rnal 'byor*), and "Unsurpassable Yoga" (Skt. *anuttarayoga*; Tib. *rnal 'byor bla med*).
6 As one anonymous reviewer has rightly noted, the term *anuttarayoga* is not actually attested anywhere in Sanskrit sources and appears to be a false back-construction of the Tibetan *rnal byor bla na med pa*. Sanskrit sources use the term *yoganiruttara*.
7 Particularly, the *Cakrasaṃvara Tantra* (Tib. *'khor lo bde mchog*), the *Hevajra Tantra* (Tib. *kye'i rdo rje*, lit. "Hail Vajra"), and the *Kālachakra Tantra* (Tib. *dus kyi 'khor lo*, lit. "The Wheel of Time Tantra") were influential in the formation of the new Tibetan identity during the Renaissance. For overviews of these systems of tantra, see Williams (2000, 202–5), Skorupski (1996, 100–2), English (2002, 2–6), Snellgrove (1959; 1987), Mayer and Cantwell (2010), Dalton (2013), Gray (2007), and Beyer (1973). While Yamāntaka and Guhyasamāja would become key deities for the Gelug school (*dge lugs*), Heruka Cakrasaṃvara became the principal deity for the Kagyü (*bka' brgyud*) and Hevajra for the Sakya (*sa skya*) (Cozort 1986, 117–33; 1996; Skorupski 1996; Gray 2007; Newman 2000; Wallace 2001). It is important to note that most of these texts are extremely obscure and only understandable with commentaries and oral instructions. Gray's comments regarding the earliest Yoginītantra, the *Cakrasaṃvara Tantra* are relevant here:

> [It] makes no overt references to Perfection Stage visualization or yoga practices involving the subtle body, although later commentators read these practices into the text, as secrets obliquely referenced by it. Elements of Perfection Stage practice are found in some of the explanatory tantras (*vyākhyatantra, bshad rgyud*) in this tradition .... However, references to these practices are quite cryptic in these texts. (Gray 2021, 7)

In the same article, Gray also notes that the reason why these practices were only described in "a cryptic manner" was "to thwart those seeking practice details without the guidance of a qualified guru" (2021, 9).
8 For more detailed discussions of such embodied forms of vitality, see Chapters 5 and 6.
9 This is one of the key arguments of Ronald Davidson (2002). It is important to remember that the New Schools themselves are not marked by a homogenous group of teachings and some of the approaches found in these traditions closely resemble Dzogchen. Consider, for instance, the Mahāmudrā tradition, which also emphasizes effortlessness, simple practice, and direct insight into the nature of the mind rather than effortful yogic exercises and monastic discipline.
10 For details on this practice, see Cozort (1986), Harding and Kongtrul (2002), Yarnall (2003), and Gray (2007).
11 Christian Wedemeyer argues that

> the central aim of this self-creation yoga is for the practitioner to do away with the perception of herself as ordinary—as well as the pride that is believed to be associated with that perception—and to replace it with a perception of herself as a divine, enlightened being, with the sense of proud empowerment and universal efficacy that characterizes such a being. (2013, 117)

"When such yogis meditate on the creation stage," so Yael Bentor writes, "their identification with the deity becomes more than nominal" as "they gradually develop through practice a greater habituation to the deity and finally reach a genuine identity with it" (2019, 10).

12 If deity yoga is the centerpiece of the "generation stage" (Skt. *utpatti-kramah*, Tib. *bskyed rim*) practices, the practitioners are subsequently engaging in the techniques of the "completion stage" (Skt. *utpanna-* or *sampanna-kramah*, Tib. *rdzogs rim*).
13 There is, of course, something paradoxical about the power and self-transformation achieved during the engagement in these tantric practices because they are extremely regulated, controlled, and governed by supra-individual institutions. Consider, for instance, the tantric "commitments" (Tib. *dam tshig*, Skt. *samaya*), vows that rule the behavior of the tantric practitioners. As van Schaik noted, "transgression is one of the main themes of the higher tantras [and] rules of purity and moral conduct are deliberately subverted in order to blur the distinction between pure and impure," while simultaneously integrating this "transgressive rhetoric of tantric ritual with proscriptions limiting the behaviour of mantrins." "The samaya vows," so van Schaik concludes, "protect the soteriological purpose of transgression, while at the same time telling tantric practitioners that they can't actually just do whatever they feel like. Here, transgression and restriction are brought into the same sphere, where they coexist, and not without some tension" (Van Schaik 2010, 65). A similar tension between restriction and freedom can be identified in the *sādhanā* as a whole, where the yogis follow strict procedures in order to generate themselves in the image of a deity. As Bhattacharyya notes, "religious *sādhanā*, which both prevents an excess of worldliness and molds the mind and disposition (*bhāva*) into a form which develops the knowledge of dispassion and non-attachment, … is a means whereby bondage becomes liberation" (2005, 174).
14 As Dominic Sur has recently suggested, according to "some promulgators of the new lineages of Buddhist practice imported to Tibet, … dismissed the religious lineages that existed in Tibet prior to the 11th-century infusion of religious and intellectual civilization from the south as 'old,' which suggested decadence, decay, and irrelevance" (2017, 2). See also Davidson (2005, 119–41, 205, 211).
15 *de ltar gnas pa'i gzhi de las/ rgyu dang 'khrul pa'i sa bon ni/ gsal ba'i cha ni phyir shor bas/ [...] yid tsam phyir 'gyus snang cha la/ yul de bdag tu bzung ba'i blos/ [...] de ltar yul la bdag bzung ba'o.*
16 *gzhi dang shes pa sbags pa dang/ gzung dang dbang po 'gor tshul lo/ rkyen ni yul dang gzung cha las/ mtha' dang mtha' yi byed pa dang/ [...] shes pa 'ju dang yal pa dang/ mched par 'dzin pa rnams yin no/ sbags pa dri mar 'dzin pa ste/ shes byas rang rgyud bcing pa'o. gzung ba ma yin sa la yang/ bden pas dam du bcing ba'o.*
17 *sngon yul rnam par dag pa rig pa'i zhing khams zhes bya ba na/ mkhar sgo brgyad dang ldan pa'i mkhar zhig yod do/ mkhar de'i rtser khye'u snang ba'i rig byed bya ba yod/ de la ma rgan mo ling tog can zhes bya ba yod/ yul de'i mda' na sdig/ spyod pa'i rgyal po grags pa dbang phyug bya ba de la bu rgyal bu lnga yod pas/ sras po lngas sku rtsed la song bas/ rgan mo ling tog can mdo na mar skyo sangs la byung bas/ sras rgyal bu lngas btson du bzung zer ba de ya cha/ de nas bu ma'i stegs ma la song ba yang bzung nas lcags su bcug zer ba te ya cha.*
18 According to contemporary Dzogchen teachers, such as Tenzin Wangyal Rinpoche, space is usually identified with the mother and the son represents light (Wangyal and Turner 2013, 41). For alternative translation, see Norbu (1995, 31), Guenther (2005, 90–1).
19 *sngon yul yangs pa can zhes bya ba na/ ston pa 'od 'gyed pa zhes bya ba yod de/ de la bu spun gnyis yod pa/ grog po stong par btson du bzung zer te ya cha/ de nas dmag mi lnga byung nas rdo' mkhar rtse nas bcom zer te ya cha/ bu gnyis dong du bcug nas rgan mo ling tog can gyis sgo bcad zer te ya cha.*

20 *yang pha ma gnyis na re 'od skad zer ro/ bu de skad ma zer bar bdud kyi yul na/ a phyi ling tog zhes bya ba yod kyis/ de khyod kyi a phyi yin gyis de la me slong la shog byas pas.*

21 *a phyi ling tog can gyis/ sgo lcags bcug nas/ 'khor rnams la sngon 'dis nga'i bu bsad pa yin pas 'di ma btang zhig byas pas/ 'khor rnams na re/ de ka ltar bgyi'o zer nas/ 'gro ba'i dbang ma byung ngo/ de nas yang bu des 'di skad ces byas so/ phyi bdag gi gnyis kyi zhal nas/ khyod kyi a phyi ling tog can bya ba de bdud kyi yul na yod kyis/ de nas me long la shog zer ba lags kyis/ bdag ma bzung bar thong byas pas/ rgan mos na re khyod mi btang ba yin/ nga'i bu khyod kyi phas bsad pa yin pas mi btang ngo zer ro/ de nas bu des 'di skad ces byas so/ bdag mi btang na dmag 'dren byas pas/ mo na re/ khyod rang dmag drongs zer nas mthar ro/ de nas khos mgron po mi gsum la phrin btang ba/ kye grogs po dag/ yul rin chen spungs pa zhes bya ba na/ gdol pa'i rigs kyi mi bzhi yod kyis/ der khyod kyi khye'u rig byed btson du bzung bas/ dmag dpung mang po chos shig cig byas pas kho na re phrin bgyi'i zer nas song nog.*

22 This quest for vitality is not only present in the story of the little children in *The Tantra of Self-Arisen Awareness*, where the parents send their son to the country of the demon so that he can ask his grandmother Cataract for fire (570.4), but also in similar stories throughout the Dzogchen scriptures. Consider, for example, *The Symbol of the Secret Seminal Nuclei Tantra*, another locus classicus for anthropomorphized myths of the Great Perfection. Here, a minister is sent "to search for five precious substances" (52) to bring them back to the king.

23 Huber made a similar observation regarding the structure of such myths. "Something is wrong in the human world; a solution must be found; a knowledgeable expert or competent agent is engaged; they either instruct how to proceed with a ritual solution, often using divination as their source of knowledge, and/or perform the ritual which effects the desired result" (2020, vol. I: 103). For another illuminating discussion of such myths, see Ramble (2015).

24 For more on this text, see Huber (2020, vol. I: 105; vol. II: 39–49), Karmay (2009, 63–4), and Dotson (2008, 61–3).

25 Huber, studying some of these texts in detail, abundantly demonstrated that "the notion of first beings as children, child-like or diminutive is widespread in cosmogonies among highland populations of the extended eastern Himalayas" (Huber 2020, vol. I: 77). See also Huber (2018).

26 It is striking that the concern for genealogical origins is also prevalent in the role of the deer itself, which not only pervades many of these narratives, but participates in the quest for lineal descent. The deer themselves repeatedly inquire about their own origins, asking about the pedigree and the identity of their fathers and mothers (e.g., *The Ultimate Vitality: The Celestial Head-Ornament, The Great Main Text of the Vitality Ritual of the Lord of the Vitality, Remedying the Lords of the Soil and Subjugating the Evil Forces of Creation through the Ground of Vitality*). Usually, the parents are identified as deer-like figures associated with the sky (Sky-Deer with Long Antlers, *Mu* Doe), or precious substances associated with the deer and heavenly vitality (White Conch Shell Mountain, Crystal Demoness).

27 This idea can already be found in old Dunhuang texts, such as *Names Occurring in the Kingly Lineage* (PT 1286), where we find a discussion of how the kings descended from a divine ancestor (*yab lha*) in the sky. The use of the term "the son of heaven" for kings is also attested among the ancient Turks and the Uighurs (Hamilton 1955, 139–44).

28 *mi la phya med snyung cig mang/ nor la g.yang med god kha sdang/ zas la bcud med phan bstobs chung/ der yab yum sras gsum bka' gros nas/ lha bon thod dkar spyan drangs ste/ dbu la dar dkar thod cig being/ 'og na za 'og gdan cig gting/ zhal du skyems phud gtsang ma drang/ phya dang g.yang du 'gug dgos zhus/ lha bon thod dkar zhal na re/ phya dang g.yang du 'gugs pa la/ phya rdzas sna dgu tshol cig gsung.*
29 *nyi zer 'phrul zhags 'phang pa yi/ rin chen sha ba sgyir gyis bzung/ rin chen sha ba'i mi skad smras/ sha ba nga phya dang g.yang gis brtan ma yin/ phya rdzas sna dgu nga la tshang/ mi khyod kyis sha ba nga yin zer.*
30 *rgan mo gcig la nor bu rin po che gcig yod pa/ rkun mo mi lngas khyer nas/ rgan mo dug bsngal gyis zin zer ba de ya cha.*
31 *de nas yang rgan mo de'i bu me lha dkar po zhes bya ba des 'di skad ces zer ro/ nga'i nor bu ma brlag gam byas pas/ mi lnga po na re/ nor bu ma brlag gis/ khyod rang gis a ma rgan mo sod cig/ ma rgan mo ma bsad par nor bu mi ster ro zer bas.*
32 *khos kho rang gi ma bsad nas sha zos khrag 'thung rus pa mur/ dngos po med par byas pas/ nor bu rkun mos byin zer ba de ya cha.*
33 *nor bu rin po che'i za ma tog gcig yod skad/ de yi nang na rin po che phra mo bsam gyis mi khyab pa yis bkang ba gcig yod skad.*
34 The term *dri* already appears in the old Tibetan manuscripts found at Dunhuang, where it seems to be associated with violent deaths (Huber 2020, vol. II: 40).
35 Besides the recent study of Gerke, for anthropological accounts on the *bla*, see Desjarlais (1992, 1996), Diemberger (1993), Holmberg (1984, 1989), Sagant (1996), and Steinmann (2001). For textual studies, see Bawden (1962), Norbu (1995), and Karmay (1998c).
36 Indeed, Jäschke includes vitality as one of his translations: "soul, life, strength, power, vitality, blessing" (1995, 383).
37 These two notions share a series of other key traits: Just like the soul, "human fortune [is] something that can escape or flee (*bros*)" (Dotson 2019, 7) or "be lost" (*g.yang shor ba*) (Karmay 1998c, 149). Like the *bla*, the *g.yang* is a profoundly relational concept that circulates and connects "gods, humans, wild animals, and domestic animals" (Dotson 2019, 1). Like the *bla*, the *g.yang* is essential for the vitality of the beings it is bound to. Ramble notes that "a horse without *g.yang* is no different from a wild ass [*kiang*], and a yak without *g.yang* is like a *'brong*, a wild yak. It is *g.yang* that gives these animals their 'horseness' and their 'yakness'" (Ramble 2015, 510). Finally, both types of life-energy are of exceptional concern to ritual practices among contemporary Himalayan communities, particularly in the form the "summoning of the soul" (*bla 'gugs*) and "summoning of good fortune" (*g.yang 'gugs*). Indeed, the two notions are sometimes even considered to be so closely related that they overlap. "The way to rectify [the loss of the *bla*]," so Dotson writes, "is to perform a ritual to summon *g.yang*, whose breadth of meaning in this way overthrows a narrow translation like 'animal fortune'" (Dotson 2019, 7). The idea of *bla* might have also merged with yet another term belonging to the semantic field of vitality, namely *srog*. As Bellezza comments, like the *srog*, the *bla* is associated with the channels within our subtle body that fulfills a "psychoenergetic function essential in the sustenance of living beings and is related to the energies of the internal and external worlds" (Bellezza 1997, 33–4). Although I was not able to find the term *bla* in Great Perfection discussions of the subtle body, it is used in such a context in the Kālacakra tantra. Cf. Berzin (2010, 16).
38 Indeed, the term *'go ba'i lha* is sometimes translated as the "companion gods." For the various possible meanings of the old Tibetan term *'go*, see (Dotson 2017). For

scholarship on the concept of the five companions, see Nebesky-Wojkowitz (1956, 318–28), Dotson (2017), Berounský (2007), Dotson (2015).

39 For examples, see Karmay and Nagano (2002, 1–33) and Berounský (2007). Like the *g.yang*, the *'go ba'i lha* are also associated with wedding ceremonies where the bride undergoes a ritual in which her personal deities are detached so she can move to her husband's house (Karmay 2007, 161).

40 For the extensive scholarship on this association, see Macdonald (1971), Stein (1972, 227), Tucci (1980, 193), and Samuel (1993, 186–7, 263–4, 268, 436, 438–42). Some scholars posits that the five protective deities had their origin as "protective souls, before they changed into protective gods on whom depend the bodily integrity of the individual" (Tucci 1980, 193; Samuel 1993, 438–9). Sumegi, similarly, writes: "In the Tibetan folk tradition, the idea of multiple souls, common in shamanic systems, is reflected in the belief that a person has five protective spirits (*gowé lha*; Tib. *'go ba'i lha*) that come to be associated with the child at birth and that reside in different parts of the body" (Sumegi 2008, 16).

41 *pha mas lasu lha mchod mchod na mgosu lha ma 'goste dmu dag dkar po gyang du bchado.* (Read *thag* for *dag*.)

42 As Norbu in his discussion of the Tibetan understanding of *g.yang* and *phya* notes, "since we have the concept of 'positive', then inevitably there is that of 'negative' … We easily notice this by observing how in our life there alternate periods of good fortune, during which everything goes well, with periods of misfortune in which we are absolutely incapable of realizing our wishes" (1995, 68).

43 *kye lha yul [*ni] gnyan g.yul du/ gshegs su ni dgyes pa ste/ sa srin ni dun 'phyam gis/ shul gis ni mdo bcad pas/ sdig dgu ni sngon dgu ru/ sku'i ni bal khrid pas/ phyva bros ni g.yang mnyam te/ yams chung ni dbugs re phra.* Alternative translation by Karmay (1998c, 315–16).

44 Note that this process of capturing souls in witchcraft involves a strikingly similar symbolism as the nourishment of humanity through heavenly vitality. Exactly like the prince casts his sun-ray noose to lasso the jewel deer that serves as the ground for *phya* and *g.yang* (*The Great Main Text of the Vitality Ritual of the Lord of the Vitality*, 525), witchcraft involves the throwing of lassoes.

45 Indeed, it appears that the *bla* is particularly vulnerable during the night as this is the time that it roams, particularly during dreams (Karmay 1998c, 315). As Huber notes, "dreams occur when the mobile vitality principle—or divisible aspects of it—departs the sleeper's body via the mouth, often in the form of a small flying insect, and travels around at night experiencing the world" (Huber 2020, vol. I: 257).

46 See also Berglie (1976b, 90–1).

Chapter 4

1 The interdisciplinary approach suggested in this chapter matured within the cognitive turn, which has swept across virtually all humanistic disciplines in recent years (Slingerland 2008; Bainbridge 2006; Bloch 2012; Carroll 2004; Cohen 2007; Dutton 2009; Hogan 2009; Richardson 2010; Smail 2007; Starr 2013; Vermeule 2011; Whitehouse 2004; Zunshine 2010). For an attempt to apply this cognitive framework in the study of religion, see Geisshuesler (2019b).

2   While there are references to the dark retreat practice in both *The Treasury of Words and Meanings* and *The Treasury of the Supreme Vehicle*, Longchenpa's most elaborate explanations on the dark retreat practice are found in two Nyingthig texts dedicated to this practice (the *nyin mtshan 'od gyi 'khor lo* and *rgya mtsho ar gtad kyi mun khrid 'od gsal 'khor lo*) as well as in his commentary on the *Guhyagarbhatantra*, titled *Dispelling all Darkness throughout the Ten Directions* (*phyogs bcu'i mun sel*).
3   Of course, the phenomenology we are speaking of here is not the one concerned with "identifying background or implicit structures of consciousness," but rather "the perceived content of experience." For the differentiation between these two types of phenomenology, see Chalmers (1996, 4, 11).
4   *de la dang po du ba lta bu dang/ sprin dkar po lang long lta bu dang/ smig rgyu lta bu dang/ skar ma lta bu dang/ me stag lta bu dang/ mar me lta bu dang/ mthing ga khyab pa chen po'i 'od re khaa nag po'i rnam pa na ro lta bu mthong ste/ 'od zer dang thig le dang dbyings rig gi stong gzugs tshad med pa 'char ro.*
5   In this context, we read about a phenomenon known as *nimitta* (lit. "sign"), visionary phenomena that appear as a consequence of the concentration achieved through sustained attention to one's breath (Ledi Sayadaw Mahathera 1999; Upatissa 1977, 157–8; Buddhaghosa 2003, 277).
6   For more on the key points, see Chapter 5.
7   *gnas pa rtsa/ g.yo ba rlung/ bkod pa byang chub sems kyi gnas lugs so.*
8   A relevant phenomenon in the experimental study of perception is the so-called Charles Bonnet syndrome, which is frequently associated with various types of visual hallucinations, particularly light-related experiences (Vukicevic and Fitzmaurice 2008; Kazui et al. 2009). However, what is striking is that the hallucinations we observe in patients with Charles Bonnet syndrome are merely an exaggerated version of the same processes that account for gap filling in patients with scotomas or even healthy individuals. Or, put differently, all of us generate a coherent picture of the world despite imperfect perception (Ramachandran and Blakeslee 1998, 111–12).
9   The eyes that see (*spyan*) are clearly referring to the Eyes of the Buddha as it is a honorific term as opposed to *mig*.
10 Similar models have been introduced: minimal and narrative (Damasio 2010; Gallagher 2000; Christoff et al. 2011), first-order and higher-order (Zelazo, Hong Gao, and Todd 2007), primary and secondary (Edelman 1992), and conscious and metaconscious (Schooler 2002). In the cognitive sciences, the emergence of our sense of self has also been a popular area of concern. In the 1960s, Paul MacLean articulated the self by means of three ingredients, speaking of a "triune brain" that explains three functions of human cognition: the control of basic bodily functions, the regulation of emotions, and the cognitive processes of memory, interpretation, and choice (Ganzevoort and Sremac 2019, 5). More recently, the three levels of selfhood have received a more in-depth treatment by Antonio Damasio (Damasio 2010, 22), who defines them as proto-, core-, and narrative selves.
11 It appears that such mythical blueprints or "archetypal expositions" already played a central in rituals performed during the Tibetan empire (Karmay 1998c, 246). During these years, ritual specialists known as the *bön* and the *gshen* performed various practices such as *gto* rituals, "divination" (*mo, phya*), ransom rites (*glud*), diagnoses (*dpyad*), funeral rites (*shid, rmang, mdad*), and other rites, mainly related to healing and death (Dotson 2013).
12 The myth, so Arguillère concludes, "gives in many ways the framework" for "the experience of the meditative practice of Skullward Leap" and "everything takes place

as if Skullward Leap had the vocation to bring us back to the original crossroads of *saṃsāra* and *nirvāṇa* so that we make the right choice this time around"(Arguillère 2007, 402). For another example, see Germano (1992, 126).

13 Here, the current project moves beyond the analysis of ritual practices, which Huber explores primarily through shamanic festivals dedicated to the "gods of procreation" or the "gods of the phenomenal world" (*srid pa'i lha*). Indeed, if Huber focuses on ritual practices and shows that they replay mythical narratives describing the descent and distribution of mobile vitality stemming from the sky, this study explores meditation techniques to demonstrate that strikingly similar priorities led to the formation of contemplative systems like the Great Perfection. My argument is, however, influenced by A. M. Hocart, who made similar claims in his studies on life-giving myths and their fundamental role for ritual practices among various religious traditions (Hocart 1953).

14 For a similar argument regarding the myths surrounding the early Tibetan kings, see Mills (2012).

15 This idea can already be found in Tucci (1980, 63–4).

16 For a discussion of these patterns and their role in human cognition, see Chapter 4.

Chapter 5

1 Again, I hasten to note that the internal division within the Great Perfection, between Breakthrough and Skullward Leap, classifies the latter as an "effortful" technique. However, this does not change the fact that the instructions regarding Tögal are premised on simplicity and effortlessness if they are compared to better-known Indo-Tibetan tantric techniques of meditation, which involve both active visualization and intense bodily movements.

2 As Anne Klein puts it, "the wisdom of meditation requires the movement of energy. This energy is the mount or steed of consciousness and experientially all but indistinguishable from knowing itself. These energies must be part of what we consider when we look into the living practices of Buddhist communities" (2013, 572).

3 bdag* dang 'dzin pa'i zhen yul ni/ dang po nyid nas chos nyid la/ 'di kun rang gis rang snang bar/ 'di kun rang gis rang snang bar/ ye nas snang ba sngar ma rig/ bdag rtogs bcings pa'i nyon mongs lnga/ ye nas rig pa rang shar bar/ lhan cig gnas pa zhal ma 'tsho (I changed *chags* to *bdag* based on *The Treasury of Words and Meanings*.)

4 sa chu me rlung 'byun ba bzhi/ ye nas rang gi lus yin par/ sus ma mthong ba mig re rtul.

5 yang gsang bsdus pa'i man ngag bcud/ bar mtshams med par rang grag pa/ gang gis 'di nyid ma thos par/ rna ba'i dbang po med dam ci. (I corrected *rags pa* for *grag pa* based on *The Treasury of Words and Meanings*.)

6 rang gnas dbyings dang rig pa'i dri/ bral ba'i skabs med rang 'khor ba/ tshor m myong ba sna 'gags sam.

7 a ho klong chen rnam nyon cig/ 'jig rten gyi khams kyi sems can thams cad de bzhin gshegs pa'i snying po til 'bru la mar gyis khyab pa bzhin du gnas so/ de yang rten ni gzugs kyi phung po la brten no/ gnas ni snying gi dkyil na kun tu bzang po gwa'u kha sbyor gyi dgons pa zhes bya ste dper na bse'i gwa'u kha sbyar ba bzhin du gnas pa'i nang na ,od kha dog lnga'i dkyil na zhi ba'i sku yungs 'bru tsam 'od khyim gyi tshul du gnas so/ de ni rig pa'i gnas so/ dper na bum pa'i sku lta bu'o.

8   Precisely because it is latent and usually "wrapped inside of the heart," so Arguillère notices, it "hinders and obscures its adequate expression" (2007, 482).
9   As Samantabhadra recognizes himself in the display of lights that lies outside of him, the outward spiraling manifestations of the ground (*phyir gsal*)—its "flickering movement" (*'gyu ba*)—is immediately reversed and the epiphany returns back into the ground where it abides as the pure potential of the "internal radiance" (*nang gsal*) (*The Tantra of Unimpeded Sound*, 107.5–107.6). Arguillère detects that "it is difficult to understand what can be the sense of this movement of exteriorization followed by interiorization [in the myth of creation and liberation of Samantabhadra], except to establish a parallel to the experience in the meditative practice of Skullward Leap." He then proceeds to associate the movement of exteriorization with the first three visions of Skullward Leap "in which the radiation of wisdom (*ye shes kyi sdang*) emerges (*shar*) in the form of luminous visions (*snang ba*) ... developing in stages until they fill the entire perceptive field of the meditator" and the movement of interiorization with the fourth vision, in which we find "similar resorptions to the ones that are described in the case of All Good One" (Arguillère 2007, 402).
10 For a similar account, see Gyatso (1998, 204). Of course, this same activating dimension is also present in the anthropomorphized allegories involving little children. As a closer look at their names reveals, the children are imbued with an inherent type of luminosity that shines even in the darkest moments of imprisoned existence. Besides the Child Performing the Awareness of Epiphany and the Child Intelligence of Epiphany, Great Perfection scriptures describe these children in a series of other ways: The Little Child Crystal, The Eyes of the Sun, The Little Child Youth, Sky Embryo, Thoroughly Radiating, or Little Child of the Inconceivable Epiphany (*The Symbol of the Secret Seminal Nuclei Tantra*, 49b-53a).
11 It is important to note that the specifics of the preliminaries as well as their individual associations with specific main practices differ significantly from lineage to lineage. For overviews, see Dahl (2008) and Laish (2017, 218).
12 "The ... preliminary practice ... of distinguishing Cyclic Existence and Transcendent Peace," so Eran Laish summarized it, "exemplifies the proactive attitude which is meant to heighten experience" (2017, 219). From a comparativist perspective, it is important to note that the "differentiation" might also be indebted to a non-Buddhist heritage. In fact, it bears striking similarities with the five levels of practice (*sādhana*) of the pāśupata Śaiva according to which the adept is first instructed to act in a normative fashion, before acting out in a "manner calculated to reap ridicule ... insane in public and court dishonor" (Davidson 2002, 184, 219).
13 Although one reviewer pointed out that the this set of preliminaries is operative both in preparation to Skullward Leap and Breakthrough practice, it needs to be noted that it receives its most thorough discussion in Longchenpa's section on the preliminaries for Skullward Leap (*The Treasury of the Supreme Vehicle*, vol. II: 112; *The Treasury of Words and Meanings*, 239–42).
14 *lus ni rgyug dang nyal ba dang/ langs dang yan lag bskyod pa dang/ bskor ba dang ni phyag bya dang/ yan lag bskor dang mgo bsgril dang/ ji ltar dran pa'i las rnams dang/ gar dang phyag rgya bsgyur ba dang/ ji ltar dmigs pa'i las rnams bya.*
15 As we will see in the latter part of this book, the sudden exclamation of the syllable *phat* also plays a role in other moments of meditative practice, particularly the so-called introductions (*ngo sprod pa*) where it serves as a sort of wake-up call to the ultimate nature of our minds.

16 *brjod pa rtog pa'i rang bzhin phyir/ sgra skad rnam pa sna tshogs pa/ ci smras bzlog pa med pa'i phyir/ lha dang klu dang gnod sbyin dang/ dri za grul bum khyab 'jug gi/ skad ni bzang ngan bye brag brjod/ mdor na 'gro ba drug gi skad/ sems kyi dran bsam ngag gis brjod.*

17 *sems kyi spyod pa brtsam par bya/ dga' dang mi dga' bde dang sdug/ rtag dang mi rtag la sogs pa/ lta sgom spyod pa'i bsam pa dang/ chos dang chos min la sogs dang/ 'dod chags zhe sdang gti mug dang/ dge dang mi dge la sogs pa'i/ bsam dpyod rnam pa sna tshogs bya.*

18 It is interesting to observe the cross-cultural continuities in this association. The association between wind-breath and soul-spirit is apparent in Hebrew (*ruach* and *nephesh*), Arabic (*nafas* and *ruh*), and Greek (*pneuma* and *psyche*).

19 *'gul ba dang 'phrig pa dang 'gro 'ong dang 'phel 'grib dang phyi'i yul la snang nus pa'i cha rnams ni rkyen rlung lnga'i byed pa ste.*

20 *'gyu dang 'gul dang 'phrig pa dang/ yang zhing bskyod pa'i bdag nyid du.*

21 *skabs su rlung gyis rang gzung bas/ shes pa dran med rmugs par yang/ [...] rlung gyis shes rab rtsal brgyed tshe/ sngon ma thos pa'i chos rnams kyang/ yid la dran zhing gsal bar 'char/ gsal dang mi gsal rtsal rnams ni/ rlung gyi g.yo 'gul nyid las 'byung/ lus dkyil rtsa nang gnas pa'o.*

22 Germano observed that "passages describing breath being inhaled via the mouth and nose, and thus becoming interior mounts of our mental activity, are very numerous" and correctly identified this is both one the most "problematic" and most "interesting" aspects of the Great Perfection meditative system (1992, 684).

23 *dbugs kyi rta la zhon nas rgyu'o/ de yang kha dang sna nas rgyu'o.*

24 *snying dang glo ba'i bar na yang/ brtsegs ma gsum du gnas pa'o/ de ni rtsa nas 'gyu ba'o/ de ni rtsa nas 'gyu ba'o/ srog pa rtsa nas lam phyung ngo.*

25 While the association between indigenous forms of vitality (*phya* or *g.yang*) with the vitality of the subtle body (*srog*) is not explicit in these texts, we find evidence that Tibetans generally did make such associations. Consider, for instance, a treasure text titled *Brief Face to Face with the Longevity and Vitality Composed by Padmasambhava of Urgyan* (*u rgyan padma 'byung gnas kyi mdzad pa'i tshe g.yang kha sprod bsdus pa*), where we find a Buddhist account of the myth of vitality that invokes tantric terminology, specifically the "vitality indestructible seminal nuclei" (*srog mi shigs pa'i thig le*).

26 *'dzum gsum gyis mi bya bar gnyis kyis tsakkhu'i 'dras bu ltems pas*. For more on this technique, see also *The Treasury of Words and Meanings* (271), *The Treasury of the Supreme Vehicle* (vol. I: 407.5–6), and *The Heart-Essence of Vimalamitra* (vol. I: 373.1).

27 *zhag gsum bzhi na ma ltems kyang snang.*

28 As Germano has shown, the vitality-channel is sometimes also identified with the spinal cord, which, together with the brain makes up the central nervous system (1992, 683–90).

29 *de las mig nam mkha' la bzlog ste rtsa gcun nas bltas na ye shes kyi 'od snang gyis nam mkha' gang bar 'gyur ro.*

30 For a discussion of how this physical practice of pressing the eyes and the aorta to stimulate the visions is downplayed by the later tradition, particularly Longchenpa, see Chapter 7.

31 *'di dag gi sngon du ngag bslab pa rgyus med pa'i sar smyon pa'i tshig ltar ci dran snga phyi thams cad bslangs nas brjod pas dub ste ci yang zer snying mi 'dod pa ni smra ba'i ngang la ngag gnas par bya zhing skabs su smra snying mi 'dod kyang lung stong la sogs pa mi med par dub pa tsam brjod nas mi smra ba'i ngang la bslab bo/ de nas gzhan*

dang gleng ba spangs te mdo kha ton sngags bzlas pa tsam las mi bya ba ni brtan par bya ba'o/ de nas de dag kyang bkag nas ci yang mi smra bar la bzla ba ni.

32 As Dotson notes: "The term [*ri*] also means 'mountain,' and emphasizes how the continuum of wild and tame is conceived of along a vertical axis. The term for wild animals, particularly those that are hunted, is *ri dags*, which means, 'belonging to the wild' or 'belonging to the mountain'" (2019, 9).

33 Consider, for instance, *The Narrative of the Deer*, where the deer flees from the hunter throughout the entire country and proclaims that it will die "at the boundary between the meadow and the forest" (379). As Huber writes,

> when the deities initially arrived within the stratified terrestrial world space, they did so at one of the crucial ecological boundaries which is always mentioned in the *rabs*, that between the alpine meadow and the forest. Above eastern Bhutanese hill villages like Changmadung, this high boundary marks the actual transition between 'wild and tame' environments in relation to human activity, and this is precisely why it is so important and fitting in the ritual sequence. (2020, vol. I: 403)

34 Several texts also describe the pursuing, capturing, and persuading of horses to serve as psychopomp animals. See, for example, Dotson (2018).

35 It has been suggested that "wildness" was a crucial trait of early Tibetan culture. "Members of the armed forces," so Walter notes, "were subsumed under the term *rgod*, indicating the unleashed 'wildness' of the forces under their leader. Non-military population, on the other hand, were literally the 'tame' (*g.yung*), i.e., subservient and even fearful of the *rgod*" (2009b, 59). Walter, in fact, describes the *btsan po* as a "sort of berserker" because he leads his troops into battle to frequently die there; moreover, he is closely associated with the *btsan* spirits, who provide him with his fierceness in battle (2009b, 59). One of the reasons why scholars of religion have been interested in berserkers lies in the idea that their *furor heroicus* is believed to be based on a ritualistic performance, an initiatory cult aimed at achieving a self-induced trance-state (Liberman 2016, 101–12). While this is not the place to discuss the association between religion and berserkers, it is nonetheless striking that the behavior of Tibetan warriors demonstrates similarities with certain shamanic practices, particularly those that involve the adaptation of animalistic behavior. Ralph Metzner points out a possible connection between yogic and shamanic practices. Drawing on an article by the Jungian scholar Marie-Louise von Franz—who suggested that the "berserker trance was a kind of visionary state, an out-of-body experience in which the soul of the warrior, sometimes in animal form, raged in battle, while the physical body lay as if asleep" (von Franz 1988)—he remarks:

> This would be comparable to what shamans and some yogi adepts report as combat in nonordinary reality or the spirit world. There are indications that combat in the spirit world was an aspect of the experience of the berserker warriors, as it is in Eurasian shamanic traditions. Shamanic warriors might have a spirit ally, in animal or humanoid form, who helps them in battle with hostile spirits and also foresees and warns of danger. (Metzner 1994, 76–7)

36 This association between the behaviors of the shaman and of the hunter is likely linked to the historical origins of shamanism within hunting communities. Furthermore, the phenomenon of the shaman acting like a hunter is also attested throughout the Eurasian steppes, particularly Siberia (Hamayon 2007, 6). Huber,

however, also points to the presence of martial performances during the festivals surrounding the gods of procreation: "These feature armed and armoured male warriors who broadcast war cries, who assume battle postures, or who engage in mock combat and vigorous—at times even aggressive—physical displays involving strutting, jumping and sometimes violent movements" (2020, vol. II: 133). He also cites the report by R. K. Billorey, who observed a group of swords-men, known as *beydungpa* in 1976, describing them as "armed men, shaking their bodies and uttering hoarse war cries, nodding their plumed heads … The dance performed on the occasion is characterized with vigour and wild energy. The dancers' bodies seem to be possessed by an uncontrollable force, making them leap, whirl and sway to the varying rhythms of music" (1978, 22).

37 In *The Excellent Chariot*, the Third Dzogchen Rinpoche, Ngeton Tenzin Zangpo (1759–1792), offers a description of what it means to perform these six forms of existence during the preliminary practices of differentiation:

> Next, act out whatever behaviors of the six realms come to mind, be they physical, verbal, or mental. Experience all the various pleasures of the gods, all of their sense pleasures, songs, dance, and music. Act out their death and fall as well, and all the suffering this entails. Next come the demi-gods. The demi-gods fight and quarrel; they are killed and dismembered. They stage battles, wage wars, and do other such things. Along the way, they experience all manner of happiness and suffering. Act all this out as well. Lamas, rulers, and other wealthy humans experience various forms of happiness, enjoyments, and sense pleasures. The middle class engages in business and agriculture, subduing their enemies and protecting loved ones, while the impoverished live in a state of misery. Act out all of this, as well as the birth, old age, sickness, and death they all experience. In a similar manner, act out the stupidity, ignorance, and enslavement that animals experience, the hunger and thirst that torture spirits, and the suffering of heat and cold that those in hell have to bear. Imagine all these forms of suffering as though you yourself are experiencing them. (Third Dzogchen Rinpoche 2008, 53)

38 *sngags dang kha ton chos kyi sgra/ yod dang med dang snang ba dang/ yid dpyod tshig ni sna tshogs brjod/ byol song sna tshogs brda skad dang/ skad ni rnam pa sna tshogs la.*

39 As Laish puts it, "in the context of the *ru shan* practices, the practitioner is instructed to act, speak, feel and think in a manner that disregards the customary distinction between wholesome and unwholesome." Moving "in an exaggerated manner," making "a variety of vocal gestures," and intentionally engaging "with the full range of human emotions," meditators perform "behavioural and mental acts, [which] are meant to overpower the force of habitual patterns related to the somatic, verbal and cognitive dimensions of human experience" (Laish 2017, 219).

40 For more on this figure and his most famous composition, see Yeshi and Dalton (2018, 2022), Achard (2018).

41 As Stein put, "in many works, we are told of the holy men, a kind of founding heroes, who 'open the gate of a place' (*gnas-sgo*). This means that they were the first to establish a holy place (*gnas-chen*) or to found a religious establishment. The site previously termed 'wild' becomes an inhabited place" (Stein 1990, 197).

42 *kye gnam … ni zhal na re/ spang snar ni g.yel gong du/ sha 'bri ni smad pa la/ sha shor ni phas kyang mchi/ lgo bdun ni chu skyang ['dri?]/ sko la ni bdag gi phyugs/ sdus cing ni ra bar stsol/ ra mtha' ni gangs gis bskor/ gangs mtha' ni brag gis bskor/ myi khyod kyang*

sdun gyod gis thogs pa las/ da nu thar bar 'ong 'o. For an alternative translation, see Dotson (2019, 10).

43   rnam dag dbyings kyi sgron mas ni/ rig pa yi ni ngo bo sdud/ lu gu rgyud kyi ra bar* snang/ 'di la sus goms don de nyid/ mthing ga mi 'gyur rang gsal ba/ mu khyud kyi ni ra bar gnas/ rang gsal phyi yi yul du snang/ ngo bo nyid ni ma bcos pa'o. (I have corrected dbar for ra bar based on TB version and *The Treasury of Words and Meanings*.)

44   rdo rje nyid ni lu gu rgyud/ 'di nyid nang du gzhug par bya/ rang gi ngo bo rtog med du/ nang gi dbyings kyi go rar yang/ ma bzung mi gnas tshul gyis ni/ 'bral ba med par rgyun du snang.

45   gnad kyis bcings dang zhags* pa dang/ dbang po** sgyur dang rtsa ba bcad/ 'dren cing gzugs la bslab par bya. (I changed bzhag to zhags and changed dngos po to dbang po based on TB and *The Treasury of Words and Meanings*.)

46   rig pa'i gnad ni mig mi 'gul sems ma yengs pa las dbyings snang lu gu rgyud dang bcas pa shar dus dbyings kyi ra bar lu gu rgyud 'khul 'phrig med par 'dzin pa ste.

47   gsum pa sems kyi mi 'gul ba gsum ni gtad pa'i 'bem dang ma bral bas rtag tu sangs rgyas kyi dgongs pa la gnas/ rig pa dbyings kyi go rar bcug pas dngos po'i gnas lugs 'khyor sa med/ rtag tu de nyid kyi ngang dang ma bral bas snang ba bzhi tshad du phyin par nges so/ de'ang 'gyu bas rtog la rtog pas 'khor ba'i las sog pa las/ 'gyu ba'i rten rtsa rlung gnad du gcun pas rtogs pa rgyun chad pa'i rang gnad gal po che'o. For almost identical formulations, see *The Treasury of the Supreme Vehicle* (vol. II: 21.1), *The Blazing Lamp Tantra* (308.2).

48   de nas mi bzhis deng pas zin te/ mi lnga rta dang phral zer te ya cha/ bu gnyis rang gis rang shor nas btson bsrung bsad zer te de yang ya cha/ bu gnyis cig char phar nyi ma can du phros nas/ 'bangs la dpya bsdus nas. For the continuation of this story, see Chapter 6, where the children are being counseled by twenty-one queens upon their return home.

49   For the continuation of this story, see Chapter 9. The notion of a cross-country expedition that leads one to return home is also present in Skullward Leap practice. It is an exploratory journey that includes a sense of discovery. Consider, for instance, another prominent set of preliminary practices, known as the "training on the four elements' sounds" ('byung ba bzhi'i sgra don la bslab pa). In these exercises, described in detail in *The Tantra of Unimpeded Sound*, the student focuses on the sound of the four elements, water, earth, fire, and wind, while moving in between various places. The fire, for example, he builds in a secluded place and to the wind he harkens in a place "where three valleys converge or on a mountain peak" (54.4–6).

Chapter 6

1   This is particularly evident in the technical term "contextualized ground" (gnas skabs kyi gzhi), a term that can be literally translated as the "temporally-abiding ground," where awareness is said to "reside" (gnas) within the hearts of our bodies. Consider, for instance, the famous *Flower Garland Sutra* (*Avataṃsaka Sūtra*) (Cleary 1983, 9).

2   In some ways, this is a direct result of the Buddhist concept of "no-self" (P. *anattā*, Skt. *anātman*), as the absence of a fixed and bounded self opens up the path toward a much more expansive type of self that is linked to its environment through a web of interdependence.

3 *de ltar sngon 'gro byas nas/ mngon sum don la blta ba'i phyir/ lus ngag yid ni rab tu gcun.*
4 According to the Oral Transmission from Zhangzhung (*zhang zhung snyan rgyud*), one of the Dzogchen lineages in the Bön tradition, there are five postures, which are described as follows: (1) The posture of the dignified lion, sitting like a dog on his haunches; (2) The posture of the reclining elephant, lying down on one's belly; (3) The posture of the crouching ascetic, crouching like an old man; (4) The posture of the waddling goose; (5) The posture of the crystal antelope, the most difficult of all (Reynolds 2011, 24–5).
5 *dang po gsum ni lus kyi bya ba la mi gnas par sdod pas 'khor ba'i 'khrul pa 'phel mi srid/ yan lag gi 'phen sdud sdod pas 'khrul pa'i 'khor lo rgyun chad/ by aba gzhis la phab ste rtsol med du sdod pas bsags pa las kyi rnam smin dang bral ba'o.*
6 *ngag ni bslab dang gnas pa dang/ la bzla brten par bya ba'o.*
7 *skal ba dag ni mnyam pa yin/ ngag ni ji ltar lkugs pa bzhin/ su dang brda tsam nyid mi bya/ 'di ltar su yis byas pa'i mi/ sems kyi 'phro 'du rang chod do.*
8 According to the Oral Transmission from Zhangzhung (*zhang zung snyan rgyud*), one of the Dzogchen lineages in the Bön tradition, there are five postures, which are described as follows: (1) The gaze of the Dharmakaya, looking upward; (2) The gaze of the Sambhogakaya, looking straight ahead; 93) The gaze of the Nirmanakaya, looking downward; (4) The gaze of Skilful Means, looking to the right; (5) The gaze of Discriminating Wisdom, looking to the left (Reynolds 2011, 25).
9 In the words of Christian Coseru, we could say that it is a form of "phenomenological naturalism" (2012, 3–4). Of course, the crucial role of our sensory faculties in human embodiment has also been a core theme in certain strands of Western philosophy, which can be productively compared to Buddhist speculations on experience. While this aspect is particularly central to the work of Merleau-Ponty and his followers (Merleau-Ponty 1962; Gendlin 1962; Colombetti 2014), there is no doubt that already the early phenomenologists laid the groundwork for what we could call a personified understanding of human experience. Edmund Husserl and Jean-Paul Sartre both promoted the centrality of self-consciousness, and intentionally, claiming that "we have an implicit, non-objectifying, pre-reflective awareness of our own experience as we live it through" (Gallagher and Zahavi 2008, 17, 52). This type of thinking has also found its way into cognitive science research, where Shaun Gallagher and Dan Zahavi's *The Phenomenological Mind* (2008) has left a lasting mark on future research in the field (Gallagher and Zahavi 2008). Around the same time, Mark Johnson's *The Meaning of the Body* (2007) also argued for an enactivist approach to cognition, which has since become the foundational orientation in the contemporary study of human mentation (Johnson 2007).
10 *rlung ni ci nas dal bya ste/ rab tu 'phags pa las byung ba/ lus dang sems kyi 'brel chad do/ khams gsum du yang ldog pa min.*
11 *rlung gi sdod pa gsum ni rlung phyir mi 'gro bar sdod pas snang rkyen tha dad pas sdod sa med/ rlung nang du mi 'gengs parpar sdod pas rnam rtog tha dad pa'i rten med/ rlung phyi nang du 'gro 'ong med par sdod pas 'khor'dos gnyis su 'dzin pa'i gzhi stongs pa'i.*
12 For an attempt to explore the relationship between the five *khandhas* and contemporary cognitive science, see Thompson (2007).
13 As Dotson, in a footnote to his study of the Dunhuang manuscript PT 1285, notes, both *phya* and *g.yang* mean "good fortune" or "luck," but "in a rather more visceral or substantive sense than it carries in English" (2008, 43).
14 For a careful analysis of these channels, see Scheidegger (2005).

15 *shel sbug can ni snying nas mig tu 'brel te bzang po'i rgyan dang ldan pa'i thig le rdo rje lu gu rgyud kyi snang ba grangs med pa 'char ba'i rten byed pa'o.*
16 In *The Ultimate Vitality*, similarly, we encounter an original situation of deprivation—the lack of fortune—that brings forward a courageous young prince who takes it upon himself to travel to a distant land in order to retrieve *phya* and *g.yang* in the form of a crystal-antlered deer. Ramble also notes that "it is clear that *phya* is more closely associated with humans, and *g.yang* with animals: *phya* is to humans what *g.yang* is to livestock, lustre is to turquoise, warmth to clothing and nutrition to food." He specifies further, however, that the two categories overlap such that humans can have *g.yang* and animals can have *phya* (Ramble 2015, 510–11).
17 *phywa bon g.yang bon sku la phyag 'tshal lo/ dang po srid pa phya gzhi btings pa ni/ kyai gnam snga srid pa'i dang po la/ zhe tsam bskal pa'i thog ma la/ srid pa yod med gnyis kyi 'tshams shed na/ dung sha dkar mo shel ru can cig srid/ srid ni bskal pa'i dang po srid/ 'bab ni phya dang g.yang du 'bab/ phya de yang ma 'phang khu'i gsungs/ yang de yang ma 'phang khu'i/ gsungs/ sha wa thugs kyi sprul pa la/ sprul pa de'i mgo bo la/ steng gis phywa mkhar g.yang thugs srid.* Alternative translation by Ramble (2015, 521–2).
18 We have already come across an almost identical formulation in *The Great Main Text of the Vitality Ritual of the Lord of the Vitality*, where we read that the hunter "casts his sun-ray noose and lassoes the jewel deer." Similarly, in *Remedying the Lords of the Soil and Subjugating the Evil Forces of Creation through the Ground of Vitality*, we see that the hunter uses a "miraculous lasso" to catch the deer.
19 This ambiguity can also be seen in another anonymous text, namely *The Fox, the Monkey and the Badger; the Three*, which has been found in the village of Sayul in the Phenchu region of northeastern Tibet and made accessible by Daniel Berounský. In this narrative, the process of cosmogony leads to the creation of four types of beings and their respective worlds, the most important of which is known as the Conch Shell Man. Like in the subtle body, where the conch shell house is associated with vitality, in the mythical context, the Conch Shell Man represents the divine realm. In the text in question, however, this divine realm is then flooded with demons, requiring the performance of a ritual of fumigation to purify the divine realm. It is possible that such association also led to an association between the skull in the Dzogchen subtle body and a potentially harmful dimension of vitality. In fact, if the heart is associated with quiet, tranquility, and calm—and thus hosts the palace of the forty-two peaceful deities—the *dung khang* is associated with more fierce processes, providing the home for the *maṇḍalas* of the fifty-eight wrathful deities.
20 In Chapter 3, I have shown that *bla* is closely related to other early concepts, like *lha*, *g.yang*, and *phya*.
21 Harmonized with the Buddhist conception of consciousness, the term *bla* has oftentimes been translated as "soul," which "implies a unitary, stationary and embodied principle that is exclusive to an individual" (Huber 2020, vol. I: 46). In fact, although "most Buddhist populations in the Himalayas assign one *bla* to each person" (Gerke 2007, 194), ethnographic research has shown that this interpretation is contested as lamas and shamans seem to disagree on the number of *bla* a person possesses (Steinmann 2001, 185). As Huber puts it, the "official" Buddhist version "not only contrasts strongly with notions of the *pla* being both highly mobile and divisible, and able to exist and frequently move between embodied and disembodied states, but also the idea that it can be shared between certain beings in some manner" (2020, vol. I: 46).

22. Gerke suggests that in the context where *bla* "extends its meanings into the cosmologies of the people and their interrelationship with the individual, the social and the spiritual, … these links to a geographical embodiment of spiritual forces and a spiritual embodiment of social forces may either be weakening or empowering" (2007, 198). The journey of this mobile vitality principle outside of our bodies, indeed, is frequently understood to be "a dangerous one" (Sumegi 2008, 16).
23. Karmay cites a Nyingma text, in which we not only read that the soul roams and a messenger is sent to capture it, but also the following passage: "If one practices magic what does one kill, the body or the 'mind'? The body is made of matter. Even if it is killed, it does not die. As for the 'mind,' it is empty and therefore there is nothing to kill. Neither the body nor the 'mind' is killed. It is the *bla*, which wanders like a sheep without a shepherd that must be summoned" (1998c, 315).
24. Internally, so Dorje shows in his study of Sangye Gyatso's *Blue Beryl* (*Baiḍūrya sngon po*)—in its own right, the most famous commentary on the four medical tantras—the *bla gnas* refer to "seminal points (*thig le*) or subtle generative fluids within the body that support or sustain the life-essence [*bla*]" (2001, 416). "In classical Tibetan medical and some astrological texts," so Gerke notes, we find "the 30 seats of *bla* in the body, known as *bla gnas*," which "are said to originate from the Indian *Kalacakra Tantra*" (2007, 191).
25. Gerke picks up Giuseppe Tucci's observation that Mount Kailash, the *bla ri* of the former Zhangzhung kingdom served as the "heavenly cord" that "links heaven and earth" (Tucci 1980, 213, 219) and elaborates: "Here, *bla* seems to extend from the microcosmic body to the macroscopic space and thus links heaven to earth, giving a seat to the sacred, a place to community vitality and protection to the country" (Gerke 2007, 197).
26. We have already seen this protective role of the *bla* in our discussion of the "five protective spirits" (*'go ba'i lha*). Dorje argues not only that the external *bla* is "a sacred object, a semi-divine animal or a sacred power place," but also that these objects are "imbued with the ability to protect a given individual" (2001, 416). Karmay, similarly, notes that while the *blas gnas* is a sacred "place where the *bla* takes up residence," such as "a rock or a boulder (*bla rdo*), a tree (*bla shing*), a lake (*bla mtsho*) or a mountain (*bla ri*), … it is probable that at some time in the past certain persons, especially of high social rank in the society, were able to choose the dwelling of their soul which eventually ceased to be that of a single person and become that of the entire community" (Karmay 1998c, 314). Other scholars have made similar observations. Hildegard Diemberger, through her ethnographic studies of the Khumbo in Nepal, not only sees the *bla* as a category that establishes links between religion, kinship and politics, but also argues that "*bla* mountains" (*bla ri*) and "*bla* lakes" (*bla mtsho*) are to be understood as the "protective fathers and mothers of the area" (1993, 113).

Chapter 7

1. For an overview of the biographical materials available to us, see J. M. Stewart (2013).
2. As one commentator put it, Longchenpa integrated these myths, which were previously only "brought up in pieces," into a "synthetic presentation" (Hatchell 2014, 98).
3. While his role as head engineer of Dzogchen Buddhism is particularly conspicuous in his literary output, it also took on more concrete forms. Consider, for instance, his

restoration of the "Hat Temple" (*zhwa'i lha khang*). As I noted, this temple is vitally tied to Nyingma identity as it was founded by Nyang Tingdzin Zangpo (myang ban ting 'dzin bzang po) around the late eighth or early ninth century during the royal period and then used to store *The Seventeen Tantras*, which are said to have been concealed during the time of the Great Tibetan empire and revealed in the period after its fall. In restoring the temple that supposedly enclosed the foundational scriptures during the fall of the Tibetan empire and the rise of the neo-conservatives, Longchenpa relies on architectonic means to authenticate his own tradition's philosophy of inherent enlightenment.

4 Although the dating of these texts has been a matter of controversy in the past, Stéphane Arguillère elucidated that Longchenpa wrote his two systematic treasuries between age thirty-five and thirty-eight, in 1343 and 1346, and the remainder of the treasuries in the years that followed (2007, 101).

5 We get a similar impression when we consider three other treasuries written by Longchenpa, *The Wish-Fulfilling Treasury*, *The Treasury of Instructions*, and *Treasury of Philosophical Positions*. While the third is part of the "tenet system," the former two can be loosely associated with the "stages of the path" genre of Tibetan literature, all the texts are structured by a causal logic, ethical considerations, and a gradualist picture of enlightenment. Consequently, van Schaik notes that the distinction between simultaneist and gradualist approaches is not radical and that the relationship between "the *samsaric* and the *nirvanic* is usually somewhere in between these two extremes." Particularly in the Heart-Essence, so van Schaik continues, "there is a notable tension between the belief in the immanence of the *samsaric* in the *nirvanic*, and the belief that the two need to be strongly distinguished." While the Dzogchen teachers place "a great emphasis on nonduality and assert that the enlightened state is immanent in the everyday state," figures like Longchenpa also introduce "strongly dualistic kind of instruction that distinguishes the enlightened state of awareness from the everyday state" (Van Schaik 2004b, 51).

6 The insights in this paragraph come from some of the research emerging in this field in recent years, See, in particular, Yeshi and Dalton (2018, 2022).

7 Finally, the fourteenth century was not only "the philosophical period *par excellence*" but also one of great political upheavals. Longchenpa's epoch must be interpreted in light of the amalgamation of various intellectual and sociopolitical contingencies, such as the "unachieved elaboration of dogmas," "the unfinished constitution of the canon," and "the still sought-after construction of a unified Tibetan state" (Arguillère 2007, 32). Longchenpa's biography reflects these tumultuous circumstances. Getting embroiled in political power struggles, he had to flee to Bhutan where he spent several years of his life in exile (Hillis 2003).

8 See, for example, Cabezón (1994), Van der Kuijp (1998), Cabezón (1998), Coseru (2012, 26).

9 "The 14th century," so one scholar suggested, "became a time during which the enormous mass of teachings transmitted from India was systematized" (Dreyfus 1997). "The period around the middle of the second millennium," so Yael Bentor notes, "was important for the systematization of Buddhist thought and practice in Tibet, and especially for the crystallization of tantric traditions" (Bentor 2019, 3).

10 For an interesting discussion of Butön's canonization and his own background, see Dargyay (1985).

11 Kapstein, similarly, highlights the importance of Longchenpa, writing that his compositions involve the "deliberate effort to disclose the Great Perfection as fully

harmonized with, in fact the culmination of, the Indian Buddhist inheritance of theory and practice" (Kapstein 2000, 178).

12 *rdzogs pa chen 'di nas gnad 'di lta bu bshad kyang gsal bar rtogs nas grub mtha' slong shes pa ni ding sang kho bo tsam du zad do/ 'di gnad shin tu che bar yod do.*

13 Longchenpa's confidence is—throughout his polemical writings—teetering on the edge of self-conceit as he repeatedly invokes the "motif of protest and critique of others' inadequate Buddhist conduct," while simultaneously proclaiming his "self-perception as a faithful and superior protector of pure Buddhist values" (Ifergan 2014, 57).

14 "The attempt made by the confused architect to construct its way out of imprisonment," so Lobel writes, "only adds further layers of entrapment by reifying the very techniques it designs, constructing a proliferation of confused acts in the efforts to bring karmic causality to rest. The architect's structures then become prisons" (2018, 179). Corresponding observations have been made by Arguillère, who perceived that Longchenpa rebuked Buddhist scholastics because they relied on the functioning of the ordinary mind (*sems*), which "does not give way to receptivity or passivity, through which one would open oneself up to the alterity of the world, but is rather *constructed* by itself" (2007, 389).

15 Even Dzogchen practitioners are generally encouraged to engage in practices from both sūtras and tantras, including Mahāyoga and Anuyoga techniques. Indeed, although scholarship has frequently focused on his contribution to the systematization of the Great Perfection teachings, Longchenpa wrote extensively about the practices of the "lower vehicles" and Arguillère cites more than 120 references to *anuyoga* alone in Longchenpa's writings (Arguillère 2007).

16 *'gro ba'i lam dmigs thig chen te/ rkang pa'i rjes ni rdul tshon ris/ 'gro bar 'dod pa stangs stabs nyid/ yan lag bskyod pa phyag rgya'o.*

17 For some stimulating reflections on the relationship between spontaneity and structure within the process of walking, see Geisshuesler (2021, 166–9).

18 For an example, see Zahler (2009, 130–6).

19 Tögal has, however, been compared to those tantric practices that include signs and some teachers have even preached that these techniques lead to the same result (Gen Lamrimpa 1999, 110). The completion stage practices without symbolic attributes, by contrast, emphasize the nature of mind and have therefore been associated with "formless practices such as Mahamudra and the breakthrough stage of the Great Perfection" (Dahl 2008, 29). Like Skullward Leap, the manifestation of signs follow specific rhythms of gradual progression (Nor-bzaṅ-rgya-mtsho 2004; Tsongkhapa 2012, 308–12, 345). In one example, we read that they start out as if one were "seeing a mirage," progress to become a "smoke-like vision," before turning into a "vision like flickering fireflies" and "the glow of a butterlamp," and conclude in manifestations "like a clear autumn sky pervaded by the light of the full moon" (Mullin 2006, 85).

20 Subtle body practices, of course, come in many different forms and consist of a panoply of techniques. The most grouping is known as the "Six Dharmas of Nāropa" (*na ro'i chos drug*). Generally, however, they involve "the bringing, or the ability to bring, the winds into the central channel" (Kilty 2012, 5).

21 I am currently working on an interdisciplinary research project that aims at providing a classification system that includes the various contemplative systems of Tibetan Buddhism.

22 *kun rdzob la sbyong byed lus kyi 'khrul 'khor dmigs pa'i chings la sogs pa rtsol bcas du ma dang/ yang 'bras rags pa'i lus la ting nge 'dzin bde stong du 'dod la*. For many more examples, see Germano (1994, 213, 220–3.).
23 *gsang snags kyi nye lam ni rtsa thig rlung gsum gnad bstun pa yin la/ 'di la rtsol bcas spros pa can gyi lugs dang. rtsol med spros pa dang bral ba'i lugs gnyis yin no*.
24 *de la sems kyi yul 'khrul snang 'khor ba'i chos te bsdu na gzugs sgra dri ro reg dang chos te drug go/ 'di dag sems kyi bag chags las skra shad kyi rnam par snang ba ste/ gang la snang na 'khrul pa'i sems la snang ba'o/ ye shes kyi yul ni dag pa'i chos nyid nam mkha' lta bu dang/ 'od gsal gyi snang ba sku dang ye shes kyi zhing snang rgya che ba rnams so*.
25 As Sam van Schaik notes, if the latter is a gradualist approach, which "is often associated with learning, meritorious works, and the practice of morality," the simultaneist perspective "is often held to transcend such religious and philosophical activities, in fact to transcend all ordinary activities" (Van Schaik 2004b).
26 it embraces "no method except direct insight, and no progress over time, only the single moment of realization" (Van Schaik 2004b, 11). As Keith Dowman put it, "strictly, the radical Dzogchen path is a formless path and, therefore, may be called a pathless path" (2013a, 21). Higgins, similarly, notes that "the vanishing point of the path of mind is the starting point of the path of primordial knowing" as it is "precisely this loss of one's customary sense of self and world that makes way for a more primordial kind of intelligibility and certitude" (2013, 265).
27 The sentences in parenthesis are taken from one of the most influential twentieth-century Nyingma teachers, Tulku Urgyen Rinpoche (Tulku Urgyen Rinpoche 2000).
28 *bya cha'i rim pa rnams la khrigs su med pas phyal pa dang/ lhug pa dang/ yeng pa dang*.
29 *yang snang ba 'di 'khrul bar snang bas 'do gsal 'khrul snang du thal ba dang/ snang ba sems can phal la mthun snang du yod pa'i phyir 'od gsal mthun snang du grub par thal te/ 'dod na thams cad rnal 'byor pa bzhin du grol bar thal ba dang*.
30 *de'ang ding sang rmongs pa phal pa dag gis snang ba rang gi sems yin/ snang ba chos sku yin/ ye shes sems yin zer te/ mgo 'phong yin/ me chu yin/ mun pa snang ba yin zhes ci rung rung smra ba'i smyon pa rnams dang khyad med pa las*.
31 *mdor na de skad smra na ba lang gi khyur phyogs gcig tu bzhag ste/ lung rigs kyis bzlog rin mi chog ste*.
32 Besides "nonconceptual" (*rtog med*), awareness is frequently described in other negative terms, such as "free from elaboration" (*spros bra*) or transcending intellect (*blo 'das*). As Sur remarks, the "Great Perfection is not ratiocinative in nature, … not being a domain of experience connected with the efforts of intellectual inquiry" (2017, 22). Further, this rejection of "intellectual analysis" is not only found "in the context of meditation," but even "in scholastic activities" (Van Schaik 2004b, 71). According to Higgins, Great Perfection philosophy is premised on the idea that "goal-realization (*'bras bu*), the full disclosure of wisdom (*ye shes*) and its spiritual embodiments (*sku*), occurs once the discursive proliferations of mind and mental factors have ceased" (2013, 270). Eran Laish, finally, underscores the tradition's preference for "intuitive disclosures" over "well-ordered analysis and argumentation," suggesting that Dzogchen "is mostly interested in disclosing the intuitive aspects that are primordial to human awareness and the aspects that make conceptual views intelligible in the first place" (2018, 94).
33 "According to Longchenpa's world view," so he writes, "Samye was not only a symbol but also an actual religious doctrinal reference point that was presented there by Ha-Shang, entailing the teaching known as *gcig car*, a view of immediate realization similar in nature to Dzogchen" (Ifergan 2014, 52).

34 As Germano notes,

> Longchenpa indicates that such pressure is excessive and involves fainting via its forcing blood drops back into the vitality channel (aorta), though he apparently indicates that the point of pressing the neck is to affect the luminous channel located there, which seems to suggest that he interprets statements indicating we must press the "strongly pulsating" neck artery as merely indicating the location of these luminous channels rather than that the arteries themselves are relevant here. (1992, 690)

35 *De yang sku yungs 'bru tsam la spyan phul thag tsam bshad pa 'di la kha cig sku bas spyan che ste rtsa ba phra yang rtse mo yangs par yod ces zer ba ni bsam mno ma btang bar ci rung rung bla rdul du smra ba'i tshig ste/ sku de nyid la spyan yod na sku sku las che ba mi srid cing de las phyir 'phros te yod na sku dang mi 'brel ba'am spyan lug pa zhig tu 'gyur ba'i skyon yod do/ des na 'tshams pa zhes bya ba'i yul skad rnying pa la phul thag tsam zhes zer te tshig de tsam las yungs 'bru la 'tshams pa'i spyan de skra rtse bas kyang chung dgos pas so so'i skye bo chu bur gyi mig can rnams kyis bltar mi rung ba'i.*

36 For similar formulations, see *The Treasury of Words and Meanings* (248.6-249.2) and *The Heart-Essence of the Ḍākinīs* (vol. II: 204.6).

37 Secondary scholarship has noted that *phul thag* is a term used to describe the eyes but generally just accepts Longchenpa's "translation" as "proportionate" (Achard 1999, 229; Karmay 2007, 187).

38 The term *phul* can be a form of the verb "to offer" (*dbul*) or indicates "the smallest measure of grain," but I find both of those options not very relevant to the current discussion. By contrast, there are other translations of the term *phul* that could prove pertinent for our understanding of *phul thag*, all of which seem intimately associated with pre-Buddhist ideas, particularly the connection to the sky. First, standard Tibetan dictionaries provide us with the following translations for the term: "extreme/limit" (*mtha'*), "supreme/foremost" (*mchog*), or "highest; culminating point" (*rab*). Based on this meaning, it is possible that the term *phul* indicates the eyes as the highest place of the meditator's' bodies, which is closest to the realm of the sky.

39 Interestingly, the term *phul* appears throughout early Tibetan texts on the royal tombs (Hazod 2007, 272), particularly in the expression *phul med*. Here, it has been translated in a variety of ways and has frequently been considered to be a corruption. Early translators suggested that we are dealing with errors in transcription: Hoffman suggested that the expression might really be *yul med* or *'khrul med* (1950, 6), whereas Tucci believed that it was *yod med* (1950, 75). Sørensen translates it as "without end" (Bsod-nams-rgyal-mtshan and Sørensen 1994, 153), and Dan Martin as "without skill" (Mkhas-pa-ldeu 2022, 716). While the word is "still not satisfactorily accounted for" (Bsod-nams-rgyal-mtshan and Sørensen 1994, 151), I believe that Dotson's translation as "tomb pinnacle" is the most significant for our present discussion (2007, 54).

40 The expression *mthong phul*, in fact, means as much as *mthong rgya*, and can be translated as "scene," "the scenery," or "field of vision." It must also be noted that the word *mthong* (meaning "to see") might be a corruption of the term *mthongs*, which is pronounced the same way but much more closely associated with the idea of an expansive view that one gains from the sky by ascending through the hole in the top of buildings. Indeed, as Stein suggests, words such as *dkar mthong*, *skar mthong*, *sbas mthong*, and *gnam mthong*, all of which indicate openings through which one

sees the white, the starts, the hidden, or the sky, are best translated as the "view [that one may have out over a landscape], sphere, lighted space" (Stein 1990, 156). More specifically, *mthongs* or *rgya mthongs* signifies the sphere of the sky, the expanse of the sky, as well as the roof hole of a house (Jäschke 1995, 604). Here too, we find early Tibetan references. In *The Compendium of Maṇis*, for instance, we read that when Avalokiteśvara was invited by Songtsen Gampo, he came through the "hole of heaven" (*nam mkah'i mthongs nas*) onto the roof and then entered the palace through the "roof hole" (*mthongs*) (1.229b, 239b). Not unlike the connection between the physical eyes of the meditator and the top of buildings, the term *mthongs* implies an isomorphism between the macrocosm of the roof and the microcosm of the human body. The architectural structure of the oculus (lit. "eye" in Latin), a circular or oval window, is "also seen as equivalent to the summit of the human head" (Stein 1990, 162).

41 See, brda dkrol gser gyi me long by *btsan lha ngag dbang tshul khrims*, Bejing, mi rigs dpe skrun khang, 1997, which Dan Martin describes as "a very valuable dictionary of unusual words."

42 *'di la mi shes pa dang 'khrul pa'i gshad med kyang brda la ma byang ba rnams tshig la 'khrul nas yig ge'i don phyin ci log tu 'chad pa'i dogs pas dgag pa'i phyir 'dir gsal por bshad pa'o.* By contrast, in a text titled in *The Eleven Words and Meanings*, Longchenpa himself gives a very different interpretation of the term *phul thag*, noting that it means as much as "vast" or "huge" (*The Heart-Essence of Vimalamitra*, vol. I: 10.6).

43 This idea is supported by some enigmatic dictionary entries, where the term *thod rgal* is translated as "teleportational reconcealment." See the dictionaries from The Tibetan and Himalayan Library (thlib.org).

44 *Sku yungs 'bru tsam la spyan phul thag tsam du bshad pa ni skad rnying ste 'tshams par yod ces pa'i don to/ la la nas ye shes 'pho bar bshad pa ni rlung gi spor shab yin no/ 'phos na lus sems 'dral bar 'gyur ro.*

45 Reinier J. Langelaar has recently discussed ancestor cults in Tibet and pointed out a "cosmological rift" between an indigenous religion that is "immanentist" and a Buddhist religion that is "transcendentalist." If the latter is premised on a project of "salvation" that leads the religious practitioner from the mundane realm to a radically separate realm of "the sacred," "immanentist traditions are marked by a rather monistic understanding of the cosmos, in which metapersons and everything hallowed alike inhere in the realm that man occupies" (Langelaar 2022, 291–2).

46 If scholasticism's logical discourse has been analyzed in terms of its pan-Indian currency and interpreted as a risk for the obliteration of a distinctively Buddhist identity (Davidson 2002), this is even more true in our case.

Chapter 8

1 As Yaroslav Komarovski put it, "virtually all Mahāyāna thinkers from different ages and cultures are in consensus that the highest ultimate reality is ineffable and transcends words and concepts" (2008, 2). William Edelglass observes that Buddhist philosophers have long claimed that "language and conceptual thought are insufficient for achieving awakening and [that] ultimate reality is beyond the reach of language." "For many Buddhists," so he continues, "language is not merely inadequate as a vehicle to articulate the Dharma or achieve liberation; language is often thought to reify,

necessarily, in ways that lead to aversion and attachment, and words and concepts are thus regarded as obstacles on the path to awakening" (Edelglass 2019, 212).

2 I remember sitting in a coffee shop in Rome with Mark Allon, a fellow Buddhologist engaging in groundbreaking research on Gandhāran manuscripts, who reminded me that Tibetologists have an unusually rich corpus of textual sources available to them.

3 With Luis O. Gómez we could argue that while the "critique of language" is a marking characteristic, "this concern is often found mixed, paradoxically, with a strong sense of the importance of the invariant word, the holy manifested in utterance, silence embodied in words" (Gómez 1987, 5309). José Cabezón summarized what he considers to be the "two most important points in understanding the role that language, and especially scripture … in the Buddhist scholastic tradition" as a "*necessary* but not a *sufficient* condition for enlightenment": On the one hand, "scripture is necessary" as understanding "involves a reliance on language, and the meaning of this language must ultimately be penetrated (whether or not this necessarily involves logical analysis)." On the other hand, "understanding of both the words and their meaning are but preparatory stages to the internalization of that meaning via the transformative experience of meditation" (Cabezón 1994, 47).

4 As Evan Thompson notes, Indo-Tibetan Buddhist traditions like the Great Perfection were premised on "direct perception" (*pratyakṣajñāna*) giving access to "non-conceptual cognition" (*nirvikalpajñāna*), in which "the subject-object structure of ordinary experience subsides" (2017, 54). Its embrace of practices like Skullward Leap goes hand in hand with a critique of language, logic, and conceptualization. With Gene Smith we could say that because "doing took precedent over plans for doing," Great Perfection yogis "were content to get about the task of emptying the mind of all conceptualization through the practice of higher esoteric methods, [having] little interest in formulating elaborate philosophical models of how *prajñā* was to be realized" (Smith 2001, 229). Not only that, once the nature of the mind is realized, it cannot simply be explained in words, philosophical theories, or doctrinal tenets, but must be personally experienced. See also Dunne (2013, 2015), Sharf (2014).

5 *tshig la zhen nas spyod 'jig tshogs la lta bar gol bas lta sgom grub mthas bcings pa gces so.*

6 *de bzhin nyon mongs dri ma med/ rang byung rang bzhin nyid shes na/ sems can 'ching bar ga la 'gyur/ de nyid la ni bden bzung na/ sangs rgyas nyid kyang 'ching bar 'gyur/ sems can rnams ni cis mi 'ching/ bden med rang bzhin med shes na/ dri ma rnams ni rang sar dag/ chu yi rnyog ma rang dangs ltar/ … gzung 'dzin dag gis bzung na ni/ 'khor ba nyid la yun ring gnas/ khams gsum pa yi khang pa ru/ ming dang gzugs kyi btson par tshud/ ma rig las kyi lcags kyis bsdams/ rang byung sgron ma nyid dang bral/ 'khor ba'i mun nag stug pos gyogs.*

7 For another interdisciplinary attempt to link the Buddhist five aggregates to understanding the emergence of phenomenal consciousness, see Davis and Thompson (2013).

8 *yan lag spras pa tha dad las/ thams cad ming gi bye brag tu/ 'khrul pa'i yul la rnam gnyis 'gyur.*

9 In the texts, we find various alternative orthographies for his name and Kumārādza.

10 Hillis wrote that his "quasi-nomadic lifestyle is quite consonant with tropes and metaphors commonly found in Great Perfection literature valorizing space, the absence of boundaries, natural freedom, simplicity, spontaneity, and so forth" (Hillis 2003, 122).

11 The idea that the rapport between language and non-conceptuality should be envisioned as dialectical in nature is not entirely new in Buddhist Studies. Klein,

for instance, writes that since "philosophical or symbolic expressions of a tradition relate to the mystical experiences of persons," it is only logical that language must play a key role in the way that "a given mystical experience is fostered" (Klein 1986, 13). Robert Buswell and Robert Gimello also suggest that *mārga*-texts might be less descriptive and more prescriptive in nature, serving as a sort of guidebook that can foster certain meditative experiences in the reader (Buswell and Gimello 1992). Finally, Karl Brunnholzl observed a similar logic at work in the *Prajñāpāramitā* sūtras, arguing that they are best understood as "contemplative manuals or road maps meant to be used as practice texts to facilitate the single message of emptiness sinking in through repeatedly familiarizing with it by multifaceted contemplations" (Brunnholzl 2012, 119).

12 *chos nyid zad pa'i snang ba mthong ba'i dus na lus mkha' 'gro rnyi las bton pa ltar song ba ni sems 'od gsal gyi dra bar tshud pa las 'byung ba ste/ 'di ni rdzogs pa chen po rang grol lugs kyi dmigs pa la zhugs pas nyam nga dang bag tsha dang re dogs dang dga' 'jigs med pa ste/ tshig dbang gi lus kyi las dag pas rab tu spros pa med pa'i ye shes rang byung du shar ba'o/ ngag brag ca'i rnam pa ltar brjod du med par song ba ni rtsa gnas kyi yi ge rlung gi thig ler tshud pa la 'byung ba ste/ rdzogs pa chen po brjod du med pa'i don ngag gi grag pa la zhugs te/ rab tu spros med smra bya'i yul las 'das pa'i ye shes la dbang ba'o.*

13 The mapping of syllables onto the body is also found in the *Kālacakratantra* (Wallace 2009, 184).

14 *rig pa ka dag zang ma 'di rjen par ngos ma zin na lta sgom thams cad yid dpyod sems kyi sgrib par song bas gnyen po dug tu song ba bshal sman brjings pa lta bu zhig yin no.*

15 Invoking esoteric materials (ranging from altered states of consciousness to hypnosis), Doug Osto has made a similar argument about the dynamic and dialectical movement between experience and philosophy (Osto 2019).

16 It is clear that this homeopathic logic is shared by the larger tantric tradition. As Gray put it, "although desire and sexuality were problematized in some early Buddhist sources, as a 'poison' in the case of desire, their application to the spiritual path were often justified in tantric Buddhist literature via the trope of alchemical transformation" (2021, 7).

17 *dri mas dri ma 'khrud pa bzhin/ de bzhin dag pas dag pa grol/ dug gis dug rnams 'joms pa dang/ lcags kyis lcags rnams gcod pa dang/ rdo yis rdo rnams gcog pa dang/ shing gis shing rnams bsregs pa ltar/ rang rang dgra ni rang gis byed/ rigs mi mthun pas grol ba min.*

18 Suggestions regarding the historical origin of the practice of introductions are manifold. Apple writes that it "may have its beginnings in the *siddha* culture during the Pāla dynasties (760–1142 CE) in northeastern India" (2020, 170), but also suggests that "systematized and structured 'not-specifically-tantric-practice' pointing-out instructions are intimately related to Atiśa's *Stages of the Path*, its commentaries, and the teachings found in the Pointing-Out Instructions in Sets of Five" (172–3). Kapstein, also drawing on intra-Tibetan controversies regarding the subitist assumptions underlying the introductions, suggested that there might be an unacknowledged influence from Chinese Chan Buddhism (Kapstein 2000, 77).

19 The introductions are a specialty in the non-dual religious systems, such as the Great Perfection (Germano 1994; Achard 1999, 58, 176, 197; 2002, 45). For a discussion of the pointing-out instruction in the other major non-dual system of Indo-Tibetan Buddhism, such as *Mahāmudrā*, see Jackson (1994, 2).

20 Apple notes that "currently known evidence for pointing-out instructions among *siddhas*, such as Saraha, Tilopa, and Maitrīpa suggests concise, unsystematic, and

perhaps spontaneous, direct verbal and/or nonverbal acts of revealing realization to disciples" (Apple 2020, 170–1).
21 Klein and Wangyal use the expression "attunement or resonance model of knowing" to describe this type of language, which is "not a reflection on reality but, rather, an acknowledgment of full consonance with it. ... Here, unlike in referential language, expression is embodiment. Meaning arrives with it, not through it" (Klein and Wangyal 2006, 150). Because "authentic scriptures are the direct expression *from*—not *about*—reality, [they] arise from the heart of effortlessness to express the spontaneous mindnature, the base that exists prior to any division into Buddhas and sentient beings" (154).
22 *ye shes gnad ni mig nas 'byung.*
23 *lu gu rgyud du cer mthong bas/ rnam rtog 'gyu ba'i dran pa 'gags.*
24 *chos nyid mngon sum khyod par gyis/ dbang po rno dang rtul med par/ sems can thams cad sangs rgyas las/ gzhan du gnas pa ma yin no.*
25 *khrags chod du yid kyi sgo rtog bcas kyi gdangs las ye shes 'tshol ba las 'dir rig pa rtog med 'od gsal gyi gdangs mig nas 'char ba ngos 'dzin pas kyang 'phags te.*
26 *khregs chod du yul snang tshogs drug gi snang ba 'dzin pa'i dbang pos mthong bas rtog pa sna tshogs su 'char ba rgyun mi 'chad pa las 'dir 'od rtsa dangs pa'i dbang pos lu gu rgyud cer mthong dus rtog pa dus gcig la 'gag cing ye shes kyi snang cha dpag tu med pa 'char ba ni.*
27 *khregs chod du ye shes dngos su bltar med la/ 'dir dngos su mthong bas phyis mang la gyi grong khyer rgyun gcod pa'i che bas 'phags te.*
28 *snang ba 'od kyi khyad par ni/ khregs chod du 'khrul snang las mi snang la/ 'khrul snang 'dzin pa'i shes pa ni 'khrul shes su 'gyur bas don la gzung 'dzin las mi 'da' ste.*
29 *gzhan yang yid dpyod kyi tshig dang/ shes rab la mi ltos par dbang pos mthong ba dang/ dbang po la rno rtul med pa dang/ las la bzang ngan med pa dang/ sku gsum lam du snang bas 'phags te.*
30 Similarly, the epiphany of the ground can be illustrated by the example of a crystal being hit by the intense rays of the sun (see *The Treasury of Words and Meanings*, 177.5; *The Treasury of the Supreme Vehicle*, vol. II: 133.2, 342.1–7). Klein and Wangyal note that the introductions are based on a certain ontological continuity when they say that Dzogchen language is both a "lived reality" that leads us back to an experience and a "voice" that indicates "there is something in the text that is also in the reader" (2006, 152).
31 As Samuel puts it, the "process by which the shamanic religion of Tibet was reinterpreted in Buddhist terms ... was a complex one" and it is apparent that "the new Buddhist terms must have carried over a considerable weight of pre-Buddhist associations" (1993, 450).
32 *gsangs sam gya' 'am rgya mtsho las byung ba'i man shel dri ma med pa zhig skar khung gi snang ba la phyar nas bltas na 'od kha dog lnga lhug par 'char te.*
33 This emphasis on material experience is clearly a more general trait of the Great Perfection contemplative system. Consider, for instance, the preliminary practice known as the "training on the four elements' sounds" (*'byung ba bzhi'i sgra don la bslab pa*). In this technique, described in detail in *The Tantra of Unimpeded Sound*, the student focuses on the sound of the four elements: "the roaring noise of the sound of water," "the cool and heavy sound of earth," "the drawn-out sound of fire," and "the cool and fierce sound of wind." First, the practitioner is instructed to "build a fire with wood and the like in a secluded place," until it is "roaring, whooshing, sparking, and burning." Then, the yogi should proceed to observe water "when the winds of

autumn are blowing and the crops are ripe, in an empty place where downflowing water is rushing and waves are agitated." Third, he should move to "where three valleys converge or on a mountain peak," where he constructs "a secluded hut with windows in every direction," in order to "turn his ear to whatever direction the wind is blowing." Finally, as for the "sound of earth," it is explained to be "heavy and consistent," and the practitioner is instructed to "make egg-shaped balls [of earth], to toss them back and forth in his hands while meditating [on that sound]" (*The Tantra of Unimpeded Sound*, 54.4–6).

34 "The riddle," so Norbu reflects on the anthropomorphized narratives we studied throughout this study, "is a means of training the intellectual faculties, and in a way that does not give rise to those difficulties and causes of fatigue encountered when studying a branch of knowledge." On the contrary, the efficacy of the riddle (*lde'u*), according to Norbu, is premised on its playful quality that encourages us to participate in the construction of knowledge: "One applies to the solution of a riddle with a relaxed mental attitude, and a sense of pleasure and of enjoyment in playing the game (Norbu 1995, 22).

35 *da 'dod pa'i rdzas dang 'phrad nas byung/ rtsal ba'i nor rdzas rnyed nas byung.*

36 In the words of Roland Barthes, the introductions can be described as texts of bliss, premised on a type of writing that "imposes a state of loss," "discomforts (perhaps to the point of a certain boredom)," "unsettles the reader's historical, cultural, psychological assumptions," and "brings to a crisis his relation with language" (Barthes 1975, 14). "What pleasure wants," so Barthes writes, "is the site of a loss, the seam, the cut, the deflation, the *dissolve* which seizes the subject in the midst of bliss" (7). If Barthes notes that "every kind of bliss," is ultimately subject to the same logic, "those of 'life' and those of the text, in which reading and the risks of real life are subject to the same anamnesis," we find a similar blending of textual, practical, and contemplative life in the Dzogchen introductions.

37 Indeed, scholars of ritual practices have rightly sensed that religious language—particularly the one used during ritual practices—is characterized by its highly standardized and formalized style (Bell 1997; Rappaport 1999; Tambiah 1979; Werlen 1984).

38 To once again draw on the theoretical work of Barthes, we could say that the language of the introductions is not that of representation, which he describes as "*embarrassed figuration,* encumbered with other meanings than that of desire." In the semiotics of representation, a text might take "desire itself as an object of imitation; but then, such desire never leaves the frame, the picture; it circulates among the characters; if it has a recipient, that recipient remains interior to the fiction." Unlike representation, "when nothing emerges, when nothing leaps out of the frame: of the picture, the book, the screen," the introductions bridge the discursive and performative functions of language, enabling the words to jump out of the frame to work on the reader and listener (Barthes 1975, 56–7).

39 The possibility of such a paradoxical concept like a "planned spontaneity" is certainly not unique to the Great Perfection tradition. Indeed, this idea has recently been explored in a popular book by two economists, titled *The Power of Moments: Why Certain Experiences Have Extraordinary Impact.* In their provocative investigation, Chip and Dan Heath start off by commenting on the importance of what we could call "moments of spontaneity," noting that "we all have defining moments in our lives—meaningful experiences that stand out in our memory," with "many of them ow[ing] a great deal to chance." Intrigued by the contact between spontaneity and chance or

destiny, they rhetorically ask whether it really must be that such "defining moments just happen to us?" (Heath and Heath 2017, 4). The answer of the two brothers is clear and corresponds closely to what I argued in this chapter: Moments of insight do not just have to happen to us, they can be planned.

Chapter 9

1. Barbara Aziz and William Stablein have compared spirit possession to the doctrine of "reincarnated lamas" (*sprul sku*) and the protector deity Mahākāla (Aziz 1976, 347; Stablein 1976, 368). In a slightly different cultural context, Gombrich and Obeyesekere studied meditation in Sri Lanka and argued that many of the techniques propagated by the famous vipassanā teacher Mahāsī Sayādaw can be compared to "those used for entering trance states." The "technique" that they engage in, so they put it, "could if followed to the letter take them into trance states very like possession" (Gombrich and Obeyesekere 1988, 454).
2. The continuities between different forms of shamanism across Eurasia are evident. Certain scholars have even compared the role of the shaman in Siberia with that of Nepal, see Sidky (2010, 209), Riboli (2000, 56–7), Maskarinec (1995, 98; 1998, viii), Hitchcock and Jones (1976), and Watters (1975).
3. Spirit possession is frequently geared toward curing physical and mental sicknesses and consequently involves certain techniques—such as the sucking of impurities (*grib*), or fortune- and soul calling rituals (*g.yang/ bla 'gugs*)—that are entirely absent in Dzogchen practice (Berglie 1976a, 93; Bellezza 2005; Peters 2016).
4. Play is also a key term in the Dzogchen cosmogony. In one scripture, we read: "The play (*rol pa*) of this great marvel involves no differentiation between Buddhas and sentient beings. Just as there are clouds in the sky, [the play], being self-emergent and self-perfected, is serenely calm" (*The Tantra of Unimpeded Sound*, 137.1). Reading *The Heap of Jewels Tantra*, similarly, we encounter an evocative passage in which the primordial Buddha himself explains his role in the crystallization of the universe in terms of playfulness: "In this way, everything that manifests and everything that is heard is my play, the play of Samantabhadra. Since the arising of this play is unobstructed, my qualities emerge. Just through this appearing of qualities, [my play] has never been and will never be exhausted" (109.2).
5. The perceptual effect created by the multicolored luminosities manifesting during Tögal is frequently expressed in such terms. In *The Treasury of the Supreme Vehicle*, we read that "by understanding appearances and cognition as reality itself, whatever path of behavior you may pursue, it will never be beyond reality itself. Whatever appearances may manifest, they arise as unceasing play to dawn in the self-emergent *maṇḍala*" (*The Treasury of the Supreme Vehicle*, vol. II: 198.4). Elsewhere, Longchenpa writes that it is "through looking at outer phenomena" that "whatever manifests, appears free as the play of reality" (*The Treasury of Words and Meanings*, 334.3).
6. Of course, the idea of playfulness is also associated to the particular use of language in Dzogchen introductions. As Guenther notes: "Such images are the sky, the sun, a crystal, a cloud heavy with rain, and a peacock's egg, the latter because of its opalescence particularly suited to illustrate the whole's pure and primal symbolicalness, its nothingness/intensity-'stuff' (*ngo bo ka dag*), an originary awareness mode that, as it were, 'contains' within itself the whole's two other mutually consistent originary

awareness modes, radiating from out of the whole's depth (*gting gsal*) and ready to burst forth in playful activity (*rol pa*), respectively" (Guenther 1994, 71).

7   *longs spyod rdzogs pa'i sku'i ngo sprod ni/ de bzhin gshegs pa'i sku ras la bris pa rang gi mdun du bzhag ste/ shel mig gi steng du bzhag nas mig nam mkha' la bltas na/ longs spyod rdzogs pa'i sku kha mig rna ba can mthong bar 'gyur ro/ de bzhin du longs spyod rdzogs pa'i sku'i zhing khams par mdo la 'char ba ngo shes par gyis shig.*

8   *btsun mo nyi shu rtsa gcig gis gros byas nas bsam rdugs kyi lha khang du bros te/ mi lngas phub gon nas sgo bsrungs nas sus kyang 'od ma nus zer te ya cha/ de nas mi bzhis me long bzhir byad bltas pas/ rang ngo rang gi shes zer te ya cha/ de nas khang pa gcig la sgo brgyad yo pa mthong bas/ rang la rang gad mo shor zer te yang ya cha/ de bzhin brda' yi rnam pa kun/ mtshon nas ye shes don la sbyor.*

9   Of course, the mirror is a symbol that plays an important role in many Buddhist traditions. For a discussion of some of its functions, see Dagyab (1995). As I will show throughout this study, while the study of "symbols" is important, scholarship oftentimes underestimates the truly practical dimensions of mirrors, lamps, and so forth.

10 As Kapstein noted, "In relation to Buddhist meditation ... it is a frequently employed metaphor for the mind, as is underscored in Mahāyāna gnoseology by the concept of the buddhas' 'mirror-like gnosis' (*ādarśajñāna*)." He even cites Longchenpa's *Natural Freedom of the Nature of Mind*, where he translates: "Like a small child seeing a mirror, an infantile person refutes or proves outer objects. Like his mother who sees [the child playing with the mirror] and then wipes it clean, the causal vehicle seeks to transform the external. But when the coquette gazes [in that mirror] she uses it to make up her face; so, too, one who knows just what is, looks to the mind alone" (2001, 158).

11 *me long lta bu'i ye shes kyi ngo sprod gang zhe na/ me long gnyis kyi bar du rdul tshon gyis dkyil 'khor bri ste/ phar 'gram tshur 'gram gnyissu me long re gzug ste/ de la bltas na snang ba gnyis 'char ro.*

12 Mirrors give rise to various visions as they are said "to hold or reflect everything in the universe" (Bellezza 2005, 437) and thus "symbolize the mystic vision of the wearer, who could equally look into the past, present, and future" (Bellezza 2014, 263). For other studies, on spirit-mediums and soul-journeys, see Berglie (1976b, 1978, 1980), Peters 1981; Holmberg (1989), Mumford (1989), Diemberger (2006).

13 Bellezza notes that the mirror is so crucial because it "functions as the residence of the possessing deities and their retinue of remedial spirits, and as the abode of the spirit-medium's *rnam-shes* (consciousness), *bla* (soul) or *thugs* (mind) during the trance" (Bellezza 2005, 23).

14 In this context, future research might fruitfully explore the role of playfulness as the term "play" (Hin. *khelnā*, Nep. *khelnu*) is invoked to describe the moment of possession (Smith 2006, 112–17). Not unlike in the Great Perfection tradition, where the "play" can sometimes be interpreted as a description of the agency and impact of some alterity (the cosmos during the moment of the creation of the universe or the visionary experiences, or the religious teacher during the introductions), *khelnā* is used to explain how the deity is playing with the possessed individual.

15 Bellezza explains that "it is believed that the *'od-zer* of the higher deities ... take up their respective positions in the *me-long* and on the *lha-pa*'s body [because] this facilitates the arrival of the possessing deity and his retinue." Then, during the

moment of possession, "the possessing deity's radiant consciousness envelops him in rainbow light. … It is reported that during the possession, the *'od-zer* of the possessing deity occupies any of the 80 *rtsa* (subtle energy channels) of the body, as well as points on the headdress, costume, *dam-gsal me-long*, and the hairs of the body" (Bellezza 2005, 129). This association between mirrors, the play of light rays, and specific points of vitality contained in our bodies is also corroborated by Peters, who writes that "during the ritual refuge process, … the lights reflecting in the altar [mirror] from a candle or the lights in the room become ever larger and brighter, indicating that the deities invoked have descended." At the culmination of the séance, so the spirit-medium reports, "the fiery radiance" of the deity "is seen to emerge from the mirror and enter the [shaman's] body through the *ro ma tsa* and *kyang ma tsa*; and, when it reaches the *saug tsa* [*srog rtsa*] in the heart, there is a momentary flash of intense heat that causes the pau to shake." Finally, the deity's radiance continues "its course up the *uma tsa* to the head and down again to the *saug tsa*, to infuse the entire body through thousands of smaller veins" (Peters 2016, 21–2).

16 As comparative archeology has shown, some Tibetan mirrors resemble those found in Scythian archeological sites of north Inner Asia, many of which are dating to the first millennium BCE (Smoljak 1984, 246; Bellezza 2014, 290).

17 In fact, in the eleventh century, the Persian historian Gardīzī's reports that the Tibetan *btsan po* came from heaven and that he wore a "cuirass of light" (Martinez 1982, 129–30). In *The Compendium of Maṇis*, we similarly read that the "golden armor" (*gser khrab*) of the first Dharma king, Songtsen Gampo, was studded with jewels and decorated with an image of a *lha* (199–200). In light of such references, Walter not only insinuates the possible connection with the Iranian sun shield (Melikian-Chirvani 1992), but also highlights the ancient Indo-Tibetan association between the sun, gold, and Avalokiteśvara; leading him to speculate that the cuirasses "were meant to be symbolic of the presence of Amitābha or the action of Avalokiteśvara" and that they "may have considered themselves under the latter's protection, or even to have been his creation." Furthermore, "individual soldiers could likewise have been seen as 'rays' of the sun." (Walter 2009b, 260). See also, MacDonald and Imaeda (1977, 64).

18 As we saw, the early history of Tibet was marked by moments of intense military activity and it was particularly during the Yarlung dynasty, when Tibet was an expanding Buddhist empire that dominated much of the region, that "Tibetan armor and weapons were praised for both their high quality and their great effectiveness" (LaRocca et al. 2006, 6).

19 Walter explains that "their value was very likely as magical as practical, since areas of the torso remained exposed around them" (Walter 2009b, 132).

20 The vertical exchange of vitality is widespread among shamanic communities. See, for example, Hamayon (2007, 12).

21 The headdress of the shaman has recently been described as "the most ritually important aspect of [the shamans'] overall costume [and] the strongest marker of their professional identity" (Huber 2020, vol. I: 198).

22 Huber specifies that the deities "travel down from the sky world during the vertical ritual journey seated upon the head, neck, shoulders and upper back of the bon shaman, and they are often said to hold onto or be supported by his headgear" (2020, vol. I: 197).

23 "In Tibetan Plateau societies and their cultural-historical extensions into high Himalayan areas," so Huber elaborates, "the head and shoulders, and sometimes

armpits, are the abodes of a person's principal innate patron deities (*'go ba'i lha*)" (2020, vol. I: 198).

24   The crown of the shamans is frequently decorated by peacock feathers, which represents another symbolic and practical tool found throughout the Dzogchen tradition. Besides being used during the introductions, the peacock's variegated colors also symbolize the rainbow-colored manifestation of light during the epiphany and the visionary manifestations, while its dotted markings are also believed to stand for the eyes.

25   For a discussion of the birdhorns in the context of contemporary shamanic rituals, see Huber (2020, vol. I: 278–82).

26   The *bya ru* are said to be part of *stūpas* (Martin 2005, 119–20).

27   For a discussion of the *bya ru*, see Martin (2005, 126–30) and Vitali (2008, 384–7).

28   The birdhorns represent yet another liminal concept that operates in between the logic of vertical and spherical vitalities. Just like the mirrors, the birdhorns are closely associated with the symbolism of light, and the headdress of the kings is frequently described as radiating with light (Vitali 2008, 392). Like with Walter's invocation of the Iranian sun shield, the potential links between Persian culture and the Zhangzhung kings has been premised on this shared emphasis on radiant light. Vitali, for instance, believes that the *bya ru* crowns "being radiant with light" associates them to "the crowns of several Indo-Iranic kings from the same broad period in which the kings of Zhang zhung bearing horned crowns purportedly lived." He notes that the "luminous feature of the helmets of the Indo-Iranic kings is represented by a filigree/relief dotted pattern around their crown" and that "the radiant feature of the Zhang zhung crowns finds parallels as early as the Indo-Scythians and Indo-Parthians" (Vitali 2008, 394). While scholarship is right in pointing out the Indo-Iranian parallels in this context, it must also be noted that the shape created by a circular human face donning vertically rising structures like feathers, horns, or antlers point to a profound intermingling between a spherical model of vitality grounded in a vegetative fertility cult and a vertical model of vitality premised on the quest for the sky-deer and its precious attributes.

29   Norbu, in his book on pre-Buddhist Tibetan culture, dedicates extensive analysis to certain rites surrounding deer—such as the "deer with large antlers" (*sha ba ru rgyas*)—which he believes "to lie at the basis … of the magic powers of flight astride a drum attributed to the Bönpos" (Norbu 1995, 183).

30   Although today many different materials (such as cotton, silk, or plant matter) are used to make the headdress, historically, the "'woolen turban' (*bal thod*) has the highest mythical and ritual status of any turban." This particular turban "has a documented history in parts of central and southern Tibet dating back at least to the fourteenth century" (Huber 2020, vol. I: 184–5).

31   For various Naxi images of the flying sheep in myth and ritual, see Oppitz and Mu Chen (1997, 111), Rock (1952, vol. II: 404, 408–9; 1963, 84, 171).

32   Put differently, we could say that the shamanistic traditions exteriorized the quest for vitality by refining a mythical-ritual complex that emerged together with the practical activities of hunting and herding, which frequently involved the attaching of animal antlers or horns to the forehead for the imitation of the prey. As Roberte Hamayon showed in the case of Siberia, in its archaic form, shamanism is profoundly linked to the life of the hunters, who needed the mediating figure of the shaman because they believed that the wild animals had a spirit akin to our souls (Hamayon 2007, 6).

33 It can also be noted that another indication for this shared cultural heritage is the name of the mountain in central Tibet where Longchenpa wrote many of his treatises, the "White Skull Mountain" (*gangs ri thod dkar*).

34 Note that the headdresses of the kings is frequently adorned with both conch and crystal. One of the crowns is described as decorated with a "crystal heron" (*kang ka shel gyi bya ru*). Interestingly, Namkhai Norbu (*Light on Kailash*, 164) decodes the term *kang ka* not as "heron," but rather as crystal. The expression *kang ka shel gyi bya ru can* is strikingly close to another one of those exceedingly mysterious Dzogchen terms used to describe a crucial dimension of the subtle body, namely "the *kati* crystal tube" (*ka ti shel gyi sbu gu can*). While I do not propose that it is providing us with a solution to the particular terminology of the luminous channels in Dzogchen, there is no doubt that further investigation of these parallels is warranted.

35 The *gshen*, of course, were Bönpo priests, ritual specialists that played an important role during the early history of Tibet (Dotson 2008).

36 In *A History of Buddhism in India and Tibet* by the mysterious scholar Deyu, which has recently been translated by Dan Martin, the stag is described as one who "knows how to go in the sky (*sha ba nam mkha' la 'gro shes pa*)" (Mkhas-pa-ldeu 2022, 569). Martin also notes that the same phrase is used in another history of Tibet, *The Feast for the Learned* written by Pawo Tsuklak Trengwa (1504–1566, Tib. dPa' bo gTsug lag phreng ba), where the ancient funerary rites are described as involving the priests playing drums and bells, traveling into the sky on stags or by riding their drums (164).

37 The texts have been published by the Tibetan scholars pa tshab Pa sangs dbang 'dus and glang ru nor bu tshe ring. For a discussion of this discovery, see Karmay (2009). For the issue of dating these antecedent tales, see Huber (2020, vol. I: 38).

38 For partial translations and discussions, see Bellezza (2013, 167–92) and Berounský (2015, 3).

39 During the empire, such convictions likely lead to the practice of equipping tombs of nobility with silk yarn of great length to allow them to return to heaven.

40 For other examples regarding this phenomenon in northern Asia, see Curtin (1909, 107–8), Czaplicka (1914, 186–90), and Harva (1938, 488–94).

41 Huber specifies: "The list of thirteen deity titles and names above only exists as orally transmitted material at Changmadung, although one can frequently find variations on this list recorded in manuscripts in this same form at other cult sites in the Kheng region from where ancestral migrations to Changmadung occurred" (2020, vol. I: 402–3).

42 *rma them pa cig yar ru rgal te gshegs pa.*

43 For a discussion of this idea in relationship to the cult of the gods of the phenomenal world, see Huber (2020, vol. II: 46–7).

44 *Thod rgal gyi rdul phran dengs na 'od du gsal bas skye ba dang 'jug pa la dbang zhing slar 'pho ba'i skur bzhengs thub la.*

45 *'pho ba'i skur bzhengs lugs ni snang snang ba rim gyis zad dus lag pa'i sor mo lnga skabs su 'od kyi dkyil na bkram bkram snang ba la shes pa gtad pas snang ba de las log nas 'gro drug gi snang ba chu zla dang rmi lam ltar mthong dus rang gi lus kyang chu'i zla ba tsam du zang thal bar rang snang du mthong la/ gzhan gyis de snga'i lus der mthong la.*

46 This part of my study, seeking to adumbrate the contours of an alternative model of the transference body in early Tibet by pointing to important associations with a larger Eurasian substratum of shamanic currents, is inspired by this excellent article by Georgios Halkias. Of particular relevance is the following sentence: "The phowa

sādhana is well-established in Hindu and Buddhist tantric scriptures but that should not deter us from searching for fruitful parallels in spiritual traditions across Eurasia relating visionary ascensions to celestial realms and shamanic transferences to other bodies" (Halkias 2019, 86).
47 In the cults that he studied, the term is also used during the invocation of helping figures, which are first "summoned to 'arise' or 'manifest' (*bzhengs*)" (Huber 2020, vol. I: 246–7), then invited to be part of the ritual, and finally deployed to assist the shaman during the journey into the sky realm.
48 This vertical perspective could be worth exploring more detail as all three types of texts studied in this book—the Dzogchen scriptures, Longchenpa's commentaries, and the Bönpo ritual texts—also rely heavily on terms like *steng du*, *steng na*, and *steng nas* to describe and locate beings on various levels of the sky.
49 *snang srid gzhi* bzhengs dpangs re mtho/ 'bad med rang grol rgya re che/ ye thog chen po 'khor re mkhas.* (I have corrected "bzhi" for "gzhi" based on *The Treasury of Words and Meanings*.)
50 Scholarship frequently identifies the *Envoy of Phywa to Dmu* (PT 126), which I have related to the Dzogchen contemplative system, as the earliest historical evidence for spirit-mediumship in Tibet (Bellezza 2014, 289–90).
51 Many of these practices appear to be distributed well beyond Tibet, including vast areas of the Himalayas, as well as Siberia. Consider, for instance, that the ancient myths of the return to the sky upon death and contemporary rituals surrounding the summoning of fortune are particularly widespread in Mongolia (Berounský 2014; Sumegi 2008, 22). Similarly, the use of ropes and ribbons to establish a passageway between earth and sky is common in various Central Asian cultures, such as the Tungus or the Buryats (Shirokogorov 1935, 352; Eliade 1964, 118).

Conclusion: Meditation and the Adventure of Life

1 The future of the field of Dzogchen studies could also benefit from a fresh look at the work of Herbert Guenther (1917–2006), whose work has been neglected or dismissed by many. Although there is no doubt that his idiosyncratic translations, his mixing of various methodological discourses ranging across space and time, and his rootedness in Heideggerian philosophy make his work both challenging and problematic, he might be the interpreter who best understood what Dzogchen was truly about. Becoming increasingly fascinated by the allegories of the little children being captured by Lady Cataract, he published—particularly in the latter part of his life—books with such titles as *Wholeness Lost and Wholeness Regained: Forgotten Tales of Individuation from Ancient Tibet* (1994) and the hardly known, self-published *Down and Up Again: Allegories of Becoming and Transcendence* (2005). Besides emphasizing the dialectical flow of vitality—between abundance and loss, between heaven and earth, between crisis and recovery—his later work also maintained an earlier fascination with meditation as a process. See, for example, Guenther (1989).
2 Commentators have explicitly emphasized the parallels between contemporary meditation and the teachings of Dzogchen. Thus, although the sky-gazing practice looks exotically different from contemporary practices upon first sight, Skullward Leap is surprisingly similar in orientation to mindfulness. The first expert to point out these parallels was likely John Dunne, who notes that Dzogchen practices represent

an example of "effortless mindfulness" (*rtsol med kyi dran pa*) (Dunne 2013, 84). Robert Sharf, similarly, argues that various key terms related to Skullward Leap, such as "awareness" (*rig pa*), "wisdom" (*ye shes*), or "luminosity" (*'od gsal*), should all be understood as Dzogchen expressions of mindfulness (Sharf 2017, 206). Finally, Tessa Watt takes a closer look at the relationship between non-dual Buddhist traditions and contemporary mindfulness practice in order to show the centrality of the notion of "spacious awareness" in both of them (Watt 2017).

REFERENCES

Works in Tibetan

Brief Face to Face with the Longevity and Vitality Composed by Padmasambhava of Urgyan (*u rgyan padma 'byung gnas kyi mdzad pa'i tshe g.yang kha sprod bsdus pa*). In *Gter chen rdo rje gling pa'i zab chos phyogs bsdebs*. Kathmandu: khenpo shedup tenzin and lama thinly namgyal, 2019. A treasure-text (*gter ma*) revealed by Dorje Lingpa (1346–1405).

Eleven Words and Meanings on The Great Perfection (*rdzogs pa chen po tshig don bcu gcig pa*) by Nyi ma 'bum. Lhasa: Bod ljongs mi dmangs dpe skrun khang, 2008.

Extracting Vitality in Nine Sections (*phywa g.yang g.yang len dgu bskor bzhugs- s+ho*). In Ramble (2015, 251–3).

Extensive Elimination and Offering Rites for the Gods of the Four Groups of Little Humans (*mi'u rigs bzhi lha sel*). In Karmay and Nagano (2002, 1–33).

The Feast for the Learned (*Chos 'byung mkhas pa'i dga' ston*) by Pawo (dpa' bo gtsug lag phreng ba), vol. I: 1–855; vol. II: 859–1531. Beijing: Mi rigs dpe skrun khang, 1986.

Inviting Vitality from the Four Directions Phyogs (*bzhi'i g.yang 'bod*) by sBbra btsun mu la, Katen 104-4.

Light on Kailash (*zhang bod lo rgyus ti se'i 'od*) by Nam mkha'i nor bu, Zi Ling: krung go bod kyi shes rig dpe skrun khang. 1996.

mDzod bdun: The Famed Seven Treasuries of Vajrayāna Buddhist Philosophy, 2 vols. Gangtok, Sikkim: Sherab Gyaltsen and Khyentse Labrang, 1983.

Methods of Subduing Crisis-Spirits (*rnel dri 'dul ba'i thabs*)." Edited by Pa tshab Pa sangs dbang 'dus and Glang ru Nor bu tshe ring. A Selection and Presentation of Ancient Bon Manuscripts Retrieved from 'Bum pa che at dGa' thang in gTam shu (*gTam shul dga' thang 'bum pa che nas gsar rnyed byung ba'i bon gyi gna' dpe bdams bsgrigs*), 28–59. Lhasa: Bod ljongs dpe rnying dpe skrun khang.

Mirror of Royal Genealogies (*rgyal rabs gsal ba'i me long by bsod nams rgyal mtshan*). Beijing: Mi rigs dpe skrun khang, 1981.

rNam par rgyal ba (gter ma). *The Coiled Sky Lasso Vitality* (*rnam par rgyal ba'i phya g.yang dmu zhags 'khyil ba*). In S. G. Karmay and Nagano (2001, 104–3).

Pillar Testament (*Bka' chems ka khol ma*). Lanzhou: Kan su'u mi rigs dpe skrun khang, 1989.

Relaxation in the Nature of the Mind (*sems nyid ngal gso 'grel*) by Longchenpa. In *The Trilogy of Resting at Ease* (*ngal gso skor gsum*), vol. I: 113–729; vol. II: 1–439. Gangtok, Sikkim: A 'dzom chos sgar par khang, 1973.

Remedying the Lords of the Soil and Subjugating the Evil Forces of Creation through the Ground of Vitality (*g.Yang gzhi srid gshed dbang sdud sa bdag bcos pa*), Katen, 6–75.

Remedying the Agitation of the Lords of the Soil (*Sa bdag 'khrug bcos*), Katen, 84-24, 84-25, 84-26.

Showing the Way to the Deer with Antlers (*sha ru shul ston rabs la sogs pa*). Edited by Pa tshab Pa sangs dbang 'dus and Glang ru Nor bu tshe ring. A Selection and Presentation of Ancient Bon Manuscripts Retrieved from 'Bum pa che at dGa' thang in gTam shu (*gTam shul dga' thang 'bum pa che nas gsar rnyed byung ba'I bon gyi gna' dpe bdams bsgrigs*), 60–75. Lhasa: Bod ljongs dpe rnying dpe skrun khang.

The Absence of Letters Tantra (*yi ge med pa'i gsang ba rgyud chen po*). In *Rñiṅ ma'i rgyud bcu bdun: Collected Nyingmapa Tantras of the Man ṅag sde Class of the A ti yo ga (Rdzogs chen)*, 3 vols.; vol. II: 215–44. New Delhi: Sanje Dorje, 1973.

The Adamantine Song of Definitive Examples and Meaning by Longchenpa. (*dpe don nges don rdo rje'i mgur*) in *Klong chen gsung 'bum*, vol. XXIV. Dege: Sde dge par khang chen mo).

The Autobiography of Guru Chöwang (*ghuru chos dbang gis sku'i rnam thar skabs brgyad ma, dharma shwara'i rnam thar*). In *The Autobiography and Instructions of Gu-ru Chos-kyi dbang-phyug*, 8 vols.; vol. I: 1–53. Paro: Ugyen Tempai Gyaltsen (Rin chengter mdzod chenpo'i rgyab chos,), 1979.

The Blazing Lamp Tantra (*sgron ma 'bar ba'i rgyuds*). In *Rñiṅ ma'i rgyud bcu bdun: Collected Nyingmapa Tantras of the Man ṅag sde Class of the A ti yo ga (Rdzogs chen)*. 3 vols.; vol. I: 281–313. New Delhi: Sanje Dorje, 1973.

The Chronicle of the Kings (*rgyal po bka'i thang yig by u rgyan gling pa*). In *The Five Chronicles (bka' thang sde lnga)*. Lhasa: Ki rigs dpe skrun khang, 1997.

The Coiled Sky Lasso Vitality (*rnam par rgyal ba'i phya g.yang dmu zhags 'khyil ba*). In Karmay and Nagano (2001, 104–3).

The Compendium of Maṇis (*chos rgyal srong btsan sgam-po'i ma ṇi bka' 'bum bzhugs so*). Xining: [s.n.], 1991.

The Deer Way-Stations (*Sha slungs*). In John V. Bellezza (2013, 30–77).

The Five Chronicles (*bka' thang sde lnga*). Lhasa: Ki rigs dpe skrun khang, 1997.

The Fox, the Monkey and the Badger; the Three (*wa sbrel grum gsum dbu lags+ho*). In Berounský (2019, 1–32).

The Great History of Buddhism (*chos 'byung chen mo bstan pa'i rgyal mtshan*) by lde'u jo sras. In Aris (1986, 12–77).

The Great Main Text of the Vitality Ritual of the Lord of the Vitality (*srid pa yab lha bdal drug gis phya gzhung chen mo gzhugs s+ho*). In Ramble (2015, 253–6).

The Heap of Jewels Tantra (*rin chen spungs pa'i yon tan chen po ston pa rgyud kyi rgyal po*). In *Rñiṅ ma'i rgyud bcu bdun: Collected Nyingmapa Tantras of the Man ṅag sde Class of the A ti yo ga (Rdzogs chen)*, 3 vols.; vol. III: 73–114. New Delhi: Sanje Dorje, 1973.

The Heart-Essence in Four Parts (*snying thig ya bzhi*). Edited by Trulku Tsewang, Jamyang, and L. Tashi. New Delhi: A 'dzom chos sgar par khang, 1971.

The Heart-Essence of the Ḍākinīs (*mkha' 'gro snying thig*). In *The Heart-Essence in Four Parts (snying thig ya bzhi)*, vols. IV–VI, edited by Trulku Tsewang, Jamyang, and L. Tashi. New Delhi: A 'dzom chos sgar par khang, 1971.

The Heart-Essence of Vimalamitra (*bi ma snying thig*). In *The Heart-Essence in Four Parts (snying thig ya bzhi)*, vols. VII–IX, edited by Trulku Tsewang, Jamyang, and L. Tashi. New Delhi: A 'dzom chos sgar par khang, 1971.

The Mirror of the Heart of Vajrasattva (*rdo rje sems dpa' snying gi me long*). In *Rñiṅ ma'i rgyud bcu bdun: Collected Nyingmapa Tantras of the Man ṅag sde Class of the A ti yo ga (Rdzogs chen)*, 3 vols.; vol. I: 315–88. New Delhi: Sanje Dorje, 1973.

The Narrative of the Deer (*sha ba rabs*). In Huber (2015, 379).

The One Hundred Thousand Tantras of Eternal Bön (*g.yung drung bon gyi rgyud 'bum*). In *Sources for a History of Bon: A Collection of Rare Manuscripts from Bsam-gling*

Monastery in Dolpo (northwestern Nepal), 1–46. Dolanji: Tibetan Bompo Monastic Centre, 1972.

The Pearl Necklace Tantra (*mu tig rin po che phreng ba'i rgyud*). In *Rñiṅ ma'i rgyud bcu bdun: Collected Nyingmapa Tantras of the Man ṅag sde Class of the A ti yo ga (Rdzogs chen)*, 3 vols.; vol. II: 417–537. New Delhi: Sanje Dorje, 1973.

The Six Spaces Tantra (*kun tu bzang po klong drug pa'i rgyud*). In *Rñiṅ ma'i rgyud bcu bdun: Collected Nyingmapa Tantras of the Man ṅag sde Class of the A ti yo ga (Rdzogs chen)*, 3 vols.; vol. II: 111–214. New Delhi: Sanje Dorje, 1973.

The Symbol of the Secret Seminal Nuclei Tantra (*thig le gsang ba'i brda' rgyud*), sde dge edition, vol. XXV: 49b–53b.

The Tantra on the Difference between Mind and Awareness According to the Great Perfection (*rdzogs pa chen po sems dang rig pa dbye ba'i rgyud*). In *The Unimpeded Realization of Samantabhadra* (*kun tu bzang po'i dgongs pa zang thal*) by Rig 'dzin rgod kyi ldem 'phru can, vol. II: 633–50. Simla: thub bstan rdo rje brag e wam lcog sgar.

The Tantra of Great Beauty and Auspiciousness (*bkra shis mdzes ldan chen po'i rgyud*). In *Rñiṅ ma'i rgyud bcu bdun: Collected Nyingmapa Tantras of the Man ṅag sde Class of the A ti yo ga (Rdzogs chen)*, 3 vols.; vol. I: 207–32. New Delhi: Sanje Dorje, 1973.

The Tantra of Self-Arisen Awareness (*rig pa rang shar chen po'i rgyud*). In *Rñiṅ ma'i rgyud bcu bdun: Collected Nyingmapa Tantras of the Man ṅag sde Class of the A ti yo ga (Rdzogs chen)*, 3 vols.; vol. I: 389–855. New Delhi: Sanje Dorje, 1973.

The Tantra of the Introductions (*ngo sprod rin po che spras pa'i zhing khams bstan pa'i rgyud*). In *Rñiṅ ma'i rgyud bcu bdun: Collected Nyingmapa Tantras of the Man ṅag sde Class of the A ti yo ga (Rdzogs chen)*, 3 vols.; vol. II: 77–109. New Delhi: Sanje Dorje, 1973.

The Tantra of the Lion's Perfect Dynamism (*seng ge rtsal rdzogs chen po'i rgyud*). In *Rñiṅ ma'i rgyud bcu bdun: Collected Nyingmapa Tantras of the Man ṅag sde Class of the A ti yo ga (Rdzogs chen)*. 3 vols.; vol. II: 245–415. New Delhi: Sanje Dorje, 1973.

The Tantra of Unimpeded Sound (*rin po che 'byung bar byed pa sgra thal 'gyur chen po'i rgyud*). In *Rñiṅ ma'i rgyud bcu bdun: Collected Nyingmapa Tantras of the Man ṅag sde Class of the A ti yo ga (Rdzogs chen)*, 3 vols.; vol. I: 1–205. New Delhi: Sanje Dorje, 1973.

The Treasury of Philosophical Positions (*grub mtha' mdzod*) by Longchenpa. In *mDzod bdun: The Famed Seven Treasuries of Vajrayāna Buddhist Philosophy*. Gangtok, Sikkim: Sherab Gyaltsen and Khyentse Labrang, 1983.

The Treasury of Words and Meanings (*tshig don mdzod*) by Longchenpa. In *mDzod bdun: The Famed Seven Treasuries of Vajrayāna Buddhist Philosophy*. Gangtok, Sikkim: Sherab Gyaltsen and Khyentse Labrang, 1983.

The Ultimate Vitality: The Celestial Head-Ornament (*mu ye pra phud phya'i mthar thug*). In Karmay and Nagano (2002, 35–90).

Secondary References

Achard, Jean-Luc. 1999. *L'essence perlée du secret: recherches philologiques et historiques sur l'origine de la Grande Perfection dans la tradition rNying ma pa*. Turnhout: Brepols.

Achard, Jean-Luc. 2002. "La Base et ses sept interprétations dans la tradition rDzogs chen." *Revue d'Etudes Tibétaines* 1: 44–61.

Achard, Jean-Luc. 2008. *Enlightened Rainbows: The Life and Works of Shardza Tashi Gyeltsen*. Leiden: Brill.
Achard, Jean-Luc. 2018. "Zhang Nyi Ma 'bum (1158–1213) et Le Développement Des SNying Thig Au 12e Siècle." *Revue d'Etudes Tibétaines* 44: 231–57.
Achard, Jean-Luc. 2022. "Erroneous Conceptions Frequently Shared about New Bon (Bon Gsar)." *Revue d'Etudes Tibétaines* 64: 1–17.
Achard, Jean-Luc, and Tapihritsa. 2016. *The Six Lamps: Secret Dzogchen Instructions of the Bön Tradition*. Somerville: Wisdom Publications.
Alais, David, and Randolph Blake. 2005. *Binocular Rivalry*. Cambridge, MA: MIT Press.
Aldenderfer, Mark, and Zhang Yinong. 2004. "The Prehistory of the Tibetan Plateau to the Seventh Century A.D.: Perspectives and Research from China and the West Since 1950." *Journal of World Prehistory* 18 (1): 1–55.
Allen, Nicholas J. 1997. "Animal Guides and Himalayan Foundation Myths." In *Les habitants du Toit du monde: en hommage à Alexander W. MacDonald*, edited by Samten Gyaltsen Karmay and Philippe Sagant, 375–90. Nanterre: Société d'ethnologie.
Almogi, Orna. 2019. "The Human behind the Divine: An Investigation into the Evolution of Scriptures with Special Reference to the Ancient Tantras of Tibetan Buddhism." In *Unearthing Himalayan Treasures: Festschrift for Franz-Karl Ehrhard*, edited by Volker Caumanns, Marta Sernesi, and Nikolai Solmsdorf, 1–26. Marburg: Indica et Tibetica Verlag.
Ansorge, Ulrich, Gregory Francis, Michael H. Herzog, and HalukÖğmen. 2008. "Visual Masking and the Dynamics of Human Perception, Cognition, and Consciousness A Century of Progress, a Contemporary Synthesis, and Future Directions." *Advances in Cognitive Psychology* 3 (1–2): 1–8.
Apple, James B. 2020. "Kadampa Pointing-Out Instructions." *Revue d'Etudes Tibétaines* 56: 170–262.
Araujo, Draulio B. de, Sidarta Ribeiro, Guillermo A. Cecchi, Fabiana M. Carvalho, Tiago A. Sanchez, Joel P. Pinto, Bruno S. de Martinis, Jose A. Crippa, Jaime E. C. Hallak, and Antonio C. Santos. 2012. "Seeing with the Eyes Shut: Neural Basis of Enhanced Imagery Following Ayahuasca Ingestion." *Human Brain Mapping* 33 (11): 2550–60.
Arguillère, Stéphane. 2007. *Profusion de la vaste sphère: Klong-chen rab-'byams (Tibet, 1308–1364). Sa vie, son oeuvre, sa doctrine.* Leuven: Peeters Publishers.
Aris, Michael. 1997. "Foreword." In *Tibetan Histories: A Bibliography of Tibetan-Language Historical Works*, edited by Dan Martin and Yael Bentor, 9–12. London: Serindia.
Arnold, Daniel Anderson. 2012. *Brains, Buddhas, and Believing the Problem of Intentionality in Classical Buddhist and Cognitive-Scientific Philosophy of Mind*. New York: Columbia University Press.
Atran, Scott, and Ara Norenzayan. 2004. "Religion's Evolutionary Landscape: Counterintuition, Commitment, Compassion, Communion." *Behavioral and Brain Sciences* 27 (6): 713–30.
Austin, James H. 2009. *Selfless Insight: Zen and the Meditative Transformations of Consciousness*. Cambridge, MA: MIT Press.
Avant, Lloyd L. 1965. "Vision in the Ganzfeld." *Psychological Bulletin* 64 (4): 246–58.
Aziz, Barbara Nimri. 1976. "Reincarnation Reconsidered—or the Reincarnate Lama as Shaman." In *Spirit Possession in the Nepal Himalayas*, edited by John T. Hitchcock and Rex L. Jones, 343–60. Warminster: Aris and Phillips.
Bachmann, Talis, and Gregory Francis. 2014. *Visual Masking: Studying Perception, Attention, and Consciousness*. Oxford: Academic Press.

Bainbridge, William Sims. 2006. *God From the Machine: Artificial Intelligence Models of Religious Cognition*. Lanham: AltaMira Press.

Barrett, Justin L. 2004. *Why Would Anyone Believe in God?* Walnut Creek: AltaMira Press.

Barrett, Justin L., and Frank C. Keil. 1996. "Conceptualizing a Nonnatural Entity: Anthropomorphism in God Concepts." *Cognitive Psychology* 31 (3): 219–47.

Barthes, Roland. 1975. *The Pleasure of the Text*. Translated by Richard Miler. New York: Hill and Wang.

Bawden, Charles R. 1962. "Calling the Soul: A Mongolian Litany." *Bulletin of the School of Oriental and African Studies*, University of London 25 (1/3): 81–103.

Beckwith, Christopher I. 1987. *The Tibetan Empire in Central Asia: A History of the Struggle for Great Power among Tibetans, Turks, Arabs, and Chinese during the Early Middle Ages*. Princeton, NJ: Princeton University Press.

Beer, Robert. 2003. *The Handbook of Tibetan Buddhist Symbols*. Boston: Shambhala.

Bell, Catherine M. 1997. *Ritual: Perspectives and Dimensions*. New York: Oxford University Press.

Bellezza, John Vincent. 1997. *Divine Dyads, Ancient Civilization in Tibet*. Dharamsala: Library of Tibetan Works and Archives.

Bellezza, John Vincent. 1999. *Antiquities of Northern Tibet: Pre-Buddhist Archeological Discoveries on the High Plateau (Findings of the Changthang Circuit Expedition, 1999)*. Delhi: Adroit.

Bellezza, John Vincent. 2000. "Buddhist Archaeological Sites in Northern Tibet: An Introductory Report on the Types of Monuments and Related Literary and Oral Historical Sources." *Kailash: Journal of Himalayan Studies* 19 (1–2): 1–142.

Bellezza, John Vincent. 2002. *Antiquities of Upper Tibet: An Inventory of Pre-Buddhist Archaeological Sites on the High Plateau: Findings of the Upper Tibet Circumnavigation Expedition, 2000*. Delhi: Adroit Publishers.

Bellezza, John Vincent. 2005. *Spirit-Mediums, Sacred Mountains, and Related Bon Textual Traditions in Upper Tibet: Calling Down the Gods. Brill's Tibetan Studies Library*. Leiden: Brill.

Bellezza, John Vincent. 2008. *Zhang Zhung: Foundations of Civilization in Tibet: A Historical and Ethnoarchaeological Study of the Monuments, Rock Art, Texts, and Oral Tradition of the Ancient Tibetan Upland. Beiträge Zur Kultur- Und Geistesgeschichte Asiens, Nr. 61*. Wien: Östereichischen Akademie der Wissenschaften.

Bellezza, John Vincent. 2011. "The Liturgies and Oracular Utterances of the Spirit-Mediums of Upper Tibet—An Introduction to Their BSang Rituals." *Revue d'Etudes Tibétaines* 20: 5–31.

Bellezza, John Vincent. 2013. *Death and Beyond in Ancient Tibet: Archaic Concepts and Practices in a Thousand-Year-Old Illuminated Funerary Manuscript and Old Tibetan Funerary Documents of Gathang Bumpa and Dunhuang*. Vienna: Verlag der Österreichischen Akademie der Wissenschaften.

Bellezza, John Vincent. 2014. *The Dawn of Tibet: The Ancient Civilization on the Roof of the World*. Lanham: Rowman & Littlefield.

Bellezza, John Vincent. 2018. "Invocation, Possession and Rejuvenation in Upper Tibet The Beliefs, Activities and Lives of Spirit-Mediums Residing in the Highest Land." PhD dissertation, University of Kent. https://kar.kent.ac.uk/67422/.

Bentor, Yael. 2019. "Introduction." In *The Essence of the Ocean of Attainments: The Creation Stage of the Guhyasamajatantra Tantra According to Panchen Lobsang Chökyi Gyaltsen*, edited by Blo bzang chos kyi rgyal mtshan and Penpa Dorjee, 1–38. Somerville: Wisdom Publications.

Berglie, F. K. Per-Arne. 1976a. "Preliminary Remarks on Some Dpa' Bos, Tibetan 'Spirit Mediums' in Exile in Nepal." In *Buddhism and Jainism*, edited by Satya Ranjan Pal and H.C. Das, 34–318. Cuttack, India: Institute of Oriental and Orissan Studies.

Berglie, F K Per-Arne. 1976b. "Preliminary Remarks on Some Tibetan Spirit Mediums in Nepal." *Kailash: A Journal of Himalayan Studies* 4 (1): 85–108.

Berglie, F K Per-Arne. 1978. "On the Question of Tibetan Shamanism." In *Tibetan Studies: Presented at the Seminar of Young Tibetologists, Zurich, June 26-July 1, 1977*, edited by Martin Brauen and Per Kvaerne, 39–51. Zürich: Völkerkundemuseum der Universität Zürich.

Berglie, F K Per-Arne. 1980. "Mount Targo and Lake Dangra: A Contribution to the Religious Geography of Tibet." In *Tibetan Studies in Honour of Hugh Richardson Proceedings of the International Seminar on Tibetan Studies, Oxford, 1979*, edited by Michael Aris and Richardson Aung San Suu Kyi, 39–44. Warminster: Aris and Phillips.

Berounský, Daniel. 2007. "Iconography and Texts of the Tibetan Five Protecting Deities." In *Filosofija, Religija i Kul'tura Stran Vostoka: Matěrijaly Naučnoj Konferencii*, edited by S. V. Pakhomov, 331–40. St. Petersburg: Izdatělstvo Sankt-Petěrburgskogo univesitěta.

Berounský, Daniel. 2014. "Tibetan Myths on 'Good Fortune' (Phya) and 'Well-Being' (g.Yang)." *Mongolo-Tibetica Pragensia '14: Ethnolinguistics, Sociolinguistics, Religion and Culture* 7 (2): 55–77.

Berounský, Daniel. 2015. "A Dialogue between the Priest and the Deer." In *From Bhakti to Bon: Festschrift for Per Kværne*, edited by Hanna Havnevik and Charles Ramble, 97–112. Oslo: Novus Press.

Berounský, Daniel. 2017. "The Nyen Collection (Gnyan 'bum) and Shenrab Miwo of Nam." In *Mapping Amdo: Dynamics of Change*, edited by Jarmila Ptáčková and Adrian Zenz, 211–53. Archív Orientální. Supplementa; 10. Prague: Oriental Institute, The Czech Academy of Sciences.

Berounský, Daniel. 2019. "Burning the Incestuous Fox. A Tibetan Fumigation Ritual (Wa Bsang)." *Études Mongoles et Sibériennes, Centrasiatiques et Tibétaines* 50 (March): 1–32.

Bertrand, Christian. 2011. *Im Licht ursprünglicher Buddhaschaft: Die Dzogchenlehren von Longchenpa*. München: Zupan, A.

Berzin, Alexander. 2010. *Wise Teacher, Wise Student Tibetan Approaches to a Healthy Relationship*. Ithaca, NY: Snow Lion.

Beyer, Stephan V. 1973. *The Cult of Tārā: Magic and Ritual in Tibet*. Berkeley: University of California Press.

Beyer, Stephan V. 2010. *Singing to the Plants: A Guide to Mestizo Shamanism in the Upper Amazon*. Albuquerque: University of New Mexico Press.

Bhattacharyya, Narendra Nath. 2005. *History of the Tantric Religion: An Historical, Ritualistic, and Philosophical Study*. New Delhi: Manohar.

Bialek, Joanna. 2015. "Dasselbe Mit Anderen Worten? Sprache, Übersetzung Und Sprachwissenschaft, Akten Des 2. Symposiums Des Zentrums Historische Sprachwissenschaften (ZhS) München, 11. Und 12. April 2014." In *Dasselbe Mit Anderen Worten? Sprache, Übersetzung Und Sprachwissenschaft, Akten Des 2. Symposiums Des Zentrums Historische Sprachwissenschaften (ZhS) München, 11. Und 12. April 2014*, edited by Peter Schrijver and Peter-Arnold Mumm, 21–42. Bremen: Hempen Verlag.

Bialek, Joanna. 2018. *Compounds and Compounding in Old Tibetan. A Corpus Based Approach*. Marburg: Indica et Tibetica Verlag.

Billorey, R. K. 1978. "The Phlha Festival of the Monpas." *Journal of the Assam Research Society* 24: 21–5.

Birket-Smith, Kai. 1929. *The Caribou Eskimos*. Copenhagen: Gyldendalske boghandel.

Blezer, Henk. 2000. "The 'Bon' dBal mo Nyer bdun(/brgyad) and the Buddhist dBang phyug ma Nyer brgyad, a Brief Comparison." In *New Horizons in Bon Studies*, edited by Samten Gyaltsen Karmay, 117–78. Osaka: National Museum of Ethnology.

Blezer, Henk. 2008. "STon Pa GShen Rab: Six Marriages and Many More Funerals." *Revue d'Etudes Tibétaines* 15: 421–79.

Blezer, Henk. 2011a. "It All Happened in Myi Yul Skyi Mthing: A Crucial Nexus of Narratives Pointing at the Proto-Heartland of Bon?" In *Buddhist Himalaya: Studies in Religion, History and Culture Volume I: Tibet and The Himalaya*, edited by Alex McKay and Anna Balikci-Denjongpa, 157–78. Sikkim: Namgyal Institute of Tibetology.

Blezer, Henk, ed. 2011b. "The Bon of Bon: Forever Old." In *Emerging Bon: The Formation of Bon Traditions in Tibet at the Turn of the First Millennium AD, 207–46. Beiträge Zur Zentralasienforschung*. Halle: IITBS, International institute for Tibetan and Buddhist studies.

Blezer, Henk. 2012. "Light on the Human Body: The Coarse Physical Body and Its Functions in the Aural Transmission from the Zhang Zhung on the Six Lamps." *Revue d'Etudes Tibétaines* 23: 117–68.

Bloch, Maurice. 2012. *Anthropology and the Cognitive Challenge*. Cambridge: Cambridge University Press.

Blondeau, Anne-Marie, and Samten Gyaltsen Karmay. 1988. "Le Cerf a La Vaste Ramure: En Guise d'introduction." In *Essais Sur Le Rituel*, edited by Anne-Marie Blondeau and Kristofer Schipper, 119–46. Louvain: Peeters.

Bloom, Paul. 2004. *Descartes' Baby: How the Science of Child Development Explains What Makes Us Human*. New York: Basic Books.

Bodhi, Bhikkhu. 2011. "What Does Mindfulness Really Mean? A Canonical Perspective." *Contemporary Buddhism* 12 (1): 19–39.

Boroojerdi, Babak, Khalaf O. Bushara, Brian N. Corwell, Ilka Immisch, Fortunato Battaglia, Wolf Muellbacher, and Leonardo G. Cohen. 2000. "Enhanced Excitability of the Human Visual Cortex Induced by Short-Term Light Deprivation." *Cerebral Cortex* 10 (5): 529–34.

Boyer, Pascal. 2001. *Religion Explained: The Evolutionary Origins of Religious Thought*. New York: Basic Books.

Braun, Erik. 2013. *The Birth of Insight: Meditation, Modern Buddhism, and the Burmese Monk Ledi Sayadaw*. Chicago: University of Chicago Press.

Breitmeyer, Bruno G. 2007. "Visual Masking: Past Accomplishments, Present Status, Future Developments." *Advances in Cognitive Psychology* 3 (1–2): 9–20.

Broz, Ludek, and Rane Willerslev. 2012. "When Good Luck Is Bad Fortune: Between Too Little and Too Much Hunting Success in Siberia." *Social Analysis* 56: 73–89.

Bruneau, Laurianne, and John Vincent Bellezza. 2013. "The Rock Art of Upper Tibet and Ladakh: Inner Asian Cultural Adaptation, Regional Differentiation and the 'Western Tibetan Plateau Style.'" *Revue d'Etudes Tibétaines* 28: 5–161.

Brunnholzl, Karl. 2012. "Introduction." In *Gone Beyond (Volume 1)*, 21–203. Ithaca, NY: Snow Lion.

Bsod-nams-rgyal-mtshan, and Per K. Sørensen. 1994. *The Mirror Illuminating the Royal Genealogies Tibetan Buddhist Historiography; an Annotated Translation of the XIVth Century Tibetan Chronicle: rGyal-rabs gsal-ba'i me-long*. Wiesbaden: Harrassowitz Verlag.

Buddhaghosa, Bhadantacariya. 2003. *The Path of Purification: Visuddhimagga*. Translated by Bhikkhu Ñāṇamoli. Onalaska: Pariyatti.
Bu-ston. 1931. *History of Buddhism (Chos-Hbyung)*. Translated by Eugène Obermiller. Heidelberg: Harrassowitz.
Buswell, Robert E., and Robert M. Gimello. 1992. "Introduction." In *Paths to Liberation: The Marga and Its Transformations in Buddhist Thought*, edited by Robert E. Buswell and Robert M. Gimello, 1–36. Honolulu: University of Hawaii Press.
Cabezón, José Ignacio. 1994. *Buddhism and Language: A Study of Indo-Tibetan Scholasticism*. Albany: State University of New York Press.
Cabezón, José Ignacio. 1998. *Scholasticism Cross-Cultural and Comparative Perspectives*. Albany: State University of New York Press.
Calkowski, Marcia. 1985. "Power, Charisma, and Ritual Curing in a Tibetan Community in India." Dissertation, Vancouver: University of British Columbia. https://open.library.ubc.ca/soa/cIRcle/collections/ubctheses/831/items/1.0097119.
Cantwell, Cathy, and Rob Mayer. 2008. "Enduring Myths: Smrang, Rabs and Ritual in the Dunhuang Texts on Padmasambhava." *Revue d'Etudes Tibétaines* 15: 289–312.
Carroll, Joseph. 2004. *Literary Darwinism: Evolution, Human Nature, and Literature*. London: Routledge.
Carter, Olivia L., David E. Presti, C. Callistemon, Y. Ungerer, Guang Bin Liu, and John D. Pettigrew. 2005. "Meditation Alters Perceptual Rivalry in Tibetan Buddhist Monks." *Current Biology* 15 (11): R412–13.
Chalmers, David John. 1996. *The Conscious Mind in Search of a Fundamental Theory*. New York: Oxford University Press.
Christoff, Kalina, Diego Cosmelli, Dorothée Legrand, and Evan Thompson. 2011. "Specifying the Self for Cognitive Neuroscience." *Trends in Cognitive Sciences* 15 (3): 104–12.
Cleary, Thomas F. 1983. *Entry into the Inconceivable: An Introduction to Hua-Yen Buddhism*. Honolulu: University of Hawaii Press.
Coblin, W. South. 1987. "A Note on Tibetan Mu." *Linguistics of the Tibeto-Burman Area* 10 (1): 166–8.
Cohen, Emma. 2007. *The Mind Possessed: The Cognition of Spirit Possession in An Afro-Brazilian Religious Tradition*. Oxford: Oxford University Press.
Colombetti, Giovanna. 2014. *The Feeling Body: Affective Science Meets the Enactive Mind*. Cambridge, MA: MIT Press.
Coseru, Christian. 2012. *Perceiving Reality: Consciousness, Intentionality, and Cognition in Buddhist Philosophy*. New York: Oxford University Press.
Cosmelli, Diego, Olivier David, Jean-Philippe Lachaux, Jacques Martinerie, Line Garnero, Bernard Renault, and Francisco Varela. 2004. "Waves of Consciousness: Ongoing Cortical Patterns during Binocular Rivalry." *NeuroImage* 23 (1): 128–40.
Cozort, Daniel. 1986. *Highest Yoga Tantra*. Ithaca, NY: Snow Lion.
Cozort, Daniel. 1996. "Sādhana (sGrub thabs): Means of Achievement for Deity Yoga." In *Tibetan Literature: Studies in Genre*, edited by José Ignacio Cabezón and Roger R. Jackson, 331–43. Ithaca, NY: Snow Lion.
Crick, Francis. 1994. *Astonishing Hypothesis: The Scientific Search for the Soul*. New York: Scribner.
Cuevas, Bryan J. 2003. *The Hidden History of the Tibetan Book of the Dead*. Oxford: Oxford University Press.

Cuevas, Bryan J. 2013. "Some Reflections on the Periodization of Tibetan History." In *The Tibetan History Reader*, edited by Gray Tuttle and Kurtis R. Schaeffer, 48–63. New York: Columbia University Press.

Curtin, Jeremiah. 1909. *A Journey in Southern Siberia: The Mongols, Their Religion and Their Myths*. Boston: Little, Brown.

Cutler, Nathan S. 1991. "The Early Rulers of Tibet: Their Lineage & Burial Rites." *Tibet Journal* 16 (3): 28–51.

Czaplicka, Mary Antionette. 1914. *Aboriginal Siberia; A Study in Social Anthropology*. Oxford: Clarendon Press.

Dagyab, Loden Sherap. 1995. *Buddhist Symbols in Tibetan Culture: An Investigation of the Nine Best-Known Groups of Symbols*. Somerville: Wisdom.

Dahl, Cortland J. 2008. "Translator's Introduction." In *Great Perfection, Volume Two: Separation and Breakthrough, by Third Dzogchen Rinpoche*, edited by Cortland J. Dahl, 1–40. Ithaca: Snow Lion.

Dalton, Jacob P. 2013. *The Taming of the Demons: Violence and Liberation in Tibetan Buddhism*. New Haven, CT: Yale University Press.

Damasio, Antonio R. 2010. *Self Comes to Mind: Constructing the Conscious Brain*. New York: Pantheon Books.

Dambrun, Michaël, and Matthieu Ricard. 2011. "Self-Centeredness and Selflessness: A Theory of Self-Based Psychological Functioning and Its Consequences for Happiness." *Review of General Psychology* 15 (2): 138–57.

Dargyay, Eva K. 1985. "A Rnin-Ma Text: The Kun Byed Rgyal Po'i Mdo." In *Soundings in Tibetan Civilization*, edited by Barbara Nimri Aziz and Matthew T. Kapstein, 283–93. New Delhi: Manohar.

Das, Sarat Chandra. 1970. *Contributions on the Religion and History of Tibet*. New Dehli: Mañjuśrī Publishing House.

Davidson, Ronald M. 2002. *Indian Esoteric Buddhism: A Social History of the Tantric Movement*. New York: Columbia University Press.

Davidson, Ronald M. 2005. *Tibetan Renaissance: Tantric Buddhism in the Rebirth of Tibetan Culture*. New York: Columbia University Press.

Davis, Jake H., and Evan Thompson. 2013. "From the Five Aggregates to Phenomenal Consciousness: Toward a Cross-Cultural Cognitive Science." In *A Companion to Buddhist Philosophy*, edited by Steven M. Emmanuel, 165–88. London: Blackwell.

Dehaene, Stanislas. 2014. *Consciousness and the Brain: Deciphering How the Brain Codes Our Thoughts*. New York: Viking.

Desjarlais, Robert R. 1992. *Body and Emotion: The Aesthetics of Illness and Healing in the Nepal Himalayas*. Philadelphia: University of Pennsylvania Press.

Desjarlais, Robert R. 1996. "Presence." In *The Performance of Healing*, edited by Carol Laderman and Marina Roseman, 143–64. New York: Routledge.

Diemberger, Hildegard. 1993. "Blood, Sperm, Soul and the Mountain. Gender Relations, Kinship and Cosmovision among the Khumbo (N.E. Nepal)." In *Gendered Anthropology*, edited by Teresa del Valle, 88–127. London: Routledge.

Diemberger, Hildegard. 2006. "Female Oracles in Modern Tibet." In *Women in Tibet: Past and Present*, edited by Janet B. Gyatso and Hanna Havnevik, 113–68. New York: Columbia University Press.

Doctor, Andreas. 2005. *Tibetan Treasure Literature: Revelation, Tradition, And Accomplishment In Visionary Buddhism*. Ithaca, NY: Snow Lion.

Doney, Lewis. 2023. "On the Margins: Between Beliefs and Doctrines within Tibetan-Ruled Dunhuang Scribal Culture." *BuddhistRoad Paper* 1.6 (February): 1–42.

Dorje, Gyurme. 2001. *Tibetan Elemental Divination Paintings: Illuminated Manuscripts from the White Beryl of Sangs Rgyas RGya Mtsho with the Moonbeams Treatise of Lo Chen Dharmāsrī*. London: John Eskenazi in association with Sam Fogg.

Dotson, Brandon. 2007. "Administration and Law in the Tibetan Empire: The Section on Law and State and Its Old Tibetan Antecedents." PhD dissertation, University of Oxford. https://eprints.soas.ac.uk/3358/.

Dotson, Brandon. 2008. "Complementarity and Opposition in Early Tibetan Ritual." *Journal of the American Oriental Society* 128 (1): 41–67.

Dotson, Brandon. 2011. "Theorising the King: Implicit and Explicit Sources for the Study of Tibetan Sacred Kingship." *Revue d'Etudes Tibétaines* 21: 83–103.

Dotson, Brandon. 2013. "The Dead and Their Stories: Preliminary Remarks on the Place of Narrative in Tibetan Religion." In *Tibet after Empire: Culture, Society and Religion between 850–1000: Proceedings of the Seminar Held in Lumbini, Nepal, March 2011*, edited by Christoph Cüppers, Robert Mayer, and Michael Walter, 85–115. Lumbini: Lumbini International Research Institute.

Dotson, Brandon. 2015. "The Call of the Cuckoo to the Thin Sheep of Spring: Healing and Fortune in Old Tibetan Dice Divination Texts." In *Tibetan and Himalayan Healing: An Anthology for Anthony Aris*, edited by Charles Ramble and Ulrike Roesler, 148–60. Kathmandu: Vajra.

Dotson, Brandon. 2017. "On 'Personal Protective Deities' ('go Ba'i Lha) and the Old Tibetan Verb 'go." *Bulletin of the School of Oriental and African Studies* 80 (3): 525–45.

Dotson, Brandon. 2018. "The Horse and the Grass-Grazing Man: Domestication, Food, and Alterity in Early Tibetan Cosmologies of the Land of the Dead." *History of Religions* 57 (3): 270–87.

Dotson, Brandon. 2019. "Hunting for Fortune. Wild Animals, Goddesses and the Play of Perspectives in Early Tibetan Dice Divination." *Études Mongoles et Sibériennes, Centrasiatiques et Tibétaines* 50 (March): 1–27.

Dotson, Brandon. 2022. "How to Read Like a Dead Horse Listens: Audience and Affect in 'The Tale of the Separation of Horse and Kiang.'" *Journal of Tibetan Literature* 1 (1): 47–73.

Dowman, Keith. 2013a. "Introduction." In *Spaciousness: The Radical Dzogchen of the Vajra-Heart, by Longchenpa*, translated by Keith Dowman, 15–34. Kathmandu: Vajra Publications.

Dowman, Keith. 2013b. *Spaciousness: The Radical Dzogchen of the Vajra-Heart*. Kathmandu: Vajra Publications.

Dreyfus, Georges B. J. 1997. *Recognizing Reality: Dharmakirti's Philosophy and Its Tibetan Interpretations*. Albany: State University of New York Press.

Dreyfus, Georges B. J. 2011. "Self and Subjectivity: A Middle Way Approach." In *Self, No Self? Perspectives from Analytical, Phenomenological, and Indian Traditions*, edited by Mark Siderits, Evan Thompson, and Dan Zahavi, 114–56. Oxford: Oxford University Press.

Dudjom Rinpoche Jikdrel Yeshe Dorje. 1991. *The Nyingma School of Tibetan Buddhism: Its Fundamentals and History*. Translated by Gyurme Dorje and Matthew T. Kapstein. Boston: Wisdom Publications.

Dunne, John D. 2013. "Toward an Understanding of Non-Dual Mindfulness." In *Mindfulness. Diverse Perspectives on Its Meanings, Origins and Applications*, edited by Mark G. Williams and Jon Kabat-Zinn, 71–88. London: Routledge.

Dunne, John D. 2015. "Buddhist Styles of Mindfulness: A Heuristic Approach." In *Handbook of Mindfulness and Self-Regulation*, edited by Brian D. Ostafin, Michael D. Robinson, and Brian P. Meier, 251–70. New York: Springer.
Dutton, Denis. 2009. *The Art Instinct: Beauty, Pleasure, and Human Evolution*. Oxford: Oxford University Press.
Dux, Paul E., and René Marois. 2009. "The Attentional Blink: A Review of Data and Theory." *Attention, Perception, & Psychophysics* 71 (8): 1683–700.
Eagleman, David. 2011. *Incognito: The Brains behind the Mind*. New York: Pantheon.
Edelglass, William. 2019. "'That Is Why The Buddha Laughs': Apophasis, Buddhist Practice, and the Paradox of Language." *Journal of Dharma Studies* 1 (2): 201–14.
Edelman, Gerald M. 1992. *Bright Air, Brilliant Fire: On the Matter of the Mind*. New York: Basic Books.
Ehrhard, Franz-Karl. 1990. *"Flügelschläge des Garuḍa": literar- und ideengeschichtliche Bemerkungen zu einer Liedersammlung des rDzogs-chen*. Stuttgart: Franz Steiner.
Ehrhard, Franz-Karl. 1999. "The Role of 'Treasure Discoverers' and Their Writings in the Search for Himalayan Sacred Lands." In *Sacred Spaces and Powerful Places in Tibetan Culture: A Collection of Essays*, edited by Toni Huber, 227–39. Dharamsala: Library of Tibetan Works and Archives.
Eliade, Mircea. 1949. *Le Mythe de l'éternel Retour*. Paris: Gallimard.
Eliade, Mircea. 1958. *Patterns in Comparative Religion*. Translated by Rosemary Sheed. London: Sheed & Ward.
Eliade, Mircea. 1964. *Shamanism: Archaic Techniques of Ecstasy*. Translated by Willard R. Trask. London: Routledge & Kegan Paul.
Ellis, Ralph D. 1995. *Questioning Consciousness the Interplay of Imagery, Cognition, and Emotion in the Human Brain*. Philadelphia, PA: J. Benjamins.
English, Elizabeth. 2002. *Vajrayogini: Her Visualization, Rituals, and Forms*. Somerville: Wisdom Publications.
Epley, Nicholas, Adam Waytz, and John T. Cacioppo. 2007. "On Seeing Human: A Three-Factor Theory of Anthropomorphism." *Psychological Review* 114 (4): 864–86.
Ermakov, Dmitry. 2008. *Bø and Bön: Ancient Shamanic Traditions of Siberia and Tibet in Their Relation to the Teachings of a Central Asian Buddha*. Kathmandu: Vajra Publications.
Ffytche, Dominic H., Jan Dirk Blom, and Marco Catani. 2010. "Disorders of Visual Perception." *Journal of Neurology, Neurosurgery & Psychiatry* 81 (11): 1280–7.
Ffytche, Dominic H., Robert J. Howard, Michael J. Brammer, Anna David, Peter Woodruff, and Steven C. R. Williams. 1998. "The Anatomy of Conscious Vision: An FMRI Study of Visual Hallucinations." *Nature Neuroscience* 1 (8): 738–42.
Fierro, Brigida, Filippo Brighina, Gaetano Vitello, Aurelio Piazza, Simona Scalia, Giuseppe Giglia, Ornella Daniele, and Alvaro Pascual-Leone. 2005. "Modulatory Effects of Low- and High-Frequency Repetitive Transcranial Magnetic Stimulation on Visual Cortex of Healthy Subjects Undergoing Light Deprivation." *Journal of Physiology* 565 (Pt 2): 659–65.
Fitzhugh, William W. 2009. "Stone Shamans and Flying Deer of Northern Mongolia: Deer Goddess of Siberia or Chimera of the Steppe?" *Arctic Anthropology* 46 (1/2): 72–88.
Fontana, David. 2013. "Authority in Buddhism and in Western Scientific Psychology." In *The Authority of Experience: Readings on Buddhism and Psychology*, edited by John Pickering, 28–50. Hoboken: Taylor and Francis.

Franz, Marie-Louise von. 1988. "The Transformed Berserk: Unification of Psychic Opposites." In *Human Survival and Consciousness Evolution*, edited by Stanislav Grof, 18–35. Albany: State University of New York Press.

Galambos, Imre. 2020. *Dunhuang Manuscript Culture: End of the First Millennium*. Berlin: De Gruyter.

Gallagher, Shaun. 2000. "Philosophical Conceptions of the Self: Implications for Cognitive Science." *Trends in Cognitive Sciences* 4 (1): 14–21.

Gallagher, Shaun, and Dan Zahavi. 2008. *The Phenomenological Mind: An Introduction to Philosophy of Mind and Cognitive Science*. New York: Routledge.

Ganzevoort, Reinder Ruard, and Srdjan Sremac. 2019. "Trauma and Lived Religion: Embodiment and Emplotment." In *Trauma and Lived Religion: Transcending the Ordinary*, edited by Reinder Ruard Ganzevoort and Srdjan Sremac, 1–14. Cham: Springer International Publishing.

Garb, Jonathan. 2011. *Shamanic Trance in Modern Kabbalah*. Chicago: University of Chicago Press.

Gayley, Holly. 2007. "Ontology of the Past and Its Materialization in Tibetan Treasures." In *The Invention of Sacred Tradition*, edited by James R. Lewis and Olav Hammer, 213–40. Cambridge: Cambridge University Press.

Geisshuesler, Flavio A. 2019a. "A Parapsychologist, an Anthropologist, and a Vitalist Walk into a Laboratory: Ernesto de Martino, Mircea Eliade, and a Forgotten Chapter in the Disciplinary History of Religious Studies." *Religions* 10 (304): 1–22.

Geisshuesler, Flavio A. 2019b. "The 7E Model of the Human Mind: Articulating a Plastic Self for the Cognitive Science of Religion." *Journal of Cognition and Culture* 19: 450–76.

Geisshuesler, Flavio A. 2019c. "When Buddhas Dissociate: A Psychological Perspective on the Origins of Great Perfection Buddhism (RDzogs Chen)." *Cogent Psychology* 6 (1): 1707055.

Geisshuesler, Flavio A. 2020a. "From Grounded Identity to Receptive Creativity: The Mythical-Historical Formation of the Nyingma School and the Potential of Collective Trauma." *International Journal of Buddhist Thought and Culture* 30: 233–69.

Geisshuesler, Flavio A. 2020b. "Luminous Bodies, Playful Children, and Abusive Grandmothers: Trauma, Dissociation, and Disorganized Attachment in the Early History of Great Perfection (RDzogs Chen) Buddhism." *Religions* 11 (3): 114.

Geisshuesler, Flavio A. 2021. *The Life and Work of Ernesto De Martino: Italian Perspectives on Apocalypse and Rebirth in the Modern Study of Religion*. Numen Religion Series. Leiden: Brill.

Gen Lamrimpa. 1999. *Realizing Emptiness: The Madhyamaka Cultivation of Insight*. Translated by B. Alan Wallace and Ellen Posman. Ithaca, NY: Snow Lion.

Gendlin, Eugene T. 1962. *Experiencing and the Creation of Meaning: A Philosophical and Psychological Approach to the Subjective*. New York: Free Press of Glencoe.

Gentry, James Duncan. 2017. *Power Objects in Tibetan Buddhism: The Life, Writings, and Legacy of Sokdokpa Lodrö Gyeltsen*. Leiden: Brill.

Gerke, Barbara. 2007. "Engaging the Subtle Body: Re-Approaching Bla Rituals in the Himalayas." In *Proceedings of the Tenth Seminar of the IATS, 2003. Volume 10: Soundings in Tibetan Medicine*, edited by Mona Schrempf, 191–212. Leiden: Brill.

Gerke, Barbara. 2012. *Long Lives and Untimely Deaths: Life-Span Concepts and Longevity Practices among Tibetans in the Darjeeling Hills, India*. Leiden: Brill.

Germano, David. 1992. "Poetic Thought, the Intelligent Universe, and the Mystery of Self: The Tantric Synthesis of rDzogs Chen in Fourteenth Century Tibet." PhD dissertation, Madison: University of Wisconsin.

Germano, David. 1994. "Architecture and Absence in the Secret Tantric History of rDzogs Chen." *Journal of the International Association of Buddhist Studies* 17 (2): 203–335.
Germano, David, and Janet B. Gyatso. 2000. "Longchenpa and the Possession of the Dakinis." In *Tantra in Practice*, edited by David Gordon White. Princeton, NJ: Princeton University Press.
Gibson, James Jerome. 1986. *The Ecological Approach to Visual Perception*. Hillsdale: Lawrence Erlbaum Associates.
Gombrich, Richard, and Gananath Obeyesekere. 1988. *Buddhism Transformed: Religious Change in Sri Lanka*. Princeton, NJ: Princeton University Press.
Gómez, Luis O. 1987. "Language: Buddhist Views of Language." In *The Encyclopedia of Religion*, edited by Mircea Eliade, 5308–13. New York: Macmillan.
Goodale, Melvyn A., and David A. Milner. 2004. *Sight Unseen: An Exploration of Conscious and Unconscious Vision*. Oxford: Oxford University Press.
Gray, David B. 2007. *The Cakrasamvara Tantra: A Study and Annotated Translation*. New York: Columbia University Press.
Gray, David B. 2021. "Bodies of Knowledge: Bodily Perfection in Tantric Buddhist Practice." *Religions* 12 (2): 89.
Griffiths, Gordian, Arvid Herwig, and Werner X. Schneider. 2013. "Stimulus Localization Interferes with Stimulus Recognition: Evidence from an Attentional Blink Paradigm." *Journal of Vision* 13 (7): 7–15.
Guenther, Herbert V. 1989. *From Reductionism to Creativity: rDzogs-Chen and the New Science of Mind*. Boston, MA: Shambhala.
Guenther, Herbert V. 1992. *Meditation Differently: Phenomenological-Psychological Aspects of Tibetan Buddhist (Mahāmudrā and Snying-Thig) Practices from Original Tibetan Sources*. Delhi: Motilal Banarsidass Publishers.
Guenther, Herbert V. 1993. *Ecstatic Spontaneity: Saraha's Three Cycles of Doha*. Berkeley, CA: Asian Humanities Press.
Guenther, Herbert V. 1994. *Wholeness Lost and Wholeness Regained: Forgotten Tales of Individuation from Ancient Tibet*. Albany: State University of New York Press.
Guenther, Herbert V. 1996. *The Teachings of Padmasambhava*. Leiden: Brill.
Guenther, Herbert V. 2005. *Down and Up Again: Allegories of Becoming and Transcendence*. Published electronically by the author. http://www.buddhistischer-studienverlag.de/shop/downloads/DownUp.pdf.
Guthrie, Stewart E., Joseph Agassi, Karin R. Andriolo, David Buchdahl, H. Byron Earhart, Moshe Greenberg, Ian Jarvie, Benson Saler, John Saliba, Kevin J. Sharpe, Georges Tissot. 1980. "A Cognitive Theory of Religion [and Comments and Reply]." *Current Anthropology* 21 (2): 181–203.
Gyatso, Janet B. 1986. "Signs, Memory and History: A Tantric Buddhist Theory of Scriptural Transmission." *Journal of the International Association of Buddhist Studies* 9 (2): 7–36.
Gyatso, Janet B. 1993. "The Logic of Legitimation in the Tibetan Treasure Tradition." *History of Religions* 33 (2): 97–134.
Gyatso, Janet B. 1996. "Drawn from the Tibetan Treasury: The gTer ma Literature." In *Tibetan Literature: Studies in Genre*, edited by Jose Ignacio Cabezon and Roger R. Jackson, 147–69. Ithaca, NY: Snow Lion.
Gyatso, Janet B. 1998. *Apparitions of the Self: The Secret Autobiographies of a Tibetan Visionary*. Princeton, NJ: Princeton University Press.

Haarh, Erik. 1969. *The Yar-Luṅ Dynasty. A Study with Particular Regard to the Contribution by Myths and Legends to the History of Ancient Tibet and the Origin and Nature of Its Kings*. Koebenhavn: Gad's forlag.

Halkias, G. T. 2019. "Heavenly Ascents after Death Karma Chags Med's Commentary on Mind Transference." *Revue d'Etudes Tibétaines* 52: 70–89.

Halkias, Georgios T. 2016. "The Mirror and the Palimpsest: The Myth of Buddhist Kingship in Imperial Tibet." In *Locating Religions: Contact, Diversity, and Translocality*, edited by Reinhold Glei and Nikolas Jaspert, 123–50. Leiden: Brill.

Hamayon, Roberte N. 1996. "Game and Games, Fortune and Dualism in Siberian Shamanism." In *Shamanism and Northern Ecology*, edited by Juha Pentikäinen, 61–6. Berlin: De Gruyter.

Hamayon, Roberte N. 2007. *Le chamanisme ou l'art de gagner sa chance grâce à des partenaires imaginaires*. Pékin: Ecole Française d'Extrême Orient.

Hamilton, James Russell. 1955. *Les Ouïghours à l'époque Des Cinq Dynasties d'après Les Documents Chinois*. Paris: Presses Universitaires de France.

Hamilton, Sue. 2000. *Early Buddhism: A New Approach: The I of the Beholder*. London: Routledge.

Harding, Sarah, and Jamgon Kongtrul. 2002. *Creation and Completion: Essential Points of Tantric Meditation*. Boston, MA: Wisdom Publications.

Harva, Uno. 1938. *Die religiösen Vorstellungen der altaischen Völker*. Helsinki: Suomalainen tiedeakatemia.

Hatchell, Christopher. 2014. *Naked Seeing: The Great Perfection, the Wheel of Time, and Visionary Buddhism in Renaissance Tibet*. New York: Oxford University Press.

Hazod, Guntram. 2007. "The Grave on the 'Cool Plain'. On the Identification of 'Tibet's First Tomb' in Nga-Ra-Thang of 'Phyong-Po." In *Pramāṇakīrtiḥ: Papers Dedicated to Ernst Steinkellner on the Occasion of His 70th Birthday*, edited by Birgit Kellner, Helmut Krasser, Horst Lasic, Michael Torsten Much, and Helmut Tauscher, 259–84. Wien: Arbeitskreis für Tibetische und Buddhistische Studien.

Hazod, Guntram. 2009. "Imperial Central Tibet: An Annotated Cartographical Survey of its Territorial Divisions and Key Political Sites." In *The Old Tibetan Annals. An Annotated Translation of Tibet's First History*, edited by Brandon Dotson, 12:161–203. Veröffentlichungen zur Sozialanthropologie. Vienna: Verlag der Österreichischen Akademie der Wissenschaften.

Hazod, Guntram. 2012. "Tribal Mobility and Religious Fixation: Remarks on Territorial Transformation, Social Integration and Identity in Imperial and Early Post-Imperial Tibet." In *Visions of Community in the Post-Roman World: The West, Byzantium and the Islamic World, 300–1100*, edited by Walter Pohl, Clemens Gantner, and Richard K. Payne, 43–57. Farnham: Ashgate.

Hazod, Guntram. 2013. "The Plundering of the Tibetan Royal Tombs: An Analysis of the Event in the Context of the Uprisings." In *Tibet after Empire: Culture, Society and Religion between 850–1000: Proceedings of the Seminar Held in Lumbini, Nepal, March 2011*, edited by Christoph Cüppers, Robert Mayer, and Michael Walter, 85–115. Lumbini: Lumbini International Research Institute.

Hazod, Guntram. 2016. "Burial in the Landscape: Remarks on the Topographical Setting of the Grave Mounds in Early Central Tibet." In the 14th Seminar of the International Association for Tibetan Studies, June 19–25, 2016, Bergen, Norway.

Hazod, Guntram. 2020. "Review of Toni Huber's Source of Life: Revitalisation Rites and Bon Shamans in Bhutan and Eastern Himalayas." *Revue d'études Tibétaines* 56: 293–304.

Heath, Chip, and Dan Heath. 2017. *The Power of Moments: Why Certain Experiences Have Extraordinary Impact*. London: Bantam Press.
Heft, Harry. 2001. *Ecological Psychology in Context: James Gibson, Roger Barker, and the Legacy of William James's Radical Empiricism*. Mahwah: L. Erlbaum.
Higgins, David. 2013. *The Philosophical Foundations of Classical rDzogs Chen in Tibet: Investigating the Distinction Between Dualistic Mind (sems) and Primordial Knowing (ye shes). Wiener Studien zur Tibetologie und Buddhismuskunde 78*. Vienna: Arbeitskreis für Tibetische und Buddhistische Studien.
Hill, Nathan. 2006. "The Old Tibetan Chronicle—Chapter One." *Revue d'Etudes Tibétaines* 10: 89–101.
Hill, Nathan W. 2008. "Verba Moriendi in the Old Tibetan Annals." In *Medieval Tibeto-Burman Languages III*, edited by Christopher I. Beckwith, 71–86. Bonn: International Institute for Tibetan and Buddhist Studies.
Hill, Nathan W. 2013. "Come as Lord of the Black-Headed: An Old Tibetan Mythic Formula." In *Tibet after Empire: Culture, Society and Religion between 850–1000: Proceedings of the Seminar Held in Lumbini, Nepal, March 2011*, edited by Christoph Cüppers, Robert Mayer, and Michael Walter, 169–80. Lumbini: Lumbini International Research Institute.
Hillis, Gregory. 2002. "Khyung Texts in the Rnying Ma Rgyud 'bum." In *The Many Canons of Tibetan Buddhism: Piats 2000: Tibetan Studies: Proceedings of the Ninth Seminar of the International Association for Tibetan Studies, Leiden 2000*, edited by Helmut Eimer and David Germano, 313–34. Leiden: Brill.
Hillis, Gregory Alexander. 2003. *The Rhetoric of Naturalness: A Critical Study of the GNas Lugs Mdzod*. Ann Arbor, MI: UMI Dissertation Service.
Hitchcock, John T., and Rex L. Jones, eds. 1976. *Spirit Possession in the Nepal Himalayas*. Warminster: Aris and Phillips.
Hocart, Arthur Maurice. 1953. *The Life-Giving Myth and Other Essays*. New York: Grove Press.
Hoffman, Donald D. 1998. *Visual Intelligence: How We Create What We See*. New York: W.W. Norton.
Hoffmann, Helmut. 1950. *Die Gräber der tibetischen Könige im Distrikt 'P'yons-rgyas*. Göttingen: Vandenhoeck & Ruprecht.
Hogan, Patrick Colm. 2009. *The Mind and Its Stories: Narrative Universals and Human Emotion*. Cambridge: Cambridge University Press.
Holmberg, David H. 1984. "Ritual Paradoxes in Nepal: Comparative Perspectives on Tamang Religion." *Journal of Asian Studies* 43 (4): 697–722.
Holmberg, David H. 1989. *Order in Paradox: Myth, Ritual, and Exchange Amoung Nepal's Tamang*. Ithaca, NY: Cornell University Press.
Horlemann, Bianca. 2021. "A Re-Evaluation of the Tibetan Conquest of Eighth-Century Shazhou/Dunhuang." In *Proceedings of the Ninth Seminar of the IATS, 2000. Volume 1: Tibet, Past and Present: Tibetan Studies I*, edited by Henk Blezer and Abel Zadoks. Leiden: Brill.
Huber, Toni. 1999. *The Cult of Pure Crystal Mountain: Popular Pilgrimage and Visionary Landscape in Southeast Tibet*. Oxford: Oxford University Press.
Huber, Toni. 2015. "Hunting for the Cure: A Bon Healing Narrative from Eastern Bhutan." In *Tibetan and Himalayan Healing—An Anthology for Anthony Aris*, edited by Charles Ramble and Ulrike Roesler, 371–82. Kathmandu: Vajra Books.

Huber, Toni. 2018. "From Death to New Life: An 11th-12th-century cycle of existence from southernmost Tibet: Analysis of Rnel dri 'dul ba, Ste'u and Sha Slungs Rites, with Notes on Manuscript Provenance." In *Tibetan genealogies: studies in memoriam of Guge Tsering Gyalpo (1961–2015)*, edited by Guntram Hazod and Weirong Shen, 251–350. Beijing: China Tibetology Publishing House.

Huber, Toni. 2020. *Source of Life: Revitalisation Rites and Bon Shamans in Bhutan and the Eastern Himalayas*, vol. I. Vienna: Austrian Academy of Sciences Press.

Ifergan, Gidi. 2014. *The Man from Samyé: Longchenpa on Praxis, Its Negation and Liberation*. New Delhi: Aditya Prakashan.

Jackson, David Paul. 1994. *Enlightenment by a Single Means: Tibetan Controversies on the "Self-Sufficient White Remedy" (Dkar Po Chig Thub)*. Vienna: Verlag der Österreichischen Akademie der Wissenschaften.

Jackson, Roger R. 2019. *Mind Seeing Mind: Mahāmudrā and the Geluk Tradition of Tibetan Buddhism*. Somerville: Wisdom Publications.

Jacob, Pierre, and Marc Jeannerod. 2006. *Ways of Seeing: The Scope and Limits of Visual Cognition*. Oxford: Oxford University Press.

Jacobson, Esther. 2018. *The Deer Goddess of Ancient Siberia: A Study in the Ecology of Belief*. Leiden: Brill.

Jacoby, Sarah. 2014. *Love and Liberation: Autobiographical Writings of the Tibetan Buddhist Visionary Sera Khandro*. New York: Columbia.

Jäschke, Heinrich August. 1995. *A Tibetan-English Dictionary with Special References to the Prevailing Dialects: To Which Is Added an English-Tibetan Vocabulary*. Delhi: Motilal Banarsidass Publishers.

Johnson, Davin, and Hussein Hollands. 2012. "Acute-Onset Floaters and Flashes." *CMAJ: Canadian Medical Association Journal* 184 (4): 431.

Johnson, Mark. 2007. *The Meaning of the Body: Aesthetics of Human Understanding*. Chicago: University of Chicago Press.

Jolicœur, Pierre, Roberto Dell'Acqua, and Jacquelyn M. Crebolder. 2001. *The Attentional Blink Bottleneck*. Oxford: Oxford University Press.

Kapstein, Matthew T. 1992. "The Illusion of Spiritual Progress: Remarks on Indo-Tibetan Buddhist Soteriology." In *Paths to Liberation: The Marga and Its Transformations in Buddhist Thought*, edited by Robert E. Buswell and Robert M. Gimello, 193–224. Honolulu: University of Hawaii Press.

Kapstein, Matthew T. 2000. *The Tibetan Assimilation of Buddhism: Conversion, Contestation, and Memory*. New York: Oxford University Press.

Kapstein, Matthew T. 2001. *Reason's Traces: Identity and Interpretation in Indian & Tibetan Buddhist Thought*. Boston, MA: Wisdom Publications.

Kapstein, Matthew T. 2006. *The Tibetans*. New York: Wiley.

Karmay, Samten Gyaltsen. 1996. "The Tibetan Cult of Mountain Deities and Its Political Significance." In *Reflections of the Mountain: Essays on the History and Social Meaning of the Mountain Cult in Tibet and the Himalaya*, edited by Anne-Marie Blondeau and Ernst Steinkellner, 59–75. Vienna: Verlag de Österreichischen Akademie der Wissenschaft.

Karmay, Samten Gyaltsen. 1998a. "Mount Bon-Ri and Its Association with Early Myths." In *The Arrow and the Spindle: Studies in History, Myths, Rituals and Beliefs in Tibet*, 211–27. Kathmandu: Mandala Publications.

Karmay, Samten Gyaltsen. 1998b. "RDzogs-Chen in Its Earliest Text: A Manuscript from Dunhuang." In *The Arrow and the Spindle: Studies in History, Myths, Rituals and

Beliefs in Tibet, edited by Samten Gyaltsen Karmay, 91–103. Kathmandu: Mandala Publications.
Karmay, Samten Gyaltsen. 1998c. *The Arrow and the Spindle: Studies in History, Myths, Rituals and Beliefs in Tibet*. Kathmandu: Mandala Publications.
Karmay, Samten Gyaltsen. 2001. *The Treasury of Good Sayings: A Tibetan History of Bon*. Delhi: Banarsidass.
Karmay, Samten Gyaltsen. 2007. *The Great Perfection (rDzogs Chen): A Philosophical and Meditative Teaching of Tibetan Buddhism*. Leiden: Brill.
Karmay, Samten Gyaltsen. 2009. "A New Discovery of Ancient Bon Manuscripts from a Buddhist 'Stūpa' in Southern Tibet." *East and West* 59 (1/4): 55–84.
Karmay, Samten Gyaltsen. 2010. "Tibetan Indigenous Myths and Rituals with Reference to Ancient Bön Texts: The Nyenbum (Gnyan 'bum)." In *Tibetan Ritual*, edited by José Ignacio Cabezón, 53–68. New York: Oxford University Press.
Karmay, Samten Gyaltsen, and Yasuhiko Nagano. 2001. A Catalogue of the New Collection of Bonpo Katen Texts. Osaka: National Museum of Ethnology.
Karmay, Samten Gyaltsen, and Yasuhiko Nagano. 2002. *The Call of the Blue Cuckoo: An Anthology of Nine Bonpo Texts on Myths and Rituals*. Osaka: National Museum of Ethnology.
Kazui, Hiroaki, Ryouhei Ishii, Tetsuhiko Yoshida, Koji Ikezawa, Masahiko Takaya, Hiromasa Tokunaga, Toshihisa Tanaka, and Masatoshi Takeda. 2009. "Neuroimaging Studies in Patients with Charles Bonnet Syndrome." *Psychogeriatrics: The Official Journal of the Japanese Psychogeriatric Society* 9 (2): 77–84.
Kilty, Gavin. 2012. "Translator's Introduction." In *A Lamp to Illuminate the Five Stages: Teachings on Guhyasamaja Tantra, by Tsongkhapa*, edited by Thupten Jinpa, 1–16. Boston, MA: Wisdom Publications.
Kjellgren, Anette, Fransica Lyden, and Torsten Norlander. 2008. "Sensory Isolation in Flotation Tanks: Altered States of Consciousness and Effects on Well-Being." *Qualitative Report* 13 (4): 636–56.
Klein, Anne Carolyn. 1986. *Knowledge and Liberation: Tibetan Buddhist Epistemology in Support of Transformative Religious Experience*. Ithaca, NY: Snow Lion.
Klein, Anne Carolyn. 2013. "Seeing Mind, Being Body: Contemplative Practice and Buddhist Epistemology." In *A Companion to Buddhist Philosophy*, edited by Steven M. Emmanuel, 572–84. London: Blackwell.
Klein, Anne Carolyn, and Tenzin Wangyal. 2006. *Unbounded Wholeness: Dzogchen, Bon, and the Logic of the Nonconceptual*. Oxford: Oxford University Press.
Klimburg-Salter, Deborah, Elizabeth Würzl, and Charles Ramble. 2013. *Bön - Geister aus Butter: Kunst & Ritual des alten Tibet*. Wien: Museum für Völkerkunde. http://www.univie.ac.at/boen_geisterausbutter/e-publikation.
Kolmaš, Josef. 1967. *Tibet and Imperial China*. Canberra: Centre of Oriental Studies. The Australian National University.
Komarovski, Yaroslav. 2008. "Encountering Ineffability-Counting Ineffability: On Divergent Verbalizations of the Ineffable in 15th Century Tibet." *Acta Tibetica et Buddhica* 1: 1–15.
Kongtrul, Jamgon. 1995. *Myriad Worlds: Buddhist Cosmology in Abhidharma, Kālacakra, and Dzog-Chen*. Ithaca, NY: Snow Lion.
Kosslyn, Stephen Michael. 2000. "Shared Mechanisms in Visual Imagery and Visual Perception: Insights from Cognitive Neuroscience." In *The New Cognitive Neurosciences*, edited by Emilio Bizzi and Michael S. Gazzaniga, 975–85. Cambridge, MA: MIT Press.

Kraus, Paul. 1942. *Jabir ibn Hayyan: contribution à l'histoire des idées scientifiques dans l'islam*. Cairo: Imprimerie de l'Institut français d'archéologie orientale.

Kroeber, A. L. 1970. *Handbook of the Indians of California*. Washington, DC: Government Printing Office.

Kvaerne, Per. 1980. "Mongols and Khitans in a 14th-Century Tibetan Bonpo Text." *Acta Orientalia Academiae Scientiarum Hungaricae* 34 (1/3): 85–104.

Kvaerne, Per. 1995. *The Bon Religion of Tibet: The Iconography of a Living Tradition*. Boston, MA: Shambhala.

Kvaerne, Per. 2013. "The Bön Religion of Tibet." In The Tibetan History Reader, edited by Gray Tuttle and Kurtis R. Schaeffer, 183–95. New York: Columbia University Press.

Laish, Eran. 2017. "Perception, Body and Selfhood: The Transformation of Embodiment in the Thod Rgal Practice of the 'Heart Essence' Tradition." In *Chinese and Tibetan Esoteric Buddhism*, edited by Yael Bentor and Meir Shahar, 215–29. Leiden: Brill.

Laish, Eran. 2018. "The Ground of Knowing: On the Different Modes of Knowing According to the 'Great Perfection' (RDzogs Pa Chen Po)." *Journal of Indian Philosophy* 46 (1): 83–112.

Lalou, Marcelle. 1952. "Rituel Bon-po des Funérailles Royales." *Journal Asiatique* 240 (1): 339–63.

Langelaar, Reinier J. 2022. "Buried Bones and Buddhas Beyond: Ancestor Cults, Buddhism and the Transcendentalisation of Tibetan Religion." In *The Social and the Religious in the Making of Tibetan Societies*, edited by Guntram Hazod, Mathias Fermer, and Christian Jahoda, 30: 221–82. Veröffentlichungen zur Sozialanthropologie. Vienna: Verlag der Österreichischen Akademie der Wissenschaften.

LaRocca, Donald J., John Clarke, Amy Heller, and Lozang Jamspal. 2006. *Warriors of the Himalayas: Rediscovering the Arms and Armor of Tibet*. New Haven, CT: Yale University Press.

Ledi Sayadaw Mahathera. 1999. *Manual of Mindfulness of Breathing: Anapana Dipani*. Edited by U Sein Nyo Tun. Sri Lanka: Buddhist Publication Society.

Li, Fang Kuei, and W. South Coblin. 2013. "The Linguistic and Historical Setting of the Old Tibetan Inscriptions." In *The Tibetan History Reader*, edited by Gray Tuttle and Kurtis R. Schaeffer, 123–32. New York: Columbia University Press.

Liberman, Anatolij Simonovic. 2016. *In Prayer and Laughter: Essays on Medieval Scandinavian and Germanic Mythology, Literature, and Culture*. Moscow: Paleograph Press.

Lifshitz, Michael, Emma P. Cusumano, and Amir Raz. 2014. "Meditation and Hypnosis at the Intersection Between Phenomenology and Cognitive Science." In *Meditation Neuroscientific Approaches and Philosophical Implications*, edited by Stefan Schmidt and Harald Walach. Cham: Springer Verlag.

Liljenberg, Karen. 2012. "A Critical Study of the Thirteen Later Translations of the Dzogchen Mind Series." PhD dissertation, SOAS, University of London.

Lillard, Angeline, and Lori Skibbe. 2005. "Theory of Mind: Conscious Attribution and Spontaneous Trait Inference." In *The New Unconscious*, edited by Ran R. Hassin, James S. Uleman, and John A. Bargh, 277–305. Oxford Series in Social Cognition and Social Neuroscience. Oxford: Oxford University Press.

Lilly, John Cunningham. 1977. *The Deep Self: Profound Relaxation and the Tank Isolation Technique*. New York: Simon and Schuster.

Lindahl, Jared R., Christopher T. Kaplan, Evan M. Winget, and Willoughby B. Britton. 2014. "A Phenomenology of Meditation-Induced Light Experiences: Traditional Buddhist and Neurobiological Perspectives." *Frontiers in Psychology* 4 (January): 1-16.
Lloyd, Donna M., Elizabeth Lewis, Jacob Payne, and Lindsay Wilson. 2012. "A Qualitative Analysis of Sensory Phenomena Induced by Perceptual Deprivation." *Phenomenology and the Cognitive Sciences* 11 (1): 95-112.
Lobel, Adam S. 2018. "Allowing Spontaneity: Practice, Theory, and Ethical Cultivation in Longchenpa's Great Perfection Philosophophy of Action." PhD dissertation, Cambridge, MA: Harvard University.
Loftus, Geoffrey R., Aura M. Hanna, and Lorraine Lester. 1988. "Conceptual Masking: How One Picture Captures Attention from Another Picture." *Cognitive Psychology* 20 (2): 237-82.
Lopez, Donald S. 1988. *The Heart Sutra Explained: Indian and Tibetan Commentaries*. Albany: State University of New York Press.
Luhrmann, Tanya Marie. 2013. "Building on William James: The Role of Learning in Religious Experience." In *Mental Culture: Classical Social Theory and the Cognitive Science of Religion*, edited by William W. Mccorkle Jr. and Dimitris Xygalatas, 145-63. Durham: Acumen.
Lutz, Antoine, John D. Dunne, and Richard J. Davidson. 2007. "Meditation and the Neuroscience of Consciousness." In *The Cambridge Handbook of Consciousness*, edited by Philip David Zelazo, Morris Moscovitch, and Evan Thompson, 499-554. Cambridge: Cambridge University Press.
Macdonald, Ariane. 1971. "Une lecture des Pelliot Tibétain 1286, 1287, 1038, 1047, et 1290: Essai sur la formation et l'emploi des mythes politiques dans la religion royale de sron-bcan sgam-po." In *Études tibétaines dédiées à la mémoire de Marcelle Lalou*, edited by Marcelle Lalou and Ariane Spanien, 190-391. Paris: Librairie d'Amérique et d'Orient.
MacDonald, Ariane, and Yoshiro Imaeda. 1977. "Tibetan costume, seventh to eleventh centuries." In *Essais sur l'art du Tibet*, 64-81. Paris: Librairie d'Amérique et d'Orient.
Maffei, Arianna, and Gina G. Turrigiano. 2008. "Multiple Modes of Network Homeostasis in Visual Cortical Layer 2/3." *Journal of Neuroscience: The Official Journal of the Society for Neuroscience* 28 (17): 4377-84.
Mar, Raymond A., and C. Neil Macrae. 2007. "Triggering the Intentional Stance." In *Empathy and Fairness*, edited by J. Goode, 111-19. Novartis Foundation Symposium 278. Chichester: John Wiley & Sons.
Martens, Sander, and Brad Wyble. 2010. "The Attentional Blink: Past, Present, and Future of a Blind Spot in Perceptual Awareness." *Neuroscience and Biobehavioral Reviews* 34 (6): 947-57.
Martin, Dan. 2001. *Unearthing Bon Treasures: Life and Contested Legacy of a Tibetan Scripture Revealer, with a General Bibliography of Bon*. Brill's Tibetan Studies Library. Boston: Brill.
Martin, Dan. 2005. *The Emergence of Bon and the Tibetan Polemical Tradition*. Ann Arbor, MI: UMI.
Martin, Dan. 2010. "Zhangzhung Dictionary." *Revue d'Etudes Tibétaines* 18: 5-253.
Martin, Dan. 2014. "The Gold Drink Rite. Indigenous, but Not Simply Indigenous." *Mongolo-Tibetica Pragensia '14: Ethnolinguistics, Sociolinguistics, Religion and Culture* 7 (2): 79-95.
Martin, Dan. 2017. "Crazy Wisdom in Moderation: Padampa Sangyé's Use of Counterintuitive Methods in Dealing with Negative Mental States." In *Chinese*

and Tibetan Esoteric Buddhism, edited by Yael Bentor and Meir Shahar, 193–214. Leiden: Brill.

Martin, Dan, and Yael Bentor. 1997. *Tibetan Histories: A Bibliography of Tibetan-Language Historical Works*. London: Serindia.

Martinez, A. P. 1982. "Gardīzī's Two Chapters on the Turks." *Archivum Eurasiae Medii Aevi* 2: 109–217.

Martynov, Anatoli I. 1988. "The Solar Cult and the Tree of Life." *Arctic Anthropology* 25 (2): 12–29.

Maskarinec, Gregory G. 1995. *The Rulings of the Night. An Ethnography of Nepalese Shaman Oral Texts*. Madison: University of Wisconsin Press.

Maskarinec, Gregory G. 1998. *Nepalese Shaman Oral Texts*. Cambridge, MA: Harvard University Press.

Mason, Oliver J., and Francesca Brady. 2009. "The Psychotomimetic Effects of Short-Term Sensory Deprivation." *Journal of Nervous and Mental Disease* 197 (10): 783–5.

Mayer, Robert. 2019. "Rethinking Treasure (Part One)." *Revue d'Etudes Tibétaines* 52: 119–84.

Mayer, Robert, and Cathy Cantwell. 2010. "Continuity and Change in Tibetan Mahayoga Ritual: Some Evidence from the Tabzhag (Thabs Zhags) Manuscript and Other Dunhuang Texts." In *Tibetan Ritual*, edited by José Ignacio Cabezón, 69–88. New York: Oxford University Press.

McKay, Alex, ed. 2003. *Tibet and Her Neighbours: A History*. London: Edition Hansjörg Mayer.

McMahan, David L. 2008. *The Making of Buddhist Modernism*. Oxford: Oxford University Press.

Melikian-Chirvani, Assadullah Souren. 1992. "The Iranian Sun Shield." *Bulletin of the Asia Institute* 6: 1–42.

Merabet, Lotfi B., Denise Maguire, Aisling Warde, Karin Alterescu, Robert Stickgold, and Alvaro Pascual-Leone. 2004. "Visual Hallucinations during Prolonged Blindfolding in Sighted Subjects." *Journal of Neuro-Ophthalmology: The Official Journal of the North American Neuro-Ophthalmology Society* 24 (2): 109–13.

Merleau-Ponty, Maurice. 1962. *Phenomenology of Perception*. New York: Humanities Press.

Metzinger, Thomas. 2009. *The Ego Tunnel: The Science of the Mind and the Myth of the Self*. New York: Basic Books.

Metzner, Ralph. 1994. *The Well of Remembrance: Rediscovering the Earth Wisdom Myths of Northern Europe*. Boston, MA: Shambhala.

Mills, Martin A. 2012. "Ritual as History in Tibetan Divine Kingship: Notes on the Myth of the Khotanese Monks." *History of Religions* 51 (3): 219–20.

Mkhas-pa-ldeu. 2022. *A History of Buddhism in India and Tibet: An Expanded Version of the Dharma's Origins Made by the Learned Scholar Deyu*. Translated by Dan Martin. Somerville: Wisdom Publications.

Mullin, Glenn H. 2006. "Handprints of the Profound Path of the Six Yogas of Naropa: A Source of Every Realization." In *The Practice of the Six Yogas of Naropa*, 71–92. Ithaca: Snow Lion.

Mumford, Stan. 1989. *Himalayan Dialogue: Tibetan Lamas and Gurung Shamans in Nepal*. Madison: University of Wisconsin Press.

Myers, L. Daniel. 1997. "Animal Symbolism Among The Numa: Symbolic Analysis Of Numic Origin Myths." *Journal of California and Great Basin Anthropology* 19 (1): 32–49.

Mykhailova, Nataliia. 2008. "The Deer in the Palaeolithic Franko–Cantabrian Rock Art Researches of the Fine Arts." *Kyiv* 1 (21): 30–41.
Mykhailova, Nataliia. 2015. "Deer Offerings in the Archaeology and Art of Prehistoric Eurasia." *Expression* 10: 53–9.
Mykhailova, Nataliia, and Alan P. Garfinkel. 2018. "Horned Hunter—Shaman, Ancestor, and Deity." *Origin of Language and Culture: Ancient History of Mankind* 5 (1): 5–26.
Napper, Elizabeth. 2003. *Dependent-Arising and Emptiness A Tibetan Buddhist Interpretation of Madhyamika Philosophy*. Boston, MA: Wisdom Publications.
Nebesky-Wojkowitz, René de. 1956. *Oracles and Demons of Tibet; The Cult and Iconography of the Tibetan Protective Deities*. 's-Gravenhage: Mouton.
Newman, John. 1998. "Islam in the Kalacakra Tantra." *Journal of the International Association of Buddhist Studies* 21 (2): 311–71.
Newman, John. 2000. "Vajrayoga in the Kālacakra Tantra." In *Tantra in Practice*, 587–94. Princeton, NJ: Princeton University Press.
Nieuwenstein, Mark R., Mary C. Potter, and Jan Theeuwes. 2009. "Unmasking the Attentional Blink." *Journal of Experimental Psychology. Human Perception and Performance* 35 (1): 159–69.
Noë, Alva. 2004. *Action in Perception*. Cambridge, MA: MIT Press.
Noë, Alva. 2012. *Varieties of Presence*. Cambridge, MA: Harvard University Press.
Norbu, Chögyal Namkhai. 1995. *Drung, Deu and Bon: Narrations, Symbolic Languages and the Bon Tradition on Ancient Tibet*. Dharamsala: Library of Tibetan Works and Archives.
Nor-bzaṅ-rgya-mtsho. 2004. *Ornament of Stainless Light: An Exposition of the Kālacakra Tantra*. Boston, MA: Wisdom Publications in association with the Institute of Tibetan Classics.
Ooi, Teng Leng, and Zijiang J. He. 1999. "Binocular Rivalry and Visual Awareness: The Role of Attention." *Perception* 28 (5): 551–74.
Ooi, Teng Leng, and Zijiang J. He. 2006. "Binocular Rivalry and Surface-Boundary Processing." *Perception* 35 (5): 581–603.
Oppitz, Michael. 1997. "The Bull, the Ox, the Cow and the Yak. Meat Division in the Himalayas." In *Les habitants du Toit du monde: en hommage à Alexander W. MacDonald*, edited by Samten Gyaltsen Karmay and Philippe Sagant, 515–42. Nanterre: Société d'ethnologie.
Oppitz, Michael. 2013. *Morphologie der Schamanentrommel*. Zürich: Edition Voldemeer.
Orofino, Giacomella. 1990. *Sacred Tibetan Teachings on Death and Liberation: Texts from the Most Ancient Traditions of Tibet*. Bridport: Prism.
Ortner, Sherry B. 1995. "The Case of the Disappearing Shamans, or No Individualism, No Relationalism." *Ethos* 23 (3): 355–90.
Osto, Douglas. 2019. "Altered States and the Origins of the Mahāyāna." In *Setting out on the Great Way: Essays on Early Mahāyāna Buddhism*, edited by Paul M. Harrison, 177–205. Sheffield: Equinox Publishing.
Panksepp, Jaak. 2007. "Affective Consciousness." In *The Blackwell Companion to Consciousness*, edited by Max Velmans and Susan Schneider, 114–29. Malden: Blackwell Publishing.
Pasarić, Maja. 2018. "For the Love of Antlers: Heads on a Wall or Antlers on a Bride." *Studia Mythologica Slavica* 21 (October): 217–35.
Paul, Robert A. 1979. "Dumje: Paradox and Resolution in Sherpa Ritual Symbolism." *American Ethnologist* 6 (2): 274–304.

Pelliot, Paul. 1961. *Histoire ancienne du Tibet*. Paris: Librairie d'Amérique et d'Orient.

Petech, Luciano. 1994. "The Disintegration of the Tibetan Kingdom." In *Tibetan Studies: Proceedings of the 6th Seminar of the International Association of Tibetan Studies, Fagerness, 1992*, edited by Per Kvaerne, 652–6. Oslo: Institute for Comparative Research in Human Culture.

Peters, Larry. 1981. *Ecstasy and Healing in Nepal an Ethnopsychiatric Study of Tamang Shamanism*. Malibu: Undena Publications.

Peters, Larry. 2016. *Tibetan Shamanism: Ecstasy and Healing*. Berkeley, CA: North Atlantic Books.

Pitskel, Naomi B., Lotfi B. Merabet, Ciro Ramos-Estebanez, Thomas Kauffman, and Alvaro Pascual-Leone. 2007. "Time-Dependent Changes in Cortical Excitability after Prolonged Visual Deprivation." *Neuroreport* 18 (16): 1703–7.

Premack, David, and Guy Woodruff. 1978. "Does the Chimpanzee Have a Theory of Mind?" *Behavioral and Brain Sciences* 1 (04): 515–26.

Punzi, Valentina. 2021. "Burying Gold, Digging the Past: Remembering Ma Bufang Regime in Qinghai (PRC)." In *Dealing with Disasters: Perspectives from Eco-Cosmologies*, edited by Diana Riboli, Pamela J. Stewart, Andrew Strathern, and Davide Torri, 233–54. Cham: Palgrave Macmillan.

Ramachandran, Vilayanur S., and Sandra Blakeslee. 1998. *Phantoms in the Brain: Probing the Mysteries of the Human Mind*. New York: William Morrow.

Ramachandran, Vilayanur S., and William Hirstein. 1996. "Three Laws of Qualia: What Neurology Tells Us about the Biological Functions of Consciousness." *Journal of Consciousness Studies* 4 (5–6): 429–57.

Ramble, Charles. 2013. "Both Fish and Fowl? Preliminary Reflections on Some Representations of a Tibetan Mirror-World." In *Nepalica-Tibetica: Festgabe for Christoph Cüppers*, edited by Franz-Karl Ehrhard and Petra Maurer, 75–89. Andiast: IITBS, International Institute for Tibetan and Buddhist Studies.

Ramble, Charles. 2015. "The Deer as a Structuring Principle in Certain Bonpo Rituals: A Comparison of Three Texts for the Acquisition of Good Fortune (g.Yang)." In *Cultural Flows across the Western Himalaya*, edited by Patrick Mc Allister, Cristina Anna Scherrer-Schaub, and Helmut Krasser, 499–528. Wien: Verlag der Österreichischen Akademie der Wissenschaften.

Rappaport, Roy A. 1999. *Ritual and Religion in the Making of Humanity*. Cambridge: Cambridge University Press.

Rey, Amandine Eve, Benoit Riou, Dominique Muller, Stéphanie Dabic, and Rémy Versace. 2015. "'The Mask Who Wasn't There': Visual Masking Effect with the Perceptual Absence of the Mask." *Journal of Experimental Psychology: Learning, Memory, and Cognition* 41 (2): 567–73.

Reynolds, John Myrdhin. 2011. "Outlines of the Contents of the Texts." In *The Practice of Dzogchen in the Zhang-Zhung Tradition of Tibet: Translations from the Bonpo Dzogchen Practice Manual: The Gyalwa Chaktri of Druchen Gyalwa Yungdrung and the Seven-Fold Cycle of the Clear Light, the Dark Retreat Practice from the Zhang-Zhung Nyan-Gyud*, 19–64. Kathmandu: Vajra Publications.

Riboli, Diana. 2000. *Tunsuriban: Shamanism in the Chepang of Southern and Central Nepal*. Kathmandu: Mandala Book Point.

Richardson, Alan. 2010. *The Neural Sublime: Cognitive Theories and Romantic Texts*. Baltimore, MD: Johns Hopkins University Press.

Richardson, Hugh. 1989. "The Origin of the Tibetan Kingdom." *Bulletin of Tibetoloogy* 3: 5–19.

Richardson, Hugh E. 1981. "Khri Gtsug-Lde-Brtsan's Illness." *Bulletin of the School of Oriental and African Studies* 44 (2): 351–2.

Richardson, Hugh E. 2003. "The Origin of the Tibetan Empire." In *The History of Tibet*, edited by Alex McKay, 1:156–64. London: RoutledgeCurzon.

Rock, Joseph Francis Charles. 1952: *The Na-khi Nàga Cult and Related Ceremonies*, 2 vols. Roma: Istituto Italiano per il Medio ed Estremo Oriente (*Serie Orientale Roma*, 4).

Rock, Joseph Francis Charles. 1963. *ANa-khi—English Encyclopedic Dictionary*, Parti. Roma: Istituto Italiano per il Medio ed Estremo Oriente (*Serie Orientale Roma*, 28).

Romain, William F. 2018. "Geomantic Entanglements in Central Tibet: Royal Tombs of the Chongye Valley." *Tibetan Journal* (blog). September 17. https://www.tibetanjournal.com/geomantic-entanglements-central-tibet-royal-tombs-chongye-valley/.

Rosch, Eleanor. 2016. "Introduction to the Revised Edition." In *The Embodied Mind: Cognitive Science and Human Experience*, edited by Francisco J. Varela, Evan Thompson, and Eleanor Rosch, xxxv–lvi. Cambridge, MA: MIT Press.

Rossi, Donatella. 1999. *The Philosophical View of the Great Perfection in the Tibetan Bon Religion*. Ithaca, NY: Snow Lion.

Roux, Jean-Paul. 1956. "Tängri Essai Sur Le Ciel-Dieu Des Peuples Altaïques." *Revue de l'histoire Des Religions* 149 (1): 49–82.

Ruegg, David Seyfort. 1989. *Buddha-Nature, Mind, and the Problem of Gradualism in a Comparative Perspective: On the Transmission and Reception of Buddhism in India and Tibet*. London: School of Oriental and African Studies, University of London.

Sagant, Philippe. 1996. *The Dozing Shaman: The Limbus of Eastern Nepal*. Delhi: Oxford University Press.

Samuel, Geoffrey. 1993. *Civilized Shamans: Buddhism in Tibetan Societies*. Washington, DC: Smithsonian Institution Press.

Sapir, Edward. 2002. *The Psychology of Culture a Course of Lectures*. Edited by Judith T. Irvine. Berlin: De Gruyter.

Schaeffer, Kurtis R., Matthew T. Kapstein, and Gray Tuttle, eds. 2013. *Sources of Tibetan Tradition*. New York: Columbia University Press.

Scheidegger, Daniel. 2005. "Lamps in the Leaping Over." *Revue d'Etudes Tibétaines* 8: 40–64.

Scherrer-Schaub, Cristina Anna. 2002. "Enacting Words. A Diplomatic Analysis of the Imperial Decrees (Bkas Bcad) and Their Application in the SGra Sbyor Bam Po Gñis Pa Tradition." *Journal of the International Association of Buddhist Studies*, June, 263–340.

Scherrer-Schaub, Cristina Anna. 2012. "Tibet: An Archaeology of the Written." In *Proceedings of the Tenth Seminar of the IATS, 2003. Volume 14: Old Tibetan Studies: Dedicated to the Memory of R.E. Emmerick*, edited by Cristina Anna Scherrer-Schaub, 217–47. Leiden: Brill.

Schooler, Jonathan W. 2002. "Re-Representing Consciousness: Dissociations Between Experience and Meta-Consciousness." *Trends in Cognitive Sciences* 6 (8): 339–44.

Schuh, Dieter. 2013. "Tibetischen Inschriften Ins Maul Geschaut: Beobachtungen Zu Stein- Und Felsinschriften Sowie Den Schriften Des 7. Bis 9. Jahrhunderts in Tibet." In *Nepalica-Tibetica: Festgabe for Christoph Cüppers*, edited by Franz-Karl Ehrhard and Petra Maurer, 143–84. Andiast: IITBS, International Institute for Tibetan and Buddhist Studies.

Schwieger, Peter. 2000. "Geschichte Als Mythos: Zur Aneignung von Vergangenheit in Der Tibetischen Kultur. Ein Kulturwissenschaftlicher Essay." *Asiatische Studien: Zeitschrift Der Schweizerischen Asiengesellschaft* 54 (4): 945–73.

Schwieger, Peter. 2013. "On the Appropriation of the Past in Tibetan Culture An Essay in Cultural Studies." In *The Tibetan History Reader*, edited by Gray Tuttle and Kurtis R. Schaeffer, 64–86. New York: Columbia University Press.

Schwieger, Peter. 2015. *The Dalai Lama and the Emperor of China: A Political History of the Tibetan Institution of Reincarnation*. New York: Columbia University Press.

Sehnalova, Anna. 2022. "Tombs and Treasures: Tibetan Empire and Ancestor Cults in Present East Tibet." In *The Social and the Religious in the Making of Tibetan Societies*, edited by Guntram Hazod, Mathias Fermer, and Christian Jahoda, 30: 221–82. Veröffentlichungen zur Sozialanthropologie. Vienna: Verlag der Österreichischen Akademie der Wissenschaften.

Shakabpa, Tsepon W. D. 1967. *Tibet: A Political History*. New Haven, CT: Yale University Press.

Shapiro, Kimron L., Jane E. Raymond, and Karen M. Arnell. 1997. "The Attentional Blink." *Trends in Cognitive Sciences* 1 (8): 291–96.

Sharf, Robert H. 2014. "Mindfulness and Mindlessness in Early Chan." *Philosophy East and West* 64 (4): 933–64.

Sharf, Robert H. 2017. "Is Mindfulness Buddhist? (And Why It Matters)." In *Meditation, Buddhism, and Science*, edited by David L. McMahan and Erik Braun, 198–212. New York: Oxford University Press.

Shirokogorov, Sergei Mikhailovich. 1935. *Psychomental Complex of the Tungus*. London: Kegan, Paul, Trench, Trubner.

Sidky, Homayun. 2010. "Ethnographic Perspectives on Differentiating Shamans from Other Ritual Intercessors." *Asian Ethnology* 69 (2): 213–41.

Sigman, Mariano. 2017. *The Secret Life of the Mind: How Your Brain Thinks, Feels, and Decides*. London: William Collins.

Skorupski, Tadeusz. 1996. "The Canonical Tantras of the New Schools." In *Tibetan Literature: Studies in Genre*, edited by José Ignacio Cabezón and Roger R. Jackson, 95–110. Ithaca: Snow Lion.

Slingerland, Edward G. 2008. *What Science Offers the Humanities: Integrating Body and Culture*. Cambridge: Cambridge University Press.

Smail, Daniel. 2007. *On Deep History and the Brain*. Berkeley: University of California Press.

Smith, E. Gene. 2001. *Among Tibetan Texts: History and Literature of the Himalayan Plateau*. Edited by Kurtis Schaefer. Boston: Wisdom Publications.

Smith, Frederick M. 2006. *The Self Possessed: Deity and Spirit Possession in South Asian Literature and Civilization*. New York: Columbia University Press.

Smoljak, A. V. 1984. "Some Elements of Ritual Attire of Nanai Shamans." In *Shamanism in Eurasia*, edited by Mihály Hoppál, 244–53. Göttingen: Herodot.

Snellgrove, David Llewellyn. 1959. *The Hevajra Tantra: A Critical Study*. New York: Oxford University Press.

Snellgrove, David Llewellyn. 1961. *Himalayan Pilgrimage: A Study of Tibetan Religion by a Traveller through Western Nepal*. Oxford: Cassirer.

Snellgrove, David Llewellyn. 1987. *Indo-Tibetan Buddhism: Indian Buddhists and Their Tibetan Successors*. 2 vols. Boston, MA: Shambhala.

Sørensen, Henrik Hjort. 2019. "Guiyijun and Buddhism at Dunhuang." *BuddhistRoad Paper* 4.2 (November): 1–31.

Sørensen, Jesper. 2007. "Acts That Work: A Cognitive Approach to Ritual Agency." *Method & Theory in the Study of Religion* 19 (3–4): 281–300.
Stablein, William. 1976. "Mahākāla the Neo-Shaman—Master of the Ritual." In *Spirit Possession in the Nepal Himalayas*, edited by John T. Hitchcock and Rex L. Jones, 361–75. Warminster: Aris and Phillips.
Starr, G. Gabrielle. 2013. *Feeling Beauty the Neuroscience of Aesthetic Experience*. Cambridge, MA: MIT Press.
Stein, Rolf Alfred. 1959. *Les tribus anciennes des marches sino-tibétaines: légendes, classifications et histoire*. Paris: Bibliothèque de l'Institut des Hautes Études chinoises.
Stein, Rolf Alfred. 1971. "Du récit au rituel dans les manuscrits Tibétains de Touen-houang." In *Études tibétaines: dédiées à la mémoire de Marcelle Lalou*, edited by Ariane MacDonald, 479–547. Paris: Librairie d'Amérique et d'Orient A. Maisonneuve.
Stein, Rolf Alfred. 1972. *Tibetan Civilization*. Stanford: Stanford University Press.
Stein, Rolf Alfred. 1987. "Sudden Illumination or Simultaneous Comprehension: Remarks on Chinese and Tibetan Terminology." In *Sudden and Gradual: Approaches to Enlightenment in Chinese Thought*, edited by Peter N. Gregory, 41–66. Honolulu: University of Hawaii Press.
Stein, Rolf Alfred. 1988. "Tibetica Antiqua V. La Religion Indigène et Les Bon-Po Dans Les Manuscrits de Touen-Houang." *Bulletin de l'École Française d'Extrême-Orient* 77: 27–56.
Stein, Rolf Alfred. 1990. *The World in Miniature: Container Gardens and Dwellings in Far Eastern Religious Thought*. Translated by Phyllis Brooks. Stanford: Stanford University Press.
Steinmann, Brigitte. 2001. *Les Enfants Du Singe et de La Démone: Mémoires Des Tamang, Récits Himalayens*. Nanterre: Société d'ethnologie.
Steward, Julian Haynes. 1941. *Culture Element Distributions: XIII: Nevada Shoshone*. Berkeley: University of California Press.
Stewart, Charles. 2012. *Dreaming and Historical Consciousness in Island Greece*. Cambridge, MA: Harvard University Press.
Stewart, Omer Call. 1942. *Culture Element Distributions: Ute-Southern Paiute*. Berkeley: University of California Press.
Suedfeld, Peter. 1980. *Restricted Environmental Stimulation: Research and Clinical Applications*. New York: John Wiley & Sons.
Sulek, Emilia Roza. 2019. *Trading Caterpillar Fungus in Tibet: When Economic Boom Hits Rural Area*. Amsterdam: Amsterdam University Press.
Sumegi, Angela. 2008. *Dreamworlds of Shamanism and Tibetan Buddhism: The Third Place*. Albany: State University of New York Press.
Sur, Dominic. 2017. "Translator's Introduction." In *Entering the way of the great vehicle: Dzogchen as the culmination of the Mahāyāna*, by Rong-zom Chos-kyi-bzang-po, translated by Dominic Sur, 8–38. Boulder, CO: Snow Lion.
Surya Das. 2005. *Natural Radiance: Awakening to Your Great Perfection*. Boulder, CO: Sounds True.
Takata, Tokio. 2000. "Multilingualism in Tun-Huang." *Acta Asiatica* 78: 49–70.
Tambiah, Stanley Jeyaraja. 1979. *A Performative Approach to Ritual*. London: Oxford University Press.
Tashi, Kelzang. 2020. "Contested Past, Challenging Future: An Ethnography of Pre-Buddhist Bon Religious Practices in Central Bhutan." Australian National University: Canberra.

Taves, Ann. 2009. *Religious Experience Reconsidered: A Building-Block Approach to the Study of Religion and Other Special Things*. Princeton, NJ: Princeton University Press.

Terrone, Antonio. 2014. "The Earth as a Treasure in Tibetan Buddhism: Visionary Revelation and Its Interactions with the Environment." *Journal for the Study of Religion, Nature and Culture* 8 (4): 465–82.

Third Dzogchen Rinpoche. 2008. *Great Perfection, Volume Two: Separation and Breakthrough*. Translated by Cortland J. Dahl. Ithaca, NY: Snow Lion.

Thompson, Evan. 2007. *Mind in Life: Biology, Phenomenology, and the Sciences of Mind*. Cambridge, MA: Harvard University Press.

Thompson, Evan. 2015. *Waking, Dreaming, Being: New Light on the Self and Consciousness from Neuroscience, Meditation, and Philosophy*. New York: Columbia University Press.

Thompson, Evan. 2017. "Looping Effects and the Cognitive Science of Mindfulness Meditation." In *Meditation, Buddhism, and Science*, edited by David L. McMahan and Erik Braun, 47–61. New York: Oxford University Press.

Thondup, Tulku. 1986. *Hidden Teachings of Tibet: An Explanation of the Terma Tradition of the Nyingma School of Buddhism*. Translated by Harold Talbott. London: Wisdom Publications.

Tooby, John, and Leda Cosmides. 1995. "Foreword." In *Mindblindness: An Essay on Autism and "Theory of Mind,"* by Simon Baron-Cohen, xi–xviii. Cambridge, MA: MIT Press.

Tsongkhapa. 2012. *A Lamp to Illuminate the Five Stages: Teachings on Guhyasamaja Tantra*. Edited by Thupten Jinpa. Translated by Gavin Kilty. Boston, MA: Wisdom Publications.

Tucci, Giuseppe. 1949. *Tibetan Painted Scrolls*. Roma: Libreria dello Stato.

Tucci, Giuseppe. 1950. *The Tombs of the Tibetan Kings*. Roma: Istituto Italiano per il Medio ed Estremo Oriente.

Tucci, Giuseppe. 1955. "The Secret Characters of the Kings of Ancient Tibet." *East and West* 6 (3): 197–205.

Tucci, Giuseppe. 1980. *The Religions of Tibet*. Translated by Geoffrey Samuel. London: Routledge & Kegan Paul.

Tulku Urgyen Rinpoche. 2000. *As It Is*. Volume II. Boudhanath: Rangjung Yeshe Publications.

Upatissa. 1977. *The Path of Freedom (Vimuttimagga)*. Translated by N. R. M Ehara, Thera Kheminda, and Tipiṭaka Sanghapāla. Kandy: Buddhist Publication Society.

Van der Kuijp, Leonard W. J. 1992. "Dating the Two Lde'u Chronicles of Buddhism InIndia and Tibet." *Asiatische Studien: Zeitschrift Der SchweizerischenAsiengesellschaft* 46: 468–91.

Van der Kuijp, Leonard W. J. 1998. "Review of J. I. Cabézon, Buddhism and Language." *Journal of the American Oriental Society* 128 (4): 563–67.

Van der Kuijp, Leonard W. J. 2013. "On the Edge of Myth and History: Za hor, Its Place in the History of Early Indian Buddhist Tantra, and Dalai Lama V and the Genealogy of its Royal Family." In *Studies on Buddhist Myths: Texts, Pictures, Traditions and History*, edited by Bangwei Wang, Jinhua Chen, and Ming Chen, 114–64. Shanghai: Zhongxi Book Company.

Van Schaik, Sam. 2004a. "The Early Days of the Great Perfection." *Journal of the International Association of Buddhist Studies* 27 (1): 165–206.

Van Schaik, Sam. 2004b. *Approaching the Great Perfection: Simultaneous and Gradual Methods of Dzogchen Practice in the Longchen Nyingtig*. Somerville: Wisdom Publications.

Van Schaik, Sam. 2010. "The Limits of Transgression: The Samaya Vows of Mahāyoga." In *Esoteric Buddhism at Dunhuang: Rites and Teachings for This Life and Beyond*, edited by Matthew Kapstein and Sam Van Schaik, 61–83. Leiden: Brill.

Van Schaik, Sam. 2011. "A New Look at the Tibetan Invention of Writing." In *New Studies of the Old Tibetan Documents: Philology, History and Religion*, edited by Yoshiro Imaeda, Matthew T. Kapstein, and Tsuguhito Takeuchi, 45–96. Tokyo: Research Institute for Languages and Cultures of Asia and Africa, Tokyo University of Foreign Studies.

Van Schaik, Sam, and Imre Galambos. 2012. *Manuscripts and Travellers the Sino-Tibetan Documents of a Tenth-Century Buddhist Pilgrim*. Berlin: De Gruyter.

Vander, Judith. 1997. *Shoshone Ghost Dance Religion: Poetry Songs and Great Basin Context*. Urbana: University of Illinois Press.

Varela, Francisco J. 1979. *Principles of Biological Autonomy*. New York: North Holland.

Vermeule, Blakey. 2011. *Why Do We Care about Literary Characters?* Baltimore, MD: Johns Hopkins University Press.

Vitali, Roberto. 1990. *Early Temples of Central Tibet*. London: Serindia Publications.

Vitali, Roberto. 1997. *The Kingdoms of Gu.Ge Phu.Hrang According to MNga'.Ris Rgyal. Rabs by Gu.Ge Mkhan.Chen Ngag.Dbang Grags.Pa*. London: Serindia.

Vitali, Roberto. 2008. "A Tentative Classification of the Bya Ru Can Kings of Zhang Zhung." *Revue d'Etudes Tibétaines* 15: 379–419.

Vogliotti, Guido. 2019. "Kings of Yore and Mounds of Earth A Reassessment of the Tibetan Royal Necropolis of 'Phyong Rgyas." In *Wind Horses: Tibetan, Himalayan and Mongolian Studies*, edited by Giacomella Orofino, 569–92. Napoli: Università degli studi di Napoli "L'Orientale."

Von Fürer-Haimendorf, Christoph. 1978. "Foreword." In *Himalayan Anthropology: The Indo-Tibetan Interface*, edited by James F. Fisher, ix–xii. The Hague: Mouton.

Vukicevic, Meri, and Kerry Fitzmaurice. 2008. "Butterflies and Black Lacy Patterns: The Prevalence and Characteristics of Charles Bonnet Hallucinations in an Australian Population." *Clinical & Experimental Ophthalmology* 36 (7): 659–65.

Vul, Edward, Deborah Hanus, and Nancy Kanwisher. 2008. "Delay of Selective Attention During the Attentional Blink." *Vision Research* 48 (18): 1902–9.

Wackermann, Jirí, Peter Pütz, and Carsten Allefeld. 2008. "Ganzfeld-Induced Hallucinatory Experience, Its Phenomenology and Cerebral Electrophysiology." *Cortex; a Journal Devoted to the Study of the Nervous System and Behavior* 44 (10): 1364–78.

Wackermann, Jiri, Peter Pütz, Simone Büchi, Inge Strauch, and Dietrich Lehmann. 2002. "Brain Electrical Activity and Subjective Experience during Altered States of Consciousness: Ganzfeld and Hypnagogic States." *International Journal of Psychophysiology: Official Journal of the International Organization of Psychophysiology* 46 (2): 123–46.

Waddell, Laurence A. 1895. *The Buddhism of Tibet or Lamaism with Its Mystic Cults, Symbolism and Mythology, and in Its Relation to Indian Buddhism*. London: Allen.

Wallace, Vesna. 2001. *The Inner Kalacakratantra: A Buddhist Tantric View of the Individual*. New York: Oxford University Press.

Wallace, Vesna A. 2009. "The Body as a Text and the Text as the Body: A View from the Kālacakratantra's Perspective." In *As Long As Space Endures: Essays on the Kalacakra Tantra in Honor of the Dalai Lama*, edited by Edward A. Arnold, 179–92. Ithaca: Snow Lion.

Walter, Michael L. 2009a. *Buddhism and Empire: The Political and Religious Culture of Early Tibet*. Leiden: Brill.

Walter, Michael L. 2009b. *Buddhism and Empire: The Political and Religious Culture of Early Tibet*. Brill Academic Publishers.

Wangdu, Pasang, and Hildegard Diemberger. 2000. *DBa' Bzhed: The Royal Narrative Concerning the Bringing of the Buddha's Doctrine to Tibet*. Wien: Verlag der Österreichischen Akademie der Wissenschaften.

Wangyal, Tenzin. 2000. *Wonders of the Natural Mind: The Essence of Dzogchen in the Native Bon Tradition of Tibet*. Translated by Andrew Lukianowicz. Ithaca, NY: Snow Lion.

Wangyal, Tenzin, and Polly Turner. 2013. *Tibetan Yogas of Body, Speech, and Mind*. Boston, MA: Snow Lion.

Watt, Tessa. 2017. "Spacious Awareness in Mahāyāna Buddhism and Its Role in the Modern Mindfulness Movement." *Contemporary Buddhism* 18 (2): 455–80.

Watters, David E. 1975. "Siberian Shamanistic Traditions among the Kham-Magars of Nepal." *Contributions to Nepalese Studies* 2: 123–68.

Wedemeyer, Christian K. 2013. *Making Sense of Tantric Buddhism: History, Semiology, and Transgression in the Indian Traditions*. New York: Columbia University Press.

Werlen, Iwar. 1984. *Ritual und Sprache: zum Verhältnis von Sprechen und Handeln in Ritualen*. Tübingen: Narr.

Westerhoff, Jan. 2010. *Twelve Examples of Illusion*. New York: Oxford University Press.

Whitehouse, Harvey. 2004. *Modes of Religiosity: A Cognitive Theory of Religious Transmission*. Walnut Creek: AltaMira Press.

Williams, Mark A., Adam P. Morris, Francis McGlone, David F. Abbott, and Jason B. Mattingley. 2004. "Amygdala Responses to Fearful and Happy Facial Expressions under Conditions of Binocular Suppression." *Journal of Neuroscience: The Official Journal of the Society for Neuroscience* 24 (12): 2898–904.

Williams, Paul. 2000. *Buddhist Thought: A Complete Introduction to the Indian Tradition*. London: Routledge.

Yarnall, Thomas. 2003. "The Emptiness That Is Form: Developing the Body of Buddhahood in Indo-Tibetan Buddhist Tantra." PhD dissertation, New York: Columbia University.

Yeshe De Project. 1986. *Ancient Tibet: Research Materials from the Yeshe de Project*. Berkeley: Dharma Publishing.

Yeshi, Khenpo, and Jacob P. Dalton. 2018. "Signification and History in Zhang Nyi Ma 'bum's RDzogs Pa Chen Po Tshig Don Bcu Gcig Pa." *Revue d'Etudes Tibétaines* 43: 256–73.

Yeshi, Khenpo, and Jacob P. Dalton. 2022. "Early Developments in Snying Thig Practice: The Eighth Topic of Zhang Nyi Ma 'Bum's Rdzogs Pa Chen Po Tshig Don Bcu Gcig p." *Revue d'Etudes Tibétaines* 63: 95–130.

Zahler, Leah. 2009. *Study and Practice of Meditation: Tibetan Interpretations of the Concentrations and Formless Absorptions*. Ithaca, NY: Snow Lion.

Zeisler, Bettina. 2011. "For the Love of the Word: A New Translation of Pelliot Tibétain 1287, the Old Tibetan Chronicle, Chapter I." In *New Studies of the Old Tibetan Documents: Philology, History and Religion*, edited by Yoshiro Imaeda, Matthew Kapstein, and Tsuguhito Takeuchi, 97–213. Old Tibetan Documents Online Monograph Series. Tokyo: Research Institute for Languages and Cultures of Asia and Africa, Tokyo University of Foreign Studies.

Zelazo, Philip David, Helena Hong Gao, and Rebecca Todd. 2007. "The Development of Consciousness." In *The Cambridge Handbook of Consciousness*, edited by Philip David Zelazo, Morris Moscovitch, and Evan Thompson, 405–34. Cambridge: Cambridge University Press.

Zubek, John P., G. R. Hughes, and J. M. Shephard. 1971. "A Comparison of the Effects of Prolonged Sensory Deprivation and Perceptual Deprivation." *Canadian Journal of Behavioural Science / Revue Canadienne Des Sciences Du Comportement* 3 (3): 282–90.

Zubek, John P., Dolores Pushkar, Wilma Sansom, and J. Gowing. 1961. "Perceptual Changes after Prolonged Sensory Isolation (Darkness and Silence)." *Canadian Journal of Psychology/Revue Canadienne de Psychologie* 15 (2): 83–100.

Zunshine, Lisa, ed. 2010. *Introduction to Cognitive Cultural Studies*. Baltimore, MD: Johns Hopkins University Press.

INDEX

Note: Endnotes are indicated by the page number followed by "n." and the endnote number e.g., 150 n.1 refers to endnote 1 on page 150.

abhidharma
  cosmology 44
  literature 31, 114
The Absence of Letters Tantra 105
Achard, Jean-Luc 147 n.17, n.21, n.22, 152 n.11, 157 n.2, 158 n.15, 170 n.40
"adamantine body" (*rdo rje'i lus*), see "subtle body"
The Age of Decline 52, 79, 154 n.32, n.35, n.40
Aldenderfer, Mark 18, 152 n.17
Allen, Nicholas J. 148 n.28
Allon, Mark 180 n.2
Almogi, Orna 157 n.11
Ancient School (*rnying ma*, Nyingma) 15–16, 18, 27, 29, 31, 32, 41, 44–5, 50, 95, 129, 147 n.21, 150 n.42, 151 n.2, 159 n.4, 175 n.3
  see also New Schools (*gsar ma*, Sarma)
antecedent tale (*smrang, rabs, lo rgyus*) 9, 24, 51–2, 55, 57, 69, 86, 121, 128, 137, 139
anuttarayoga 43, 44, 101, 160 n.6
anuyoga 14, 85, 146 n.14, 176 n.15
Apple, James B. 181 n.18, n.20
Arabic 168 n.18
Arguillère, Stéphane 35, 152 n.11, 165 n.12, 167 n.8, n.9, 175 n.4, 176 n.14, n.15
Atiśa Dīpaṃkara Śrījñāna (982–1054) 96, 181 n.18
Avalokiteśvara 179 n.40, 186 n.17
avaskandha 8, 148 n.36
awareness (Tib. *rig pa*, Skt. *vidyā*) 14–18
Aziz, Barbara 184 n.1

Barthes, Roland 183 n.36, n.38
Bawden, Charles R. 163 n.35

Beckwith, Christopher I. 151 n.3, 157 n.6, n.7
Bellezza, John Vincent 6, 16, 18, 24, 36, 78, 132, 148 n.27, n.29, 149 n.38, 153 n.27, 155 n.37, n.41, 156 n.49, n.51, n.52, n.53, 163 n.37, 185 n.13, n.15, 188 n.38
Bentor, Yael 160 n.11, 175 n.9
Berglie, F. K. Per-Arne 164 n.46, 185 n.12
Berounský, Daniel 52, 147 n.24, 148 n.27, n.31, 149 n.38, 164 n.38, n.39, 173 n.19, 188 n.38
Bertrand, Christian 152 n.11
Berzin, Alexander 155 n.39, 163 n.37
Beyer, Stephan V. 160 n.7
Bhattacharyya 161 n.13
Bhutan 149 n.40
Bialek, Joanna 148 n.35
Billorey, R. K. 169 n.36
"birdhorns" (*bya ru*) 133, 187 n.26, n.27
The Blazing Lamp Tantra 81
Blezer, Henk 16–17, 49, 148 n.35
Blondeau, Anne-Marie 148 n.31
Bodhi, Bhikkhu 146 n.12
Bön tradition 11, 17, 28, 29, 70, 172 n.4
  and Buddhism 6
Britton, Willoughby 61
Broz, Ludek 80
Bruneau, Laurianne 78, 148 n.27, 156 n.49
Brunnholzl, Karl 181 n.11
Buddhicization of Dzogchen 99
Buddhism 14, 21, 97, 99, 151 n.4, 159 n.3
  Chinese Chan 181 n.18
  Dzogchen 52, 113–18, 121, 142
  esoteric traditions of 1
  Indian 32, 43
  modern 146 n.9, 151 n.9
  Nyingma School of 29

spherical vitality of 27
tantric 41, 43, 135
Tibetanization of 27, 32, 52, 127, 157 n.11
Buddhist
 modernism 2–3
 monocentrism 55, 99, 106, 110
 tantric practices 128
Buswell, Robert 181 n.11
Butön Rinchen Drup 97–8

Cabezón, José Ignacio 116, 175 n.8, 180 n.3
Cakrasaṃvara Tantra (Tib.*'khor lo bde mchog*) 44, 160 n.7
Calkowski, Marcia 54
Cantwell, Cathy 69, 149 n.38, 160 n.7
Chalmers, David John 165 n.3
channels (T. *rtsa*, S. *nāḍī*) 85
Charles Bonnet syndrome 165 n.8
The Chronicle of the Kings 31
Chetsün Senge Wangchuk 31
China 14
Chinese Chan Buddhism 5–6, 181 n.18
Chonggye ('Phyong rgyas) 28, 36
Coblin, W. South 155 n.39
The Compendium of Maṇis 179 n.40, 186 n.17
conch shell
 antlers or horns 22, 24, 52, 141, 155 n.40
 conch shell egg 20
 Conch Shell Mountain 24, 162 n.26
 Conch Shell Deer with Crystal Antlers (*dung sha shel ru*) 88–90, 121, 123
 Conch Shell House (*dung khang*) 88–9
 Conch Shell Man 173 n.19
Coseru, Christian 172 n.9, 175 n.8
Cosmides, Leda 67
Cozort, Daniel 160 n.10
crystal
 antlers or horns 23–5, 48, 87–90, 121, 123, 134, 141, 173 n.16, 188 n.34
 as contemplative paraphernalia 60, 87, 142
 "crystal tube channel" (*shel gyi sbu gu can*) 87–9, 92, 121–3, 129, 131, 138, 141, 188 n.34
 demoness 24, 162 n.26

 and epiphany of the ground 182 n.30
 Little Child Crystal 167 n.10
 palace of five lights 73, 86–7, 121
Cuevas, Bryan J. 153 n.20
Curtin, Jeremiah 188 n.40
Cutler, Nathan S. 157 n.3
Czaplicka, Mary Antionette 188 n.40

Dagyab, Loden Sherap 185 n.9
Dahl, Cortland J. 167 n.11
ḍākinī 38, 89, 101
Dalton, Jacob P. 97, 106, 107, 160 n.7
Damasio, Antonio 165 n.10
Dangma Lhungyi Gyaltsen 31
Dargyay, Eva K. 175 n.10
dark retreat (*mun mtshams*) 60, 165 n.2
Dar-stellung 124
Das, Lama Surya 123–4, 129
Davidson, Richard 68
Davidson, Ronald M. 35, 43, 160 n.9, 161 n.14
Davis, Jake H. 180 n.7
Deer Way-Stations (*Sha slungs*) 25, 49, 149 n.40, 149 n.41, 156 n.46, 156 n.50
"deity yoga" (Skt. *devatā yoga*, Tib. *lha'I rnal byor*) 43, 161 n.12
Desjarlais, Robert R. 163 n.35
Deyu 188 n.36
Dharma kings 42
Diemberger, Hildegard 128, 163 n.35, 174 n.26, 185 n.12
Dilgo Khyentse 129
Doctor, Andreas 157 n.11
Dölpopa Sherap Gyeltsen 97
Doney, Lewis 18
Dotson, Brandon 24, 53, 77, 79, 80, 149 n.38, 154 n.34, 156 n.52, 157 n.13, 162 n.24, 163 n.37, 164 n.38, 169 n.32, n.34, 171 n.42, 172 n.13, 178 n.39
Dowman, Keith 177 n.26
Dromtönpa Gyelwa Chungne 96
Dunhuang texts 9, 133, 139, 154 n.32, 155 n.38
 "Library Cave" (Chin. *Cangjing dong*) 149 n.39
Dunne, John 180 n.4, 189 n.2

Dzogchen (Great Perfection) Buddhism 2, 28, 37, 45, 57, 63, 72-4, 78, 83, 93, 108, 113-14, 135, 137, 145 n.3, 151 n.1, 166 n.13, 174 n.3, 175 n.11, 189 n.2
  conceptions of origins 13-19
  cosmogony 1517, 30-1, 46, 50, 73, 87-8, 129, 137, 141, 184 n.4
  experience in 113-19
  Heart-Essence/Nyingthig 6, 8, 55, 73, 93, 145 n.3, 150 n.45
  language in 113-19
  "mind series" (*sems sde*) 5
  riddles 45-7
  scriptures 41, 147 n.23, 152 n.14
  "space series" (*klong sde*) 5
  status of the body in 84
  systematization of 10, 95-8, 114, 139, 176 n.15
  yogis and the forgotten shamans 127-34

Edelglass, William 179 n.1
"effortless mindfulness" (*rtsol med kyi dran pa*) 189-90 n.1
Ehrhard, Franz-Karl 119, 120, 157 n.11
"elephant" (*glang chen*) 84
The Eleven Words and Meanings on the Great Perfection 79
Eliade, Mircea 135, 147 n.25
English, Elizabeth 160 n.7
Ermakov, Dmitry 147 n.20, 148 n.27, 155 n.39
Eurasian religions 7, 13, 23, 25, 31, 41, 50, 54, 78, 80, 128, 133-4, 141, 142, 147-8 n.26, 155 n.39, 169 n.33, 184 n.2, 188 n.46
  Central Asian 6-7, 13, 18, 23, 25, 31, 148 n.26, 155 n.39, 189 n.51
  Northern Asian 6-7, 17, 22, 23, 25, 31, 156 n.49
  Siberian 4, 7, 22, 25, 78, 79, 131, 133, 169 n.36, 184 n.2, 187 n.32, 189 n.51
  South Asian 27, 31, 32, 137-8
The Excellent Chariot 170 n.37
"expanse" (Tib. *dbyings*, Skt. *dhātu*) 1-2, 17, 45, 61, 72, 81-2, 178 n.40
eyes (*tsakshu/ briguta*) 72, 76, 81, 84-91, 105-6, 108-10, 120-3, 134-6, 165 n.9
  pressing of the 76, 105-6, 122, 137

"First Buddha", *see* Samantabhadra
Fitzhugh, William W. 147 n.26
"four mirrors" (*me long bzhi*) 132
"four visions" (*snang ba bzhi*) 59, 61, 63, 66, 73, 76, 81-2, 90, 116-17, 167 n.9
Franz, Marie-Louise von 169 n.35
"freedom" (Skt. *mokṣa, mukti*) 2, 145 n.5
  "naked freedom" (*cer grol*) 145 n.5
  "natural freedom" (*rang grol*) 145 n.5
  "primordial freedom" (*ye grol*) 2, 145 n.5
  and sky 1-5, 57, 64, 102, 109, 111, 117, 142-3
  "unbounded freedom" (*mtha' grol*) 145 n.5
  "unique freedom" (*gcig grol*) 145 n.5

Gallagher, Shaun 62, 172 n.9
"gap filling" 62-3
Gardīzī 186 n.17
gates (*sgo'i gnad*) 84
Gayley, Holly 158 n.27
Geisshueseler, Flavio A. 145 n.3, 146 n.11, 164 n.1, 176 n.17
Gentry, James Duncan 121
Gerke, Barbara 163 n.35, 174 n.22, n.24, n.25
Germano, David 45, 64, 104, 108, 115, 137, 150 n.44, 152 n.11, 158 n.17, 168 n.22, n.28, 177 n.22, 178 n.34
Gimello, Robert 181 n.11
Gombrich, Richard 184 n.1
Gómez, Luis O. 180 n.3
Gray, David B. 44, 160 n.7, n.10, 181 n.16
Greek 168 n.18
ground (*gzhi*) 15, 20, 23, 136-7, 161 n.16, 189 n.49
  "contextualized ground" (*gnas skabs kyi gzhi*) 171 n.1
  "ground of vitality" (*g.yang gzhi, phya gzhi*) 20, 21, 23, 42, 52, 54, 87-8, 153 n.29
  "initial ground" (*thog ma'i gzhi*) 34-5
  "manifestation of the ground" (*gzhi snang*) 15, 17, 20, 28, 37, 45, 46, 69, 83, 182 n.30
  "original ground" (*gdod ma'i gzhi*) 34-5
  phenomenal existence rising (*bzhengs*) from 136-7
  "primordial ground" (*ye gzhi*) 34-5

Guenther, Herbert V. 34, 46, 65, 161 n.18, 184 n.6, 189 n.1
Guru Chöwang 37–8
Gyatso, Janet B. 29, 34, 38, 60, 157 n.11, 158 n.17, 167 n.10
Gyeltsen, Tashi 30

Haarh, Erik 16, 148 n.29, 157 n.3, 158 n.22
Halkias, Georgios 5, 188 n.46
Hamayon, Roberte 24, 131, 186 n.20, 187 n.32
Hamilton, Sue 85
Harding, Sarah 160 n.10
Harva, Uno 188 n.40
Ha-Shang 177 n.33
Hatchell, Christopher 64, 82, 150 n.44, 158 n.17
Hazod, Guntram 36
The Heap of Jewels Tantra 72, 184 n.4
heart (*tsitta*) 86–7
The Heart-Essence of the Ḍākinīs 89
Heath, Dan 183 n.39
Hebrew 168 n.18
Heller, Amy 148 n.30
Heshang Moheyan 104, 105
Hevajra Tantra (Tib. *Kye'i rdo rje*, lit. "Hail Vajra") 160 n.7
Higgins, David 2, 102, 146 n.8, 151 n.1, 177 n.26, n.32
Hill, Nathan W. 136, 155 n.39, 157 n.3
Hillis, Gregory 180 n.10
Himalayan folk traditions 92
    Himalayas 1, 4, 189 n.51
    cult of animal guides 7
A History of Buddhism in India and Tibet 188 n.36
Hitchcock, John T. 184 n.2
Hocart, A. M. 166 n.13
Hoffman, Donald D. 66, 178 n.39
Holmberg, David H. 163 n.35, 185 n.12
Horlemann, Bianca 149 n.39
Huber, Toni 6, 22, 33, 35, 50, 52, 78, 110, 135, 148 n.29, n.37, 149 n.41, 153 n.27, 155 n.39, n.41, 156 n.46, n.50, 159 n.31, 162 n.23, n.24, n.25, 164 n.45, 166 n.13, 169 n.33, n.36, 173 n.21, 186 n.22, n.23, 187 n.25, 188 n.37, n.41, n.43
Husserl, Edmund 172 n.9

Ifergan, Gidi 105
Imaeda, Yoshiro 186 n.17
India 14, 32, 41–3, 95, 104, 137, 149 n.40
Indian Buddhism 32, 43, 119
Indigenous Tibetan Practice of Transference 134–40
Indo-Scythian communities 7
Indo-Tibetan Buddhism 181 n.19
Indo-Tibetan tantric techniques 24, 43, 44, 166 n.1
interiorization of shaman's headdress 131–4
IOL (India Office Library) 149 n.39
Iranian cultures 7

Jackson, Roger R. 181 n.19
Jacobson, Esther 31, 147 n.25, 147 n.26
Jacoby, Sarah 29, 158 n.26
James J. Gibson 65
Jäschke, Heinrich August 163 n.36
Jigme Lingpa 127
Johnson, Mark 172 n.9
Jones, Rex L. 184 n.2

Kagyü 119, 159 n.3, 160 n.7
Kālachakra Tantra (Tib. *dus kyi 'khor lo*, lit. "The Wheel of Time Tantra") 160 n.7, 181 n.13
Kamalaśīla 104
Kapstein, Matthew T. 14, 33, 116, 152 n.11, 157 n.3, 158 n.28, 175 n.11, 181 n.18, 185 n.10
Karmapa Rangjung Dorje 93
Karmay, Sonam Gyaltsen 14, 22, 23, 33, 147 n.21, 148 n.31, 149 n.38, 151 n.1, 153 n.19, 155 n.39, 157 n.3, n.6, 158 n.18, n.22, n.24, 162 n.24, 163 n.35, 164 n.39, n.43, 174 n.23, n.26, 188 n.37
key points
    of Skullward Leap 85, 100, 101
    "six key points" (*gnad drug*) 84, 85
    "three key points" (*gnad gsum*) 84
Khandro Pelchen Lhamo 30
khelnā 185 n.14
Klein, Anne Carolyn 122, 146 n.6, 166 n.2, 180 n.11, 182 n.21, n.30
Klimburg-Salter, Deborah 156 n.51
Kolmaš, Josef 151 n.7

Komarovski, Yaroslav 179 n.1
Kongtrul, Jamgon 152 n.11, 160 n.10
Kosslyn, Steven 66
Kuijp, Van der 152 n.15, 158 n.21, 175 n.8
Kumārādza 116, 180 n.9
Kvaerne, Per 153 n.22, 153 n.24, 157 n.4, 158 n.15

Laish, Eran 167 n.11, n.12, 170 n.39, 177 n.32
Lalou, Marcelle 148 n.29
Langelaar, Reinier J. 179 n.45
Lha Thothori Nyantsen (*lha tho tho ri gnyan*, fifth century) 151 n.4, 154.n.33
Liljenberg 146 n.16
Lindahl, Jared 61
"lion" (*seng ge*) 84
Lobel, Adam 44, 176 n.14
Longchen Nyingthik 127
Longchen Rabjam 95
Longchenpa (1308-1364) 2, 10, 76-7, 81, 84, 96-7, 100-11, 114-25, 127, 136-7, 142, 146 n.6, 150 n.47, 152 n.11, 175 n.5, 176 n.13, 176 n.15, 184 n.5
Lopez, Donald S. 157 n.11
"luminous channels" (*'od rtsa*) 1, 5, 57, 63-4, 83, 86-90, 108, 117, 120, 131, 134, 141, 178 n.34, 188 n.34
Lutz, Antoine 68

Macdonald, Ariane 157 n.3, 164 n.40, 186 n.17
MacLean, Paul 165 n.10
Mahākāla 184 n.1
Mahāmudrā 99, 181 n.19
Mahāyāna Buddhism 93, 98
Mahāyoga 14, 146 n.14, 176 n.15
maṇḍala 66, 100, 130
Mantrayāna, *see* tantric Buddhism
Martin, Dan 5, 109, 118, 133, 155 n.39, 157 n.11, 178 n.39, 179 n.41, 187 n.27, 188 n.36
de Martino, Ernesto (1908-1965) 146 n.13
Martynov, Anatoli I. 147 n.25
Maskarinec, Gregory G. 184 n.2
Mayer, Robert 149 n.38, 160 n.7
McKay, Alex 151 n.7

McMahan, David L. 2, 146 n.9, n.10, 151 n.9
meditation 1, 5, 26, 39, 43, 60, 61-2, 67, 68, 69, 73, 74, 79, 82, 84, 86, 95, 99, 101, 103, 117-19, 122, 135, 142, 146 n.10, 166 n.13, 176 n.15, n.17, 184 n.1, n.3
contemplative paraphernalia 5, 121, 122, 130, 131
contemplative system 3, 6, 8, 9, 10, 15, 57, 79, 89, 95, 113, 128, 137, 156 n.1, 166 n.13, 182 n.33
modernist construction of 3-4
and myth 3, 6, 8, 9, 11, 15, 19, 55, 57, 69-70, 73-4, 81-3, 85-91, 107, 113, 124, 128, 137, 141, 166 n.13
and vitality 71-6
see also Dzogchen; Skullward Leap meditation
Merleau-Ponty, Maurice 172 n.9
Metzner, Ralph 169 n.35
Mills, Martin A. 166 n.14
The Mirror of the Heart of Vajrasattva 14, 72, 108, 130
mirror
as contemplative paraphernalia 130-1
of the Shaman 127-9, 131, 185 n.15
Mongol dynasty in China 42-3
Mongolia 7, 14, 189 n.51
Mount Kailash 174 n.25
mthong phul 178 n.40
mthongs 179 n.40
"Mu Doe" (*dmu sha yu mo*) 87
Mumford, Stan 128, 185 n.12
muscae volitantes (flying flies) 62
myths
crisis and crisis management 48-54, 123
of cosmogony 15-17, 30-1, 46, 50, 73, 87-8, 129, 137, 141, 184 n.4
and embodiment 85-92
as history 18-19
Khumbo myths 33
and rituals 6-11, 19-20, 22-5, 29, 34-5, 41, 49-50, 52-5, 78, 86-8, 107-10, 124, 128, 131, 135-7, 148 n.31, 149 n.40, 162 n.23, 166 n.13, 173 n.19, 187 n.30
reality of 10, 15, 18-19, 27-8, 47, 55
Sherpa myths 33

Nagano, Yasuhiko 164 n.39
"naked vision" (*cer mthong*) 59
Nampar Gyalwa 153 n.24
The Narrative of the Deer 54, 169 n.33
Nebesky-Wojkowitz, René de 164 n.38
Nepal 14, 128, 149 n.40, 174 n.26
New Schools (*gsar ma, Sarma*) 41, 98, 99
   see also Ancient School
Ngagpa 116
nimitta (lit. "sign") 165 n.5
nirvāṇa 73–4, 95, 97, 106, 121
Noë, Alva 63
Norbu, Chogyal Namkhai 53, 152 n.16, 153 n.19, 157 n.4, 161 n.18, 163 n.35, 164 n.42, 183 n.34, 187 n.29, 188 n.34
"no-self" (P. *anattā*, Skt. *anātman*) 171 n.2
Nyang Tingdzin Zangpo 31, 175 n.3

Obeyesekere, Gananath 184 n.1
The Old Tibetan Annals 136
Oppitz, Michael 148 n.32, 156 n.47, 187 n.31
Orgyen Lingpa 37
Ortner, Sherry 128
Osto, Douglas 181 n.15
Özer, Drime 116

Padmasambhava 116
Pāla dynasties 181 n.18
Pasarić, Maja 25
Path of Freedom (Upatissa) 151 n.8
Paul, Robert 19
Pawo Tsuklak Trengwa 188 n.36
The Pearl Necklace Tantra 100, 114, 118
"perfectibilism" of Buddhism 14
Peters, Larry 185 n.12, n.15
phul 108–9, 178 n.38
phul thag 108–10, 139, 178 n.35, 178 n.38, 179 n.42
planned spontaneity 125, 183 n.39
Prajñāpāramitā sūtras 181 n.11
pre-Buddhist 5, 16, 17, 19, 32, 106, 108, 113, 127
   beliefs and practices 20, 26, 29, 95, 110–11, 135
   and Bön 6–7, 158 n.13
   cosmologies 26, 134, 141

   culture 9, 11, 145 n.1
   deities 128
   heritage 109, 139
   motifs 34
   origins 6
   religion of Tibet 86, 110
   society 6
   substratum 134
   Tibetan culture 6, 11, 138–9, 155 n.39, 187 n.29
   valorization 28
PT (Pelliot Tibetain) 149 n.39
Punzi, Valentina 158 n.14

"rainbow" (*dmu ru rgyud*) 61, 155 n.39, 186 n.15
   body ('*ja' lus*) 5, 83, 137, 139, 143
   body of the great transference ('*ja' lus'pho ba chen po*) 83, 136, 137, 139
   colored headdress 132
   colored lights 15, 28, 34
   colored manifestation of light 187 n.24
   flaps 132
   Zhangzhung term for 92
Ralpacen 14, 151 n.6
Ramble, Charles 14, 20, 23, 36, 88, 148 n.31, 153 n.28, 154 n.29, 156 n.51, 162 n.23, 163 n.37, 173 n.16, n.17
Religions of Tibet (Tucci, Giuseppe) 157 n.7
rGyud (*skye rgyud, rus rgyud, pha rgyud*) 50
Riboli, Diana 184 n.2
Richardson, Alan 60
Richardson, Hugh 154 n.36
rnal dri 51–2
Rock, Joseph Francis Charles 187 n.31
Romain, William 36
Rosch, Eleanor 115

sādhanā (Tib. *sgrub thabs*, lit. "means of achievement") 43, 161 n.13
Sagant, Philippe 163 n.35
"sage" (Tib. *drang srong*, Skt. ṛṣi) 84
Samantabhadra (lit. "All Good One," Tib. *kun tu bzang po*) 15, 30, 37, 70, 96, 124, 167 n.9, 184 n.4
Sambhogakaya 172 n.8
saṃsāra 46, 73–4, 95, 97, 121

Samuel, Geoffrey 128, 154 n.33, 158 n.25, 164 n.40, 182 n.31
"sanctuaries" (*gnas pa rtsa*) 85
Sangphu Neutok 99, 115
Sangye Gyatso 174 n.24
Śāntarakṣita 96
Sartre, Jean-Paul 172 n.9
scala contemplationis 66
Schaik, Sam van 14, 998, 151 n.2, 159 n.35, 161 n.13, 175 n.5, 177 n.25
Scheidegger, Daniel 172 n.14
Schwieger, Peter 16, 98, 99, 106, 152 n.15, 158 n.27
scriptural originality 44
Scytho-Siberian cultures 7
Secret Nucleus Tantra (*Guhyagarbhatantra*) 14
seminal nuclei (T. *thig le*, S. *bindu*) 85
"sensory deprivation" 60
The Seven Treasuries 150 n.46
  Treasury of the Supreme Vehicle 107
  Treasury of Words and Meanings 102
The Seventeen Tantras 9–10, 30, 33, 79, 95, 97, 99, 100, 141, 150 n.42, n.45, 175 n.3
shaman(ic/ism) 7, 78, 94, 128, 131–2, 187 n.24
  cults 35
  festivals 166 n.13
  headdress of 131–4, 186 n.21
  and hunting 143, 169 n.36, 187 n.32
  and lamas 173 n.21
  material culture of 147 n.25
  objectives of 7
  outfits 127
  practice 169 n.35
  practitioners 128, 130, 136, 155 n.39
  in Siberian context 7, 24, 148 n.32, 184 n.2
  societies 13
  soul-journeys 136, 139
  and spirit world 131, 133
  system 164 n.40
  Tibetan 137
  traditions 127, 128, 134, 187 n.32
  trance ritual 132
  transference 188–9 n.46
  visionary journey 128

Shangpa Kagyu 99
Sharf, Robert H. 180 n.4, 189–90 n.1
Siberia 184 n.2, 187 n.32, 189 n.51
Siberian religions 7
siddha culture 181 n.18
siddha' (Tib. *grub thob*) 14
Sidky, Homayun 184 n.2
Sigman, Mario 62
Six Dharmas of Nāropa 176 n.20
skandhas 115
Skorupski, Tadeusz 160 n.7
skull (*dung khang/ dung khang dkar*) 86, 145 n.1
  "turban/headdress" (*thod, lha thod*, or *thod dkar*) 8, 133–4, 135, 187 n.30
Skullward Leap meditation (*thod rgal*, Tögal) 1, 8, 11, 13, 67–9, 76, 109, 127, 129, 145 n.1, 166 n.1, 176 n.19, 189 n.2
  preliminary practices (Tib. *Sngon 'gro*) 71
"sky" (Tib. *Nam mkha'*, Skt. *Ākāśa/ gagaṇa*) 2
  and freedom 1–5, 57, 64, 102, 109, 111, 117, 142–3
  as source of vitality 5–11, 13–39, 50–5, 70, 76, 79
  and deer 7–11, 21–6, 29, 31, 41, 48–55, 79–80, 87–90, 135–7, 147 n.26, 155 n.39, 155 n.40, 162 n.26
"Sky Embryo" (*nam mkha'i snying po*) 135
"Sky Ladder Rock" (*gnam skas brag*) 38
"Sky-Deer with Long Antlers" (*gnam sha ru ring*) 87
  Zhangzhung term for 147 n.19
Smith, Gene 180 n.4
Snellgrove, David Llewellyn 160 n.7
Songtsen Gampo 151 n.4, 179 n.40, 186 n.17
Sørensen, Henrik Hjort 149 n.39, 178 n.39
Sørensen, Jesper 67
Source of Life (Huber, Toni) 6
"space" (Tib. *klong*, Skt. *dhātu*) 2
Stablein, William 184 n.1
Stein, Rolf Alfred 37, 148 n.29, 148 n.35, 149 n.38, 155 n.39, 157 n.8, 158 n.23, 159 n.33, 164 n.40, 170 n.41, 178 n.40

Steinmann, Brigitte 163 n.35
Stewart, J. M. 174 n.1
"subtle body" (Skt. *sūkṣma śarīra*, Tib. *lus 'phra, phra ba'i lus*) 44, 57, 74, 83, 84–5, 86, 88, 89, 95, 101, 108, 121, 131, 134, 138, 141, 160 n.7, 163 n.37, 168 n.25, 173 n.19, 176 n.20, 188 n.34
Sumegi, Angela 164 n.40
Sumpa Khenpo 153 n.22
Sur, Dominic 158 n.19, 161 n.14, 177 n.32

The Tantra of Self-Arisen Awareness 46–7, 51, 81, 130, 162 n.22
The Tantra of the Self-Emergent Teaching 74
The Tantra of Unimpeded Sound 45, 74, 85, 96, 115
tantric Buddhism 41, 133
    Mantrayāna 101
    Vajrayāna 93, 98
tantric practices 176 n.19
tantric techniques 101
Tapihritsa 147 n.22
Taves, Ann 65
Tenzin Wangyal Rinpoche 161 n.18
Terrone, Antonio 30, 157 n.12
The Testament of Ba 105
"Theory of Mind" 67
Thompson, Evan 68, 172 n.12, 180 n.4, n.7
Thondup, Tulku 157 n.12
"three key points" (*gnad gsum*) 84
"three unwavering states" (*mi 'gul gsum*) 84
Tibet 41
    Bön tradition 1, 9
    Dharma Kings 14
    Indian Buddhism in 32
    Ralpacen (*ral pa can*, 802–838) 14
    Songtsen Gampo (*srong btsan sgam po*, 569/605–649) 14
    Trisong Detsen (*khri srong lde btsan*, 5 reigned 755–797/804) 14
    vocabulary 11
    writing system 14
Tibetan anthro-cosmology 111
Tibetan Buddhism 1, 32, 52, 95, 98, 127, 128, 137, 157 n.11, 176 n.21
Tibetan rock art 7
Tibetosphere 127, 149 n.40
Tögal meditation, *see* Skullward Leap meditation
Tooby 67
"transcendentalist" 179 n.45
Treasures (*gter ma*)
    and pre-Buddhist religion 29–32, 34–5
    revelation 6, 38, 91, 127
    Seventeen Tantras 9
    and Skullward Leap meditation 37–8
Tride Yumtan (*khri lde yum brtan*) 42
Trigum Tsenpo 27, 28, 157 n.3, n.7
Trisong Detsen 151 n.5
tsitta (mind) 72–3
Tucci, Giuseppe 21, 154 n.34, 157 n.7, 164 n.40, 166 n.15, 174 n.25
Tulku Urgyen Rinpoche 177 n.27
Turkic cultures 7

Ü Dumtsen (*'u'I dum btsan*) 42
Upatissa 151 n.8
Uyghur Khaganate 159 n.2

Vilayanur Ramachandran 63
Vimalamitra 9
viṣkanda 8, 148 n.36
Vitali, Roberto 133, 151 n.7, 187 n.27
vitality 52
    activation of vitality 71–6
    Buddhicization of 27–39, 48, 52, 83, 99, 121, 127, 132, 139, 142
    domestication of vitality 71–81
    embodied-technical circulation of 57, 72, 87, 139
    internalization of 5, 10, 44, 83–91, 127, 134
    language and 113–27
    lassoing 5, 23–4, 51, 89–92, 123, 134, 164 n.44
    "mobile vitality principle" (*bla*) 11, 52, 54, 86, 91, 92, 163 n.37, 164 n.45, 173 n.20, n.21, 174 n.22, n.26
    phya/g.yang 11, 19, 20, 23, 29, 30, 34, 50–1, 52, 70, 75, 86, 87, 88, 123, 133, 138, 139, 153 n.26, 155 n.39, 156 n.46, 163 n.37, 164 n.37, 164 n.39, n.42, n.44, 168 n.25, 172 n.13, 173 n.16, n.17, n.20, 184 n.3

quest for 1, 6, 8–10, 13, 16–17, 22–4, 31, 35, 45, 47–50, 53–5, 71, 75–7, 86–9, 106–10, 121, 123–5, 134–5, 141–4
  spherical model of 27, 28, 31–2, 35, 41, 187 n.28
  tantric model of 41–4, 72, 75
  vertical model of 11, 13, 19, 23, 25, 27–8, 31–7, 48, 50, 77, 83, 89–92, 132–42, 187 n.28
Vorstellung 124
vyatikrāntaka 8, 148 n.36
vyutkrānta 8

Walter, Michael L. 158 n.24, 159 n.31, 169 n.35, 186 n.17, 186 n.19, 187 n.28
Wangyal, Tenzin 122, 146 n.6, 182 n.21, n.30
Watt, Tessa 189–90 n.1
Watters, David E. 184 n.2
Wedemeyer, Christian 160 n.11
"White Conch Shell House" (*dung khang dkar*) 88
"white silk thread" (*dar dkar snal ma*) 88–9, 134
"White Skull Mountain" 117, 188 n.33
Willerslev, Rane 80

Williams, Paul 160 n.7
Würzl, Elizabeth 156 n.51

Yarlung Dynasty 42, 97, 159 n.2, 186 n.18
Yarnall, Thomas 160 n.10
Yenisei Kirghiz 159 n.2
Yeshe Tsogyal (*ye shes mtsho rgyal*) 116
Yeshi, Khenpo 97, 106, 107, 170 n.40, 175 n.6
Yinong, Zhang 18, 152 n.17
yoganiruttara 160 n.6
yogi 59–60
  as hunter and herder 76–82
Yoginītantra 160 n.7
Yuan dynasty in China 42–3
yul ("home"/"home region") 82

Zahavi, Dan 62, 172 n.9
Zahler, Leah 176 n.18
Zeisler, Bettina 157 n.3
Zhang Nyima Bum 79, 96–9, 105, 107, 121, 147 n.23
Zhangtön Tashi Dorje 31, 147 n.19, 147 n.23, 150 n.44
Zhangzhung 7, 18–19, 21, 27, 92
  kings 187 n.28

www.ingramcontent.com/pod-product-compliance
Lightning Source LLC
Chambersburg PA
CBHW071833300426
44116CB00009B/1532